# D-DAY

## PIERCING THE ATLANTIC WALL

# D-DAY

## PIERCING THE ATLANTIC WALL

### ROBERT J. KERSHAW

IAN ALLAN
Publishing

# TO MY MOTHER AND FATHER

*It's "D-Day" tomorrow, but we've known that for ages.*
*Are young lives nearly finished?*
*Can we turn back the pages?*

*['Ginger' Woodcock. British Paratrooper.*
*Written Broadwell. 5.6.44.]*

*Page 1:* Recovering from the strain of the actual landings.
*Imperial War Museum*

*Previous page:* Forming up to begin the advance inland
while tanks and other vehicles come ashore in the
background. *Imperial War Museum*

*Overleaf:* Typical scenes as British tanks and infantry fight
through Normandy towns and villages.
*Imperial War Museum*

First published 1993

ISBN 0 7110 2176 7

Designed by Richard Souper

Published by Ian Allan Publishing, an imprint of Ian Allan
Ltd, Terminal House, Station Approach, Shepperton,
Surrey; and printed by Ian Allan Printing Ltd, Coombelands
House, Coombelands Lane, Addlestone, Weybridge, Surrey
KT15 1HY

# CONTENTS

# PREFACE

The invasion of Normandy, D-Day, is an event that has been exhaustively picked over by Allied historians. What is there left to say after works by Cornelius Ryan, Alexander McKee, Max Hastings and John Keegan to name just a few? *D-Day — Piercing the Atlantic Wall* has concentrated on describing the event through the eyes and oral testimonies of the survivors themselves. The Battle of D-Day was not as Cornelius Ryan suggests 'The Longest Day', it is rather concerned with the nine days it took for the Allies to dominate the foreshore upon which they had landed. It attempts to detect that moment when the Germans thought in terms of containing the spread of an accepted bridgehead, not in 'throwing the Allies back into the sea'. This was the culminating and deciding point of D-Day, when it could be judged a success. Both sides believed the event would force the decision in the West. Yet paradoxically it resulted in stalemate, until the Allied break-out two months later. This book, beginning on the invasion eve, covers the conduct of the D-Day operation until that moment it achieved success. The battle of D-Day occurred broadly between 6-14 June 1944. The battle of Normandy followed.

An attempt has been made to redress the balance of an event viewed almost exclusively from British, Canadian and American viewpoints, and include the German in more detail. Detailed study of German sources does impact upon a number of previously accepted assumptions. Rather than attempt overall balance, credence or weight has been given to examining whichever side held the initiative at a given moment, or analysing issues that have been either inadequately assessed previously, or little known.

Developments are seen primarily through the thoughts, opinions and partisan views of the participants themselves. I have been mindful of the advice of one German veteran, who on being interviewed remarked 'bear in mind two points when you speak with these people: they were all as a minimum Lance-Corporals, and they all won the war single-handed!' Most of the sources are contemporary by preference, as near to the events in chronological terms as is possible. Veteran accounts are offered with the caveat that they truly reflect the business of combat, a highly personalised and emotional experience; which at best can only be reviewed in the 'snap-shot' fashion presented in the following pages. As a serving soldier myself, I find it almost impossible accurately to recall active service incidents twenty years — even two years — ago, without resorting to a diary. Memories are sketchy and become embellished with the re-telling. Perhaps one of the most realistic accounts of D-Day I came across, were the very honest declarations of a Canadian soldier, who said:

> *Honest to God, I don't remember a thing. I remember the outfit marching down those lanes in England near the coast and then sleeping in a big hall that night and then loading up next afternoon and then going across the Channel and it was dark ..... I don't remember going ashore. I don't really know how I did, whether we had to wade or if we just ran up the beach when they dropped the gate. If there was heavy fire I don't remember .....*
>
> *The first thing I remember, and this is the God's truth. I'm sitting with my back to a German tank and there's guys all around me and we're eating C-rations.*[1]

*D-Day — Piercing the Atlantic Wall* is really concerned with this human aspect. What was it like to drop from the skies, go ashore from a landing craft, or defend a bunker on D-Day? Accuracy is probably less important in factual data terms, than impressions, the real stuff of war. Therefore priority is given to describing and interpreting the human dimension — sight, sound, touch, smell, hearing — and the influence that such experience does have upon men in battle. As one former American paratrooper in Normandy described it:

> *Like desert warfare, hedgerow fighting became associated with the land itself, so that long afterwards the sight of them in other countries recalled the mosquitoes at evening, the taste of soil, and the ammoniac smoke in the meadows where crickets piped.*[2]

Few people today have endured warfare at the intense levels of those who experienced D-Day fifty years ago. One British officer asked forty years after the event:

*How can it have been so real then, and be so remote now?*
*What was the meaning of it, this second of history*
*overshadowing our whole lives. With whom can one share*
*the knowledge of what it was really like?*

*The answer is no one. For we all died forty years ago.*

Andrew Wilson answers the question himself, because even when the veterans get together to talk 'we are middle-aged strangers to one another. Our whole conversation is a fruitless attempt to deny this'.[3] The following pages attempt to provide some answers.

Every effort has been made to trace the source and copyright holders of the maps and illustrations appearing in the text, and these are acknowledged where possible. Similarly, the author wishes to thank those publishers who have permitted the quotation of extracts from their books. Quotation sources are annotated in the notes that follow the text. My apologies are offered in advance to those with whom, for any reason, I have been unable to establish contact.

I am particularly indebted to Dr Kehrig and Herr Meyer at the Bundesarchiv in Freiburg for their assistance in locating many of the German documents quoted in the text, and for being responsive to specific requests. Much of the American material came from Major Dan Nettling and Ms Louise Arnold-Friend of the United States Military History Institute in Pennsylvania, and my thanks also to Colonel Raymond K Bluhm Jnr from the US Center of Military History in Washington. Additional material came from the National Archives also in Washington. Mr John Harding at the British Army Historical Branch at the Ministry of Defence provided many of the official histories mentioned in the text, as well as locating papers dealing with official and unit histories of both American and German formations. Magnum Photos Incorporated provided the Robert Capa material. The Imperial War Museum in London provided information from maps and photographs, while Mrs Diana Andrews of the Aldershot Parachute Regiment and Airborne Forces Museum was able to provide some previously unseen material.

Without my typist, Miss Linda Ganter, the project would never have come to fruition; she not only accurately typed the manuscript, she rarely missed inconsistencies in content. My thanks also to Simon Forty of Ian Allan, whom I thought insane for suggesting the subject of the book in the first instance. The real victims of the pressure throughout have been my long suffering wife Lynn, and my sons: Christian, Alexander and Michael, who have had to bear the brunt of meeting deadlines; which has conflicted with everything, cricket and sailing included. Lynn, as ever provided the back up that made it all possible. We are back to normal at last!

Church Crookham
June 1993

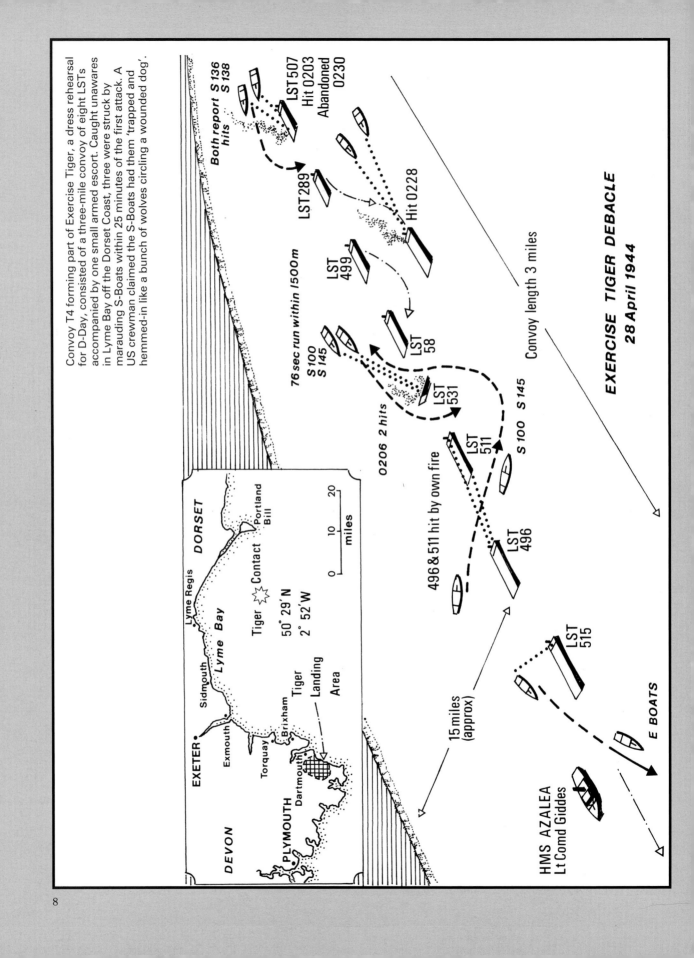

Convoy T4 forming part of Exercise Tiger, a dress rehearsal for D-Day, consisted of a three-mile convoy of eight LSTs accompanied by one small armed escort. Caught unawares in Lyme Bay off the Dorset Coast, three were struck by marauding S-Boats within 25 minutes of the first attack. A US crewman claimed the S-Boats had them 'trapped and hemmed-in like a bunch of wolves circling a wounded dog'.

Both report S 136
hits           S 138

LST 507
Hit 0203
Abandoned
0230

LST 289

Hit 0228

76 sec run within 1500m

LST
499

S 100
S 145

LST
58

0206 2 hits

LST
531

LST
511

S 100   S 145

Convoy length 3 miles

496 & 511 hit by own fire

LST
496

15 miles
(approx)

LST 515

E BOATS

HMS AZALEA
Lt Comd Giddes

*EXERCISE TIGER DEBACLE*
*28 April 1944*

DEVON

EXETER

PLYMOUTH

Exmouth

Torquay

Brixham

Dartmouth

Tiger
Landing
Area

Sidmouth

Lyme Regis

*Lyme Bay*

Tiger ☆ Contact

*DORSET*

Portland
Bill

50° 29' N
2° 52' W

0        10        20
         miles

8

# CHAPTER 1

# THE NARROW CHANNEL

*'Before their eyes as they stepped shivering from their huts each morning was the channel, the grey channel, and beyond it, the grey mist.'*

A. Baron

## 'Wolves circling a wounded dog' . . . Lyme Bay 28 April 1944.

The sea was very dark with a setting quarter moon, and visibility good. Kapitänleutnant Jurgensmeyer, captain of *Schnellboot* (motor torpedo boat — known to the British as E-Boats) *S-136*, could just make out the outline of his sister craft *S-138* in the gloom, its antennae and mast intermittently breaking the horizon line as they rose and fell in the inky blackness on a gentle swell. It was chilly. Some members of Jurgensmeyer's 21-man crew were below decks where there was some warmth. Others wrapped arms around themselves, or thrust them deeper into pockets to ward off the damp chill as they silently rode the Lyme Bay waves. Visibility was almost 15,000 metres, with Portland Bill almost due west, but there was still no sign of life apart from distant searchlights. These were of interest. As Jurgensmeyer was to report:

*Searchlights in Lyme Bay in recent times had always been regarded as "E-Boat warning signs", spiral and criss-cross light beams would show up in likely target areas.[1]*

Something was up, had to be.

Jurgensmeyer scanned the surface of the sea yet again, pausing here and there, almost willing the darker shadows to stop teasing and merge into the tell-tale silhouette of an enemy ship. The tension on the bridge was palpable. The previous night's wait had also proved fruitless. As the deputy commander of the 5th E-Boat Flotilla he had had four boats stood by from dusk to dawn to intercept a convoy like the one anticipated this night. They had missed it. Poor visibility in any case had aborted the mission. One more of a series of frustrations like the maintenance problems that had plagued the 5th Flotilla, tying up an average of six boats out of ten already this month. The best they had achieved was a successful mine-laying operation off the Isle of Wight

with the 9th S-Boat Flotilla, employing six boats. Tonight, however, was different. They had been galvanised into action by the short terse message from S-Boat command based at Wimereux near Boulogne. Kapitän zur See Rudolf Petersen, Führer der Schnellboote, had directed that

*The 5th and 9th S-Boat Flotillas are to depart as soon as possible to intercept an enemy convoy identified 10 sea miles west of Portland Bill.[2]*

Two nights now of enemy convoy activity. Air intelligence had reported further naval activity. Korvettenkapitän Klug, Jurgensmeyer's flotilla commander had sent them out. 'Targets are likely in square BF2398'. The Invasion perhaps, but no sign yet.

Two groups of E-Boats, six from the 5th Flotilla and three from the 9th Flotilla had departed Cherbourg at 22.00 in two columns. Clearing the harbour mole, they accelerated to 35 knots. Radio silence was maintained, even radars were not switched on, to avoid being detected by the enemy.

This was a potentially powerful force. Each of the sleek, low-silhouetted craft was over ninety feet long. Armament was a 20mm cannon forward, twin 20mm amidships and 40mm gun aft, with two fixed torpedo tubes forward and a further reload pair of torpedoes on board. All boats could make 35 knots with their Daimler-Benz engines, those with super-chargers, more. On arrival in the area of operations, the 5th Flotilla boats split into pairs (or *Rotten*)[3] and began, with the 3-boat group from 9th Flotilla, to comb their sectors.

It was often useful, as Jurgensmeyer knew, simply to switch off engines and concentrate on the sights and sounds around them, bobbing up and down, a low silhouette, shrouded in inky blackness. Such ambush tactics were proven against British convoys. Oberleutnant zur See Stohwasser's crew in *S-138* similarly strained their ears and stared into the darkness. There were doubts but it appeared that some shadows were moving independently of the dark sea mass. Some even imagined they heard a slow rhythmic throb like a distant aeroplane. Taking his eyes off the shadowy spots identifiable only through binoculars, Stohwasser grimaced,

*Above:* 'The 5th and 9th S-Boat Flotillas are to depart as soon as possible to intercept an enemy convoy identified 10 sea miles west of Portland Bill'. Casting off from Cherbourg.

*Below:* Conditions were cramped and crowded. 'You lived on top of one another.' Speculation varied between 'another dry run' and the actual invasion of France. Troops ready for sailing.

wiped his eyes, blinked hard and rested them. Changing direction he peered intently at the nearer dark mass, that must be Jurgensmeyer's *S-136*. Had he seen it too? Forward and off the port bow was 'a destroyer with two smoke stacks, beyond that to the north west was a further destroyer in sight moving west'.[4] 'Start engines', he ordered.

Convoy T4 preceded by the corvette HMS *Azalea* seemed an unlikely herald for an invasion force. She appeared more like a converted trawler. Nevertheless following on behind was a column of eight Landing Ship Tank (LST) vessels.[5] They were powering through the night at between 6-7 knots, throwing up a considerable splashing turbulent wake. The column stretched nearly three miles, broken only by the fifth vessel, *LST 58*, towing two pontoon causeways, to ease beach unloading operations. On board were American troops, elements from the 1st Special Engineer Brigade, rehearsing for their planned landing on Utah Beach. The ships were packed with amphibious trucks and combat engineers whose task was to manage the landing beaches and keep traffic moving smoothly. They were following the 6th Special Engineer Brigade, who had sailed in the first wave.[6]

LSTs were dubbed 'Large Slow Targets' with typical black humour by those who had already served in the Pacific and Mediterranean campaigns. Regarded individually as disposable war-horses, yet collectively indispensable, they took on average only four months to build. The LST was in effect the forerunner of the modern roll-on, roll-off ferry. At the bow were doors and a ramp that could be lowered to let out men and vehicles. They were built to contain as much as possible so the 322-foot length lacked a proper reinforcing system of bulkheads and ribs. As one former crewman Emanuel Rubin declared it was almost all hold, 'just a big welded box', and the hull was like 'a thin piece of fabric between you and the fish'. Conditions were 'cramped and crowded'.

*You lived on top of one another. When there were soldiers aboard, you couldn't move. It smelt always of people.*[7]

*LST 507* bringing up the rear of the convoy, carried the 478th Amphibian Truck Company, the 557th Quartermaster Railhead Company, the 33rd Chemical Company, the 1st Platoon of the 440th Engineer Company, and the 3891st Quartermaster Truck Company, 282 US Army troops in all. Aboard were two ¼ ton trucks, one ¾ ton truck, thirteen 2½ ton trucks, and 22 amphibious DUKWs. These were also fully fuelled and carrying additional supplies. The vessel was crewed by 165 officers and men. The other LSTs carried similar loads. Soldiers on board had cumbersome backpacks with weapons slung over their shoulders. They were equipped for the forthcoming beach assault. There was sufficient space for life-belts to be worn, but only incorrectly around the waist.

Weeks of bored inaction waiting in pre-invasion assembly areas, interspersed by sudden embarkation flaps and practices had fuelled inevitable rumours. Most participants were ignorant of what was going on. German planes had appeared over Plymouth the morning before and air raid sirens had howled. But no bombs were dropped, apparently another photographic mission. These were so common as to be unexceptional. Some of the sailors had told the GIs they were on yet another dry run but the Assistant Executive Officer of *LST 531*, the fifth ship in line, believed that 'most of the men thought they were embarked on the actual invasion of France'. Another crewman thought 'Poland!' Quartermaster Eugine Carney of the US 4th Infantry Division on the lead LST had complained on arriving in Plymouth — 'not another dry run!' But when he saw that the ship's tank deck 'was loaded with small planes and trucks filled with machine guns' he knew this was 'no routine practice'.[8]

It was certainly no drill for the second S-Boat *Rotte* led by Oberleutnant zur See Goetschke. *S-140* and *S-142* had crash started engines and were on an attack run. Stumbling on the convoy from a different sector, shadows had been identified nine miles out:

*Three small steamers (of 600-800 tons, with funnels to the rear) were identified running on a south easterly course.*

Goetschke gave his sister vessel commanded by Oberleutnant Ahrens permission to open fire at 2,000 metres in order to cloak his own attack run out of the moonlight. Five torpedoes were launched, close in, at ranges varying between 1,400-1,500 metres. They knew they had achieved surprise; at this range they could not miss. Anticipating retaliatory fire they broke off the action and sped off into the darkness. The torpedoes ran, but nothing — no impacts.[9]

The time was shortly after midnight. Convoy T4 ploughed on oblivious to the danger. Quartermaster Wendell Hoppler on board the lead *LST 515* recorded routinely in his log that the sea was 'very dark', the weather 'clear and calm' with 'a faint slip of setting moon'.[10]

Goetschke and Ahrens pulled alongside each other and conducted a short discussion boat-to-boat by megaphone as their vessels rose and fell on the dark mass of the swell. What had gone wrong? Goetschke subsequently reported:

*It could not be ruled out that the torpedoes had undershot (Tank Landing Craft). Two torpedoes were observed exploding on land.*

The feint and attack tactic was further pursued. This time the aim was 'to show the convoy's position to other S-Boats thereby creating further attack opportunities'. Their 40mm cannon began to thump out spiralling trails of greenish and yellow tracer lacerating identified convoy vessels. Goetschke described how at 01.30:

*Concentrated fire was directed from all weapons on the two northerly vessels from ranges between 600 to 300 metres ..... 60 rounds of 40mm cannon were fired from each boat. Good strikes. No response.[11]*

This four minute attack run was discerned by the third LST (*LST 511*) in the convoy line who reported: 'firing was seen astern, believed to be part of exercise'. The fifth, *LST 58*, was not so sure, shells were passing overhead and erupting in multiple ripples, slashing the water only 400 metres to port. Nobody could pinpoint the source of the firing. Both S-Boats, low silhouettes blending perfectly with the dark sea mass, were using flashless powder. Tracer ignited well away from the guns. An occasional flare lit the sky, and jets of molten tracer flickered ominously throughout the column as American sailors gazed anxiously about, trying to discern whether this was part of rehearsal realism or mistaken identity. General Quarters was sounded and reluctantly, in some cases enquiringly, soldiers and sailors within the convoy moved to battle stations.

Kapitänleutnant Jurgensmeyer and Oberleutnant zur See Stohwasser in *S-136* and *S-138* were roaring across the dark surface of the sea intent only on lining up on the dark silhouettes before them. 'Los!' ordered Stohwasser as he approached to within 2,000 metres of the rear right hand 'destroyer'. Two torpedoes ejected from his bows in an explosive discharge of compressed air. Almost concurrently two more erupted from Jurgensmeyer's boat directing a similar salvo at the lead destroyer. Taking rapid evasive action both roared off in a wide sweeping curve back into the inky blackness. No fire was returned.

Both boats stopped. Jurgensmeyer transmitted a short signal giving the convoy position. There was no reply. Peering intently at watch faces the crews counted off the seconds, willing success. The time was 02.03. Stohwasser estimated a running time of 95-100 seconds to reach the rear destroyer. All was black, until, as '95-96-97-98' was counted off, there was a flash, followed after a pause by a crack and roar. Jurgensmeyer observed:

*A huge fiery explosion, strongly audible in our own boat. S-138 observed the strike in line with the second funnel ..... simultaneously accompanied by the detonation of both torpedoes from S-136 after a running time of approximately 40 seconds.*

The forward enemy ship 'fired poorly directed tracer to the north east'.[12]

American Naval Corpsman Arthur Victor was on the port stern of *LST 507*, the last in the column, when it was hit.

*I was lifted from my feet and hurled back against a bulkhead. Although my head hit so hard I almost passed*

*out, my helmet absorbed most of the shock .....[13]*

Officers and men on the bridge of *LST 289* immediately ahead, saw an enormous flash, which reflected off their upturned faces. Darkness briefly intervened after the flash of the strike until a fire-ball arose, sucking in cold night air, before merging into a violently ascending light coloured bulbous column of smoke. Flames spread almost instantly from bow to stern. One torpedo slamming into the auxiliary engine room on the starboard side of the ship cut all electric power. The main engine stopped, and the ship, dead in the water, was engulfed in flames. Control at the rear end of the convoy now began to disintegrate. *LST 499* third from the end began to pull alongside the port side of the LST ahead of it. *LST 289* immediately to the front of the stricken *507* sheered off to port.[14] Damage control parties on *507* had no power to operate their pumps, so by 02.30 the order to Abandon Ship was given.

With four S-Boats committed, the remaining five became alerted, by degree, to the possibility of potential prey. The 1st *Rotte (S-100 and S-143)* just outside Lyme Bay intercepted Jurgensmeyer's initial contact transmission: 'Silhouettes. Two Destroyers off port bow.' Oberstormann Borkenhagen reported that:

*A few minutes later I observed a huge explosion at approximately 110 degrees, with two high white waterspouts. The impact could not be felt within the boat. After a while a loud sharp crack came through the air.*

Shortly after, two tracer rounds were observed curving languidly 'very high into the sky'. Borkenhagen considered the possibility of aircraft attacks, and immediately radioed his flotilla chief after the explosion 'What was that?' But he received no answer, from either *S-136* or *S-138*.[15]

The other three S-Boats from the 9th Flotilla picked up 'a short flash of light at 70 degrees'. They attempted to close in on the source. Presently they saw 'red tracer at 40 degrees, probably enemy'. Not realising this was the colour being used by the 5th Flotilla, they moved closer. Borkenhagen could still observe nothing 'despite very good visibility'. Until the situation regarding the engagement being fought clarified, he was keeping *S-100* and *S-143* out of Lyme Bay. This changed dramatically with the partial intercept of *S-138*'s signals traffic. A report of 'two destroyers in square 2393' was confirmed by a similar message from C-in-C E-Boats Wimereux, that they were 'coming from the east'. Then came the electric report from Jurgensmeyer, 'Destroyer sinking'. Gaining speed rapidly, the 1st *Rotte* began to accelerate into Lyme Bay, radioing both its own position and that of the enemy convoy they had been seeking all night. This message was intercepted by the remaining three S-Boats of the 9th Flotilla, tying in with the directional clue already provided by distant tracer fire.[16] The wolves were now gathering. But the slaughter, which was to continue throughout the night, had already begun.

The stricken and burning hulk of *LST 507* guided in the captains of S-Boats *S-100* and *S-140*. Borkenhagen saw that

*A larger tanker had been torpedoed by another boat in the north, which burnt brightly raising huge clouds of black smoke. The southern part of the bay lay within this dense smoke.*[17]

They sped toward the source of the activity at full speed. Random firing in all directions by various vessels could be identified through the smoke. Roaring through the obscuration at 35 knots, both S-Boats approached to within 1,500 metres of *LST 531*, ploughing on in the centre of the convoy. 'Los!' two torpedoes were fired from each. After a run of 76 seconds the first hit.

It was difficult to identify which vessel it was. The American bridge watch on *LST 58* following immediately behind cowered beneath the explosion, but when there were no flames, realised all the damage was to the ship ahead. Emanuel Rubin, crewman on *LST 496*, just ahead, saw:

*A gigantic orange ball explosion, like something from the movies, a flame like it had come from hell, with little black specks round the edges which we knew were jeeps or boat stanchions, or men.*[18]

Two ships had now been mortally wounded within the space of thirteen minutes. The stern of *LST 507*, the first hit, was now 'wild with confusion' according to Ensign Tom Clark on board, with men yelling 'we're gonna die!'[19] Soldiers and crew began leaping from the high side of a ship into a sea that was at once cold and burning with oil, dark yet already lit up in places by leaping flames. James Murdoch another officer on board later reported:

*All of the Army vehicles naturally were loaded with gasoline, and it was the gasoline which caught fire first. As the gasoline spread on the deck and poured into the fuel oil which was seeping out of the side of the ship, it caused fire on the water around the ship.*[20]

But 'the greatest horror' for medic Lieutenant Eugene Eckstam, which could still give him nightmares forty years later, were the agonising screams for help of the Army men trapped in the 'high roaring furnace fire' where trucks were exploding on *507*'s tank deck.[21]

Kapitänleutnant Jurgensmeyer was certain the 'tanker' was crippled and sinking. But he wanted to make certain. In a boat-to-boat discussion with *S-138* they decided to re-enter the engagement zone and finish the crippled vessel off 'in case it had not sunk, with 40mm gunfire, and pick up any crew as prisoners'.[22]

The demise of the second mortally wounded vessel *LST 531*, was even more swift than her sister ship *507*, and spectacularly violent. US Naval Medical Corpsman Arthur Victor, already floundering helplessly in the water saw the ammunition explode from *531*'s bow 'like a fourth of July celebration' and 'bodies flung in all directions like rag dolls'. Within six minutes she began to capsize and sink. He continues:

*We were in a state of unbelieving shock, as we knew that there were hundreds of guys on board whose losses were even greater than ours. More men became hysterical, screaming that the Germans were going to kill us all. Most were convinced that the entire convoy would be destroyed. Others cried that the Germans would come back and shoot us in the water. I kept screaming "Don't panic! Stay put!"*[23]

This view was shared by those at the front end of the convoy. On board the second vessel, *LST 496*, everybody was 'petrified'. Emanuel Rubin could hear the 'men in the half-tracks and trucks crying hysterically'.[24] The guns on the lead three LSTs were all firing. Two E-Boats swept from port to starboard on supercharge at 40 knots. None of the ships' guns could bear low enough to fire on this high speed threat throttling out of the darkness, sounding like approaching low flying aircraft. One passed directly in front of the third vessel, *LST 511*. The after port guns of *LST 496* ahead swept the decks of *511* wounding 18 officers and crewmen. Firing ceased when it was realised they were getting strikes on a superstructure too high for an S-Boat.

Convoy T4 began now to break up and scatter. By twelve minutes after the second strike Lieutenant Mettler, the commander of *LST 289*, now last in line was running for his life. Churning along at emergency speed, the ship was steering left full rudder then right at five minute intervals. The only defence against E-Boat attack was to expose the smallest target, the rear, and keep hostile shrieking engine noises behind. Several gun crews reported torpedo wakes astern, on the starboard quarter, then another across the port bow. Then yet another, running shallow, struck the stern high above the propellers. Thirteen men were killed at once, including most officers on the bridge, and 21 were wounded. The whole of the stern area was reduced to a mangled wreck, with the rear gun tub hanging over the edge of the superstructure at a ninety degree angle to the deck. The entire ship shuddered and reverberated following the flash and crack of the explosion. Small fires began to break out as the ship lay momentarily dead in the water. *S-145* from the 9th Flotilla, despite receiving random fire from enemy ships, roared jubilantly off into the darkness. Its commander reported

*Hitting with a surface runner, despite pronounced evasive manoeuvring by the Landing Craft ..... In technical shooting terms, this launch could be counted as the best of all.*[25]

*Below:* 'The whole of the stem area was reduced to a mangled wreck, with the rear gun tub hanging over the edge of the upperstructure at a ninety degree angle to the deck'. *LST 289*, shown here after the action, was struck in the stern. Thirteen men were killed instantly.

*Above:* 'Darkness briefly intervened after the flash of the strike until a fire-ball arose...' Torpedo strike on a 'large landing craft' photographed from a German S-Boat and displayed in the *Wehrmacht* illustrated propaganda magazine in June 1944. Quite possibly, they are pictures of the Tiger action.

*Below:* Kapitänleutnant Freiherr von Mirbach, commander of the 9th S-Boat Flotilla (standing centre), assessed that he had sunk three ships, two of which were LSTs.

The crew of *LST 289* restarted their propellers but were only able to turn to port. She was crippled.

The E-Boat assaults had now virtually engulfed the whole convoy line. *S-150* and *S-130* attacked a single LST, while *S-145* went after some small 'armed escorts'. The action could be likened to a shark feeding frenzy, command and control was lost as the E-Boat pairs strove to capitalise on individual successes. *S-100* and *S-142* were on the point of torpedo release, when their intended target, probably *LST 531*, burst into a fiery conflagration, hit by another boat. They themselves had difficulty keeping track of target 'steamers' that 'disappeared in dense smoke and mist'. At the height of the sinkings Borkenhagen, commander of *S-100*, complained:

*I could not run at speed because of our other boats in the immediate vicinity. Two boats from the 9th Flotilla were actually in sight. I decided therefore at 02.42 to retire.*[26]

Thirty five minutes later he collided with his sister boat *S-143* during an attack run, damaging the latter's superstructure. Borkenhagen understandably decided enough was enough, and broke off the attack to return to base. The convoy had been totally cowed. It was clear to one crewman on the third ship in line that the E-Boats had them 'trapped and hemmed in like a bunch of wolves circling a wounded dog'.[27]

Darkness and relative inactivity descended once again after 03.20. The glow of the burning vessels was snuffed out as they slipped scalding, bubbling and groaning beneath the surface of the sea. By 04.40 the E-Boats had broken off the action and were returning to Cherbourg, which they reached shortly before dawn, under the threat of retaliatory air-strikes. Only *S-100* and *S-143* were straddled by a stick of bombs as they made good their escape.[28] It had been their most successful mission to date.

It was not the invasion, but it did produce a scare along the German-occupied Normandy coast. The 9th Flotilla boats had been closer to assessing the significance of the action, and the first to identify and report landing craft at 03.25. German coastal defences had immediately been placed on alert. *S-100* eventually radioed during its return to base that 'beyond reported destroyers, nothing of significance'. 9th Flotilla reported an enemy destroyer 'bringing a landing craft under heavy fire'. It was evident to the German commander 'that the destroyer was not aware of the whereabouts of the landing craft in its sector, and that therefore it was more likely they were stragglers from a unit on an exercise'. The commander of the 9th Flotilla, Kapitänleutnant Freiherr von Mirbach assessed that his men had attacked a landing craft unit, sinking two LSTs, one of 4,600 tons another of 3,000, and hitting a further smaller vessel of 200 tons.[29]

The fact that this heavy skirmish had not heralded an anticipated Allied Second Front came as no surprise. There had been so many false alerts and alarms during April that, with the passing of favourable tide, moon and weather conditions, it was becoming increasingly likely that the Allied invasion would be coincidental with the anticipated Soviet summer eastern offensive.

Dawn on 29 April 1944 exposed the tragic failure of Exercise 'Tiger', the final dress rehearsal for some units before Overlord, the invasion of Europe, which was actually scheduled for 5 June. Julian Perkin aboard one of the rescue ships, the destroyer HMS *Obedient* reported:

*We arrived in the area at daybreak and the sight was appalling. There were hundreds of bodies of American servicemen in full battle gear, floating in the sea. Many had their limbs and even their heads blown off ..... Of all those we took on board, there were only nine survivors.*

Doctors were pushing those pronounced dead back into the sea. Not as callous as it appears because Perkin added that by this time 'small American landing craft with their ramps down were literally scooping up bodies. It was a ghastly sight'.[30]

## 'It will be all right on the night' . . . England, spring 1944.

The successful outcome of the invasion was dependent upon the ability of the Allies to project military power across the narrow channel. Tiger had shown palpably that this might not be possible. The exercise debacle summed up the problems of D-Day. Nothing on this scale had ever been previously attempted. This final dress rehearsal for the Force U, US VIIth Corps' landings on Utah Beach had not gone well in other respects also. General Bradley, commander of the US First Army, asked General Collins to assign a new beach commander to the engineers, based on their inadequate beach landing performance. He was not aware at that moment that the 1st Special Engineer Brigade alone had lost 413 dead and missing with 16 wounded. One unit, 3206th Quartermaster Company, had been completely wiped out. Total deaths were in the region of 749.[1]

'Tiger' and the following 'Fabius 1' exercise with Force O were held at Slapton Sands on the coast of Devon. Fabius 2 with Force G was held at Hayling Island, Fabius 3 with Force J in Bracklesham Bay and Fabius 4 with Force S to the west of Littlelampton. These large scale exercises were designed to test assault techniques and co-ordination between the joint US and British armies, smoothness of staff work in all phases of the operation, and techniques of mounting, marshalling, loading and unloading. With only six weeks to go before the actual invasion 'Tiger' revealed a disturbing and depressing spectrum of unresolved problems. Postponement of H-Hour ruined the air and naval bombardment programme. Units landed in the wrong place, there were insufficient maps, communications between landing craft and engineers on shore were non-existent. Traffic direction on the beach was chaotic, vehicles bogged down, medical evacuation and resupply were poor. Naval craft were motionless and bunched off the beaches, a potentially inviting target for coastal artillery. Perhaps worst of all, troops were 'unenthused' during the landings, to them it was 'just an exercise'.

US and British liaison revealed serious shortcomings. The fault lay on both sides, and both blamed each other for the tragic massacre that resulted in Lyme Bay. Convoy T4 had only a single British escort, which could not communicate directly with the American LSTs it was tasked to protect. The naval security screen had been penetrated by the E-Boats, and radar reports of impending disaster were passed on too slowly. The division of guilt for the disaster has been debated endlessly since.[2] It inevitably led to bitterness and recrimination. Coxswain Joseph McCann of *LST 515* was enraged whilst searching for survivors when

*We observed three British motor torpedo boats moving very fast from the north to the south. I felt sure they would move out and around all of the bodies and debris in the water, but they did not. Instead they cut right through and were churning up bodies in their screws.*

He had not had a chance to check them for life. 'We were very unhappy with the British Navy and that feeling still persists' he stated.[3] That the survivors were handled insensitively is indisputable. Infantryman Eugine Carney's experience was typical:

*We were told to keep our mouths shut and taken to a camp where we were quarantined. When we went through the mess line we weren't even allowed to talk to the cooks.[4]*

In the build up to D-Day, the Americans and British could allow no serious rift to open between them. Nothing — whatever the nature — could be allowed to weaken the Anglo-American alliance. But the strain of the impending operation was beginning to tell. The strategic decision that American forces were to attack on the right flank of the invasion had a profound effect upon the ordinary GI, now usually based in south-west England, and the civilian population that lived there. Units were relocated as required to the coastline fronting the English Channel from the eastern tip of Dorset to the far edge of Cornwall. US sailors took over ports like Falmouth and Plymouth, Dartmouth and Weymouth, and, almost overnight it seemed, the small towns and villages in Dorset, Devon, Somerset and Cornwall, felt the full impact of the American occupation. As one US battalion commander wrote to his wife, shortly after arrival in England. 'The British people seem very queer to us, and I suppose we seem just as queer to them.' He continued:

*There are so many of the ..... ordinary everyday things of the American way of life that I miss a great deal. Funny papers, magazines, cokes, just any one of the million and one things that we accept as the usual thing are gone, and I have suddenly realized that I don't know when I'll see them again.[5]*

Lack of understanding caused frictions. Lieutenant John Downing an American infantryman felt the underlying tensions. The British he felt:

*Outwardly retained their quiet courtesy, but there were signs that they were becoming testy about being crowded out of their pubs, their buses, and their cinemas and having their girls monopolised by Americans.[6]*

Americans *were* strange to the British. Not only were there divisions between Allies, there were racial divides within the US Army. White and black American soldiers were segregated. Quarters were separated on troop ships sailing to Europe. Black soldiers and white soldiers often could not even go to the same pubs or cinemas or dance halls when off duty in England. Timuel Black, a coloured (as the expression of the time would put it) GI in the Quartermaster Corps, commented paradoxically:

*The ordinary British were absolutely amazed, looking at these two armies. I guess they hadn't thought about their two armies, too: the colonial and the regular. But they were chagrined by this racial situation, which they'd never seen.*

White soldiers would say 'Don't have anything to do with those niggers'. Blacks seemed to be given the least desirable towns to go to. British girls were encouraged to accuse young blacks of rape if they had developed a relationship. Black remembers the outcome of such cases: 'We had one in our outfit who was hanged'.[7]

The longer the troops waited for the invasion, the more complicated life became in England. There were differences also with the Canadians. As one Canadian soldier commented 'initially we didn't like the Americans.' The British found this difficult to believe, since to them all the newcomers came from the same continent and shared the same language and similar culture. The difficulty was principally over money, the same problem dogging Anglo-American relations at the ordinary soldier's level. Combat pressures were subsequently to mellow differences, which were all too apparent within the restricted confines of troop concentration areas. The same Canadian soldier complained:

*It used to brass us off to see some Yank come in to a pub flashing five-pound notes, and try to buy the one bottle of whiskey in the place plus a place in the dart game plus the barmaid plus everything. I'd say most of the fights occurred because the Yanks had too much money and didn't understand the climate of England in those days, and they often got their faces pounded in for it.[8]*

American feelings were perhaps summed up by the final verse of a poem that appeared on the company bulletin board of a unit in the US 18th Infantry Division one day in May 1944:

*This Isle's not worth saving, I don't think*
*Cut those balloons loose — let the damn thing sink.*
*I'm not complaining but I'll bet you know*
*Life's rougher than hell in the E.T.O.*[9]

The flow of American men and supplies into Britain accelerated markedly from January 1944 onwards. In July 1943 it had already reached a rate of 750,000 tons per month, this now rose, in 1944, towards a D-Day peak of 2 million tons. To handle this vast flood, the supply organization — Com Z or Communications Zone — expanded to 31,500 officers and 350,000 enlisted men representing one quarter of the maximum 1,526,965 US troop strength (excluding sailors) in the United Kingdom[10] just before D-Day. Nonetheless, in the final months, a high proportion of the new arrivals were combat troops.

These men were immediately swallowed up in the large scale manoeuvres conducted during the last few months, a grim and weary business. One British helper in a Red Cross club in Exeter remembers how, at this time:

*Men would arrive on the Saturday night, with no bookings ..... muddy, tired and glad of a rest. As soon as eleven o'clock came and the dance was over mattresses would be laid on the floor in the main rooms, even in the cloakroom, and along the wide passages, so that there was somewhere for them to sleep.*[11]

Some of these men were veterans of North Africa, Sicily or Italy but the majority had never heard a gun fired in anger, having just completed six months training in the United States. Two months before that they had been civilians. Their usual age was 18-20 years. They were insignificant cogs in a remorseless build up that was to reflect the American way of waging war. There were to be no unnecessary, wasteful or superficially glorious heroics. The war was to be won surgically by an overwhelming preponderance of hardware and manpower, utilising technology to the full. George S. Patton the future commander of the US Third Army complained the anti-heroic impulse had been overdone 'that in our attempts to prevent war, we have taught our people to belittle the heroic qualities of the soldier'.[12]

Nevertheless these soldiers were human and subject to normal frailties; one of which was fear of the unknown. The large dress-rehearsal exercises unfolded in an atmosphere of dread and foreboding, which deepened as the winter of 1944 turned into spring, and with it the prospect of the invasion. Hitler's Atlantic Wall propaganda attained significance because its aura of invincibility, however unlikely, could not easily be laid psychologically to rest. Ralph Ingersoll, an American liaison officer on General Montgomery's staff, wrote:

*Everything across the Channel was mysterious ..... what we were doing had no precedent. The veterans of Africa and Sicily — and even they were a small minority — had no comfort to offer. The more they knew, in fact, the less reassuring they were — for they seemed only to remember the confusion and the wreckage and the terrible dependence of the amphibious operation on chance, on the luck of weather and the enemy's mistakes after the landing.*[13]

General Bradley felt, however, that such experience was indispensable. When the American beachhead was expanded during the Overlord planning to include Utah as well as Omaha, he decided to include the only veteran assault division he had 'rather than chance a landing with two inexperienced divisions', the 4th and 29th Infantry. He chose the 'Big Red One':

*By this time the 1st Infantry Division had swallowed a bellyful of heroics and wanted to go home. When the Division learned that it was to make a third D-Day assault, this time in France, the troops grumbled bitterly over the injustices of war. Among the infantrymen who had already survived both Mediterranean campaigns, few believed their good fortune could last them through a third.*[14]

Many were to be proved correct. The veterans understood the odds, and did not share the enthusiasm of those seeking their first combat ribbon. The 29th Division who, in Bradley's words, 'had staked out squatters' rights on Omaha Beach' having been in England since October 1942, did not impress the 1st Division's old sweats. 'Twenty-nine, let's go!' was the 29th Division battle cry, often earning the 1st Division response 'Go ahead, twenty-nine, we'll be right behind you!'[15]

Gloomy rumours about what fighting would be like began to permeate the 29th Division. Platoon and company level leaders, the gossips argued, would not last long in combat. Bradley felt he should visit the unit 'infected with a despondent fear of the casualties it was predicted they would suffer in the assault. Some talked of 90%.' He tried to be realistic, referring to casualty experiences in the Mediterranean.

*"This stuff about huge losses is tommyrot," I told them. "Some of you won't come back — but it'll be very few."*[16]

The unit was to sustain some of the heaviest casualties on D-Day. Lieutenant Bentz Carroll of the 16th Infantry Regiment, 1st Division made no secret of his preference:

*If I was going to be in combat I would rather be with combat-hardened troops than with people who were mostly untrained and inexperienced.*[17]

The Americans were not alone in their despondency. The British had been at war since 1939. Following milestones such as Dunkirk, the Battle of Britain and Alamein, the forthcoming Second Front was an emotional event. Its delayed start had begun to oppress both civilians and soldiers. They shared the forebodings of their allies. Waiting had gone on for so long. The inevitable mystery and secrecy of the operation added to the difficulties. As war correspondent Alan Moorehead expressed it:

*Although there was a general certainty that the landing would occur, people were without any technical knowledge of how it would be done; they had no means of estimating the chances; and as the talk and conjecture continued the fears increased. All that one could see ahead was a deliberately planned massacre.*[18]

A dead, heavy mood settled over the country, and this was communicated to the army. It would have been easier if more people were aware of the minute detailed preparation that had gone into this vast undertaking. Submarines had charted the coast, commandos had landed on beaches to gather information, hundreds of ships were collecting in the ports, five thousand aircraft were preparing for the day. Science in all its complexity and mystery was being applied to solve the assault problem at the minimum cost in lives.

The British 79th Armoured Division was, for example, an entirely new creation equipped with tanks specifically designed to meet particular invasion problems. So odd and diverse were they that the 79th was called the 'Funny Division', and the tanks themselves 'Funnies'. Lieutenant Ian Hammerton found himself commanding a Crab, or Flail tank. This had a large drum mounted at the front with stout chains attached with a metal end. Its task was to advance through minefields, chains flailing the ground. General Sir Percy Hobart, commander of 79th Armoured, briefed Hammerton's Regiment on its new role, leaving behind

*A sad and disillusioned collection of men. No sweeping across the fields of France at cavalry speed in our Cruiser tanks — just sweeping mines. But surely, came the thought, after we have cleared a few mines, we will be able to be let loose and Tally-ho! after the foe? Surely, after all our training .....*

Of course their training had to be shrouded in secrecy. As Hammerton's name was connected to that of a famous brewer — Hammertons' Stout — their activities became known as 'stouting'.[19]

Concrete pillboxes could hold up armoured advances, so a flame-throwing variant of the Churchill tank, the Crocodile, was developed, able to drive right up to a target and neutralise it by drenching it with flaming jelly. Lieutenant Andrew Wilson, soon to be a troop leader in such a unit, mystified as to why so many of his colleagues in C Squadron 141st Regiment RAC were 'on a course' he knew nothing of, asked for further information one mess night. He had heard of AVREs, Congers, and 'other devices' but was mystified by Crocodiles which

*Sounded dramatic — like a vast machine weighing thousands of tons which advanced with steel jaws to scoop up battalions of infantry.*

His curiosity overcame all else, and he asked 'Can someone please tell me, just what the hell is a Crocodile?' He was immediately invited to sign the Official Secrets Act.[20]

AVREs (Armoured Vehicles Royal Engineers) were modified Churchills fitted with demolition mortars instead of guns and provision for a wide range of special fittings from bridges to the 'Congers', rocket propelled mine clearing hosepipes. Others were equipped with huge 'bobbins' designed to lay hessian carpets reinforced with steel tubes to cross soft patches of clay. Turretless Churchill ARKs with ramps at each end could be driven into wide ditches to allow other vehicles to drive over them. 79th Armoured would be a vital factor in victory from Normandy all the way into Germany. Other specialist armour included old Crusader tanks with twin 20mm AA guns to provide protection from the expected air threat and little Tetrarch light tanks to be dropped in specially designed Hamilcar gliders. Above all however, there were the amphibious versions of the Sherman. Lance Corporal Patrick Hennessy of 13th/18th Hussars remembers:

*The notion that we would swim our tanks across the water was difficult for us to understand. A tank is a solid steel object and very heavy. "Surely," we said, "it will sink like a stone?" "Not so," said the Boffins, "consider this stone of which you speak. If you place it in a canvas bucket, and put that bucket into the water, it may go down an inch or two, but it will float."*[21]

A canvas screen supported by struts was the bucket, and Duplex Drive (DD) propellers provided the propulsion for the D-Day tanks. Underwater escape training was provided, but even during exercises 'panic was not far off'. All this was 'fine in theory — but we had grave doubts!' Like many of the other projects, the development of DD tanks was shrouded in obsessive secrecy. They were to provide the Germans with an unpleasant technological surprise.

A Canadian Lieutenant, W.D. Little of the Fort Garry Horse, described the impact of the first DD tank he saw, soon to be issued to his unit.

*This little barge turned and headed toward us, and as it rolled you could see it struck the bottom of the pond or lake, and started to roll up. Lo and behold — tracks! This was a tremendous surprise. Then as it rolled forward the tracks kept coming higher; and then as it got to the edge of the water, down came the screen and there was the gun. This was a terrific surprise and shock.*[22]

Hennessey, Little and their crew members were well aware of the risks, as was also the chief petty officer at Gosport responsible for the escape equipment; who said 'Rather you than me, mate!'[23]

As with the Americans there was a desire to bolster the inexperienced units within assault divisions by veterans.

The 7th Armoured Division, 'The Desert Rats', had been returned from overseas to participate in the forthcoming invasion. These men had few idealistic or romantic notions of what lay ahead. Some were war weary. Norman Smith, a tank crewman in the 5th Royal Tank Regiment (RTR), joined 22 Armoured Brigade on its return to England. The desert men he remembers:

*Felt they had not been exactly generously treated with home leave passes after all their years fighting so far from home ..... Graffiti began to appear on walls and railway carriages, "no leave, no second front". As someone said, "They can put us in prison if they like but someone else will have to do the fighting."[24]*

There were inevitably problems with wives, who had been left at home alone during years of overseas service. 'Jacked me in for a civvy,' said one soldier. 'I got home; no one there, no furniture, nothing.'[25] These soldiers were inevitably unimpressed with morale-raising visits by senior officers, unlike some units as yet untried in battle. Alan Moorehead, listening to General Montgomery's pre-invasion addresses, felt that:

*Monty was all right. He didn't talk a lot of cock about courage and liberty. He knew what it was like. And perhaps one had been taking the whole thing a bit too seriously. It wouldn't be so bad.[26]*

'Montgomery is a bit of a bull-shitter' was the unsolicited view of one old regular army desertman in B Squadron 5 RTR. Private Norman Smith was dubious that 'This "party",' referred to in Montgomery's speech, ..... 'was not going to be too bad'.

*"Not too bad, for those who are going to be dead?" muttered someone close to me.*

The General's rousing speech 'served only to increase our suspicions'. They knew what was required of them. 'We would rather have had someone just tell it straight.'[27]

Part of the problem of waiting was over-training. Men were confident and ready. By May their kit was packed to assault scales, with pouches full of ammunition ready to go. Frustrations were not eased by the 'flaps' or test embarkation exercises that were conducted in late May. Startled villagers and citizens of sea port towns would suddenly see columns of infantry trudge down to the docks and file aboard landing craft. A rumour would spread through the town that 'it' had started. Troops would then return and civilians would argue in groups at their front doors, declaring it had been called off yet again, or it had all been done to fool 'Jerry spies', or that it was only a practice. Trooper Duce of the 8th Hussars remembered:

*We had one false alarm at the end of May when we were paraded in Battle Order and marched down to the seafront to our respective vehicles with the intention of moving off,*

*but after having mounted up and kept hanging about for orders, it was suddenly cancelled. So back we went to our billets.[28]*

Lieutenant Colonel Moulton CO of 48 Commando, part of the initial assault wave, felt:

*We could certainly do with some more training but we could never recapture the old intensity; there is a limit to the time you can train the way we had been doing, and the tension would now be snapped. Better to go and have it over.[29]*

There was still a nagging doubt whether they would pull it off. General Eisenhower observed on the eve of the invasion 'the whole mighty host was tense as a coiled spring'.[30] Yet having prepared so long, so thoroughly, so intimately, it appeared at times the spirit to put the plan into operation might be lacking. It was a hot May, and still the waiting continued. Alan Moorehead declared: 'One felt only an emptiness and a mental weariness and overburdening ennui.'[31]

Convoys roared through the countryside day and night moving men and supplies into areas, from which in indeterminate stages, they would move to the embarkation ports and then into loading zones. Successive manoeuvres rehearsed every aspect of the invasion. Constant practice brought with it less tolerance of the everyday mundane mistakes that add up to what Clausewitz described as the friction of war. Even so, errors such as those exposed on 'Tiger' were dismaying. There would not be another opportunity on this scale before they went to put it right. Ralph Ingersoll wrote of a mood of gloom and pessimism before the invasion:

*With every amphibious exercise, through the winter and early spring, we seemed to get worse at it instead of better ..... vital equipment got lost, plans seemed forgotten and all sense of coherence disappeared ..... Demonstrably it could not be done.*

Resolve, nevertheless, had to be kept up at all costs. In the final resort, whatever the problems it was 'to hell with everything except getting on the beaches'.[32] Or as the theatrical profession might say: 'It will be all right on the night'.

All along the Channel coast lived the soldiers of the great Allied hosts. Most wrapped in their thoughts, listened day and night to the undertones of the wind, to the crack and groan of corrugated iron roofing and the mutter of loose doors in the camps, or the slap of canvas in their tents. Every morning as they awoke they saw the problem, the narrow Channel, the embodiment of their fears. Alexander Baron described the feelings of one such unit waiting pensively for the invasion:

*Before their eyes as they stepped shivering from their huts each morning was the Channel, the grey Channel, and beyond it — the grey mist.[33]*

# CHAPTER 2

# THE FAR SHORE

*'The day will yet come when the bells herald German victory, and we'll have peace again'*

*German soldier*

## ... The German Army in the West.

On the far shore, across the grey Channel, Grenadier Robert Vogt of the 1st Battalion 726th Regiment was hard at work, constructing so called 'Rommel Asparagus' on a strip of sand, soon to be called Gold Beach, next to Arromanches-les-Bains. This was the visible manifestation of the Atlantic Wall so feared by the Allied soldiers waiting on the southern coast of England. Vogt and his comrades worked hard on the beach obstacles. Like their enemies, German soldiers generally believed in the effectiveness of their Channel defences. Fed a diet of invincibility via impressive newsreel reports of massive coastal batteries in the Pas de Calais area, there was little reason to doubt that the Atlantic Wall was truly formidable. Indeed reassurance that, despite massive losses in the east, at least the west was secure enough, was what the Germans were seeking. Vogt was hard at work thickening up these defences, because unlike soldiers inland who had not seen it, those occupying the line were aware of its shortfalls. The obstacles were designed to ensnare landing craft. As Vogt recalled:

*We did all this at low tide when the sea retreated a few km. We put in a wooden stake and then, at a distance of, I'd say four to five metres, another stake. On top of these we attached a third stake with clamps — all of it done by hand — and secured by more clamps. Teller mines were attached to the tips of the stakes or beams, so that, at high tide, the mines were just beneath the water's surface, so that even a flat-bottomed boat would touch them and be destroyed.[1]*

The invasion was anticipated, but when and where nobody knew. Meanwhile as Vogt recalled: 'We worked in shifts around the clock'.

The German Armies in the west were commanded by Generalfeldmarschall Gerd von Rundstedt. Forward and right, on the Channel opposite the Straits of Dover was the Fifteenth Army, stretching from the Scheldt eastwards almost to the river Orne. To the left and west stood Seventh Army covering Normandy and Brittany. This element – *Heeresgruppe* (Army Group) B – was commanded by Generalfeldmarschall Erwin Rommel. In depth in the French interior was Heeresgruppe G consisting of the First and Nineteenth Armies.

German strategy for 1944 rested on the realization that decisive offensives could no longer be mounted in the east and that the growing strength of the Western Allies made a major invasion attempt almost certain before the end of the year. But those in the front line were aware that should the blow fall soon, they might not be ready. As Grenadier Vogt said:

*All this construction went on under great pressure because there were virtually no bunkers at our location, only dugouts. Generalfeldmarschall Rommel said at the time in his famous statement "You must stop them, here, forward, on the first day, if you don't, it's all over for us."[2]*

The invasion would prove a turning point. If an Allied landing could be deflected from the heart of Germany, and the beachheads annihilated, it was unlikely a new attempt could be made for a long time to come. As many as fifty German divisions might thereby be released to pursue the struggle against the Soviet Union.[3]

By early 1944 it had been acknowledged by the German Armed Forces Supreme Command (OKW), that no matter how critical the defence of the west was declared, there could be no question of withdrawing forces from the hard-pressed Russian front to strengthen it. The best that could be hoped for was to hold onto forces already in the various occupied territories outside of Russia, and devote the bulk of new resources in men and equipment that became available to the west, in the time before the Allies attacked. Originally they thought that France alone would be the target. If so an eight division force was to be raised from Norway, Denmark, Italy and the Balkans to repel it. However, by January 1944 OKW began to suspect that, although indicators pointed to an invasion across the narrowest part of the English Channel, it might be supported by subsidiary thrusts from other directions — Portugal or the Balkans. If so, the Germans could not afford to weaken sectors not immediately under attack in order to prepare for one main invasion. This belief was reinforced by Allied landings at Anzio, which resulted in the transfer of the highly mobile 715th Infantry Division from France, when this formation had formerly been included with the reserve armoured force. Supreme Command West (OB West) by this time had had its original eight-division reinforcement force diluted by a new policy providing support from within certain Replacement Army units in Germany. The new concentration consisted now of a corps HQ, two reinforced panzergrenadier regiments, one reinforced infantry training regiment, combat teams (*Kampfgruppen*) of those infantry regiments providing cadres for new divisions, a motorised artillery training regiment, five *Landesschützen* (infantry) battalions, and one *Nebelwerfer* (automatic mortar launcher) training battalion.[4] In effect a compromise solution born of strategic uncertainty, and certainly less than the original eight divisions.

A succession of crises on the Eastern Front further dissipated the original aspiration to grant the west priority of resources to face an inevitable challenge. On 10 March the 361st Division was ordered out of Denmark and replaced with a division of inferior combat value. Two weeks later the 349th Division in France was substituted by a new weak 331st Division from the Replacement Army (under training) in Germany. Four further divisions under OB West[5] were ordered to give up their assault guns to the Eastern Front. On 26 March the complete IInd SS Panzer Corps consisting of the 9th and 10th SS Panzer Divisions was despatched from France to assist First Panzer Army in Russia. This departure left OB West with only one fully mobile division (21st Panzer).

The end of March 1944 marked one of the low points of preparedness in the west, but during the following six weeks, and a stabilisation of the Russian Front, the west did much to recoup its losses. An opportunity may have been missed to launch the Invasion at the moment of least resistance, but the Allies as witnessed by Exercise Tiger were still not ready. By the end of the month the Panzer Lehr Division returned from Hungary and the 1st SS Panzer Division from the Eastern Front: both units were attached to OB West for rebuilding. Further the XLVIIth Panzer Corps under the very experienced and able General der Panzertruppen Hans Freiherr von Funck was also transferred from the east to serve under Rundstedt.

As was to be demonstrated again later during the war, the recuperative powers of the German forces in the west were remarkable despite the strain of supplying transfusions to the east. Between November 1943 and June 1944, the total number of combat divisions under von Rundstedt's command was to actually increase

from 46 to 58. This increase was achieved in part by the transfer of burnt-out units from Russia but mainly by the formation of new units. Sore pressed for manpower, by autumn 1942 the German Army was already adopting a policy of combining training with occupation duties. As the operational responsibilities of these training units increased, they also came under pressure to provide fillers for regular units before eventually being re-designated as infantry or armoured divisions. Six of OB West's reserve divisions, including all three reserve panzer divisions, had been thus upgraded before the Invasion.[6]

The steady drain of units from the west to other theatres, primarily the Russian Front, had an impact upon the organization and character of the remaining units awaiting the invasion. It produced broadly two kinds of units: old divisions which had lost much of their best personnel and equipment, and new divisions, some of potent combat value and others only partially equipped and trained. The rationale influencing the organization of the new units was to use the fewest possible men to produce the maximum firepower.

It would be to these units that the focus of German expectation would swing in the event of 'Der Invasion' or as the Allies referred to it: 'The Second Front'. Even as early as the summer of 1943 Generalfeldmarschall Rommel had declared:

*The West is the place that matters. If we once manage to throw the British and Americans back into the sea, it will be a long time before they return ...*[7]

Hope was still not lost so far as the German soldier was concerned; particularly the impressionable teenagers, schooled in National Socialist ideals, who had yet to experience combat. Fanatical Nazis were considerably more numerous among NCOs and particularly junior officers than the rank and file, and these represented the backbone of fighting power.[8] A young 18-year old, Grenadier Kurt Maier under training in Bessarabia, wrote to his mother during the spring of 1944:

*The war to be sure is not over for us yet. You see, the day will yet come when the bells herald German victory, and we'll have peace again.*[9]

## 'As for as the Atlantic Wall ... It was sheer humbug.' The Defence Debate.

Despite setbacks in the east, the German soldiers still broadly believed in the professional ability of the generals who led them. The coming battle in the west was, however, producing a conflict between two schools of thought — Rommel versus von Rundstedt — over the way this future decisive defensive battle should be planned. Successful defence with the means available was going to be difficult. All accepted that the armoured divisions with their great mobility and striking power were the decisive weapon, and the outcome would depend on the manner of their deployment. In addition the high ranking commanders agreed that in theory the optimum defence should be to smash the Allied attack before, or when, it reached the beach. The dilemma was how to reconcile the design with reality.

Neither von Rundstedt, von Sodenstern (C-in-C Nineteenth Army in southern France) nor Geyr von Schweppenburg (C-in-C Armoured Forces West) believed this was possible. Their plan was to cause as much attrition as possible during the landings by coastal artillery and a thin cordon of troops stationed on the coast. Enemy forces were bound to gain beachheads which would be counter-attacked by local reserves. Even this resistance it was anticipated would be overcome by the enemy, but he would then be thrown back into the sea by concentrated motorized and panzer forces. There were still differences within this school of thought over the conduct of the decisive phase. Von Rundstedt envisaged an invasion battle near the beach, von Schweppenburg planned it further inland, with his panzer divisions hidden in the forests of southern Normandy and around Paris. Von Sodenstern saw the counter-stroke occurring between the Seine and Loire, luring the Allies into a trap north west of Paris.

Rommel, with more recent experience, particularly of Allied air power, disagreed completely with this. He looked for ways of defeating the landings on the beaches, thereby achieving a strategic respite that could be exploited politically. He saw the imminent possibility of the V-1 flying bomb bombardment of England 'creating particularly adverse conditions for the enemy's attack'.[1] German coastline defences as presently configured would suffer severely from the overwhelming Allied material superiority, which would also negate the effectiveness of counter attacks by the few German reserves. With such a thinly held coastline the enemy would succeed in creating bridgeheads. Once on land the Allies would be difficult to remove. Rommel reflected pessimistically:

*Bearing in mind the numerical and material superiority of the enemy striking forces, their high state of training and tremendous air superiority, victory in a major battle on the continent seems to me a matter of grave doubt.*[2]

Therefore he concluded it was essential to fight the decisive battle from a fortified coastal strip. This involved the dual task of both defending the coast against amphibious landings and holding a strip 5 to 6 miles inland against enemy airborne troops. Rommel felt the number of direct fire weapons forward on the beaches, in particular machine guns and anti-tank guns was too small. Reserve panzer divisions would need to be deployed a short distance from the coast.

The conflict between Rommel's and Rundstedt's defence theories were never to be resolved definitely in favour of one or the other, and led to troop dispositions on D-Day which were not suitable for the practice of either theory. Von Rundstedt was to be even more emphatic after the war. 'As for the Atlantic Wall itself,' he said:

*It had to be seen to be believed. It had no depth and little surface. It was sheer humbug. At best it might have proved an obstacle for twenty-four hours at any one point, but one day's intensive assault by a determined force was all that was needed to break any part of this line.*[3]

An ineffective command network added further complications to the nuances and compromises that characterised the defence plan. Rommel had been tasked by Hitler specifically to review and improve upon defences in the west at the end of 1943. Initially he had right of inspection only, able to give advice, but not orders. This inevitably caused delays in the enactment of policies accepted eagerly at low level, but not palatable to superior staffs. Rommel was subsequently given command of Heeresgruppe B, which included Seventh Army in Normandy, Fifteenth Army in northern France and LXXXVIIIth Army Corps in Holland. Under command of von Rundstedt, Rommel could still only inspect the defences of other areas outside his command. Von Schweppenburg, C-in-C Panzer Forces West, was directly under von Rundstedt, parallel to Rommel, as was Generaloberst Blaskowitz for the south west and south of France. Neither von Rundstedt nor Rommel could give any orders to Generalfeldmarschall Hugo Sperrle, C-in-C Third Air Fleet, or to Admiral Thedore Krancke, C-in-C Navy Group West, nor were they permitted to move any of the armoured and other divisions without asking Armed Forces High Command (OKW). To add to the difficulties, the *Kampfgebiet* or fighting area and with it the jurisdiction of Army Group B and the armies defending the coast, did not reach more than 20 miles inland. All the interior was under a military governor who resided in Paris and received orders partly from OKW and partly from von Rundstedt. There was no recognised supreme authority, apart from Adolf Hitler, able to coordinate the coming decisive battle. Elements on land could not jointly interact with those at sea and in the air. It was a recipe for confusion.

## 'It is essential to prepare for hard times here ...' Normandy Defences. Spring 1944.

The German High Command did not know where or when the blow would fall. Normandy began to be considered an option only in terms of second guessing. The stronger the defences in the Pas de Calais, the less sensible it appeared to attack there. But the strategic

*Above:* We put in a wooden stake and then, at a distance of, I'd say four to five metres, another stake....' said Robert Vogt, 'Teller mines were attached to the tips of the stakes or beams'. Beach obstacles under construction. They were to prove particularly effective.

*Left:* Von Rundstedt declared the Atlantic Wall 'had to be seen to be believed...' This was sheer humbug. Much of it was only field defence shown here being frantically constructed.

advantages to the Allies of a short dash to Germany appeared to transfix the German mind and attract it to this area. It therefore became the *Schwerpunkt* or 'main point of effort' so far as defence resources were concerned, attracting the best quality units and equipment, and heavier fortifications. Alternative options could not, however, be ignored. It is in such a context that the defences of Normandy should be considered. They formed a part, albeit a subsidiary section, of the Atlantic Wall.

Forward on the Normandy coast were so-called 'static' ground-holding divisions. The war seemed far away to many of these soldiers, who as in the case of the 736th Infantry Regiment, had been manning defences in front of St Aubin since 1942. Oberleutnant Gustav Pflocksch thinking back on his 60-strong garrison reminisced later in halting English:

> St Aubin was a happy place for us. The soldiers were young people. They had their girl friends and made music in the private houses, they danced even, and they drank. I think that the soldiers were rather happy ...[1]

The 736th Regiment formed part of 716th Infantry Division, soon to be subjected with the rest of Seventh Army to the main weight of the Allied assault. To their right was 711th Division, the most westerly formation of Fifteenth Army, to their left was the 352nd (an infantry line division) and 709th Division covering Cherbourg. Also on the Contentin Peninsula was 243rd Division, a further static ground holding formation, and 91st Air-landing Division in depth.

The 'static divisions', which made up the bulk of von Rundstedt's infantry, had first been formed in 1942 in order to retain a nucleus of divisions not subject to transfer to the east. They were a triangular organization of nine rifle battalions, but substantially weaker than a line infantry division (such as the 352th), because they lacked a reconnaissance battalion, and had only three battalions of artillery. Although designed as permanent western garrison troops, by the end of 1943 many had lost their third regiments, sucked in by manpower crises on the Russian front. Generalmajor Dr Hans Speidel, Rommel's Seventh Army Chief of Staff, did not rate them highly, despite the fact they represented his main combat strength, complaining:

> They consisted of the older age groups, with a very weak veteran element. Training, because of a surfeit of over age commanders at all rank levels did not match their anticipated task. They were inadequately equipped in logistic terms, resembling an infantry division type from the end of the First World War. Lack of horses rendered them virtually immobile; they were hardly able to re-supply themselves.[2]

Moreover, differences in total strengths and the number and variety of combat units, meant static divisions bore little resemblance to one another. Whereas the 716th Division around Caen had six battalions and only one regimental headquarters under its control on D-Day, the 709th Division occupying two and a half times more coast line, around Cherbourg, had eleven battalions under three regiments.

The average age of soldiers in the Allied divisions poised to cross the Channel was 25. In 709th Division it was 36. German naval gun crews along the Invasion front were generally 45, with men of 56 and more.[3] These men had been in place for a considerable time and were becoming complacent. Life was comfortable. Relations between the French and the garrisons of these forward coastal zones were generally correct. Feldwebel Karl Schieck was posted from Paris to a battalion headquarters in the 736th Infantry Regiment as a master tailor. He remembers life in St Aubin, and contacts with the locals:

> We were stationed in the country and Herr Cassigneuel was our neighbour. As I was responsible for the shopping, I obviously went to him and asked if he would be able to help us out in any way, with various kinds of foodstuffs. I bought milk there for example, and out of this there developed a friendly relationship.

His sentiments were echoed by his French acquaintance Monsieur Cassigneuel who admitted:

> Our Germans were fine. We had no problems at all. We had horses on the farm and they had horses too. Many of the Germans were farmers and we were all the same age, we did the same kind of work, and we talked a lot about the way things were done. They told us about German methods and we told them about the way we did things in France. We swapped information. It was quite good really!

Bruno Skupski in the same regiment was also billeted 'in amongst the population' where by 1943 he had met and married his wife. There was an underlying feeling that the invasion, if and when it did come, would not arrive on the shores of Normandy.

Relationships were not always this comfortable. Life was harder within the hinterland of occupied France. Frenchmen were deported as labourers to the Reich. Jews were under investigation. People simply vanished without trace. Marie Josephe Houel worked in the St Aubin post office. She was under no illusions. 'They were our enemies you understand'. Her view was:

> I didn't like them one bit, I worked against them whenever I could. I did not even look at them. I turned my head away. I hated the Nazis. In fact we did not even call them Germans, we had our own names for them — "Les Boches".

The Germans, including Oberleutnant Gustav

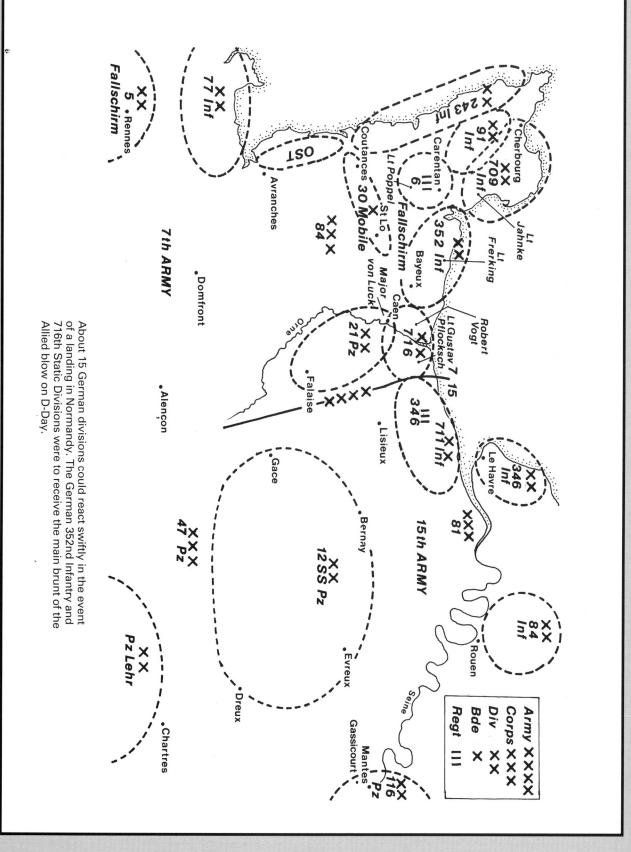

About 15 German divisions could react swiftly in the event of a landing in Normandy. The German 352nd Infantry and 716th Static Divisions were to receive the main brunt of the Allied blow on D-Day.

| Army | XXXX |
| Corps | XXX |
| Div | XX |
| Bde | X |
| Regt | III |

Pflocksch, were not insensitive to all this. The attitude of the French was in military terms largely irrelevant. 'Yes I heard of that', he stated 'but isn't that a natural reaction? They would hardly call us darling!' he added, not without a touch of humour.[4] Geneviève Duboscq an eleven-year old French girl living on the outskirts of Ste Mère-Eglise viewed the relationship through a filter of child-like simplicity.

> *They didn't strike me as particularly friendly. But then why should they be? What did we represent to these fair-haired, grey-eyed men? We were poor French peasants ..... We were nothing more than slaves, ants in a conquered ant-hill.*[5]

German complacency was to have a negative tactical impact. Rommel writing to his son, a Luftwaffe auxiliary at the end of January 1944, was sensitive enough to identify during his tour of coastal defences that 'people get lazy and self satisfied when things are quiet'. It was a characteristic discerned by veterans newly posted to the west from more active fronts. Rommel continued:

> *The contrast between quiet times and battle will be tough and I feel it is essential to prepare for hard times here.*[6]

Leutnant Arthur Jahnke, newly appointed commander of a strong-point – WN (*Widerstandsnest*) 5 – in the 709th Division's sector facing what was to become Utah Beach, had just arrived, on convalescence, after being wounded in Russia. He discovered to his amazement that French fishermen were authorized to stroll along the road right through his strong-point on their way to the shore. He forbade it.[7] Major Hans von Luck a seasoned veteran posted to the 21st Panzer Division was similarly concerned that the civilian population in his tactical area of operations could move about freely. He complained:

> *We even had to leave passages open in the minefields, so that the peasants could go about their business. Evacuation was not considered. Why should it be?*

The paradoxical reason was that German units manning strong-points along the coastal belt were engaged in peace-time occupation duties. Apart from the occasional air raid nothing happened. Luck's assessment was scathing:

> *Through this the Resistance, which was certainly active in Normandy, had the chance to let the British know our positions, where our tank and artillery parks were, and the location of the mine fields. And indeed we later found campaign maps on prisoners with precise indications of our positions.*[8]

Average division frontages reflected the German High Command's intuitive assessment that the invasion would come across the Pas de Calais and not Normandy. The Fifteenth Army with its 18 infantry and two panzer divisions was responsible for covering a 550km coastal sector. Seventh Army with its 14 infantry divisions and one panzer, was required to secure 1,600 kilometres. This represented in real terms a 40km divisional average in Fifteenth Army to something varying between 40 and 270km in Normandy and Brittany. The 716th Division in Normandy covered 40 kilometres, 709th around Cherbourg was stretched over 110 kilometres, while 77th Infantry Division in Brittany covered 270 kilometres. It was generally accepted that an infantry division could effectively cover a 10-kilometre frontage.[9] The Normandy defences therefore amounted to little more than an attempt to coordinate resistance between a series of widely dispersed strong-points, strategically placed at likely landing points along the coast.

Just how weak the Normandy defences were in comparison to Fifteenth Army's sector is revealed by a Seventh Army staff report prepared by Oberst Oehmichen, released four weeks before the invasion.[10] It disclosed that while Fifteenth Army disposed 22 anti-tank weapons for every 1-10 kilometres of front, of which three were heavy guns, Seventh Army could site only 12.25 of which 1.75 were heavy. Few of these could therefore be mutually supporting. The figures moreover reveal a misappreciation of the Allied ability to push armour in support of infantry into the assault, across beaches using both LCTs (of which the Germans were aware) and DD tanks of which they were not). This Allied technological capability was to produce a nasty tactical surprise, and moreover, the sector to which it was being directed had less than half the anti-tank resources of Fifteenth Army.[11]

The Normandy defences were a shell-like crust, only slowly thickening by virtue of Rommel's energetic attempts to harden it. Mine-laying continued apace but it took time to increase the deliveries of mines. So engineers designed simple gadgets under Rommel's direction to convert heavy shells into mines, and to produce makeshift mines from materials at hand. Up to the end of 1943, 1.7 million land mines had been laid in France. In 1944, over 4 million were laid, with a target of 50 million more.[12] Rommel felt able to write to his wife in January 1944:

> *I saw a lot and was very satisfied with the progress that has been made. I think for certain that we'll win the defensive battle in the west, provided only that a little more time remains for preparation.*[13]

Oberst Oehmichen's survey reveals that 750,000 T-Mines had been laid in the Seventh Army area by the end of May. 6,000 of these had been laid forward on the beaches. These figures represent a figure of approxi-

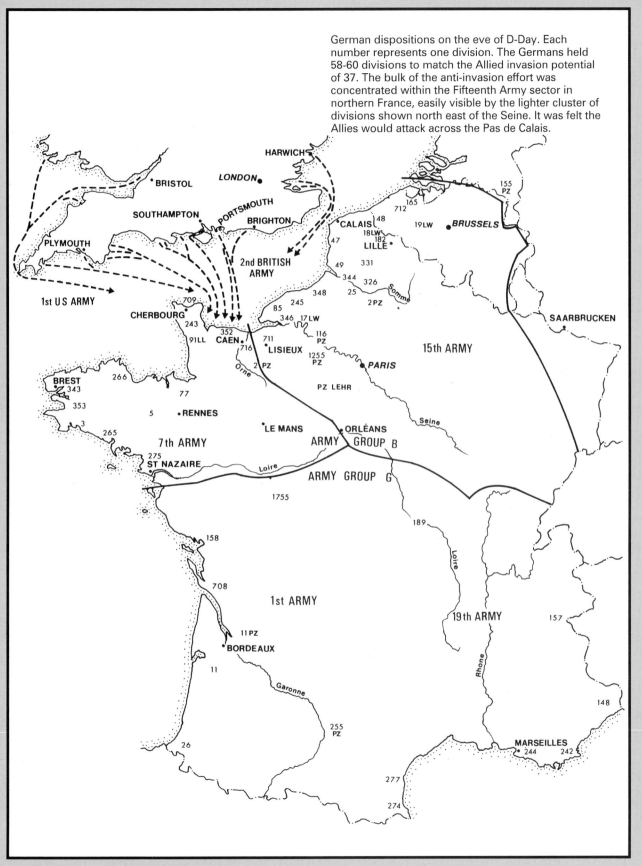

German dispositions on the eve of D-Day. Each number represents one division. The Germans held 58-60 divisions to match the Allied invasion potential of 37. The bulk of the anti-invasion effort was concentrated within the Fifteenth Army sector in northern France, easily visible by the lighter cluster of divisions shown north east of the Seine. It was felt the Allies would attack across the Pas de Calais.

mately 440 T-Mines per kilometre of front, in fact 30 mines per kilometre were laid among the beach obstacles actually breached during the invasion.[14]

Getting more guns to the coast and putting all the artillery there under bomb-proof shelters was slow work. Most of the effort, like all other defence preparations, had been in Fifteenth Army's sector, along the Channel coast. In the Pas de Calais and Seine-Somme sectors, 93 of 132 heavy guns had been casemated. Normandy had 47 heavy guns, 27 of which were under concrete at the end of April. As for fixed anti-tank positions, 16 of the 82 guns had been covered in the Fifteenth Army area. The nine guns in the Seventh Army sector were all open.[15] By the end of May, the LXXXIVth Army Corps estimated that its programme of construction was about half complete. On the east coast of the Contentin Peninsula, strong-points and resistance nests (*Widerstandsnester*) were spaced about 875 yards apart; between the Orne and Vire rivers, the interval was 1,300 yards. In the 352nd Infantry Division sector, only 15 percent of the shelters were bomb-proof. According to the commander of the 716th Division, soon to receive the main blow, the 40 to 50 fortified resistance centres in his sector were beaded along the coast like 'a string of pearls'.[16] Fortifications along the Normandy coast had no depth whatsoever. Plans to build a secondary line (*Zweite Stellung*) had to be shelved due to lack of resources, which indeed were insufficient to complete the first line. Rommel's inability to complete the Atlantic Wall was to compromise his basic strategic tenet to fight the battle forward in the coastal sector. All would therefore depend upon the forces in the interior.

## 'Your objective is not the coast. Your objective is the sea!' ... The Panzers.

Although the ideal would be to destroy the invasion forward on the coast, many senior German commanders accepted that resources to achieve this, would not be forthcoming. The panzer divisions, the instrument of crushing victories in 1940 and 1941, would provide the means for a decisive counter-stroke that could check inevitable penetrations of the Atlantic Wall, and throw the Allied invasion back into the sea.

The 21st Panzer Division was the nearest armoured unit to the Normandy coast. Owing to lack of sufficient supplies, it was mainly equipped with obsolete French war material taken after the French surrender in 1940. It had been reformed in Brittany in 1943 following the capitulation in North Africa. Built around veteran cadre units reconstituting after heavy losses on the Russian Front, it was filled out with replacements from Germany. The unit was in many respects an unorthodox panzer division, and still far from well equipped. Commanders were cursing their old French Somua tanks that had been captured in 1940 in which they had

to be both commander and gunner. Only slowly were Panzer Mark IVs reaching the division but even a few of these were old models with short 75mm guns, also dating back to the early years of the war. By the time of the invasion however there were about 90 late model long-barrelled Mark IVs with 21st Panzer Division, over 70 percent of its strength. Major Becker of the Division's Assault Gun Battalion 200 was a gifted engineer and reserve officer who had personal links with the armaments industry. He had improvised a highly effective force using his family company in Krefeld to modify French Hotchkiss and Lorraine tracked chassis to carry 75mm anti-tank guns and 105mm field howitzers. Between them the Assault Gun Battalion and divisional Panzer Artillery Regiment had 44 Hotchkiss conversions and 45 Lorraines. Major Hans von Luck commanding Panzergrenadier Regiment 125 within the division commented: 'at first, we laughed at the monstrous looking assault-guns, but we soon came to know better'.

Von Luck, a veteran panzer commander, had his reservations concerning the coming battle. Conditions within the motorised infantry regiments were little better than the tank units. Only one of von Luck's two battalions was equipped with armoured half-tracks, the other was truck borne. Oberleutnant Höller commanding a company in 192nd Panzergrenadier Regiment commented 'our best weapons are our old corporals, sergeants and NCOs'.[1] Von Luck's commander had made it clear that the anticipated Allied landing was not expected in Normandy, but rather in the Pas de Calais. Yet Caen, an important industrial city, had to be defended, because it was a key point. Luck's regiment was stationed north east of Caen, east of the river Orne, while his sister panzergrenadier regiment, 192, was located north of the city, west of the Orne. To the south of Caen was the panzer regiment, artillery, and the division's other units. The threat was reckoned to be 'airborne landings or large-scale commando operations, which would serve as a diversion from the actual landing'. Von Luck was disturbed at the curbs placed upon their flexibility to react. 'Our division,' he remembered, had 'strict orders not to intervene in the event of enemy landings until cleared by *Heeresgruppe B*.'[2]

Routine training continued, including terrain familiarisation and regular field exercises, many by night. General Feuchtinger the divisional commander, appears not to have inspired great respect. Von Luck categorized him as 'a live and let live person' adding:

*He was fond of all the good things of life, for which Paris was a natural attraction. Knowing that he had no combat experience or knowledge of tank warfare, [he was an artilleryman] Feuchtinger had to delegate most things, that is, leave the execution of orders to us experienced commanders.*[3]

The division although located near the coast, offered a

flawed tactical potential, as its freedom of action was limited by Army Group B. Inexperience might further inhibit its commander from exercising initiative for fear of making a mistake. As the invasion was not expected in Normandy this might be of only limited significance. Rommel addressing von Luck prophetically during one of his numerous visits did not, however, encourage complacency:

*I know the British from France in 1940 and from North Africa. They will land at the very place where we least expect them. It might be here.*[4]

If this was the case, the next nearest panzer formation to Caen was the 12th SS Panzer Division 'Hitlerjugend', located in a large assembly area due east of Falaise, encompassing Bernay, Gureux, Dreux and Gace. The majority of units could march to Caen, if unimpeded, within 1.5 to 9 hours.[5] The division was some 20,500 all ranks strong, with 149 tanks and tank destroyers (48 Panthers, 91 Mark IVs and 10 Jagdpanzer IVs) 333 armoured personnel carriers, 52 artillery pieces and some 2,750 vehicles.[6] A considerable force.

The so called 'milk-sop' division of youths varying from 16½-17½ years-old were to eventually earn the nickname 'Crack-Babies' from the popular German press.[7] They had ominously been moved from a training organisation in Flanders for the Ist SS Corps, as a fully fledged SS panzer division into France in April 1944. These recruits represented an identifiable cross-section of German youth whose background made them particularly susceptible to National Socialist ideals, and thereby good material for fanatical resistance. They had little to lose. After five years of war, a large number had lost fathers, killed and wounded or missing. Their mothers were often obliged to work away from home, sustaining the war effort. Teachers and Hitler Youth instructors had already been called up. Many boys had already witnessed the horrors of war first hand, serving as young Luftwaffe auxiliaries in cities feeling the full brunt of the Allied bomber offensives. Bombed out, or evacuated from their homes, the military offered succour of a sort. Some teenagers were undernourished and many found to be physically weak on reporting for duty.[8] Their condition was reflected in the initial training priorities set by the 'Hitlerjugend' Division for its recruits: firstly physical fitness, then 'character development' and finally weapon handling and field training.

Paul Kamberger a volunteer recruit for the 12th SS remembers this indoctrination, leaving 'unlit empty stations in the midnight hours' from Germany in November 1943 'heading west', for the recruit depot in Belgium.

*The train filled up on the way as, at many stations, similarly aged boys with cardboard suitcases or small bags climbed aboard. Not too difficult to work out where they had to go!*

Before long 'sections and squads had already formed up' so that by morning when the train arrived at its destination 'a super atmosphere reigned'. The recruits soon found themselves standing in the barracks' square waiting for the inevitable onslaught of instructors — 'and they came!' Trying to move off the square towards voluntary collection stands for the divisional unit of their choice, Kamberger with a group of colleagues headed towards the tanks. They were stopped.

*"Who are schoolboys?" Ten to twelve arms flew in the air, and thereby the divisional motor despatch-rider section was called into being.*[9]

Training for the division began in earnest, directed towards their future role. 50 Wehrmacht officers were drafted in as replacements to compensate for the inevitable shortage of experienced officers and NCOs among the teenagers.[10] Hard unbroken training continued mainly at battalion level, hindered only by a shortage of fuel. Three day exercises were routinely conducted each week. Call-out 'Alarm' exercises and anti-airborne training predominated. Much of it was conducted by night to avoid Allied air activity, an ominous portent for what was to come. New equipments and weapons arrived constantly throughout this training period as the division came together. Panther tanks were delivered during the first week of June.[11]

By 1 June 1944 Ist SS Panzer Corps announced the division 'ready for offensive operations'. Lacking only its anti-tank (*Panzerjäger*) and rocket launcher (*Werfer*) battalions, the 'Division was fully prepared for any task in the west'. This formation could present a potentially lethal check against any sector of the invasion coast. Its soldiers, nearly all teenagers steeped in National Socialism, with little to lose, viewed their approaching task with equanimity. SS-Sturmmann Jochen Leykauff felt he spoke for many in identifying the mood at that time:

*All waited for the attack across the Channel. It was clear that the decisive battle was upon us. Our first operation was imminent, and we were tense about it.*
*We wanted to sort out the "Milk-sop" label given us by the Allies. But we were not uneasy. Ja, occasionally we were even a little cocky. After thorough training on our weapons we believed we could handle ourselves.*[12]

These young fanatical recruits were issued sweets instead of cigarettes in their ration packs.[13] But they were no less lethal than their adult counterparts.

Deep within the French hinterland, occupying an assembly area 80 kilometres by 100 kilometres around Chartres, Le Mans and Orleans was the Panzer Lehr Division, recently returned from operations in Hungary. Panzer Lehr was the Wehrmacht show-piece. With 189 tanks (Mark IVs, Panthers and even a few Tigers), 40 assault guns and Jagdpanzer IVs and 658 armoured half-

*Right:* In 1944 over four million mines were laid in France. The target was 50 millions more. Rommel believed 'we'll win the defensive battle in the West, provided only that a little more time remains for preparation'. He had four months. Mining beach exits.

*Below:* The 'Milksop' Division - the 12th SS 'Hitlerjugend' took recruits aged between 16 and 17 years. They received sweets instead of cigarettes in their ration packs, but they were as lethal as their adult counterparts. A young 12th SS Panzergrenadier.

'*Above:* Bayerlein, your objective is not the coast, your objective is the sea'. In the past the panzers had swept all before them. Panzer Lehr Panthers in Normandy.

*Below:* The perennial question 'when will the Allies come?' remained an enigma. There were many false alerts. Observing from field defences.

tracks it was the only division within the German Army that was fully 100 percent armoured. Its commander Generalleutnant Fritz Bayerlein was under no illusion as to the importance of his coming task. Generaloberst Heinz Guderian, the Inspector General of the Panzer Arm, had expressed it succinctly during a recent visit: 'Bayerlein, your objective is not the coast, your objective is the sea!'[14]

Bayerlein, a veteran of the North African campaign, was — unlike many of his contemporaries who had experience mainly of the Russian Front — well aware of the destructive potential of the Allied Air Forces. Even now his units were located outside barracks, divided amongst woods, small farms and villages within his assembly area. To avoid Allied air reconnaissance, vehicles were forbidden to move by day, unless the weather was bad, even for urgent maintenance reasons. Much training, including camouflage and dispersal was directed at emphasizing and countering the Allied air threat, which daily flew reconnaissance missions across the assembly area. Bayerlein's division was ready for action. Stocks of petrol, ammunition and supplies were full. There was some concern at the shortfall of re-supply vehicles — some 23 percent — but 95 percent of the division's fighting vehicles were combat ready. The division on 1 June was pronounced 'ready for any offensive operations'. Furthermore 'training standards amongst all divisional arms had reached a good standard', achieved as a result of the division's bloodless intervention in Hungary. Dispersal among the French community was causing no problems. They had not been hindered by the French Resistance, and 'although the local populace was generally reserved, they were not unfriendly to the troops'.[15] There was still a requirement to train, but 'exercise opportunities on the whole, are not available'. Panzer Lehr, like the rest of the German Army in the west, waited.

## Cry 'Wolf!' ... Spring 1944.

German agents in England had been nervously passing on warnings of an invasion since early April. When April had come and gone and nothing had happened, they picked early May and then late May for the likely enterprise. The intelligence staffs cried 'wolf' so often, that by June, the general opinion at von Rundstedt's headquarters was that no invasion was likely now until July or August. There was in effect a crisis of credibility experienced by the German Army waiting in the west. This phenomenon, already apparent in the underlying tensions and complications bedevilling relations between American, British and Canadian soldiers in the Allied armies, began to manifest itself within the Wehrmacht also.

Static ground-holding German infantry battalions were supplemented by the inclusion of so called *Ost* (East) battalions, consisting of former Soviet soldiers, captured and paroled in exchange for service with the German army. There were two Ost battalions attached to 716th Division in Normandy. The 77th Infantry Division had an Ost artillery battery and a Volga–Tarter battalion. Richard Blinzing, a 36-year old Wehrmacht artillery forward observer serving in the small port of Binic near Saint-Brieux, remembers in the absence of an impending external threat, how volatile inter unit frictions could become. 'It was rumoured at this time' he recalled 'that the invasion was impending, but nobody believed it was going to be played out in this decidedly quiet sector of the Front'.

Hostilities on the contrary were to take a different form with the arrival 'probably April or May 1944' of Russians of the pro-German 'Vlassov Army' who replaced the local German strong-point garrison. Directly beneath the strong-point at this small Brittany port was 'a Nissen-hut cafe', often frequented by the local German soldiery, due to the fact that the proprietor had two very attractive daughters – 'Jacqueline' eighteen years old, and 'Mimi' an alluring twenty year old. The inevitable happened during the first visit by the Russian commander, who on leaving the worse for drink, insisted an understandably reluctant Mimi accompany him. Blinzing recalled 'the great tumult' that resulted as the kidnap attempt was foiled. The Russian commander and his accompanying adjutant were set upon by the German soldiery present, 'beaten and thrown out of the door'. Cursing, the Russians retired to their strong-point and sounded the alarm. All three 50mm guns within the strong-point were directed at the Cafe. Blinzing who had witnessed the whole incident with his team of artillery observers, was able to telephone the regimental commander and avert a catastrophe. The hapless Russian strong-point garrison was confined to its quarters, but Blinzing recalls that even three days later, 'the gun barrel nearest to the "Nissen Hut Cafe" was always directed against it'.[1]

The perennial question 'when will the Allies come?' remained an enigma. Rommel visited 21st Panzer Division on 30 May, exhorted the division to be extremely vigilant, and prophetically concluded 'You shouldn't count on the enemy coming in fine weather and by day.'[2] Many wondered if they would come at all. Major von Luck of the same division commented upon the torpor beginning to affect the troops in Normandy:

*The weeks went by. For a Panzer division, which in the campaigns so far had been accustomed to a war of movement, the inactivity was wearisome and dangerous. Vigilance was easily relaxed, especially after the enjoyment of Calvados and cider, both typical drinks of the region. There was, in addition, the uncertainty as to whether the landing would take place at all in our sector.*[3]

# CHAPTER 3

# OBJECTIVES

*'Dash and doggedness no longer make a soldier.'*

*Rommel*

## The Race to the Fore-shore …
## Objectives and Plans.

*Eisenhower's address was simple, straightforward and to the point. We would invade the Continent by way of the Normandy beaches on the morning of the fifth of June. [Later changed to the sixth.]*

Group Captain Desmond Scott commanding 123 Wing of the 2nd Allied Tactical Airforce (2 ATAF) had been given privileged information to enable forward planning. 'The preparations,' he recalls 'were staggering …The scale and precision of it all made our past efforts look insignificant'. Both the Allied and Axis powers were awaiting this decision. To be privy to it was a sobering experience.

*When the briefing was over there was no conversation, no laughter. No one lingered and we filed out of the [briefing] cinema as though we were leaving church. Old friends seemed oblivious of each other. Expressions remained solemn … The task ahead outweighed all our previous experiences and sent a shiver down the spine. With a mind full of doubts, hopes, fears and excitement, I climbed into my station wagon and set off for 123 Wing.*[1]

General Sir Bernard L. Montgomery was tasked by General Eisenhower to prepare and manage the coming assault and land battle. His headquarters, therefore, was an allied one, exercising operational command initially over four armies. The First American and Second British Armies were to conduct the assault, with the Third American and First Canadian Armies following up. On 15 May 1944 Montgomery gave the final presentation of the 'Overlord' plan to a select audience of the King, Prime Minister, Chiefs of Staffs and numerous generals in St Paul's School in London.

The plan was briefed in outline, followed by Montgomery's concept of operations. Five assault divisions were to be put ashore on D-Day. They would attack simultaneously from west to east. Two American divisions would be landed at Utah and Omaha Beaches immediately north of the Carentan estuary, forming the van of the First US Army under Lieutenant General Omar N. Bradley. Then between the Carentan estuary and the river Orne, one British division was to land on Gold Beach, a Canadian division at Juno and a further British division on Sword Beach near Ouistreham. These were the three leading divisions of Second British Army under Lieutenant General Sir Miles Dempsey. All five divisions were reinforced by armour, anti-aircraft units and several battalions of commandos and rangers. The attack was to be preceded by an airborne insertion of three divisions to protect the flanks of the intended lodgement. Two US airborne divisions would drop onto the Contentin Peninsula directly behind Utah Beach, and one British immediately east of the Orne river, north of Caen. The overall aim of the coordinated assaults was to secure a lodgement area which would quickly expand to include airfield sites and the port of Cherbourg. Within six days, seven more divisions were to be landed across the beaches, followed by five more supplemented by a number of armoured battalions and brigades over the next six day period. The Allied Expeditionary Air Force composed of 3,500 heavy bombers, 2,300 medium and light bombers, and 5,000 fighters would provide fire support. 1,400 troop carriers and 3,300 gliders had been made available for airborne operations.[2] There was limited scope for tactical manoeuvre. The Allies intended to smash their way onto the Continent of Europe by the mass application of sea and air supporting fire, and utilizing the momentum of the sheer violence of the initial assault.

Once ashore, Montgomery highlighted the operational dilemma taxing Allied and German minds alike. Who would win the subsequent race, following the break-in, to secure the fore-shore, the coastal strip, vital to the establishment of an allied lodgement? This was certainly not the problem taxing the minds of the commanders of the assault divisions, who sought primarily to get ashore in some semblance of order. The fundamental problem having breached the Atlantic Wall, was how to hold the rampart, until sufficient force

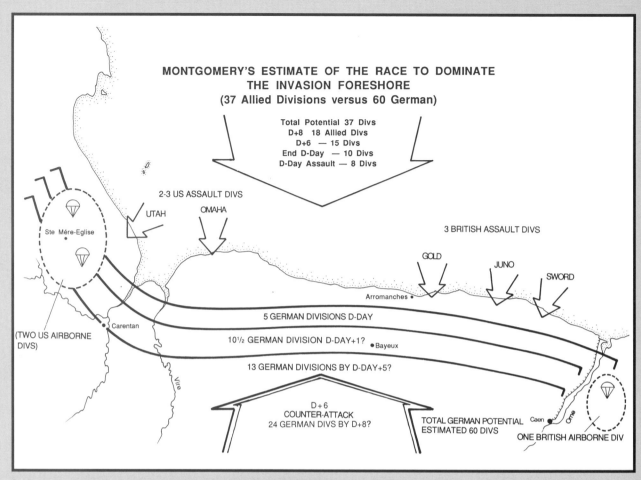

## MONTGOMERY'S ESTIMATE OF THE RACE TO DOMINATE
## THE INVASION FORESHORE
### (37 Allied Divisions versus 60 German)

Total Potential 37 Divs
D+8  18 Allied Divs
D+6 — 15 Divs
End D-Day — 10 Divs
D-Day Assault — 8 Divs

2-3 US ASSAULT DIVS

UTAH

OMAHA

Ste Mére-Eglise

3 BRITISH ASSAULT DIVS

GOLD

JUNO

SWORD

Arromanches

5 GERMAN DIVISIONS D-DAY

(TWO US AIRBORNE DIVS)

Carentan

$10\frac{1}{2}$ GERMAN DIVISION D-DAY+1?

Bayeux

Vire

13 GERMAN DIVISIONS BY D-DAY+5?

D+6
COUNTER-ATTACK
24 GERMAN DIVS BY D+8?

TOTAL GERMAN POTENTIAL
ESTIMATED 60 DIVS

Caen

Orne

ONE BRITISH AIRBORNE DIV

By D+5 Montgomery estimated 13 divisions could be on the move.

Battalion sectors within the 716th Division thickened up to regimental areas. More field defences, including wiring shown here, were constructed. A defensive crust was beginning to emerge.

could be built up to break out.

Montgomery identified a total of 60 German divisions in France, 10 of which were panzer and 12 mobile field infantry divisions. His intelligence estimate was only two divisions short.[3] His immediate concern was the five German divisions in situ, who could offer opposition to his proposed initial launch of five divisions (plus three airborne) in the assault waves, before reinforcements built up. It was assessed that 716th Infantry Division 'was expected to be completely influenced by the landings to the point of disruption'. This left 711th Division — assessed at 40 percent of the efficiency of a first class infantry division, and like 716th Division only 15 percent in the counter-attack role[4] — a field infantry division (the 352nd), assessed as being in the area of St Lô, another division at Coutances, and 21st Panzer near Caen.[5]

The risk, as identified by Montgomery, was immense. Apart from the immediate opposition that could be expected from the five German divisions in place; a total of four panzer divisions (12th SS, 17th SS, 21st and Lehr), could influence operations in the invasion area. At worst case 12th SS could arrive by 12.00 hours on D-Day and 17th SS Panzergrenadier Division by the evening. This would produce a ratio of 7⅔ Allied divisions facing six German, with 17th SS en route. On D+1 the Allies would have 10½ divisions ashore which could be matched by nine German, (five of which would be panzer).[6] The first conceivable critical point to the invasion could come when within 48 hours, with 12 divisions to 12, the Germans might match the Allied strength. By this stage Overlord would have become an overriding menace, requiring the concentration of all available German formations.

By D+5 Montgomery estimated 13 German divisions might be on the move.[7] They may not all have arrived completely, but the necessary ingredients for a full scale counter-attack, following reconnaissance and deployment, with infantry holding essential ground, and perhaps 10 panzer divisions available for the blow, would be present. A full blooded counter-attack would therefore be likely at any time after D+6. Eight days after the landings 18 Allied divisions could be confronted by 24. In addition to these identified disparities, there were the inevitable 'friction of war' limitations that the Allies would be required to overcome. There were 160km of sea between Portsmouth and Arromanches to cross. Several weeks would be required to land the 37-division strong Allied order of battle. This would be dependent upon the capacity of Allied shipping, the weather, and the tactical situation within the lodgement area itself. Small wonder Rommel felt able to confide to his wife that 'I believe we'll be able to beat off the assault'.[8]

Montgomery had few illusions concerning the task ahead. The enemy he felt, 'will do his level best to "Dunkirk us",' and attempt to 'force us from the beaches'.[9] The battle would be fought around three nodal points: Caen, Bayeux and Carentan. If these three towns were held by one side, the other would be awkwardly placed: the Germans to split the invader and 'rope off' the Allied salient; the Allies to hold a lodgement area sufficiently large to break out. Thereafter the Allies needed to secure the important ground dominating and controlling road axies in the close and easily defended 'bocage' country in order to go on the offensive. These areas were the high ground east of the river Dives, between Falaise and St Lô (between the rivers Orne and Vire), and further high ground west of the river Vire. Montgomery was relying upon the sheer violence of the Allied assault, supported by a great weight of fire from sea and air, coupled with his simple plan, to win through. The key to all this was to win the race in establishing superior combat ratios in the projected lodgement area. All Allied strategy was directed to this central tenet, win the race to the shore-line.

Deception was a means to this end. Allied freedom of manoeuvre was limited by the need to concentrate for a frontal assault to breach the Atlantic Wall, and restricted by the limited amphibious capability. Feints in other areas could only be achieved by deception. The extent of the success of Ultra in achieving this for the Allies has already been well publicised.[10] The code for enemy signals mechanically enciphered by Enigma machines had been regularly broken from earlier in the war. Messages had long been intercepted and rendered intelligible. Translated texts were distributed by secure means to appropriate Allied headquarters. Ultra facilitated deception on a strategic scale, and was to have a fundamental impact upon the course of the subsequent campaign.

The 'bending' of German spies in England contributed to the same end. So successful was this that an English-run Spaniard code-named 'Garbo' was awarded the Iron Cross by the Germans in June 1944, for the quality of his information. Six months later he was awarded the British MBE for the same work![11] 'Fortitude North', forming part of the Normandy 'Bodyguard' deception plan contained all German divisions in Scandinavia until well after D-Day, by assembling Allied 'ghost' divisions in Scotland. 'Fortitude South', perhaps the greatest orchestration of strategic deception in military history, achieved the decisive coup of reducing German strength in Normandy. Carefully simulated wireless traffic supplemented by double-agents' reports, incorporating the well-advertised presence of General Patton in England, built up a solid conviction in the German mind of the existence of First US Army Group or FUSAG in south east England. It was anticipated this powerful force would spearhead an assault on the Pas de Calais. The result was a total German intelligence misappreciation of Allied strength. German appreciations of May 1944 record a vast order of battle numbering 85 to 90 divisions plus seven airborne divisions.[12] The true figures were 35, plus three airborne divisions — an overestimate verging on 60 percent. The Fifteenth Army opposite the Pas de Calais was the sword of Damocles hanging over Montgomery; should it move westward in concert with the combined might of the Panzer divisions in reserve, then the race to secure an Allied lodgement beyond the fore-shore would never succeed.

## Realignment ... 'The situation did not look promising'.

In March, Rommel partially succeeded in increasing the number of divisions in or behind the coastal belt he considered as vital to blunt the invasion. The consequence was the moving forward of higher class field infantry divisions, the 352nd from St Lô and the 243rd Division near La Haye du Puits, nearer the coast, so that they could be committed in the first hours after an enemy landing. In some areas, particularly to the west or American side of the invasion sector, it doubled the number of troops, as the 352nd Division took over the left half of the 716th Infantry Division sector. Battalion sectors within 716th Division thickened up to regimental areas. Although not a decisive measure, it did represent a trickling forward of the combat power needed. Significantly Allied intelligence missed the realignment of 352nd Division.

Second-guessing the likely location of the invasion became an inevitable consequence of the build up of German forces opposite the Pas de Calais in the Fifteenth Army sector. While German military leaders were nearly unanimous in predicting the landings in this area, Hitler in March 1944 suddenly decided the Allies were likely to land on the Contentin and Brittany peninsulas. Records do not reveal how he arrived at this decision. German generals commenting after the war admit they were unable to see the military advantages of a Contentin assault compared to an attack against the *Kanalküste*. Hitler did not undertake any analysis of possible military benefits. It may well have been a degree of intuition, coupled with a mind that refused to be cluttered by general staff analysis, which could not accept, despite the success of Allied deception, that they would really attack at the defence main point of effort. A naval report by Admiral Kranke, Commander Navy Group West, concluded on 26 April, that Allied air attacks against batteries, radar installations and rail traffic; coinciding with naval mine-sweeping and mine-laying operations — hinted at the possibility of an invasion between Boulogne and Cherbourg. The main effort might well be against the Contentin, or the Seine or Somme estuaries. Cherbourg and Le Havre alone, it was pointed out, had been spared heavy Allied air attacks.[1]

Whatever the influences, in late April Hitler began to insist upon the need to reinforce defences in Normandy. On 6 May Seventh Army was ordered to deploy the 6th Fallschirmjäger (Parachute) Regiment, 206th Panzer Battalion and Seventh Army Sturm Battalion in the immediate vicinity of Cherbourg. Additional individual supplementary battalion moves followed. At the same time it was decided to switch 91st Airlanding Division, a Luftwaffe formation, en route from Germany to Nantes to the Contentin, where it was to take the 6th Parachute Regiment under command. All of these major units were ordered to prepare defences against airborne landings. The Contentin was thus substantially reinforced and fully alerted one month before two US Airborne divisions were due to be dropped there. Brigadier General James M. Gavin, second in command of the 82nd US Airborne Division, having formulated two plans already, was obliged to consider a third airborne plan as German units began to establish themselves on his proposed drop zones. As he recalled 'The situation did not look promising' following this further realignment of the German defence.

*Indeed, it looked so unpromising that it was decided to change our landing areas. On May 26 we received new orders, moving the Division further east.[2]*

There remained only 10 days to refine and brief the new plan.

The 6th Parachute Regiment began to menace not only proposed drop zones, it was within reasonable striking distance of Utah Beach, the most westerly of the proposed US amphibious landing points. Its 15-company order of battle, numbering some 3,457 men, made it larger and better armed than its corresponding Wehrmacht infantry equivalents.[3] Battle-seasoned veterans formed the core of this unit. Oberleutnant Martin Pöppel, a company commander, recalled the recruitment of officers for the new regiment after the battles for Monte Cassino between January to May 1944:

*One of the "Old Men" (Major Freiherr von der Heydte, the Regimental Commander) is looking for battle tested and experienced men from among the convalescents for the new 6 Regiment. We do our best to decline, but when he discovers that we're both "Heavies" from support weapons companies, that's it ... we have to join.[4]*

The unit was formed entirely from volunteer trained parachutists, aged on average 17½ years, possessing excellent fighting morale. Rifle companies had twice as many light machine guns as normal infantry division companies, while heavy weapons support companies were also superior with 12 heavy machine guns and six medium mortars. Pöppel's regiment took up positions in the Carentan-Le Plessie region. Each of the three battalions formed a sub-sector in regions 'which seem particularly favourable for an airborne landing operation by the enemy'.[5] As with any unit relocation, Pöppel described the frantic activity following the move, suggesting that the invasion was imminent:

> *The Regiment with all its units is established in its field positions, which we have worked tirelessly to complete. Alarm exercises by day and by night increases our combat readiness. The whole terrain has been surveyed for the heavy weapons, almost every eventuality has been considered.*[6]

A defensive crust was at last beginning to emerge along the Normandy coastline.

## 'The day of the dashing cut-and-thrust tank attack … is past and gone.'

Fundamental to the race to secure the coastline by both sides, was the nature of the units to be employed. Both the Allies and Germans were mesmerised by the location and potential combat power that could be generated by tank divisions. The German defence plan was based upon an appreciation of factors more relevant to its victories in 1940 and 1941, rather than the threat in 1944. There was an underlying premise that the panzers would sweep all before them, once they had been concentrated and been directed onto any Allied bridgehead. The Allies fearful of early *Blitzkrieg* lessons, hard learned, sought to match tank with tank formation; although the increasing effectiveness of anti-tank guns, *Pak* fronts, learned in the desert, had not escaped them. Nevertheless priority was still given to disembark armour formations, instead of infantry, to match the German panzer reserves. As Montgomery reiterated during the St Paul's briefing:

> *Armoured columns must penetrate deep inland, and quickly, on D-Day; this will upset the enemy's plans and tend to hold him off while we build up strength.*[1]

However, these combat appreciations paid scant attention to the nature of the terrain on the objective. Although the geography of northern France, opposite the Pas de Calais, was perhaps more suited to armoured operations, Normandy — quite patently a secondary possibility — was not. Flooded, hilly or close 'bocage' terrain, ideally suited to infantry defence, characterised the coastal strip inland from the proposed American beachheads to the west of the invasion sector. Similarly, apart from a strip of territory north of Caen, the British area in the east was subject to the same restrictions. The 21st Panzer Division was due to cover this area of 'good going', also identified within the German Oemichen Study as suitable for mobile armoured operations. However, behind the British lodgement area, to the south, were thickly wooded ridges, and to the east around the Orne estuary, further flooded terrain. Misappreciation of these terrain factors by both sides would favour the

Allies initially, as following an assault it would be difficult to mass armour successfully against the bridgeheads. Should fortunes change however, it would favour a German defence seeking subsequently to 'rope-off' Allied attempts to break out.

The 'bocage' or 'hedgerow' country in Normandy had not been fought over in 1940. Most German officers had previous experience of the rolling steppelands of Russia against a relatively unsophisticated yet immensely strong opponent. Ground in Normandy was different, and so too would be the enemy. The veterans knew war only in its two-dimensional form. They were unable to appreciate the impact that British and American command of the air had already achieved in the southern war theatre. There was therefore a misappreciation of Allied technological capabilities, matched by an unwillingness or incapability to adopt a combat task organisation more suited to this close terrain. German veterans regarded the British and Americans as comparatively incompetent at mobile warfare, considering that the western enemy would be no match for Eastern Front combat experience. Yet rolling panzer attacks would be no substitute for a balanced mix of tanks supported by infantry. 'Static' divisions were in essence unsuited. Mobile infantry, with firepower akin to the quality field divisions operating in Russia was what was required. The 352nd Division, due to be moved opposite the American sector was just such a division. Rommel was concerned at the German inability to manoeuvre, claiming 'the day of the dashing cut-and-thrust tank attack of the early war years is past and gone'.[3] The Panzer Lehr Division, fully mechanised, was not necessarily the most appropriate formation for the task ahead, as suggested by its regimental history:

> *Such a division, deployed in Russia, able to manoeuvre and apply the appropriate combat capability, possessed an equivalent value of three other fully equipped panzer divisions. But in the Normandy hedgerow terrain, with the French road network, and fighters as enemy, its position was untenable.*[4]

Allied tactics based upon the application of technological and material superiority in some areas, and supplemented by deception in others, was to produce a shock. Bayerlein, the commander of Panzer Lehr, recalled Rommel's prophetic analysis of the nature of the coming campaign:

> *Our friends from the east cannot imagine what they're in for here. It's not a matter of fanatical hordes to be driven forward in masses against our line, with no regard for casualties and little recourse to tactical craft; here we are facing an enemy who applies all his native intelligence to the use of his many technical resources, who spares no expenditure of material and whose every operation goes its course as though it had been the subject of repeated*

*rehearsal. Dash and doggedness no longer make a soldier ...* [5]

The spectre ahead was to come out of the third dimension — air.

## 'Jägerschreck' — Fear of Fighters.

Air power had not been a particular problem on the eastern steppes, where vehicles under threat could get off the roads quickly and disperse. Road systems in the west were not so easily accessible. While the Germans were to miss the potential significance of air dominance, the Allies were dependent upon it to win the race for combat parity and then ultimate superiority on the shore line, prior to breakout. 'Air must hold the ring,' explained Montgomery during his St Paul's address:

> *and must hinder and make very difficult the movement of enemy reserves by train or road towards the lodgement area.* [1]

To this end the Allied 2nd Tactical Air Force was given a two-fold objective: achieve air superiority, to allow unmolested ground support while denying it to the enemy, and provide a high degree of air support to army tactical operations. In April the Allied Expeditionary Air Forces (AEAF) commenced pre-invasion attacks, beginning with a series of assaults upon the western European transport system, demolishing railway workshops, marshalling yards and particularly bridges. Starting on 10th May, the tempo was increased to include systematic attacks on coastal radar stations between Ostend and the Channel Islands, followed one day later by attacks on airfields throughout the same area. Key points — night fighter direction and gun-laying control bunkers — were assaulted on a ratio of two sites outside for every one within the invasion area. After 21 May locomotives and rolling stock on French railways were rocketed and cannoned wherever they could be found. The French rail system was reduced to 40 percent capacity. [2]

The AEAF consisting of the RAF 2TAF, the US 9th and 8th Air Forces and Home Defence, amounted to some 7,520 aircraft. Opposing them were 891 German aircraft from Luftflotte 3 commanded by Generalfeldmarschall Hugo Sperrle. Inexorably the Luftwaffe was ground down by this superior force. By the end of May only 497 of these aircraft, of which 266 were fighters and 200 bombers, were operational. [3]

Göring's Luftwaffe Headquarters adopted the term *Jägerschreck* — fear of fighters — which summed up the reeling blow dealt to the Luftwaffe in the west. Allied intercepts of the once feared *Kanalgeschwader* (Channel Squadron) JG26 'the Abbeville Kids' of Battle of Britain days, observed that previous exhortations of 'Sieg Heil' and 'Horrido!' on radio nets had been replaced by more cautious transmissions of 'close up' and 'look out!'

Pilots it seemed were more interested in avoiding escort fighters than locating bombers. German fighter pilots were aggrieved at the *Jägerschreck* label. Ordered to attack bombers only, their only sensible course of action as Allied fighter screens perceptibly thickened, was to avoid contact. Young German fighter pilots in time lost their natural aggressiveness, obliged as they often were to run before the enemy.

As combat exhaustion took its toll, so did horrific casualties. By May 1944, Luftflotte Reich, responsible for German home defence, lost 38 percent of its pilots the preceding month; Luftflotte 3 on the Channel lost 24 percent. During this April period the entire Luftwaffe lost 489 fighter pilots and was able to replace only 396. JG26 on the invasion front lost 16 pilots in combat and a further six in accidents. The dead included two experienced squadron leaders. Such a casualty rate was ruinous, considering the low state of Germany's manpower reserves and despite an accelerated programme, so too was the length of time needed to train pilots. [4] During May the German fighter arm lost 25 percent of its pilots and 50 percent of its aircraft. By this time JG26 had lost 106 pilots since the beginning of 1944. Although representing 50 percent of the wing establishment the figure actually represented 140 percent of the average number of pilots actually available for combat duty during the period. Eleven *Staffel* (i.e. Squadron) commanders had been killed; irreplaceable combat experience. [5]

The US 8th Air Force lost 409 bombers alone during April 1944, 25 percent of its average strength, but unlike the Luftwaffe, their losses could be replaced. [6] However, a price was being paid. Group Captain Desmond Scott RAF, commanding 123 Wing of 2TAF, recalled the requirement to destroy all enemy radar stations between Ostend and the Channel Islands, in order to blind and deceive the enemy as to the main Allied invasion effort:

> *As our squadrons weaved their way into the strongest parts of the Atlantic Wall, the radar site defenders fought back like demented tigers. In attacking heavily defended ground targets there was no rule of thumb, no helpful advice to give. The experienced pilot shared the same deadly flight path as the inexperienced.*

His squadrons based on Thorney Island lost six commanding officers in three weeks. [7]

Some elements of the German Army in the west were beginning to experience for the first time the appalling ferocity of the assault from the new third dimension — the air. Radar stations, because of their technical requirements, were surrounded by clear fields of fire. On 24 May, four aircraft attacked the radar station at Joburg on the Cap de la Hague. Squadron Leader Niblett of No198 Squadron RAF led the assault. His report read:

> *Thirty-two 60lb rockets and cannon were fired. One*

*Above:* Locomotives and rolling stock on French railways were rocketed and cannoned wherever they could be found.

*Left:* During May the German fighter arm lost 25 percent of its pilots and 50 percent of its aircraft. A camera gun records the destruction of one victim.

*Left:* 'He dived below the level of the radar structure, fired his rockets into it and then tried at the last minute to clear it.' Pilot's-eye view of a rocket attack on a German coastal radio installation in northern France. *IWM*

*Below:* A German gun battery crew relaxes in the spring sunshine. The invasion was due to commence within one week.

*aircraft was seen to crash at the base of the installation. Flight Sergeant Vallely crashed on target.*

Niblett was killed one week later leading a similar attack on a radar installation at Dieppe. Months later a captured German soldier so impressed by the experience, insisted on recounting the desperate assault on Joburg to his interrogators:

*Three Typhoons came in from the valley, flying very low. The second aircraft received a direct hit from 37mm flak which practically shot off the tail. The pilot, however, managed to keep some sort of control and continued on straight at the target. He dived below the level of the radar structure, fired his rockets into it and then tried at the last moment to clear it. The third aircraft, in trying to avoid the damaged Typhoon, touched the latter's fuselage, and both crashed into the installation. This radar site was never again serviceable. Of the cables leading up to the target, 23 out of the 28 major leads were severed.[8]*

Only selected elements of the German Wehrmacht had any conception how violent this assault would be, when it came. SS Sturmmann Jochen Leykauff in one of the assembly areas of the 12th SS-'Hitlerjugend' Division inland, echoed the sentiments of many of his comrades, claiming:

*That the swarms of bombers daily droning their way overhead, could unload their "blessings" upon us, had us worried. Above all else, one kept an eye out for low level fighters. But then, certainly, our own fighters would come — we thought.[9]*

Still, nobody on the German side could predict when or where the invasion would some. An Ultra encription of a message from von Rundstedt's Headquarters on 29 May revealed little more than routine discussion with OKW on the fuel requirement to support Atlantic Wall defence construction that summer.[10] The invasion was due within one week.

# WAITING

*'Once the gate was closed ... You were committed irrevocably to the landing, perhaps tomorrow, perhaps the day after: no one knew for certain.'*

*War correspondent*

## 'Eternal Father Strong to Save' ... The Camps.

The Spring of 1944 was, as one Canadian soldier remembers, the one

> *I remember most. We were going to open a Second Front. Everyone knew that and that a lot of men were going to die.*[1]

The troops began to move from their divisional assembly areas to the coast. It was the height of spring. Commander M. Miller RN, an LCT squadron commander very much involved in the modification, cancellation and re-introduction of last minute plans, commented he had 'never seen so much blossom on the trees as there seemed to be as we sped through the Sussex lanes on our way to and from conferences at Portsmouth'.[2] The senses of men who feel they might die are inevitably heightened. More attention was paid to their surroundings. 'Hedges that lined the narrow, winding roads were green and fragrant', wrote Lou Azrael, a correspondent attached to the US 29th Division en route to the coast:

> *Gorse splotched the broad and rolling moors with gold. From the tops of hills, irregular patches of farms spread in kin-folk shades of brown and green.*[3]

The same Canadian soldier vividly remembered his last days in London where, even when moving through blocks of rubble or slums in the Strand, 'there seemed to be the smell of flowers'. Men drank life greedily in their perceived last moments:

> *There was a feeling that these were the last nights men and women would love, and there never was any of the by-play or persuading that usually went on ... My God, but it was easy to fall in love in those two months before D-Day.*[4]

Orders to many units cancelling leave arrived on 5 April. This was the first indication in the Allied camps as May wore on, that the invasion was imminent. Spring this year engendered contradictory emotions. As Commander Miller saw it:

> *When the blossoms began to fall we realised that the nightmare would soon be reality and the next year's apple-blossoms a doubtful dream that many of us might never see.*[5]

Sea-borne assault troops went first to 'concentration areas', where men not taking part in the initial landings were left behind. From about 26 May they moved onto 'marshalling areas' nearer the coast, consisting of closely guarded barbed-wire enclosures patrolled by uncommunicative sentries. American soldiers called the new marshalling areas 'sausages', because of their elongated appearance on operations maps. Most of the US 29th Division, due to land in the first wave on Omaha, were to remain in the sausages for almost two weeks. Boredom was to be their worst enemy. The British experience was similar, although in some cases lengthier. Captain Stephen Sykes, a Royal Engineers officer attached to 5th Beach Group Headquarters due to land on Sword Beach, remembers staying in Camp A2 with the 5th Battalion The Kings Regiment from 11 April until 2 June.

The movement of troops towards the coast had a profound psychological effect on both civilians and soldiers alike. A 14-year old girl in Tavistock, in the 29th Division area remembers how:

> *A couple of months before D-Day things went subdued and there was a great air of secrecy and solemnity where before there had been fun and light-heartedness. Everyone I knew seemed to disappear and I felt that a phase of my life was over.*[6]

Tension began to break, replacing the previous fever of suspense. Certainty came to soldiers who believed now that the invasion really was going to happen. This suspicion was also shared by the general public. One young woman working on a farm near Chippenham, near an American camp, was caught unawares when:

*At dawn on a Sunday morning they moved off. I was on my way to work and ... got off my bike and stood and waved for a little while. Now I'm older I should probably cry with realization, but then I accepted that they had not come to Chippenham to sit the whole war out. I had never failed to see an American in the town each time I went to work or school. Now it was to seem peculiarly empty.[7]*

Patrick Hennessy, a young trooper in the 13th/18th Royal Hussars, received seven day's leave in May. 'Nobody said it was embarkation leave,' he remembers, 'but few of us thought otherwise'. Then in the last week of May his unit was strictly confined to barracks. 'We were virtually sealed in with no mail or telephone calls allowed.'[8]

Captain Stephen Sykes, Royal Engineers remembers the 'big build up' that had been given about the final assembly areas in the south, to troops training in the north. There were apparently to be all kinds of comforts and non-stop cinema shows. Predictably, however,

*The food was about the same as any other army food. The non-stop cinema turned out to be a true fact, the only snag being that it was a non-stop showing of the same film.[9]*

Isolated within their camps as if they were abroad, sealed off in coastal areas forbidden to travellers, without leave and with their mail censored by officers as if they were already overseas, left the men plenty of time to reflect. War correspondent Alan Moorehead wrote:

*Once the [camp] gate was closed you could no longer return to the normal world outside, not even to buy a packet of cigarettes at the shop on the corner of the street, nor have a haircut, nor telephone your friends. You were committed irrevocably to the landing, perhaps tomorrow, perhaps the day after; no one knew for certain.[10]*

Unlike their adversaries across the Channel, the majority of Allied soldiers had yet to experience action. Sergeant Ian Grant, a combat photographer attached to 45 Commando, remembered how he and his colleagues were separately dropped off at different camps on the outskirts of Southampton. The imminence of action hit them:

*Quite suddenly we were almost strangers to each other and managed only a gruff "See you" at each stop. But inwardly the conscience repeated "keep safe — keep safe".[11]*

Most soldiers were concerned how they would face up to their first experience of battle. Only the veterans could tell them. Trooper Hennessy asked his Squadron Sergeant Major, who had fought in France in 1940: 'what is it like in battle, Sir?' He elicited an immediate dry response: 'bloody noisy mate!'[12]

The administrative tedium of camp life was made worse if, outside the perimeter wire, soldiers could still observe civilians going about their normal business. Such glimpses of normality to men rudely severed from all personal contact, and faced with an uncertain future, could have an unsettling effect. 'Beyond the wire' Sergeant Ian Grant could see:

*People, cars and the buses turning around at this terminus point, returning to the City — a threepenny ride perhaps — to homes, shops, cinemas and pubs. Was it real — us and them?*

Whereas inside the wire there remained only 'boredom; eating, sleeping; sprawling in a tented city' with 'warm spring sunshine giving promise of the summer ahead'.[13] All kit had been reduced to assault scales; spare clothing collected by quartermasters, and personal belongings in the case of the British, stowed in men's kit-bags, labelled and sent to their homes at Army expense.

Briefings started, men played cards, short haircuts were advised to prevent lice, maps were issued and new equipments began to appear. Lieutenant Ian Hammerton, a Flail tank troop commander remembered 'a thrill of expectation' which 'zipped through the camp as we saw our "B" Echelon three-tonners arrive with tank ammunition', which they proceeded to load into their tanks.[14] The impending operation was drawing steadily nearer.

This was also the time to write last letters. Most like Hammerton wrote 'letters of farewell we hope would never have to be sent'.[15] Compositions were not imaginative, they were for the most part brief, guarded and unsentimental. Soldiers tended to write what their loved ones expected to read. There was a reluctance to tell the truth or reveal inner emotion, apart from affection, for fear this may cause pain or concern.

*Dear Mum . . . You may not hear from me for a week or two, as we shall be busy for a bit. Don't worry, whatever you read in the papers. I'll make up for it as soon as I can with a nice long one. Love and kisses, CHARLIE.[16]*

The tedious waiting in the camps continued. Fear began to take an insidious mental toll. As one soldier recalled: 'fear feeds on delay, of course, and we didn't really know just when we were going'.[17] Concern at the coming assault produced a nervous apathy in some, which was in effect a psychological defence mechanism. There was a desire not to reflect on the future. War correspondent Alan Moorehead explained:

*The mind projected itself forward as far as the embarkation, as far as the landing. Then there was a blank, a kind of wall over which the mind would not travel.[18]*

Troops were broken down into landing craft groups in their respective camps. When the time came to load, they were called forward. This in itself produced strain. Moorehead recalled how waiting hour after hour 'drove the mind into a fixed apathy. It made you reluctant to walk, to talk, to eat, to sleep,' producing an oppressive atmosphere 'like an over-rehearsed play'. His description of the call forward process is like a grotesque parody of a dentist's waiting room:

*We sat at rickety trestle tables, eating slices of cold bully beef and cold white cabbage ... A few made some attempt to talk, but most of the officers sat eating silently, and brushing the flies away from their plates. Every few minutes a loudspeaker outside the tent began calling numbers. These were the numbers of units which were to prepare themselves to go down to their ships and invasion barges. As the numbers were called the men at the table cocked their heads slightly to listen. One or two men got up and left the tent. The rest went on eating the cold cabbage.[19]*

This all changed once soldiers were told the plan and what they had to do. Lieutenant Colonel J.Moulton, CO of 48 Commando, shortly due to land at St Aubin recalls the 'atmosphere was electric'.[20] Sergeant Grant with 45 Commando wrote: 'tomorrow, June 4th, we move out at 6 a.m. Myself tense, the others not so, their faces mirror anticipation and confidence'.[21]

Southern England by now resembled a vast armed camp. Every wood held its quota of huts or tents, piles of ammunition and other stores. Troops of all kinds were everywhere, tanks, lorries, carriers, guns of all calibres and many other equipments lined roads, under trees, hidden from the air, ready to go. A 17-year old boy from Appleshaw near Tidworth saw that 'Perham and Tidworth hill were so crammed with tanks you could scarcely walk between them'.[22] Lieutenant Ian Hammerton about to move to the coast with his flail tanks noticed:

*Perhaps most impressive of all, the narrow roads had been widened, telephone poles, fences and even hedges moved back, corners strengthened, with concrete. Everything combined to give us a gigantic boost of confidence.[23]*

The civilian population could plainly see what was happening; as witnessed by a schoolboy in the Salisbury area, previously used to observing 'large convoys passing through the village on a summer evening' watched by 'us villagers from the village doorways'. Now, instead of 'as usual turning towards Tidworth' the vehicles 'continued on towards Southampton'.[24] Mile long columns of DUKWs (amphibious vehicles), three-ton lorries, jeeps and tanks and bulldozers roared out of camps and traversed urban areas. 'On the sidewalk one or two people waved vaguely' reported Moorehead:

*But for the most part the people stared silently and made no sign. They knew we were going. There had been rehearsals before but they were not deceived. There was something in the way the soldiers carried themselves that said all too clearly "This is it. This is the Invasion".[25]*

Nobody had illusions about casualties. Ian Hammerton's tank troop 'were told that on this sea-borne landing we could expect at least two-thirds casualties'. This meant that:

*At least sixteen of the troop might be wiped out. Nor were we to stop to care for any wounded. Not very cheering, but there was too much else to think about.[26]*

But not so the rank and file. Unlike the officers, once their personal equipment had been sorted and stowed, there was plenty of time to ponder the future. A housewife living in the Sussex village of Singleton remembers how this manifested itself with the departure of the US 4th Cavalry Regiment. One morning in June, 'on pulling my cottage curtains I noticed odd packages on the window sill'. They proved to be 'wallets with mothers' and girls' pictures and such like treasures, [with notes] asking me to care for them until they could call again'. The Americans reluctant to say 'Goodbye', feeling it was 'too final', preferred instead to say 'So Long'.[27]

The steady movement of troops from camp to camp approaching the embarkation ports continued remorselessly as administrative plans, rehearsed countless occasions before, were put into effect. The impact on local populations alternated between sadness and bewilderment. One Henley-on-Thames woman inured to losing one set of friends after another as units rotated through the park opposite her house, nevertheless, remembered the departure of one particular artillery regiment shortly before D-Day. It was a:

*Warm, quiet and peaceful evening my children were tucked up in bed and I leaned for a few moments out of the window, thinking about how far away war seemed, when, very quietly at first, I heard the sound of "Eternal Father Strong To Save" coming from the camp. It became louder as more voices joined the singing. It was so moving my eyes filled with tears ... That night we heard the rumble of midnight traffic. The next day ... nothing.[28]*

## Embarkation ...

Lieutenant Gregson, Royal Artillery recalls:

*Our orders came to embark on June 3rd after dark. It was a filthy night and as darkness descended we moved off in road convoy from our forest "hide" down towards the Solent shore, the air choking with dust and fumes and*

*Above:* 'On the sidewalk one or two people waved vaguely.' Cromwell tanks moving to the coast. The invasion was imminent.

*Below:* Huge choke points formed outside major British ports.

*vibrations as we crawled slowly through the forest, nose to tail.*[1]

The steady inexorable movement of traffic towards the coast continued. A resident of Dorchester saw a priest standing on the corner of one street 'all day long while he made the sign of the cross as each vehicle went by, and the men bowed their heads'.[2] Journeys were not without mishap. One British tank officer assailed by the dust and diesel fumes thrown up by so many armoured vehicles travelling head to tail, commented on the fatigue all units experience moving to the area of hostilities, even before going into action. He noticed:

*Everyone who had been in the main column was suffering from eye strain, varying from a minimum of slight soreness to Lieutenant Pothecary, who lost his sight completely and for some time had to be led about.*

This, coupled with the tiredness caused by columns crawling, and stop-starting, making no more than 5mph, produced huge choke points outside major British ports. The officer observed there was 'so much traffic that normal road discipline was abandoned'. The order was given: 'close up and get on'.[3]

Trooper Duce from the 8th Hussars, part of the 'Desert Rats', 7th Armoured Division wrote: 'we simply had to follow the tank in front with no idea where we were going'. They moved through the streets of Gosport 'in the early hours' and were ordered 'to kip down on the pavement beside our tanks after hot cocoa'. They were thankful for the rest.

*At around six o'clock next morning we were roused and gazed bleary-eyed about to find we were the centre of attention. Towns people were looking from their bedroom windows, registering amazement at the sight in their streets and obviously amused at the various state of dress of the troops.*[4]

Men moved down to the 'hards' and harbours and began to embark on the ships. Tension rose. 'There was so much going on' recalled a Canadian sailor crewing one of the transports, 'it was very confusing, very exciting, not knowing for sure all that much about anything'. There was no turning back now. 'That first night when we took on the load of troops those soldiers seemed to be a little quieter and more serious-looking'.[5] Small wonder, these would provide the initial attacking waves.

The sea-borne assault was a complex operation. Five divisions were to land from west to east on the Normandy coast. From right to left flank were the US 4th and 1st Infantry Divisions (including elements of the 29th) embarking between Falmouth, Torquay, Dartmouth, Poole and Portland; and further east: the British 50th, Canadian 3rd and British 3rd Divisions embarking between Southampton, Portsmouth and Newhaven. These five divisions would produce eight assaulting

brigade groups or regimental combat teams in American parlance. Such a task force would generally consist of 5,000-6,000 men and about 700 vehicles, allowing for differences in uniformity between British and American groups. Each of the eight assault groups was to attack with two battalions of infantry, a battalion of amphibious DD tanks, one battery of self-propelled close support artillery and special engineer parties — Navy and Army — with special armoured vehicles, designed to clear beach obstacles.

It was a major staff and logistic feat to arrange the arrival and loading of these units at the correct ports, in reverse order, enabling them to disembark in the correct assault order of battle. Commander M. Miller RN for example faced with the complexities of loading his LCT so as to achieve the correct draught and slope of keel, determining how far up the beach he could land, found himself remonstrating with commanding officers whose tanks with their 'household necessities were considerably heavier than a second lieutenant's'. They could not therefore be allowed to load forward and put the craft down at the bows. 'After much explaining' he commented

*We convinced the colonels that this was not just some nautical whimsy. But the tenacity with which this "Battle of the Baggage" was fought boded ill for the unfortunate Germans when the disgruntled losers stormed ashore.*[6]

Last minute discoveries of German defence improvements caused enormous difficulties. Major Kenneth Lord, Assistant G3 (operations officer) of the US 1st Infantry Division 'received an awful blow' when, on examining air photographs of the Omaha Beach obstacles, underwater mines were discerned, an aspect of the defences not previously considered. Two additional engineer battalions had to be found and allocated to 'lead off the division attack' and breach this new menace. Lord later reported:

*Now we had to change our entire loading plan. We went to the underground headquarters at Plymouth and worked around the clock for three days, until we had it finished. We imagine it was a great shock to those engineers to find that they were the first wave.*[7]

Many became casualties.

To carry the initial amphibious assault of 40,000-50,000 men complete with vehicles and equipment required an armada of over 4,000 landing ships, landing craft and barges of varying types. Only about half of these were capable of crossing the Channel under their own power, the remainder being towed or carried aboard larger ships. Every man and vehicle was allotted to a specific craft; all vehicles had to be 'waterproofed', and both men and vehicles had to arrive at their 'hard' (improvised landing place) at pre-planned times for loading. It was an immensely complicated task of planning and organisation. The naval effort to protect and support the assault force, code named 'Neptune', included five battleships, 23 cruisers, and 79 fleet and escort destroyers as well as a swarm of sloops, frigates, corvettes, patrol craft, mine-sweepers and a fleet of over 200 specially designed, purpose built fire support landing craft.[8]

The US 29th Division assault transports were loaded by 31 May off Plymouth and Falmouth. They sailed that night to join 'Force O' destined for Omaha, assembling off the Dorsetshire ports of Weymouth, Portland and Poole. There followed a period of several days during which transports bobbed up and down at their moorings and waited. Soldiers had little to do but ponder the future. Cramped, claustrophobic conditions coupled with the niggling frustration of over-crowding, however, gave little opportunity for considered reflection. There were the usual boisterous pastimes: 'shooting crap' and playing poker. Incredibly the Navy was serving white bread, chicken, ice cream, steak and limitless hot coffee. 'Some of us thought this to be the last meals for the condemned' remarked First Lieutenant Edward James Jnr, a member of the divisional Cavalry Reconnaissance Troop. There was no alcohol.[9]

The British experience was little different. A bombardier from 90 Field Regiment RA remembers boarding his troop ship at Tilbury docks during the afternoon of 3 June:

*In seconds racks were completely packed with bedding, … packs, haversacks, webbing equipment with pouches, water bottles, steel helmets, rifles, sten guns, etc. The temperature on board was rising rapidly, and before long men were sweating.*

The ship was a hive of activity. 'Order, counter-orders and noises soon filled the air'. It was virtually impossible to move on board after nine o'clock until reveille at five, with soldiers 'in hammocks, swinging under stairs, over tables, on tables and under tables'. Unlike the Americans, the British played housey-housey or Bingo. Most of the troops, however, 'were reading, writing, sunbathing or just watching the waves'. As might be anticipated, there were queues for everything aboard the large troopship. 'It was nothing to wait two or three hours' for the simplest of requirements, such as orderlies lining up to pick up the breakfasts to be shared at tables.[10]

Private Irwin Spandau, a US 1st Division mortarman remembers on boarding his transport in Portland, an absence of the traditional grumblings and complaints. Men appeared strangely quiet. 'They were all too preoccupied with their own thoughts and fears to make much noise'.[11] A British infantryman from the East Yorks Regiment rather resented being 'lined up at the harbour wall' and then 'shunted on [to the ships] like

cattle going for slaughter'. So as the launch moved off to their transport, they cocked a snook at authority, represented by a Military Police officer:

*From the safe distance on the boat, knowing nothing could be done about it the lads blew resounding raspberries and in a good-humoured sort of way shouted insults and profanities at the Redcap, but he never batted an eyelid. The officer came up to the salute and I swear I saw a smile on his face.*[12]

Once on board, fear was an insidious presence. It manifested itself in a number of ways: loud boisterous chatter, banal jokes and sleepiness. Fatigue, often an adjunct of fear, dulls the mind. Men preferred to succumb to tiredness rather than come to terms with a myriad of gruesome images that tended to wander across the mind. Lieutenant John Bentz Carroll of the 16th Infantry Regiment, shortly due to land on Omaha, recalled:

*There was a lot of talking when we first went aboard; by the second night, when we definitely knew we were going in on D-Day the following morning, everything became quiet. Men got out pencil and paper and started to write to their loved ones at home. Most of the crap games disappeared to a large extent, and the men started to become quite sober about what they were about to go into.*[13]

Uncertainty was the key unsettling factor, coupled with individual fears whether they would be able to cope with impending pressures. Lance Corporal Hennessey of the 13th/18th Royal Hussars recalled:

*A feeling of excited anticipation as we waited for the arrival of the LCTs, one or two, mostly the older men, were somewhat apprehensive. Individually I think, the majority of us were wondering how we would face up to our first experience of battle ..... each one of us must have asked himself just how he would cope when under fire from an equally determined enemy.*[14]

Lieutenant Colonel Michael Forrester, 7th Armoured Division, felt himself asking 'am I going to be up to this myself?' Fully realising 'it takes a certain amount of personal drive to overcome it'. But the real conundrum was:

*The unknown, which we were going into meant uncertainty. You don't know, and uncertainty very naturally leads to apprehension, and so the adrenalin is flowing.*[15]

## Postponement …

The weather, mirroring the mood of turbulent uncertainty grew worse. General Bradley, the commander of US First Army glancing at the G2 (Intelligence) weather forecast on Sunday 4 June reviewed the gloomy forecast for the next three days:

Specially-built hards were constructed to embark troops. The US 29th Division assault transports were loaded by 31 May off Plymouth and Falmouth.

'A feeling of excited anticipation', which soon changed to sober reflection. An American troop transport ready to go.

'You could have walked from the Isle of Wight to the mainland on solid ships.'

*Mist from Sunday to Wednesday, with low clouds and reduced visibility in the mornings. Winds not to exceed 17 to 22 knots. Choppy water in the Channel with five-foot breakers. A four-foot surf on the beaches.*

'Doesn't look good,' he commented. Dickson, a member of his personal staff was more emphatic: 'It stinks'.[1] General Eisenhower decided to postpone the invasion for 24 hours. Force 'O' outward bound for Omaha Beach had already departed after the previous midnight. General Bradley foresaw the impact this decision would have:

*Now the sharp edge of those troops would be dulled and seasickness would take its toll in another day on the choppy Channel. We checked the weather forecast that had been posted in our journal. It was even less promising than the one on June 3: five-foot waves in the Channel and no sign of a break in the overcast until June 7 or 8.[2]*

Destroyer Squadron 18 commanded by Commodore Harry Sanders aboard the USS *Frankford* battered on through heavy seas toward the French coast. The recall signal although encoded, was contained within a message pile-up. Squadron 18 was screening one of the Omaha-bound convoys commanded by Captain Sabin. Just before the convoy was scheduled to turn south, which would have provided confirmation to radar-watching Germans that the invasion fleets were heading for the Bay of the Seine, the message was discovered by the communications officer aboard the USS *Frankford*. Two destroyers were despatched post-haste to bring Sabin's ships back to Poole harbour; here they were kept waiting outside the harbour overnight. A false start had been bad enough, but now a despatch boat, which had developed a leak, sank. The remaining ships were tossed about all night by the stormy weather. Lieutenant John Bentz Carroll of the 116th Infantry Regiment had seen 'all kinds of vintage 1920 boats; anything that floated was carrying troops' and 'some of those poor devils were on those ships a week to ten days'.[3]

Postponement had a stultifying effect on the whole army. A British Yeomanry officer wrote that the last minute delay 'made them all glum and depressed'. Moreover the outlook did not appear promising:

*There seemed no break in the sequence of depressions coming in from the Atlantic. As they embarked there had been something like jubilation. But now spirits fell as they had nothing to do but study the heaving grey sea, and feel their precariousness, anchored out in deep water.[4]*

Sergeant Ian Grant with 45 Commando remembers 'the decision to abort was not accepted with pleasure'.

Inevitably 'men were sullen and critical of the higher echelons of command'.[5] Inland light breezes gave no indication of their impact upon stormy Channel waters. Troops returned to their tents and relaid bedding. Captain Stephen Sykes, Royal Engineers 'utterly sick of the waiting period' had seen landing craft assemble off the coast and drop anchor; but saw then 'to our dismay ... that we were heading back to Newhaven'.[6] For others the moment brought a transitory sense of relief. Lieutenant Gregson, Royal Artillery, recalled:

*We were well out into the Channel and it was dark and rough, when the code message same through — "Return to Base". The tension evaporated and I for one heaved a sigh of relief that the great trial of strength was postponed for the moment.[7]*

But for the majority, including Lieutenant Colonel Moulton, CO of 48 Commando, it was 'better to go and have it over'. Any relief could only be fleeting,

*Somewhere in the back of my mind must have been the thought of reprieve from the responsibility for others' lives and danger for my own. In that electric atmosphere, that did not seem to matter much, our main wish was to go, and we felt flat and disappointed that we were not to.[8]*

Lieutenant Holbrook also experienced 'dismay and perplexity'.

*But there was nothing more the men could do. They felt a depressing sense of flop. They tried to rest, but were anxious and downcast.[9]*

The delay heightened the perception of vulnerability. Captain Sykes, picturing harbours choked with ships all along the south coast, remarked that 'surely at least one German reconnaissance plane would get a glimpse of it and the whole operation become known',[10] because daylight in June lingered until 22.00. A crew member aboard an anti-aircraft landing craft observed the 'confusion' of ships caused by the postponement decision, which was 'so great you could have walked from the Isle of Wight to the mainland on solid ships'. His view was that 'if the enemy missed this golden opportunity to bomb us, which they did, they never could or would'.[11] He was to be proven correct.

General Eisenhower met again with his subordinates at Southwick House on the evening of 4 June A more favourable weather report was presented. At 02.00 on 5 June, the order putting convoys in motion again for Normandy was re-issued. Sergeant Ian Grant remembered the activation of 45 Commando:

*Next morning there was no hesitation and we sped away*

*in trucks, racing through Southampton's streets, with passers-by knowing full well what was about to happen — blowing kisses, weeping and cries of good luck.*[12]

Members of the US 29th US Infantry Division who had been recalled and had just returned to port hardly had time for a hot meal and a decent cup of coffee before putting out to sea again. The invasion was on.

Men had few illusions over what now lay ahead. Soldiers of the 116th Regiment outward bound for Omaha were able to reflect upon their Regimental Commander's last word prior to embarkation:

*There is one certain way to get the enemy out of action and that is to kill him. War is not child's play and requires hatred for the enemy. At this time we don't have it. I hope you get it when you see your friends wounded and killed. Learn to take care of yourself from the start. Remember the Hun is a crafty, intelligent fighter and will not have any mercy on you. Don't have it on him.*[13]

Within 24 hours they would meet the enemy face-to-face.

# CHAPTER 5

# IT'S D-DAY TOMORROW

*'It's "D-Day" tomorrow, but we've known that for ages,
Are young lives nearly finished?  Can we turn back the
pages?'*

*British Paratrooper 5 June*

## Manning the West Wall ... 5 June

Unteroffizier Hans Rudolf Thiel of *Fallschirmjäger*
(Parachute) Regiment 6, greeted the dawn of 5 June
with some enthusiasm:

*The invasion alarm of the previous day and last night has
been lifted.  The storm has abated and it has stopped
raining.  The sun is even shining today, as if it wants to
compensate us for the unbelievable tension of the last
24 hours.[1]*

Oberleutnant Martin Pöppel commanding the 12th
(Support Weapons) Company was reasonably satisfied
with the positions they had just occupied in the
Carentan-Periers area. They were situated on the edge
of the proposed American airborne landing zones. Much
had been achieved since arriving two days before but
'more arduous labour to extend the positions, put up
camouflage nets and set up sniper posts' would be
needed. 'Then the Regiment can wait calmly for the
expected attack from the enemy'. Major von der Heydte
the Regimental Commander felt confident enough to
conduct a map exercise on 5 June involving all battalion
officers down to platoon commander:

*In which the possibilities of an airborne landing by the
enemy are played through. We disperse amid laughter and
no one has any idea how near we are to the real situation.[2]*

They were to be in action within hours.

Unteroffizier Thiel was thankful not to be planting
further anti-glider obstacles. While the officers were
involved in their map exercise, the soldiers were
conducting low level field training. Thiel and his men
conducted a machine gun siting exercise in the
surrounding meadows, which provided a welcome
break:

*Oberfeldwebel Geiss our platoon commander, allows us to
catch up on the sleep we missed last night. As well as we
can, we all seek out a place with good cover in the hedges,
or sunbathe.[3]*

Enemy air activity remained all pervasive. Major von
Luck, commander of Panzergrenadier Regiment 125,
based north of Caen, recalled that 'in the first days of
June, British aerial reconnaissance over the Normandy
coast increased considerably'.[4] Unteroffizier Thiel
observed how:

*At high altitude above us one enemy bomber squadron
after another flies into the hinterland, and from there we
can hear a terrible thundering.[5]*

Increased air activity appeared to herald a sinister portent of what was to come. Its true significance was difficult to assess. There had been so many false alarms in
the Seventh Army sector that soldiers were beginning to
question the credibility of a spring invasion. Indications
there were aplenty, logical acceptance of these warnings
there was not. On 5 June Headquarters Seventh Army
reported:

*Since the 30 May the enemy has been systematically
destroying the Seine bridges between the estuary and Paris
from the air, in order to cut off troop deployments from the
south or north.*

The appreciation concluded this might be the preparatory phase of the forthcoming battle in the west, beginning with 'the destruction of traffic centres and the
break-up of the railway network', enabling the enemy to
mount his main offensive either north or south of the
Seine.[6]

Grenadier Robert Vogt of the 726th Infantry Regiment dug in opposite the future Gold Beach near Arromanches said later, 'we knew certainly that something
was coming; but where, when and how, that we could
not imagine'.[7] Unteroffizier Thiel at the base of the
Cherbourg Peninsula shared this general unease. 'Our
morale is good', he recalled, 'but the old front veterans

have 'something in their water'. Something was afoot, an intangible threat, loosely interpreted, possibly, as the calm before the storm.

*Even I can't conceal a sense of unease. After the relative calm of the last few weeks I turn my thoughts to the massive bombardments of the hinterland. Something is going to come down on us.*[8]

Many eye-witness accounts of the German Army in the west on the eve of the invasion are wise after the event. There was a general feeling of insecurity; a psychological state deliberately fostered by Allied deception measures, and false alarms since the beginning of spring. Major von Luck, an experienced panzer commander 'felt our lot was highly unsatisfactory', explaining:

*Like most of my men, I was used to mobile actions, such as we had fought in the other theatres of war; this waiting for an invasion that was undoubtedly coming was enervating.*

Yet Normandy was still a peacetime occupation zone, in which training alongside defence preparations was still the major activity, and had been thus for almost four years. On 5 June von Luck gave his IInd Battalion clearance to release its 5th Company for its routine night exercise. His policy was to rotate a different company into the field on manoeuvres every night. The trucks departed shortly after last light. As usual the troops had been issued with blank ammunition. 'The evening of the 5 June 1944', as von Luck was later to write, 'was unpleasant. Normandy was showing its bad side; during the day there had been rain and high winds.'[9]

Generalfeldmarschall Rommel had departed his Army Group B Headquarters the previous evening, driving to Germany for discussions at Hitler's Headquarters. Although the timing was partly influenced by bad weather, his real aim was to brief the Führer personally on his misgivings over the coming invasion battle. Despite 'imminent danger', Supreme Command West (OB West) held the 'Alarm State' at the lowest level, declaring in its assessment of the situation, released during the evening of 5 June that 'the immediate prospect of an invasion is not yet identifiable'.[10] Indeed so low was regard for the threat, that Generaloberst Dollmann, Commander Seventh Army, was en route to Rennes in Brittany for a 'war games' map exercise. Also making their way along various routes were the commanders of the 91st, 77th, 709th, 352nd and 716th Divisions — all holding sectors about to be struck by the Allied assault. The absence of these key commanders was arguably due less to prevailing weather conditions than to the psychological success scored by the Allied deception plan. While most of the indicators for the coming attack were discernible, their credibility to those sifting the facts were not.

Major Friedrich Hayn, the Intelligence Officer (IO) on the staff of General Erich Marcks's 84th Corps in St Lô, wrote after the event, that weather reports for 6 June 'forecast such heavy sea states that a landing would appear practically impossible'.[11] This information appears to have been passed to combat units on the ground. Major von Luck commanding his regiment near Caen recalls:

*The general weather conditions worked out every day by naval meteorologists and passed on to us by [21st Panzer] Division, gave the "all clear" for 5 and 6 June. So we did not anticipate any landings, for heavy seas, storms, and low flying clouds would make large scale operations at sea and in the air impossible for our opponents.*[12]

A myth has arisen concerning a German misappreciation of the weather that assisted the Allied invasion of Normandy.[13] It is based on the premise that, denied weather reports from the British Isles and ocean areas to the west and north, German forecasters were kept in ignorance of the development and movement of weather systems affecting north west and central Europe. In fact, the Germans went to great lengths, using submarine and reconnaissance aircraft reports to achieve accuracy. An examination of information compiled by Dr Müller, the Chief Meteorologist in OB West, reveals a similar picture to that already discerned by the Allies, which contributed to General Eisenhower's decision to proceed with the invasion. Conditions were marginal, but not necessarily impractical, to conduct the operation. Müller's reports of 3 June reveal that conditions for launching an airborne operation from the English mainland and over OB West 'were broadly possible'. Sea states of 2 to 3 were identifiable, up to 5 in some areas. Conditions worsened on 4 June with a deep low south of Iceland. Flying conditions deteriorated, but air operations despite some problems 'were conceivable without major difficulties' in the invasion area; but sea states in the Channel were poor, varying from 4 to 6 — even 7 — in some areas. This led to the Allied 24 hour postponement. Dr Müller's report for 5-6 June picked out the same improvement dictated by the Allies. Air operations 'were possible without substantial impediments', while sea states during the night — '3 to 5, in some areas 6' — would be 'somewhat less (3 to 4) in the morning'. Moreover, 'visibility apart from early morning mist would be generally good'. In short, an invasion attempt was conceivable. But this was not the picture apparent to the German troops on the ground.[14]

Part of the discrepancy was that both protagonists were looking for different conditions. This compounded the German error. OB West expected the invasion to start with a rising tide, one or two hours before high water and about the same time before daybreak, on not too dark a night (half moon), and of course, with little wind and sea. The actual Allied requirement was different: three hours before high water — to see the beach obstacles — and one hour after dawn, to allow time for an accurate sea and air bombardment. Moonlight was needed on the preceding night so that air transports could correctly identify the airborne landing zones.[15] The main reason for subsequent German misinterpretations, however, was that these conditions were measured against high and low tides opposite the Pas de Calais, not Normandy. Conditions for an invasion of Normandy, based on these forecasts, as identified by the Allies, were nothing like as marginal. As usual the German effort was focussed upon the narrowest part of the Channel. It represented a triumph for Allied deception.

German soldiers who had not seen action felt the same misgivings identified by their Allied adversaries, at that moment boarding ships or on the move on 5 June. The 12th SS 'Hitlerjugend' Division preparing in its assembly areas east of Falaise was largely unblooded, apart form a veteran core of officers and NCOs. They also felt uneasy at the coming test, and how they might fare under fire for the first time. SS Sturmmann Jochen Leykauff pondered immediate prospects:

*How would it go? Will I cope within myself? It is going to be deadly serious. I wrote to my father in much the same vein as they were reporting events in the newspapers. I often found, for no particular reason, that I was short-tempered. I used to try and walk alone through blossoming woods when off-duty, trying to compose myself. Self-confidence remained.[16]*

Nerves were on edge. SS-Obersturmführer Hans Siegel, a company commander in Panzer Regiment 12 related how:

*We were overflown by bomber formations every night. Nobody knew if suddenly paratroopers might sail down and slaughter us.*

These uncertain threats nevertheless concentrated efforts. Siegel recalled the high state of readiness such insecurity engendered. It meant:

*Complete camouflage and absolute stillness by day — the village a peaceful picture — with soldiers sleeping with weapons to hand. By night, crews stood by in lean-tos, ready for action, in the vicinity of their tanks. Field maintenance teams were permanently prepared for tasking. It was virtually "stand-to", everyone at their post, or nearby ready for action. This was the situation four weeks before the invasion began.*

The tempo of defence preparation increased further during the first week of June. SS-Sturmmann Willi Schnittfinke in the 5th Company of the same panzer regiment recalled night routine replaced that of day. Only light duties were carried out during the afternoons. A command-post exercise run during 3-4 June was stopped the following day, because — according to

SS-Untersturmführer Willi Kandler — 'the Allied invasion was imminent'. Petrol restrictions for training were relaxed, enabling the previous short-fall of combined arms training between tanks and panzergrenadiers (armoured infantry) to catch up. The Ist and IInd Battalions of SS Panzer Regiment 12 continued an exercise, begun 24 hours previously in their assembly areas, with the associated Panzergrenadier Regiments 25 and 26. Troops were fully equipped and moving with live ammunition.[17]

Throughout Normandy on 5 June routine peacetime training continued, albeit at a higher level, but forming part of general defence preparations, differing little from the tempo of preceding weeks. Marie Houel a French Resistance woman living in St Aubin on Juno Beach, having heard the codeword confirming the imminence of the invasion, heard:

*That afternoon the Germans announced there would be shooting exercises on the morning of 6 June. We were to leave our doors and windows open because of these shooting exercises. We laughed — just for once the Germans got it right.[18]*

As Major von Luck waited in the rain during the evening with his Adjutant for his IInd Battalion to finish its blank firing exercise in the Troarn area east of Caen, the IInd Tank Battalion of Panzer Regiment 22 (also 21st Panzer Division) was moving to a start line east of Falaise. Commanded by Major Vierzig, the unit was due to begin an exercise on 6 June. Like von Luck's soldiers, the tanks were loaded with blank ammunition.[19]

Further along the Normandy coast German soldiers settled down to another restless night. The ration run reached Unteroffizier Thiel at the base of the Cherbourg Peninsula:

*The food today was wretched once again — a lot of groats and no meat — a lot of jam and no sausage. Hopefully it will remain quiet tonight, and we're hoping that there won't be another "false alarm".*

Near Arromanches Grenadier Robert Vogt of the 726th Infantry Regiment retired to his bed, alongside the rest of his platoon in 'two or three storey bunks, self made; in a farmhouse, perhaps 400 to 500 metres from the beach', already marked as 'Gold' on Allied maps. Leutnant Arthur Jahnke in strong-point WN (*Widerstandsneste*) 5 in the 919th Infantry Regiment sector opposite Utah Beach, could not sleep. Bomb-bursts, the continuous rumble of aircraft above an overcast sky and anti-aircraft fire, encouraged him to telephone Oberleutnant Ritter in adjoining strong-point WN2. 'Something is up', commented Ritter; 'but nothing that concerns us', responded Jahnke. Ritter was doubtful. A free drink was wagered on the assessed significance of all this activity, one that Jahnke felt confident he would collect.[20]

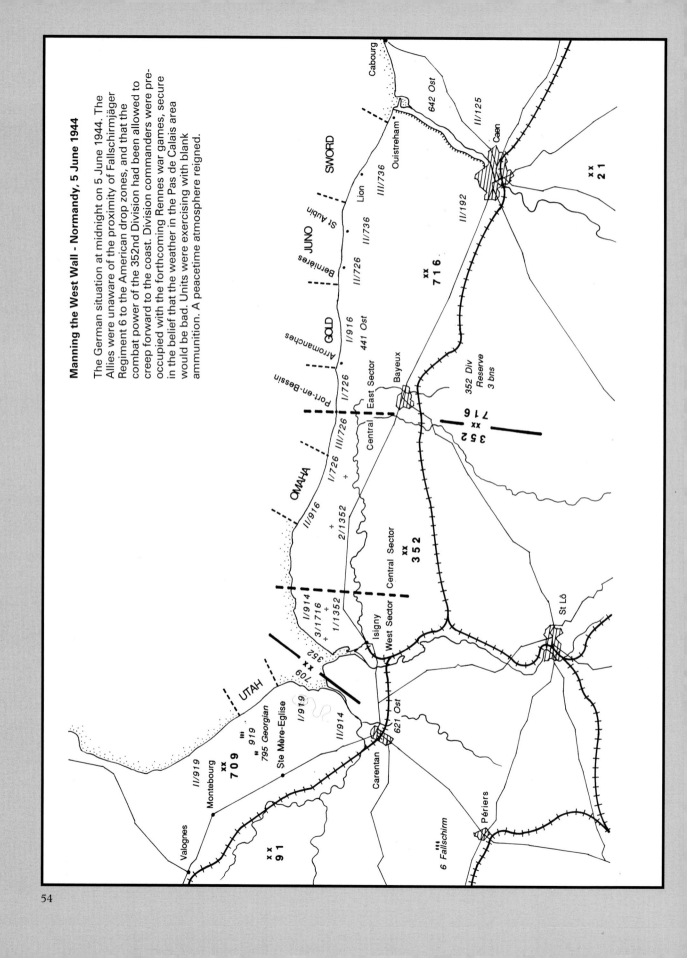

**Manning the West Wall - Normandy, 5 June 1944**

The German situation at midnight on 5 June 1944. The Allies were unaware of the proximity of Fallschirmjäger Regiment 6 to the American drop zones, and that the combat power of the 352nd Division had been allowed to creep forward to the coast. Division commanders were pre-occupied with the forthcoming Rennes war games, secure in the belief that the weather in the Pas de Calais area would be bad. Units were exercising with blank ammunition. A peacetime atmosphere reigned.

Oberleutnant Martin Pöppel having just established his Company Headquarters in a Normandy farmhouse, settled down to enjoy a break from routine. He commented in his diary how 'really homely and snug' it was 'with the warmth of the open fire lit by my batman Soser'. Feldwebel Behne his Company Sergeant suggested a nightcap before retiring. Pöppel agreed, reflecting 'he is definitely on edge, feeling that something is going to happen today'. Outside the bombing raids continued. 'They drone over our heads in large numbers'.[21] The farmhouse was on the edge of the envisaged American airborne landing zones.

In 21st Panzer Division Headquarters at Saint Pierre sur Dives south of Caen, the duty officer, Hauptmann Wagemann was handed a message. He was deputising for the Divisional Chief of Staff, accompanying the Commander, General Feuchtinger, on a trip to Paris. Any feelings of envy he may have had for his superiors, enjoying the delights of the city, evaporated when he read the contents. It was a British intercept by the Divisional Radio Company — and was clear. Transport gliders were being loaded in England.[22]

## 'We were coming over Lord' … airfields in Southern England.

Six parachute regiments from the American 82nd and 101st Airborne Divisions, including organic support, were beginning to load 822 transport aircraft at nine airfields in England. They numbered some 13,000 men. At the same time two parachute brigades from the British 6th Airborne Division, six battalions strong were loading aircraft on airfields south of Oxford. These, including divisional assets, amounted to a further 266 transport aircraft and 344 gliders to be employed ferrying troops and heavy equipments. Airlanding brigades (glider troops) both American and British, were to follow after dawn. The combined airborne strike force was to number 20,000 men.[1]

Paratroopers laboured in and around their accommodation, huts and tents to painstakingly prepare the equipment loads with which they would drop. Packing for action is a difficult and detailed undertaking. There were interminable debates over load priorities: ammunition, explosives, rations? Concern over impending action coupled with the concentration required to force bulky equipments into containers unable to accept the volume is physically and mentally demanding. Frustrations would show as troopers, stripped to the waist would thrust and push vital ammunition loads and equipments into a bundle that must be parachutable, and suspended on a harness within the claustrophobic and noisy confines of a bucking aircraft at night.

Many American soldiers could scarcely lie down on the ground once their equipments had been fitted. Private Thomas Raulston of the 506th Regiment (of the 101st Division) wrote: 'my (leg) pack had a 20lb battery, 24 pounds of rockets, a 20-30lb field bag, my shovel and a few bits of personal equipment'.[2] Restricted movement could be remedied by a slash or two with a knife on landing. It was the same also for the British. A.R. Clarke, a company commander in the 13th Parachute Battalion, remembers seeing in the gathering dusk of 5 June, off the perimeter track of Broadwell airfield, what 'could just be distinguished' as:

*Parties of what might have been men, had it not been for the shapelessness of their appearance. Perhaps a better description would have been that of many caravans of heavily laden camels silhouetted against the darkening horizon.*

Clarke was carrying 38-set radio batteries for his signaller, because he had felt pity 'at the apparent mountain of kit he was endeavouring to stow away in his kit bag'. The officers' load, which was not untypical, consisted of a Sten gun, spare magazines with 9mm ammunition, 2lb of plastic high explosive (HE), two 36 primed hand grenades, two full belts of Vickers .303 ammunition, wire cutters, radio batteries, small-pack, basic equipment webbing, 48 hours worth of rations, water, and cooking and washing kit. Spread over his clothing were further heavy items: a loaded .45 automatic pistol, medical kit, another 2lb of plastic HE, knife, escape/survival kit, toggle rope and all the additional personal items a soldier feels he needs to take into battle. His equipment probably weighed 90lb, which combined with his parachute would represent an all-up weight of 110-120lb, which he had to carry and move within the aircraft. 'I shudder now', he recalled, 'at my recollection of the weight of the equipment' but 'I suppose I should have shuddered still more at the possible result of detonation'. This was not however the immediate fear 'as long as I could hobble from my position in the plane to the exit door I felt reassured that I should be able to cope'.[3]

The additional day's wait had been a strain following the postponement 24 hours before, although veterans with one eye on the weather had already anticipated it. Cards although a popular pastime, had lost some of their humour and zest; thoughts of impending action encouraged rash betting. This underlying tension further devalued the aim of 'enforced rest'. Soldiers preferred to pass time in the company of their fellows, as expressed in verse by a paratrooper from the 9th Battalion waiting at Broadwell airfield:

*Yet another look at our watches, just four hours to go,*
*"Let's blow to the NAAFI". No-one says no,*
*It's just wet and warm, yet they call it tea,*
*And it's a cheap way of turning those four hours to three.*[4]

Soon after 21.00 on the evening of 5 June the leading troops of the airborne divisions started to move from

An overloaded American paratrooper prepares his equipment.

transit camps to airfields. Parachute troops preceded the glider borne formations. A staff captain in the US 82nd Airborne Division recalled that night:

*Getting word that tomorrow would be our departure date. There was no sleep that night and I remember our column marching out of our area about 2a.m. ... walking about an hour and finally arriving at a large airfield at the top of a long hill. We were directed to our gliders and sat around for an hour or so before entering the aircraft.*[5]

Paratroopers crowded into chilly dimly lit hangars and chattered nervously as they 'DFC'ed (drew and fitted 'chutes). Private John Weathers of the 12th (Yorks) Parachute Battalion recalled an atmosphere of 'much "brave" chit-chat etc, so that any fears one might have had were at least for the moment forgotten'. This was a nervous moment. 'No postponement this time — faces now "blacked-up"', adrenalin would surge again as 'all equipment, especially the parachute, [was] checked over many times'. One individual dilemma was whether to accept the final tea and biscuits, measured against the avoidance of air sickness or a nervous desire to urinate — both problems to avoid when fully kitted up in a crowded loaded aircraft. Weathers staggered out to his aeroplane:

*By the time emplaning took place (time of no return), about 23.00 hours, I recall everyone looking like Christmas trees without the fairy lights — 'chutes on backs, steel helmets with all the camouflage decorations on, personal weapons, and in my case I was to drop with a carrier pigeon in a cylindrical container hung about my neck.*[6]

Many had yet to come to terms with what was about to happen. Captain Gerald Ritchie, also 12 PARA, wrote shortly after the operation:

*It all seemed very unreal, it was difficult to imagine that by dawn on the next day, we should have been tipped out of our aeroplane over France and should have landed in the place where there were quite a number of evil minded Bosch, whose one object would be to liquidate us before we could do the same to them.*[7]

It was dark as the troops began to emplane. Pilots had joined their aircraft at about 22.00. Technical Sergeant John Ginter, a Dakota crew member, proceeding with pre-flight checks saw that 'the Paratroopers were sitting, standing, constantly relieving themselves — nervous, very nervous'.[8]

The final 'nervous pee' was an indulgence requiring careful consideration. Often conducted on the runway prior to emplaning, it meant the parachute harness had to be unbuckled, perhaps necessitating a re-jig of personal equipment stowage, all of which had to be re-checked by despatchers. Final orders were tied up.

Anxious eyes scanned wind movement on airfield perimeter trees as troops moved to aircraft, in an attempt to discern likely wind speeds, although all knew the winds across the Channel would be different. Captain Ritchie remembered how it still 'seemed so like an ordinary exercise'. The primary difference was 'the ceremony which was to take place', expressed by Major Clarke from 13 PARA 'at that moment', seemed 'to be the most natural in the world'. Soldiers going to battle become painfully aware of their individual mortality, often feeling a need to communicate with their God. These were no exception:

*The many shapeless caravans converged, and, like camels, sank to their knees. What matter that prayer was made by a Methodist, or a Muslim, Catholic or Congregationalist, Sadhu or Salvationist: the intention was the same. So all six hundred of our battalion, led by Padre Boy Foy, acknowledged our need and our dependence, our fear and yet our trust, our inadequacy and yet our resolve.*

The weight of their equipments caused the perimeter gravel to cut and bruise knees in the act of contrition. More than half the battalion were destined to become casualties.[9]

Men now awaited the call-forward to aircraft; eyes flickering anxiously toward any sign of movement that would indicate they were off. Numbered lorries transported the heavily laden paratroopers to their respective aircraft. Troops began to board as the all-pervasive smell of high octane fuel wafted across runways as aircraft engines burst into explosive life. Private Woodcock recalled, again in verse:

*A few scattered handshakes with the pals we know. Weak jokes with the aircrew, the Yank pilot named Joe.*[10]

Entering dimly lit aircraft interiors, troops cumbersomely struggled into their places, burdened by outsize loads. Achieving a semblance of comfort, they waited, thinking through last minute plans or lost in thoughts. Many were troubled, seeking some solace from last minute pep talks. 'Just before we pulled out', remembered Sergeant Robert Miller of the US 502nd Regiment, 'the CO read this message from Eisenhower about how we were all crusaders and all that, and it made us feel pretty good'.[11] Others listening to the 101st Division Commander's final talk were not so reassured. 'We will have no place to keep prisoners tomorrow', he said; the implication was ominously clear.[12] 'It is strange', recollected Major Clarke, sitting in his aircraft at Broadwell, 'what inconsequential matters occupy our thoughts, and indeed remain in them, during moments of stress'.[13] Trooper Brown, from the 6th Airborne Armoured Recce Regiment remembered a 'quite nonsensical' pep talk from General Montgomery during which, to sounds of applause, he

*Above:* 'How would it go? Will I cope within myself?' The 12th SS was at a high state of readiness, with soldiers sleeping with weapons to hand.

*Left:* 'It was dark as the troops began to emplane'. Troopers assisted aboard their aircraft. Nerves were stretched taut.

reiterated having pushed the Germans into the sea in North Africa, they were going to do it again:

*It seemed to me that I was the only one who realised at this time the idea was to push the Germans not into the sea but away from it.*[14]

Major Clarke, looking around the dimmed interior of the aircraft, noticed that the application of camouflage paint had totally transformed his men:

*I could not recognize a single one of the men with me. All were rendered additionally shapeless by the acquisition of a parachute on the back and a very large kit bag strapped to the right leg of each. How very disconcerting this was.*

The constant rise and fall of the roaring pitch of aircraft engines drowned out all else. Clouds of aviation exhaust produced a ghostly shroud wafting across aircraft queued on runways prior to take-off. Troops inside could discern the movement and direction of taxiing through a series of bumps, sudden accelerations, stops, and the squeaking and bird-like chatterings of rudders and control cables. Presently there was a signal pause during which engines would rise to a crescendo of noise, followed by a gathering momentum and roar as each heavily laden craft accelerated down the runway, bumping and lumbering, until with a lurch and change of engine note and vibration, they were in the air. Technical Sergeant Ginter en route to Ste Mère-Eglise said in retrospect 'we took every inch of the runway'.[15] Major Clarke:

*Felt that lack of bumping which indicated our being airborne, saw obliquely through the open door the ground which should have been below swing upward to my right, and felt the "clunk" of the wheels as they were retracted into their flying position. We were off. We were coming over Lord.*[16]

## 'What a night — dark and wet' ... the Invasion Fleet.

The sight of the massive invasion fleet underway at last produced a sense of relief, which was soon transformed into excitement. A tank officer gazing out to sea saw:

*There was no doubt now — the line of little boats was moving. It was just a line of drab, small landing craft, with silver barrage balloons aloft, coming out in a long queue, at a snail's pace, into the heaving sea. At first he wondered what they could be doing. Were they shifting place for the night? Surely they weren't setting out to sea? Gradually the snaking progress turned towards the perfect ring of the horizon ..... No doubt about it now: they were making for the open sea, and for France.*[1]

Lieutenant Ian Hammerton recalled 'at last! This was it! The long called-for Second Front. We were on our way.' As commando units cleared the Solent in their assault landing craft there were cheers. The CO of 48 Commando destined for St Aubin remarked 'we and the other commandos were on top of the world'. Captain Glover, captain of an LCI carrying elements of 45 Commando recollected:

*They're cheering us from the transports. "Give 'em hell!" I expect we all feel how few we are, how small and very much alone. Being cheered makes one feel heroic in a grand and desperate way.*[2]

The spectacle was easily recalled by the participants much later in their lives. Captain Triggs, a member of No 10 Beach Group observing the panorama with a colleague, agreed 'this was a unique moment in history and there would never be another like it'. The fleet passed familiar landmarks to the English crews: the tower at Lee-on-Solent, Portsmouth harbour, the war memorial at Southsea and as it grew darker, the cliffs at Beachy Head. Many soldiers inevitably grew reflective. 'We were very quiet', remembers an AVRE driver from an RE Assault Squadron, standing with his troop alongside their flat-bottomed barge, 'thinking should we ever see England again?' An infantry Lieutenant, P. Webber, despite being 'buoyed up by the staggering sight of the massive force' still felt uneasy:

*Most of us could not bear to think beyond the immediate landing. Perhaps our worst fear was the possibility of German "secret weapons" and particularly flame throwers.*

Most, as the dramatic scene unfolded believed like Captain Triggs who 'felt that it would be impossible for the Germans to prevent the invasion'.[3]

Valedictory addresses came across loudspeaker systems on board ships. These speeches by Prime Minister Winston Churchill, President Roosevelt and senior military commanders, were often viewed with scepticism. General Bradley in summing up his address to the US 29th Division bound for Omaha, had claimed: 'you men should consider yourselves lucky. You are going to have ringside seats for the greatest show on earth'.[4] Soldiers were not enthused by the bravado. Private Mason of the 2nd Battalion East Yorks remembered when 'Eisenhower came and gave us the once over. He was a bright and breezy person but loaded with bull'.[5] On board the US 29th Division transports men hooted derisively in response to patriotic messages coming across public address systems. 'We all thought isn't that nice?' recalled one staff officer. 'If you had a couple of violins, you could put it to music'.[6] British soldiers were similarly unimpressed:

*We read this great message from Monty about hunting in the fields of Europe and all this rubbish, and naturally being a soldier we thought what a load of cods it was.[7]*

Minds were focussed on more practical considerations. On board the leading mine-sweepers:

*No one spoke about it, but every one of us expected bombs, torpedos, gun fire, mines, E-Boats, destroyers, secret weapons of new and horrible types and gas.*

Lieutenant William Pugsley aboard HMCS *Georgian* had no chance of evasive manoeuvre, constrained as he was to minesweeping a single channel. The fear was: 'thus would we meet the Luftwaffe, out in force to protect the Atlantic Wall since surely the easiest time to stop us would be before we got a footing on the land.'[8] The Luftwaffe had, however, effectively been emasculated. German air reconnaissance had discovered shipping sufficient to carry two and a half divisions in the Plymouth-Brixham area during April and May. A further three divisions' worth had been identified between Portsmouth and Southampton, and capacity for one more division in Falmouth. The last reliable photographs taken on 24 May confirmed the Allies had assembled shipping for at least 16 divisions. Not one single reconnaissance aeroplane got through after this date until D-Day.[9]

The German Navy, or *Kriegsmarine*, was the weakest of the three services forming the Wehrmacht. Its defensive strategy by June 1944 was based upon Rommel's fore-shore obstacle belt, supplemented by coastal artillery batteries, with radar and anti-air, and mines in deeper water. Surface combat elements in the Channel area consisted of five torpedo boats (small destroyers), 23 S-boats, 116 minesweepers, 44 patrol vessels and 42 artillery barges. Beyond Brest along the Atlantic coast were five destroyers, a torpedo boat, 146 minesweepers and 59 patrol vessels. In addition, there were a number of obsolete submarines.[10] Forward observation and some harassment was the only tactical recourse to give the coastal defences some depth in an arena totally dominated by the Allied navies and air force. Obstacles were the only effective sea barrier. Coastal batteries formed a loosely coordinated part of the German ground defence plan.

Sixteen minefields had been laid between Boulogne and Cherbourg during the period August 1943 to January 1944. Not a single further mine had been laid in the Seine Bight, despite increasing demands by Army Group B on Navy Group West. This was partly due to ineffective command arrangements and poor inter-service co-operation but Allied sea and air activity made mine-laying dangerous. A new shallow water mine, the KMA (Coastal Mine A) could potentially have been very effective but the surface vessels used to lay them were hindered and many sunk. The Navy therefore preferred the idea of *Blitzsperren* or lightning mine barrages which were seen as Navy Group West's primary offensive strategy in the event of attack. But this was dependent upon the speed and ability of vessels to lay them in the identified attack area.

Another missed opportunity was the failure to lay 'Oyster' pressure mines in the invasion assembly areas. These mines were unsweepable but the whole Luftwaffe stock had been sent back to Germany on Goering's orders shortly before D-Day because of faulty intelligence. They did not return to France until over a week after the invasion. The German Navy had been reluctant to lay its pressure mines because of fear of discovery and use by the Allies. The waters off the beaches were not very suitable for pressure mines and the effectiveness of a potentially decisive weapon was completely wasted.

What mines had been laid on the approaches to the beaches might still have imposed critical delays on the landing operations and the largest minesweeping operation of the war was carried out to clear paths to the beaches. 247 minesweepers and damlayers (of which 25 were American) cleared two channels for each assault force. The 14th Minesweeper Flotilla had sighted the French coast almost three hours before it grew dark on 5 June, and approached it for more than two hours, until crews were able to discern houses and other objects with the naked eye. Nothing happened. The 16th Flotilla sighted the coast at 18 miles and closed to within 11; there was still no German reaction.[11]

Nerves aboard the leading minesweepers were stretched to breaking point. 'I'd never seen ratings taking this so seriously', recalled Lieutenant Pugsley:

*We hadn't met any opposition at all so far. We couldn't understand it. Why hadn't there been any German planes? Lordy! Maybe they were waiting to trap us close in by the coast.*

Vapour trails could be seen from aircraft that often passed overhead. 'If a man off watch and passing the time of day on deck spotted one of these trails before the nearby look-out did, he gave his shipmate a terrific blast for not keeping his eyes open'. Slowly, surely and irresistibly the armada began to close up on the minesweepers. 'Far astern, but closing on us' Pugsley 'could now see a jumbled mass of invasion ships, their balloons mere black dots against the grey sky'. Besides the infantry and tank carrying vessels, there were ocean-going tugs, landing craft towing barges laden with more landing craft, barges with heavy guns, 'and raft-like somethings barely awash with people walking about on them'. Rocket ships ploughed on through the waves 'looking like a direct steal from *Popular Science* or *Amazing Stories*'.[12] The fingers of the invasion fleet approached the Normandy coast, poised to grasp the foreshore like a gigantic mailed gauntlet.

*Above:* 'There was no doubt now - the line of little boats was moving.' Exiting Portsmouth harbour under a threatening sky. *IWM*

*Below:* They're cheering us from the transports, 'Give 'em hell!' Buoyant optimism – British Commandos.

Norman Smith a tank crewman aboard one of the LCTs, recalled how 'ominously, the weather began to deteriorate'. Lieutenant-Commander Denis Glover commanding *LCI(S) 516*, transporting elements of Lord Lovat's Special Service (Commando) Brigade, was becoming increasingly concerned at the navigational accuracy of their passage. The sea state was making it increasingly difficult to identify marker buoys:

> *What a night — dark and wet, with just the sort of sea that makes the old tub wallow like a lovesick hippopotamus. All right for sailors, but I'm thinking about the troops.[13]*

They miserably shared his concern. 'The big sea swelling up was causing our LCT to lift and bang down on the water', Smith recalled 'shaking the tanks about and straining the chains holding them to the hull' With a rise and fall of four or five feet with each wave 'it was clearly instant death to be between two tanks or between a tank and the hull of the LCT when they clanged together'.[14] Marine Neale a deckhand aboard HMS *Glenearn*, a converted cargo ship, which was carrying their landing craft remembers: 'we felt the full force of the weather' as the ship left Southampton Water. 'Waves were about thirty to thirty-five feet high and the ship although 29,000 tons, was thrown about like a cork'.[15] For those unfamiliar with such conditions, like Major Sindall of the Hertfordshire Regiment, rolling and pitching in a violent sea, aboard a landing craft 'The mood was tinged with something of anxiety' less for what might happen in the future, but 'there and now'. The deck, 'jam-packed' with tanks and self-propelled guns:

> *Seemed to be alarmingly low in the sea, in fact we shipped a torrent of water every time she rolled. "One more like that", I thought, "and we'll be in the drink.[16]*

Conditions for the soldiers became nightmarish. Flail tank commander Lieutenant Ian Hammerton 'caught a whiff of diesel exhaust and found it necessary to hang over the stern and get rid of my last meal. Since then I have never been able to stomach the smell of diesel'. Sergeant Ian Grant with 45 Commando remembers 'after the scent of clean sea air, the atmosphere below was foul'. Nauseous diesel fumes were a recurring theme to those aboard the transports. 'Some of the early arrivals were already stretched out, their faces the same shade of green as the paintwork, and their recent meal had already been deposited in the soggy bags beside them'. Hammerton, offered the use of the skipper's bunk, 'left it to be sick and sick again and again throughout the night, until I could be sick no more'.[17] The Americans suffered equally badly. One sarcastic GI in the 29th Division commented he had been trained to come ashore spewing lead, not just spewing.[18]

Despite sea-sickness, most men preferred to spend their time below. 'There was really nowhere to go,' remembers Sergeant Gilbert Gray of the US 116th Regiment, 'and no feeling to get away from the companionship of our buddies'. Fear was an insidious companion. Gray remembers, 'the ship was unusually quiet, not at all like it was on the dry runs'. There was inevitable discussion about chances ashore. 'We talked about the invasion,' said private Anthoney Ferrara, also in Gray's Regiment, 'and whether there would be many Germans defending the beach, and how hard it would be to reach our objective'.[19] Captain Sykes, Royal Engineers, indulged in similar conjecture, 'about what, in fact, would prove to be the least, or most, hazardous time to arrive' on the beach. Either it would be those in the initial assault waves benefiting from the violence of the air and sea bombardment who 'would have it easy', or successive waves who might be 'met by a recovering German defence.'[20] Lieutenant David Holbrook, a British Yeomanry tank officer knew 'they were for the real thing now', but found himself doubting the outcome. As darkness closed in, and the sea state increased, men became oppressed; and despite being surrounded by countless ships, felt insecure.[21] Holbrook tried to recall 'when had anything like it ever come off? Certainly nothing since 1588, and then an Armada in the same waters had come to grief in a similar gale'. He was a young officer, unblooded, barely at the end of his training:

> *This is what I asked for, after all. This is the last moment for thought: tomorrow would be like a whirl of maps and briefings, explosions, action, alarms and excursions. I couldn't imagine what it would be like.[22]*

The security for the invasion had been astonishingly effective. The battleship HMS *Ramillies* ploughed on through heavy seas toward her battle station off the British beaches. Petty Officer Drake recalled how 'one day we sailed for what we thought was another practice shoot but instead proceeded out to sea and not until we were out of sight of land did the captain address the ship's company over the broadcast system. I can still remember his opening words: "The die is cast and we are committed to the attack".'[23]

At RAF Group Headquarters at Hill House in Wiltshire, a young cryptographer from the US 9th Air Force reported for duty at 23.00. On arriving in the operations room 'we were told the invasion would begin on the morrow'. They would not be allowed to leave the complex until their shift was finished at 07.00 the next day.

> *We were able to watch the fascinating groupings for the Normandy Invasion right on the Op's map which was painted in front of us on a huge board. We traced the ships as they began their journey across the board. We watched with utter disbelief as the hundreds of planes left the English coast heading for the French.[24]*

Chief Wren Katherine Andrews manning her desk in the top secret maze of tunnel headquarters, controlling the D-Day landings beneath Fort Southwick in Portsmouth commented on the disappearance of the invasion host. 'One minute they were there', she said, 'and the next they had just vanished'. Required to man her switchboard post, everyone watched for 'a red light on one switchboard to signal the call to say that the landings had been made'. There was considerable anxiety waiting for the initial call from the airborne troops. 'From then on it was a case of waiting'.[25]

A Luftwaffe radio intercept company on the island of Guernsey were by 22.40 on 5 June gazing intently at their *Freya* and *Wurzburg* radar screens. Formations of four-engined Lancaster bombers had been spotted, followed immediately behind by other unidentified aircraft, at regular intervals. They appeared to be gliders. 'Altogether 180 such combinations were picked up.' Not wishing to appear unduly alarmist, the Luftwaffe company commander checked with a neighbouring Army signals unit with similar equipment, before calling an Alert. Following confirmation the Regimental Commander, Oberst Oelze, telephoned 84th Corps in St Lô direct. He wished to speak to the Chief of Staff, who proved to be unavailable. 'The Operations Officer would do', but persevering he felt he ought to personally inform the Corps Commander what he had seen. Key personnel were not available, the Duty Officer patiently explained. One was in Paris attending an Army Group Conference, another was at a birthday celebration, another quite simply on leave. Oberst Oelze now visibly frustrated ordered — indeed swore — the Duty Officer to sound the air alarm. In his opinion, a major operation directed against the mainland was imminent. The Duty Officer promised to do what he could.

Twenty minutes later a General Staff Officer rang back. 'The Gentlemen of the Staff', he said, 'wished their comrades on the Island a good night; advising them to be on the look out for small ghosts only, and urging caution before sowing any more wild oats'!

# CHAPTER 6

# SECURING THE FLANKS

*'We had a first class view of the Division coming in ...It really was the most awe-inspiring sight.'*
*British Airborne Officer*

## Coup de Main ... the Orne River
## 00.16 - 00.26.

The glider swooped low, scything through the air with a sinister whooshing sound, full of lethal intent. Its wings began clipping trees at some 90mph. Ahead lay two shining irregular, yet parallel, strips of moonlight reflected on water, the Orne river and Caen canal. All around flooded meadows, drainage ditches and small ponds, reflected a translucent eerie half lunar light. A bridge loomed up ahead. The dark mass of the ground suddenly rushed up, trees to the left, a small marshy pond to the right. Buildings now, the tower on the bridge and the irregular outline of barbed wire entanglements. With a long drawn out shrieking, squealing crash the aircraft struck the ground, momentarily checked by a billowing parachute, which was soon jettisoned. It careered along on its belly, showering sparks, snapping off tree branches and stripping the top brush off as it ploughed its way through the darkness at 60mph. It came to an abrupt grinding screeching halt, nose first, into tangled wire emplacements a few score metres from the outermost trenches. Dust, pieces of foliage and shards from the plywood frame hung momentarily in the air, and slowly began to settle.

Grenadier Romer, a 16-year old conscripted into Infantry Regiment 736, pacing the bridge, glanced around in alarm. That was loud, and extremely close! But the flak continued to thump remorselessly away in the distance, and silence returned. Yet another fragment from a doomed aircraft spiralling out of the night sky he thought, frightening but not unusual. He continued his pacing, scanning the half-light for the opposite sentry coming from the other side of the bridge.

A second crashing tearing sound could be made out in the darkness, including sparks like tracer rounds, as yet another huge piece of debris careered into and broke up around the small pond on the far bank. The incidence of these crashes, barely a minute apart was

becoming alarming when one minute later, still another shattering tearing commotion broke the silence further down the canal side. The adrenalin began to flow. The incidence of three crashes appeared threatening. Soldiers within earshot began as a precaution to warily reach for weapons and pull on equipment. What was going on?

Shaken and slightly concussed, the first airborne troops poured out of the first glider as soon as they were able. They passed the gently sobbing pilots who had been catapulted through the cockpit window. 'We could hear them moaning', recalled Major John Howard, 'but our first job was to capture that bridge intact'.[1] Wincing at the prospect of a storm of anticipated machine gun fire, they flowed up onto the canal embankment; silently and furtively moving through or over barbed wire entanglements. They paused. Within a few minutes the second platoon of the Oxford & Buckinghamshire Light Infantry closed up. Confidently expecting the third platoon to be close behind, Major Howard launched his coup de main assault. Stens and Bren guns at the ready, the two platoons of over 40 airborne soldiers approached the bridge at a determined trot, moving in irregular groups, trickling in rushes over and around obstacles, making for the trenches and pill boxes.

A single shot rang out. Romer on the bridge heard the sound of scuffling feet, and fearfully observed the first onrush of airborne troopers frantically scrambling up the embankment on to the bridge. '*Fallschirmjäger*!' (Paratroopers) he screamed, and began running. His comrade hastening to meet him from the other side, paused, fired his Verey pistol into the air, and was immediately cut down by a burst of Sten-gun fire. The flare popped and bathed the entire area in an eerie glow.

Feldwebel Heinrich Hickman from Fallschirmjäger Regiment 6 braked the open staff car on the Benouville bank on recognising the distinctive stutter of British Sten guns. He had just picked up four young inexperienced privates manning observation posts outside Ouistreham. The intention was to drop them off at his headquarters at Bréville on the east side of the canal and river. He saw:

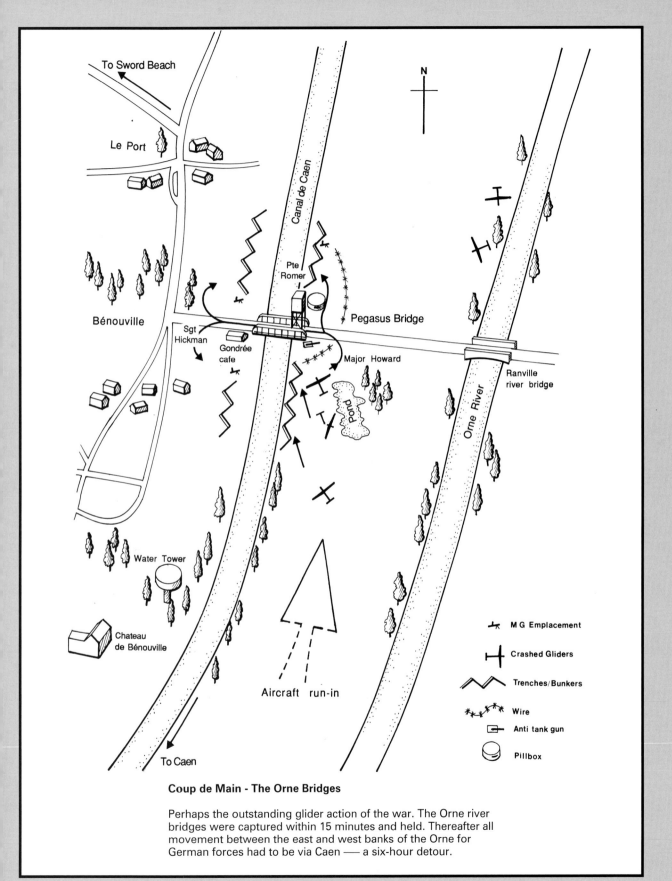

To Sword Beach

Le Port

N

Canal de Caen

Bénouville

Pte
Romer

Pegasus Bridge

Sgt
Hickman

Gondrée
cafe

Major Howard

Ranville
river bridge

Pond

Orne River

Water Tower

Chateau
de Bénouville

Aircraft run-in

To Caen

M G Emplacement

Crashed Gliders

Trenches/Bunkers

Wire

Anti tank gun

Pillbox

**Coup de Main - The Orne Bridges**

Perhaps the outstanding glider action of the war. The Orne river
bridges were captured within 15 minutes and held. Thereafter all
movement between the east and west banks of the Orne for
German forces had to be via Caen — a six-hour detour.

*Men running across the bridge. It was full moon, only a few clouds about, and then I recognized they were British soldiers. They can't be land forces, so they must have come out of the air, either Paras or glider-borne troops. So I opened up.[2]*

Shooting began, desultory at first, then building up until the noise, flashes and bangs assaulted the senses. Rapid-firing German Spandau machine guns interspersed with slower thumping Bren guns and chattering Stens shattered the stillness of the night. The noise was accentuated and magnified by the echoing concussive impact of grenade explosions, followed by shrieks and anguished cries around pill boxes, buildings, and the metal surround of the bridge esplanade itself. Ricochets whined off the metal work, and spun off the concrete surface of the road and bunkers. Hickman

*Crept slowly forward. Watched my blokes. Come on, come on, come on ..... Gave them the order, "don't fire until I fire". We made more or less more noise, than hitting anybody.*

He was uncomplimentary about the bridge defenders, too used to easy occupation duties. The weak company of Infantry Regiment 736 assigned to secure the bridge had been caught napping. Many young conscripts fled, but NCOs and officers offered determined resistance where they could. Hickman fought on about 100 metres from the Benouville end of the bridge, until 'I more or less ran out of ammunition'. It was an unequal struggle:

*I gave the order: "back". What can I do with four men? There is no hope for me.[3]*

Resistance quickly crumpled under the murderous ferocity of the assault. The attacking glider borne force offered no quarter at this stage. They set about their task with a grim well-rehearsed lethality. Private Wally Parr of D Company the 2nd 'Ox and Bucks' recalled a series of disjointed 'snap-shot' impressions of the murderous action. Just about to sprint across the bridge, he noticed:

*One of the dug-out doors half opened and closed again. I don't know if someone went in, or went to come out. By this time I had a "36" grenade with a pin out. Into the dug out. Shut the door. Explosion went: "Charlie [his team mate] — In!" Banged the door open again, and machine gun. Onto the second dug-out, and the same again. In with the grenade, door shut — the explosion. Smash the door wide open again, Charlie finished them off with the machine gun. As we came by the first dug-out, suddenly, there was a moan or a word from inside. I pulled out a "77" phosphorous, took the cap off, gave it a twirl [shaking his hand], undid the tape, and jumped in. That went off ...*

The impact of a '36' high explosive hand grenade in a confined space, among sleepy young conscripts, was devastating. Unprepared, and frantically trying to pull on equipment, they were overwhelmed by a merciless assault, that signified with shocking finality the end of their 'peacetime' occupation. The blast produced a high pressure wave which ruptured internal organs, tore limbs from bodies, and fearfully lacerated flesh with jagged spinning shards of metal. Struck by machine gun fire while still in this semi-comatose state, shocked survivors were then horrifically burnt by cascading flowers of white hot phosphorous which burst in their midst. Hair burned while molten gelatine splashes of phosphorous flared on skin still exposed to air. Oxygen sucked in by flame was replaced by bulbous clouds of acrid smoke, which further constricted lungs collapsed by the initial blast. Resistance to an attack by flame from within the confined interior of a bunker is not feasible. Parr continued [pointing]:

*There was all hell going on over there. There were blokes scrambling, they were knocking out the pill box, others were over there [indicating] sorting the gun out, and "sorting" people out. But by this time everybody was beginning to stream across [the bridge].[4]*

By 00.26 hours the action was over. It had lasted just 10 minutes. One or two German stragglers evading capture fled toward the small hamlets of Le Port and Benouville on the west bank. They were, in raising the alarm, running straight toward the projected sea-borne landing. Feldwebel Hickman remounted his small detachment in the open staff car, intending to drive to his company headquarters across the bridge near Bréville, in order to warn them. The first impact of the British coup de main soon became apparent. His 10-minute journey was to develop into a six-hour detour through the bombed out streets of Caen, before the alarm could be given. The very effect intended.

Two more gliders had landed and secured the bridge over the Orne river at Ranville. Major Howard's assault group of five platoons had secured their initial D-Day objective. One-sixth of the force, in the missing last glider mistakenly landed 20km away on the river Dives. Three platoon commanders were out of action; one dead. Casualties had been light.

Dug-outs were scoured as Howard reorganised his force to defend their positions, pending the arrival of 7 PARA which would provide the necessary substance to hold off German counter-attacks, until the sea-borne link up. One platoon commander, Lieutenant Fox, came across three Germans snoring in their bunks inside one of the dug-outs, with rifles stacked neatly nearby. The sleeping figure on top confronted by a torch and menaced by a sten gun was enjoined to surrender. 'Fuck-off' was the response from the German, who, refusing to take the prank seriously, turned over to get back to sleep. Total surprise had been achieved.[5]

*Above:* Shaken and slightly concussed the initial airborne troops poured out of the first glider as soon as they were able. All three gliders are down. The bridge is bottom left. Trenches are clearly visible, as is also the pond above and left of the second glider. *Airborne Museum*

*Above:* The Allied air armada was launched.

## The Plan ... secure the flanks.

Just four and a half hours earlier, the German weather prognosis had stated:

*Flights from English bases are in general possible without any particular difficulties, only slightly limited at particular locations by thick cloud cover. Due to widely dispersed cloud which is clear in some areas, air activity in OB West's sector is broadly possible. There are no particular limitations, except in south and south east France, due to an area of bad weather, and difficulties caused by heavy cloud over Holland.[1]*

The Allied air armada was launched. The task of the US 82nd and 101st Airborne Divisions was to drop several miles inland from the proposed amphibious beachheads and seize crossings or destroy bridges over the Merderet and Douvre rivers and secure the vital exits of causeways leading inland from Utah Beach, across areas inundated by water, thereby facilitating the expansion of the beach-head by the US 4th Infantry Division. More specifically the 101st Airborne Division was to seize the western edge of the flooded area behind Utah Beach between St Martin-de-Varreville and Pouppeville, using the 502nd Regiment supplemented by the 377th Artillery Battalion. A secondary mission was to protect the southern flank of the US VII Corps, and be prepared to exploit southward through Carentan. This was to be achieved by destroying two bridges on the main Carentan road and the railway bridge west of it, and by seizing and holding the La Barquette lock. Finally a bridgehead was to be established across the Douvre river north east of Carentan to facilitate an eventual link up at Omaha Beach. Two further parachute regiments — the 501st and 506th, were employed to achieve this.

The US 82nd Airborne Division was ordered to drop astride the Merderet river, to clear the western portion of the amphibious beach-head area between the sea and the Merderet and from the Douvre river north to Ste Mère-Eglise, and establish a bridgehead on the west bank of the Merderet. The 505th Parachute Regiment was to capture Ste Mère-Eglise, secure crossings of the Merderet near La Fière and Chef-du-Pont, and establish a defensive line to the north tying up with the 101st Division. The other two regiments — 507th and 508th — dropping west of the river, were to consolidate the 505th's bridgeheads and push out a defensive line three miles westward.

In short, the US Airborne divisions were protecting the landings by the US 4th Infantry Division on Utah, and laying the pre-conditions for a future advance up the Cherbourg peninsula: The 101st Division south east of Ste Mère-Eglise capturing vital beach exits and sealing off a possible eastern approach by the enemy, and

the 82nd blocking a possible advance from the west. The first of 822 American aircraft having taken off before midnight were bringing in the first jump serials from the west side of the Contentin peninsular. They would be flying over their respective drop zones between 01.15 and 01.30. Glider reinforcements would arrive at dawn and again at dusk on landing zones the paratroopers would have cleared of enemy. Two airborne divisions were therefore securing the western flank of the invasion.

The British 6th Airborne Division was to secure the eastern flank. Its 5th Parachute Brigade was to capture and hold the Orne crossings, and take, clear and protect glider landing zones north of Ranville. Meanwhile to the south and east 3rd Brigade Group were to cut road bridges across the river Dives and occupy the high ground commanding enemy approaches that could menace the British left flank. A key battery near Merville was also to be destroyed. Crucial to the success of the plan were subsequent link ups by the vanguard of the sea-borne forces — 1st Special Services (Commando) Brigade — who were to be passed over the Orne bridges and occupy the left forward (northern) sector of the Division, between Le Plein and Franceville Plage on the coast. The 6th Airlanding Brigade, on arrival on D-Day in the Ranville area, was to occupy the area to the south and form part of the Divisional Reserve.

Execution of the airborne phase would signal the beginning of the race to secure the invasion fore-shore already envisaged by supreme commanders on both sides. The airborne plan was designed to either neutralise or seize the key terrain features that dominated the flanks of the sea-borne invasion; which in turn was reliant upon the successful application of an echeloned frontal assault. There was little room for tactical manoeuvre; merely a brutal race for tactical supremacy. Major John Howard's coup de main seizure of the Orne crossings had raised the first flimsy hurdle, at a key point, to the German reinforcement plan. Securing airborne dominated flanks was a prerequisite for an Allied sprint start to win this race for the dominance of the vital invasion foreshore. The British feared the possible arrival of the German 352nd Division within eight hours, the 12th SS possibly in 12; they did not realise that 21st Panzer Division was virtually in-situ. Similarly, the Americans were not aware they were jumping on the edge of the 91st Division, that Fallschirmjäger Regiment 6 was virtually on the drop zones, and the 352nd Division far nearer the coast than anticipated.

Whatever the outcome, every man who jumped was aware of the risk. Should the sea-borne invasion fail, or if indeed there was another weather cancellation, there could be no evacuation.

'Go! Go! Go!' shouted despatchers as paratroopers exited into the dark night.

*Above:* The view of assaulting British troops from the anti-tank gun pit. The café Gondrée is the building to the left on the Bénouville (invasion) bank. Grenadier Romer would have run away from the camera towards Feldwebel Hickmans's group on the other side. *Airborne Museum*

## Go! Go! Go! … 'a fantastic chimera of lights and flak'.

As darkness fell the airborne armada was approaching the Normandy coast from three directions. Two American streams were approaching the Contentin from the west, and the British from north west of Le Havre. One British paratrooper described how:

*As the last light faded off the landscape that fell away into a misty horizon, the glow of our cigarettes grew brighter. Other aircraft in the formation were no longer visible, dipping and swaying in the wind-flukes. Trails of sparks were the only indication that we were not alone.[1]*

The steady rising and falling drone within the aircraft had a hypnotic effect upon many paratroopers who, mentally fatigued at the prospect of coming action, dozed off. Others attempted to read using the ambient light within the aircraft. 'It seemed like a long trip' said Sergeant Robert Miller of the 502nd Regiment, in the 16th aircraft of his stream, 'but it was only two hours'. Nevertheless:

*It was a long two hours, though, because it was so hot in the plane, and with all that 120 pounds of stuff on us, most of the guys got a little sick.*

*You don't talk much. I didn't say a damn word. And don't ask me what I was thinking, because I don't remember. I guess I was thinking a little about everything.[2]*

Many aircraft flew with open doors, anticipating flak; there should be no hurdles should misfortune strike. 'Nervousness and tension, and the cold that blasted through the open door, had its effect upon us all' recorded General Matthew Ridgeway, the commander of the US 82nd Airborne Division. Bulked out with equipment, paratroopers were unable to reach the small toilets situated at the rear of the aircraft. Neither in any case could they barely perform the function, buckled up in full combat gear. Buckets were handed around, for the desire to pass water was greater than the embarrassment noted by Ridgeway of comrades 'watching him, jeering derisively and offering gratuitous advice' Flying at 1,500ft the transports droned on in tight formation. Even at this height they could tell the Channel was rough, passing over small patrol craft, navigator check points, the lights could be seen 'bobbing like a cork in a mill race'.[3]

Having converged on the main stream from different directions, individual aircraft had both to navigate and keep in formation. As Flight Lieutenant P.M. Bristow of No 575 Squadron RAF commented, flying out of Broadwell: 'formation flying is not a normal part of a transport pilot's expertise' and 'here we were on a particularly dark night'. They were supposed to be flying in 'V' formations of threes, not easy in darkness. Bristow opened his throttle 'to catch up the others in front' to reassure himself he was on course. He 'found there were four of them', so 'I decided I should be much more relaxed if I dropped back and flew on my own'. Paradoxically disaster ahead could provide just the navigational aid that follow-on aircraft needed.

*Shortly before we made landfall something exploded on the land right ahead. A vast sheet of yellow flame lit up the sky for a second or two, and in that I saw a line of aeroplanes all going in the same way, all at the same height, and I was part of this mad game of follow-my-leader.*

The bombers had done their work. Told they should be crossing heavy gun emplacements, Bristow glancing out of the cockpit window noticed 'we passed over a number of plates of ferro-concrete'. Heat generated inside produced 'the topside of a concrete roof glowing like a red-hot plate of steel.'[4]

'Stand up! — Prepare for action!' was the command that sent adrenalin surging through the body as the British stream approached the coast. Lights dimmed as soldiers struggled in the half darkness to fit equipments, bumping into each other as they attempted to attach the dragging weight of their loads to parachute harnesses; all this accompanied by a sinking feeling in the pit of the stomach. Exertion produced sweat, and with it arose the stench of nervous flatulence, and the sour smell of vomit as aircraft began to bob and weave. All along aircraft fuselages metallic clicks sounded as parachute hooks were snapped home on cables, followed by a chattering rattle as attachments were tested. The appearance of air despatchers heralded silence, checks continued, all watched them intently for any hint of information. Major Clarke, a company commander in 13 PARA, remembers 'he said there was flak coming up ahead'. They were getting near the French coast. Now even the invasion craft far below, could be made out by those looking down nervously through open doors, 'little points of darkness made visible by their tiny white wakes' in the brilliant moonlight.[5] Lieutenant Alan Jefferson of 9 PARA saw 'a gap in the clouds had revealed the white caps of waves far below, reported by those who had the energy to look for themselves'.[6] Then came the long white line of surf, at which point the despatcher shouted 'Cabourg!'. 'Shortly afterwards' reported Clarke:

*We were into the flak. It came up at us rather like fireworks. Our aircraft instead of rising and increasing speed seemed to slow down. It dropped lower, altering course slightly a couple of times.*

This was the pilot lining up for the run-in on the drop zones. 'Something hit us,' Clarke recalled. 'The sound was rather like that of a dustbin being emptied, but there was no apparent damage at the moment.'[7]

Other aircraft took violent evasive action. Paratroopers inside were thrown about in a general melée of baggage, kit bags and weapons, which would take vital time to remedy before jumping, as aircraft broke formation. Lieutenant Richard Todd standing over the hole in the floor of the Stirling bomber was held back by his batman, but remembered 'we lost a number of people over the sea from evasive action, who fell out'[8] — a lonely death, totally weighed down by helmet, weapons and equipment.

'Five minutes to go!' Despatchers were edgy as Clarke recalls 'making frequent trips to the pilot's cabin and ceasing individual attention to us'. Most picked up the message by sign language, guessing correctly before the shouted messages reached the end of the line.

*Those nervous motions, so well known and yet unnoticed by those making them, began again; the fidgeting with and preliminary tap on quick-release boxes, the tightening of chin straps, the glance at the hooks on the static lines, verifying that the safety pin was safely home; that the kit-bag was safely fastened to the leg — all those little things we so often cursed ourselves for doing, well knowing that they were just signs of nervousness.*[9]

'Stand to the door!' A few muttered prayers 'please God let it be all right'. The first man shuffled to the door, hanging onto the side frame gazing intently firstly at the red light, then into the dark blackness punctuated by the odd light below; hoping to God he was not looking the wrong way when the green light came on. Closing up behind came the remainder of the stick, each man jostling with each other and the motion of the aircraft, to achieve that important area of space to enable a clean and controlled exit through the door. Aeroplanes throttled right back and began to vibrate as they slowed almost to stalling speed. At times there was considerable turbulence in the air from the large number of aircraft in the area, mostly at the same height.

'Mind your arm in the strap!' was another call along the stick. Another important precaution was to ensure that the strap running from the parachute pack to the aircraft cable, which would jerk open the parachute automatically on exit, did not pass beneath the inboard arm. Often overlooked by nervous paratroopers, failure to observe the rule, often resulted in a dislocated arm. Lieutenant Jefferson heard 'a sudden banging under the aircraft as though it was being hit with saucepans'. Major Clarke was almost prematurely pitched out as the plane rolled. 'God, that kit-bag was heavy' he recalled. 'All right, Sir?' enquired the despatcher. 'All I could do was nod.'

During the final run-in, the mind becomes totally absorbed and alert to the business at hand. Fear takes second place to the requirement to achieve a clean exit.

The rest of the stick behind, seeing nothing, are totally reliant upon their sensory perception of changes in engine-sound, direction and speed. Only able to see the red glow ahead, above the door, everything hinged on its transition to a green hue. At the door itself, the propeller roar and buffeting of the slip-stream has an almost surgical calming effect, as the parachutist controls all those emotions encouraging him not to jump. As Clarke explained:

*It was not easy to screw my head into the right position to see that little red light up by my left ear, when it came on. But the old butterflies in the midriff had gone. I even remember thinking amusedly that there would be no yellow light between the red one and the green like you get at the crossroads, and, there, flick, the red was on. The green followed quickly and I was away.*[10]

Lieutenant Jefferson in another aircraft could see:

*The despatcher was staring, mesmerised, at the darkened bulb of the green light. Then it glowed, and I could see its reflection on the inside of the fuselage — Green.*[11]

'Go! Go! Go!' shouted the despatchers, a cry often taken up by the whole stick, as with irresistible momentum the paratroopers shuffled and scrambled along dimmed aircraft interiors. As the door is neared there is a slight pause to gain control and then a final physical effort as each man pitched himself cumbersomely out with his weapons container into the blackness of the Normandy night. There were difficulties. Despatchers exercised caution, red lights came on again at the end of drop zones. Stanley Lee, a wireless operator with No 512 Squadron RAF, recalled some aircraft made as many as three runs in, because 'soldiers, very heavily laden and running on a metal floor in boots with smooth, rubber soles, slipped and fell, holding up the rest of the stick'.[12]

Upon exit the slip-stream strikes the face, causing a frightened exhalation of breath. The shadow of the tailplane might momentarily be glimpsed, a rush of cold air, and then the taut snap as the parachute takes the body and equipment weight. A brief glance around may reveal other shadowy shapes in the air. There is a blessed silence following the roaring aircraft crescendo of sound, which now recedes in the distance. Others follow their place, encouraging a momentary urge to duck, as successive banks of aircraft continue to fly over, shedding their loads, tumbling into the darkness overhead.

Lieutenant Jefferson's static line tightened and momentarily applied the whole weight of his body and equipment onto his left arm, a painful wrench that flung his arm up across his face. It was virtually dislocated, and now useless. Clarke, having exited, realised with dread, failing the normal tug at his harness seconds into the air, that he had lost his kit bag. He looked instead to his landing: 'it was not easy to judge the wind'. Others feeling the reassuring drag of their containers suspended below, saw there were few if any lights enabling them to pick out the line of the horizon. Some hit the ground unexpectedly with a startled cry, others could just discern the dark mass with its different hues of black and grey rushing up to meet them, and feel the thump of the container just before they hit the ground. Many to their horror realised at the first splash of equipment into deep water, that the fight for life was about to begin. 'Suddenly I was down' felt Clarke, and the canopy of his 'chute gently subsided around him. 'Planes were droning overhead. Away to the north I could hear gunfire of some sort.'[13] BBC correspondent Guy Byam found himself in the middle of a cornfield. 'I can't be sure where I am' he said, nevertheless, 'overhead hundreds of parachutes and containers are coming down'.[14]

The time was 00.50. Major John Howard already on the ground defending the Orne crossings, had noticed the German searchlights flickering on in the villages to the east and north of Ranville. Gazing up, he saw:

*We had a first-class view of the Division coming in. Searchlights were lighting up the 'chutes and there was a bit of firing going on and you could see tracer bullets going up into the air as they floated down to the ground. It really was the most awe-inspiring sight.*[15]

Guy Byam began to record his impressions. 'The whole sky is a fantastic chimera of lights and flak, and one plane gets hit and disintegrates wholesale in the sky, sprinkling a myriad of burning pieces all over the sky.'[16] The sound of receding aircraft could be made out. Inside some of these lay pathetic discarded khaki bundles including Private Richardson of C Company 8 PARA. Struck down by flak shrapnel, he had been unhooked and by-passed by his comrades, determined to exit the aircraft. He was to be buried near the airfield where he had taken off.[17] Major Howard was quite philosophical about the dramatic scene unfolding above him: 'above all', he was to subsequently record, 'it meant we were not alone'.[18]

As the British were tumbling into the night sky over the eastern flank, the American airborne formations having by-passed the Channel Islands, split into two streams, and began thundering from west to east acros the Cherbourg Peninsula. The pilots of the US 9th Air Force IXth Troop Carrier Command were less experienced than their RAF counterparts. Steering initially by bright moonlight, there were few problems. Corporal Raymond Kubista flying in a 101st Division glider saw the invasion fleet below in the 'silvery moonlight' and felt 'we couldn't lose. There was nothing going to stop that'. He spent most of the time looking out of the window.[1] Technical Sergeant John Ginter of the 92nd Troop Carrier Squadron en route for Ste Mére-Eglise was also watching, but from the cockpit with the pilot

and co-pilot as they crossed the peninsula. 'As we were going in I see tracer bullets, but they looked just like Roman candles for sure and as we approached them they were more intensive.' Seemingly out of range they continued. 'But the second Island, as we turned, all hell started to break loose. You know ...' Ginter felt unable to continue.[19] Troopers who initially were able to 'see fighter aircraft all around the plane' found as did Trooper Howard 'Goody' Goodson of the 505th Regiment, also en route to Ste Mère-Eglise that:

*All of a sudden it was just black. I thought it was cloud but it was smoke from German ack-ack fire and I believe our plane was hit, two or three times, it was shaking all over and I was scared to death.*[20]

Captain Laurence Critchell of the 501st Regiment remembers 'by the time the planes began to encounter scattered clouds near the French coast, most of us were asleep'. Brigadier General James Gavin, the US 82nd Division's deputy commander, ordered his aircraft stick to hook up as soon as he saw the French coast, which was his practice flying over hostile territory. 'If we had been hit, we would then have been able to scramble out of the aeroplane with a minimum of delay.'[21]

Flying conditions for some appeared ideal. If so, the same advantage applied to flak. Lieutenant Colonel Ekman of the 505th Regiment reported heavy ground mist had prevented Channel Island German batteries from seeing the aircraft, but afterwards, fog broke as they began crossing the peninsula.

*Before long the Douvre could be seen. We came from above the fog and at once started to lose altitude to get down to a proper jump height. The moon was bright, good for purposes of checking land marks for us, but also good for the ack-ack that was shooting at us ... now and then a plane would pitch upon getting the effect of an air-bursting shell.*[22]

For the majority, the experience appears different. Major General Ridgeway commanding the US 101st Division described their sudden penetration of 'thick and turbulent' cloud:

*I had been looking out the doorway, watching with a profound sense of satisfaction the close-ordered flight of that great sky caravan that stretched as far as the eye could see. All at once they were blotted out. Not a wing light showed. The plane began to yaw and plunge, and in my mind's eye I could see the other pilots, fighting to hold course, knowing how great was the danger of a collision in the air ... Not even our own wing lights showed in that thick murk. It was all up to the pilots now.*[23]

It was the same for Gavin in the other stream, who 'could look back and see the most comforting sight. As far as I could see there were aeroplanes, a lot of them, right across and way back.' Then 'all of a sudden, like hitting a brick wall, we hit a cloud-bank'. This was a total reversal of fortune. 'It was so thick that I could not see the wing tips of our plane', or indeed, 'any other planes'.[24] Finding the drop zone was now totally dependent upon a timed appreciation from the moment of landfall to objective, assuming they were flying on the correct heading at a constant speed; at best an approximate calculation of distance. Some of the inexperienced pilots panicked. One battalion commander receiving the 'go' signal well before the drop zone, simply ordered the crew chief to go back and tell the pilot to turn it off again until they reached the correct drop zone.[25]

Discomfort in the back of the aircraft was much the same as it had been for the British. Trooper Goodson of the 505th Regiment said, 'we were so heavily loaded that the crew chief on the plane had to come around individually and pull each man up. He couldn't rise up by himself.'[26] Private Thomas Raulston in the 506th Regiment recalled 'the door was being removed when I woke up'. In the confusion of standing up and hooking on equipment, the fact that the red light was already on was not yet noticeable. Once it was, bathed in its sullen glow, the waiting paratroopers 'didn't look like men but rather huge machines ... we weren't flesh and blood at that moment but hard, cold things of precision'. Attention was now focussed on the door, 'a black exit in our little world', because now they were subjected to violent anti-aircraft fire. Roaring aircraft engines and the howling buffeting slip-stream were interspersed with the sharp metallic crack and reverberation of flak.

*All of a sudden the night became alive with red, yellow and white flashes and streaks of light; among these tracers, one could notice the burst of explosive ack-ack. I prayed then most of the guys did; it wasn't much of a prayer but a very sincere one. Over and over I said "give me guts".*[27]

Paratroopers pressed up close against each other, enduring these pressures in silence, inside the aircraft, had difficulty maintaining balance. Aircraft would suddenly rise a hundred feet in a second or two, buckling legs under the upward pressure. Captain Laurence Critchlell described the noise of explosions:

*The distant ones made an odd, enveloping "wop", like a sound curling in on itself; close by they had the concussion of dynamite. A noise like the rattling of chains beat against the walls of the plane; it was expended shrapnel. Nothing had prepared us for the surprising discovery that flak made noise!*[28]

Formations began to disperse. Thomas Rice of the 501st Regiment noticed a glare lighting up the sky. He saw another aircraft:

*As it dipped down below him, curling off on one wing. One—two—three dark figures hurtled out of it; then the flames enveloped the cabin. In his mind's eye he saw the men shrivelling up inside ...*[29]

Under the stress of combat, transport aircraft tended to fly faster, which can magnify the opening shock of the parachute to a violent and alarming degree. Like the British, the sensory faculties of those about to jump became honed to an abnormal alertness. The desire to achieve a clean exit through the door, pervades all else. Concentrated anti-aircraft fire was, however, to deny this to many. Navigation was still largely guess work in these conditions if the area 'looked right', or if someone in the aircraft was astute enough to exercise control. Gavin, a veteran, was anxious despite incoming fire to pin-point his location before jumping. 'We began to receive small-arms fire from the ground', he recalled, sounding 'like pebbles landing on a tin roof'. They were flying at about 600ft when the green light went on. He had sighted 'another aeroplane or two', and 'directly ahead of us there was a tremendous amount of small-arms fire, and apparently buildings were burning'. This had to be Ste Mère-Eglise. He jumped.[30]

Private Thomas Raulston's stick was slowed right down by the difficulty over-encumbered paratroopers had in shuffling along the fuselage and exiting the aircraft:

*When number 4 hit the door, or about that time, we hit a thick spate of ack-ack and the plane did a fine Irish jig. The floor was jumping and we could hear a drum-drum on the plane, like when birds crawl on a tin roof. Just as I hit the door the plane rocked in such a way as to throw me from the door.*

It was a paratrooper's nightmare, a totally unbalanced exit. The aircraft was also flying too fast. If the speed of the plane was not greater than 100kts, one might experience a deceleration equivalent to five or six times gravity and have a split-second blackout. In Normandy, however, some apprehensive pilots flew in excess of 150kts, causing troopers to have parts of their equipment torn from their bodies. Lucky ones lost only a wrist-watch. Raulston pitched out head first:

*The opening shock was as easy as being hit by a truck. A quick check proved that I had no leg pack, whether the darn thing was shot off, blown off by the prop or just couldn't take the opening shock, I'll never know.*

This was not the only problem:

*We jumped too high and the trip down took a thousand years. My straps were twisted (proof of bad body position) and I couldn't slip or turn. The sky was still full of those streaks of death.*

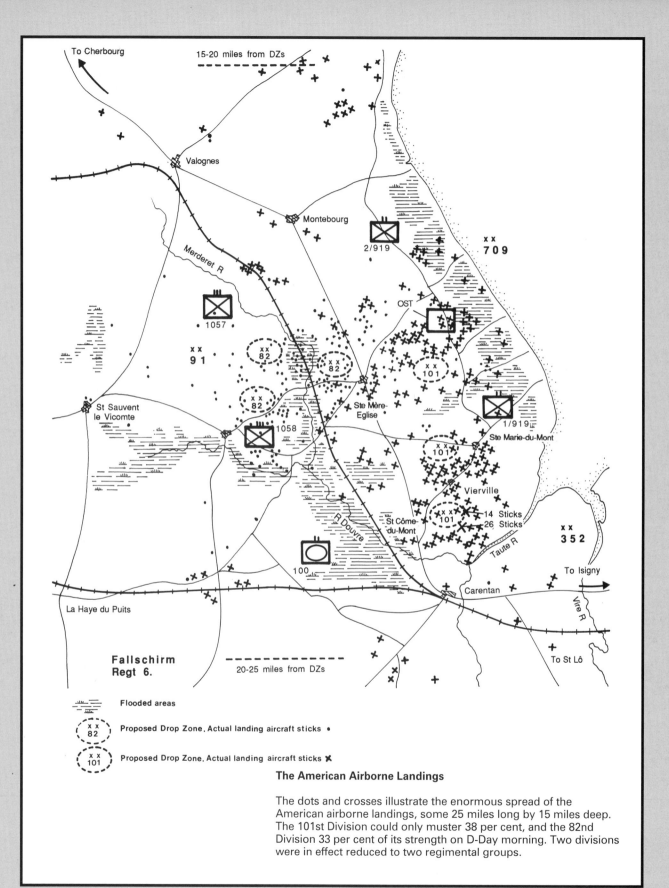

To Cherbourg

15-20 miles from DZs

Valognes

Montebourg

2/919

xx
709

Merderet R.

1057

OST

xx
91

xx
82

xx
82

xx
101

St Sauvent
le Vicomte

xx
82

1058

Ste Mère-
Eglise

1/919

Ste Marie-du-Mont

xx
101

Vierville

100

R Douvre

St Côme-
du-Mont

xx
101

14 Sticks
26 Sticks

Taute R.

xx
352

To Isigny

Carentan

Vire R.

La Haye du Puits

Fallschirm
Regt 6.

20-25 miles from DZs

To St Lô

Flooded areas

x x
82    Proposed Drop Zone. Actual landing aircraft sticks •

x x
101   Proposed Drop Zone. Actual landing aircraft sticks ✗

**The American Airborne Landings**

The dots and crosses illustrate the enormous spread of the
American airborne landings, some 25 miles long by 15 miles deep.
The 101st Division could only muster 38 per cent, and the 82nd
Division 33 per cent of its strength on D-Day morning. Two divisions
were in effect reduced to two regimental groups.

He was falling toward a river. Luck did not totally desert him, because landing on the edge, the wind filled his chute and pulled him up onto dry land. 'You can guess how sweet that ground felt', he subsequently wrote. Eight days later he was to be wounded in action.[31]

Others on entry into the slip-stream, terrified, simply closed their eyes, or blotted the frightening images from their memories. 'Don't ask me what I saw when the 'chute opened, because I don't remember that either,' said Sergeant Robert Miller. 'But I remember everything after I hit the ground. Seeing a guy burning in the air. Things like that.'[32]

The primary fears of a paratrooper follow the sequence of events that follow his aircraft exit. First of all he must ensure a clean jump through the door. Failure to achieve this will affect the next step — the flight — resulting in an entanglement within rigging lines and parachute, loss of flight control and perhaps also equipment. The next hazard is landing, and the imperative to avoid obstacles, particularly trees and buildings. Private Tony Mead of 9 PARA near Merville crashed into a massive tree and became impaled on a branch that penetrated his gut. Various soldiers broke bones, or were knocked senseless bouncing off the roofs of buildings. Yet descending over water inspires sheer terror. Many paratroopers of the 507th and 508th Regiments, attempting to land in the triangle at the confluence of the Douvre and Merderet rivers, overshot their zones, and heavily laden with equipment, dropped into the swamplands along the river. Encumbered by their containers which they had intended to cut free with knives, many perished in shallow water. Exhausted, by standing over-long periods kitted up in the aircraft, mentally drained being shot at by flak, tumbling out of aircraft ensnared in rigging lines; many did not have the strength to disentangle themselves from equipment in water they could have stood up in. Brigadier General John Gavin said:

*Well I saw at least a dozen bodies of men who landed in water which could not have been more than two or three feet above the ground. Because the parachute came right down on top of them, it sealed it to the water. And they were excited anyway, and they were being shot at as well. We lost a surprising number that way.*[33]

Thrashing around, suffocating in soaking folds of silk and rigging lines, they drowned; unable to summon sufficient presence of mind, or strength, under such claustrophobic conditions to cut themselves free.

British paratroopers landing in flooded ditches around the Dives suffered the same fate. Some splashing into deep water with full equipment and helmet simply disappeared beneath the stinking surface never to appear again. Unfortunates could be heard screaming for assistance in the mud and slime, their terrified appeals bubbling into silence before comrades could reach them. A few American aircraft, dependent upon mis-timed appreciations after crossing the coast, then being enveloped by cloud, released sticks into the Channel on the other side of the Peninsula, having flown west to east. Veteran paratroopers seeing the flooded areas approaching, reflecting the moonlight, often ignored the green light until certain firm ground was coming up. Others at the rear of sticks were not able to see. Lieutenant Sumpter Blackmon of the 501st Regiment 'saw the proper landmarks come up, but felt no tap' from the despatcher. 'Then I saw the ground disappear and then white-caps — we were back over the sea.' His aircraft turned back, and despite flak tried again. Once over the shore-line Blackmon 'decided it was now or never' and jumped.[34]

Behind the paratroopers came the gliders; groping their way through the black night. Flight Lieutenant John Macadam, RAF remembers tracer lights ahead 'like the Blackpool illuminations, and when it seemed obvious to us that we should call it a day and go back, the pilot put the nose of the aircraft into it as if it were confetti'. Macadam admired 'the tough little glider sergeant' who could do little else but hang onto the controls and follow the tug plane through the murky cloud as they descended.

*The rear-gunner yelled suddenly: "The glider's hit". The skipper said "Glider pilot, glider pilot, are you all right?" There was a short pause, and then the voice came again: "All right, we're with you".*

'Casting off', said the little gruff voice when the landing zone was identified. Macadam watched the tug lunge forward, free of the glider's weight. 'There was nothing but blankness now. But there were a lot of gliders swooshing down in the blankness.'[35]

War correspondent Chester Wilmot described as 'with grinding brakes and creaking timbers we jolted, lurched and crashed our way to a landing'. They were more successful than many around them. Looking at another glider alongside, Wilmot saw:

*The bottom of the nose was battered in … the wings and tail assembly were slashed here and there, but she came to a rest on her three wheels, even though she had mown down five stout posts that came in her path and virtually crash landed in a ploughed field. No one was even scratched.*

They 'shouted with joy … and relief'[36] and with reason. More often than not, the experience was that endured by Corporal Raymond Kubista of the US 101st Airborne Division:

*Just before we released from the plane they killed either our pilot or our co-pilot, I don't recall which. But the other man who was piloting the plane tried to hold him up by*

*Above:* Cramped conditions and over-encumbered by equipment, pensive paratroopers of the 82nd Airborne Division await the drop.

*Left:* 'I saw at least a dozen bodies of men who landed in water which could not have been more than two or three feet deep.' An entangled and drowned trooper of the 82nd Airborne Division amid the scum of the marsh edge.

*the back of his collar. The last thing I remember was he turned his head and said we "were headed right for a tree". Most of them were killed.*[37]

Once on the ground paratroopers experienced a transitory feeling of relief, mixed with the elation of having survived the experience. Adrenalin could still act as a stimulant for the first few hours before a fatigued reaction set in. Coincidental with this depressing downturn in spirits, came a realisation that many were in the wrong place. As Sergeant Robert Miller of the 502nd Regiment expressed it:

*The most terrible thing is when you hit the ground and you don't see anybody and you don't hear anything and you're all alone. Being lonely like that is the worst feeling in the world.*[38]

All commanders were aware of the imperative to rally their units quickly and get them into battle as effective integrated formations. But a sense of creeping helplessness began to afflict commanders, already worn by fatigue and in some cases shock. Difficulties appeared overwhelming. They could only be overcome by energy and personal motivation. Brigadier General Gavin recalled the appearance of a red light on the far side of the swamp, followed by a green. These were the assembly lights of the 507th and 508th Regiments 'far to the east of where they should have been'.

It soon became apparent 'we had evidently overflown our drop zone by several miles, and I had no idea where the rest of the troopers were'. It was daylight before he would gather 100 to 150 men, some wounded and injured. Many equipments had been irretrievably lost in the swamp. Moreover 'to my utter frustration, I found them completely disorganized, lacking unit organization and even unit leadership'.[39] Lieutenant Blackmon miles away near the coast admitted 'we had no idea where we were', unable to match any landmarks with his map he concluded 'we had obviously jumped off the map'.[40]

Private Weathers of 12 PARA found he was part of a smaller group of four to five men on the river Dives 'some 12 miles or so from the battalion dropping zone'. Wading across the river 'engulfed in thick oozing mud ... up to our arm pits' he summed up his initial impressions:

*I think I was more apprehensive than frightened, although there were frightening moments. Certainly I was bewildered and very frustrated indeed at being virtually of no use because we were dropped in the wrong place.*[41]

Although the drop zone was 'teeming with people' Captain Radmore a signals officer in 5 PARA Brigade, 'had no idea where I was and was convinced I'd been dropped in the wrong place'. Moreover, 'a private soldier was very indignant with me for being in the wrong

DZ — as he thought incorrectly'.[42]

By 02.30 Lieutenant Colonel Otway commanding the 9th Battalion the Parachute Regiment was beside himself with frustration. He had been given the vital mission of silencing a German battery at Merville, in a position to dominate the eastern flank of the proposed British landings on Sword Beach. Major General Gale, commander of British 6th Airborne Division had been brutally frank to Otway's Brigade Commander J. S. L. Hill: 'your attitude of mind', he instructed, 'must be that you cannot contemplate failure in the direct assault'. Otway's battalion, some 600 strong, had been incarcerated for months, training for this specific role. 'No other commitment must jeopardise success in this enterprise.'[43] A highly detailed, painstaking plan had been developed for his battalion's assault on the battery. They were prepared for high casualties, yet now, one hour and 35 minutes after the drop, only 110 men had reported in at the rendezvous. How could the plan be made to work?

## Will it suffice? ... holding the flanks.

In order to have any impact upon the forthcoming battle, the airborne divisions had to gather as formations to enact the plan. The US 101st Division drop, as subsequently plotted by sticks on maps, covered an area 25 miles long by 15 miles wide. Isolated elements dropped even further afield. Few of these aircraft sticks were to have any realistic chance of massing into a division strength formation. The 502nd Regiment was so scattered by cloud and flak that it would take more than a day to begin assembling as a unit. Although not to plan, and using smaller forces, the 506th Regiment, better able to assemble rapidly, began to move to secure the beach exits on the western edge of the flooded area west of Utah Beach. Elements of 501st Regiment moved to the line of the river Douvre, west to St Côme-du-Mont, where it came upon the enemy in unexpected strength. The division was in effect reduced to regimental strength, only 2,500 of 6,600 managing to assemble within 24 hours. Only a dimly apparent offensive pattern was beginning to emerge, led by a half-dozen colonels commanding bands of men varying between 75 to 250-men strong. These groups at least managed to clear the way inland for the amphibious landing, by securing beach exits.

The US 82nd Airborne Division fared little better. One regiment — the 505th — dropped in a fairly tight group north west of Ste Mère-Eglise. Aircraft which had been scattered by cloud and flak, persevered, circling back and finding the drop zone. It was almost devoid of enemy. Lieutenant Colonel Krause 'bounced' the town with only a quarter battalion strength and secured it by day. At least one firm base was therefore established. The other two regiments were too dispersed in order to

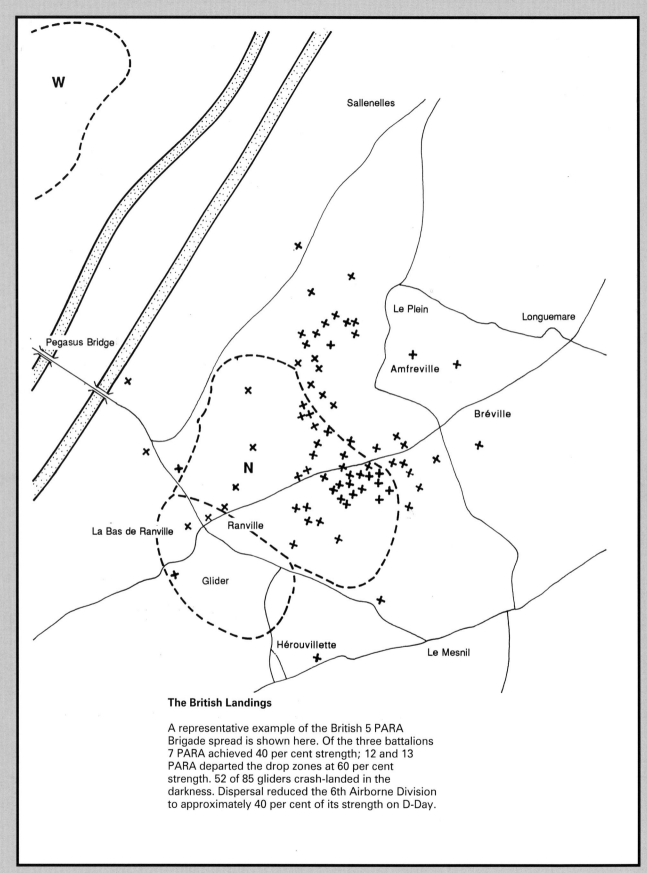

**The British Landings**

A representative example of the British 5 PARA
Brigade spread is shown here. Of the three battalions
7 PARA achieved 40 per cent strength; 12 and 13
PARA departed the drop zones at 60 per cent
strength. 52 of 85 gliders crash-landed in the
darkness. Dispersal reduced the 6th Airborne Division
to approximately 40 per cent of its strength on D-Day.

carry out their missions effectively. The 82nd had dropped on the fringe of the German 91st Airlanding Division assembly area, making their situation more precarious than that of the 101st Division. Small groups of 50 to 60 men began to fight the enemy where they found them, among ditches and hedgerows. Often these groups, only 1,000yds apart, were unaware of each other's presence, due to the dense terrain. It was these bands, like the four or so west of the Merderet river, which took much of the pressure off the mass of the division firmly ensconced around Ste Mère-Eglise. One platoon led by Lieutenant Turnball fought a desperate battle, outnumbered five to one, north of the town. Only 16 of 42 survived the day's fighting, but managed to secure the northern approach to the town while another attack was beaten off to the south. About 500 to 600 men gathered to contest the La Fière crossing of the Merderet. Only 4 percent of the force dropped on the zones west of the river, consequently both it and crossings over the Douvre could not be secured. Even at the end of the first 24 hours, the division was in control of only 40 percent of its combat infantry and 10 percent of its artillery. It had also shrunk to regimental size — less than one third of division strength — declaring 4,000 casualties to VII Corps on the first day.[1] The Allied hold on the western flank of its proposed lodgement was therefore tenuous.

It was faring only marginally better on the eastern flank. British path-finders had not been given sufficient time to mark the drop zones properly before the main stream arrived. 3rd Brigade, ordered to destroy bridges over the Dives, began its tasks at 30 percent below strength. Both 8 PARA and the 1st Canadian PARA were widely dispersed, but nevertheless continued with the plan as best they were able. 9 PARA left the drop zone 2½ hours after dropping with only 150 of 600 men. While en route to the vital Merville battery they discovered the bomber force, due to hit their objective prior to their breach of the defences, had completely missed the target. The 5th Brigade, due to reinforce and then hold the Orne crossings area, also had scattered jumps. By 03.00 only 40 percent of 7 PARA were to reach Major Howard on the canal; and 12 and 13 PARA departed their drop zones 60 percent strong to seize the glider landing zones in the Ranville area. Some 52 of the 85 British gliders crash-landed in the darkness; 16 were two or more miles out, 17 were missing.[2]

Major John Howard on the Orne Canal bridge had successfully knocked out the intermittent German traffic that had attempted to cross the bridge, since the coup de main. He had, in so doing, also captured Major Hans Schmidt, the German bridge commander. For the first hour, enemy tank and lorry movement had been monitored between the two hamlets at Bénouville and Le Port, on the western sea-borne invasion side of the bridge. The Germans were conferring. At 01.30 Howard's worst fears were confirmed. Still no British reinforcements of any substance, yet two German Mark IV tanks were squeaking and clattering remorselessly toward his bridge from Bénouville. Behind, and fortunately separated from the tanks, were German infantry. With engines revving, and tracks squealing the lead tank negotiated the T-junction adjacent to the bridge. There was a bang — and it stopped. Machine gun clips started to chatter inside the darkened silhouette, grenades crumped and suddenly a huge orange explosion blasted off turret and hatch lids, followed by a cascade of molten tracer and globules of white-hot metal as a succession of shell explosions began to tear the tank apart. A huge bulbous cloud of oily flame-tinged smoke boiled into the night air, followed by the pick-pocking of a myriad of exploding ammunition reports. The fiery conflagration, stoked by a PIAT round, blocked the junction. A roar of exhaust sounded from the second tank as it beat a hasty retreat; unable to locate the source of the anti-tank fire. Sounds of explosions and the glow in the night sky was the very beacon that members of 7 PARA, stumbling and cursing in the darkness, attempting to cross water-logged ditches, needed finally to orientate themselves. Flimsy though it was, this Allied hurdle, precariously balanced across the Orne river crossings, was holding.

General Montgomery was relying upon the rapid and initial insertion of three light airborne divisions at least to restrict the immediate options of five German divisions in-situ, until the violent frontal assault by his sea-borne divisions was successful. In order to win the vital race for the invasion fore-shore, they must hold the wings, the flanks of the great Allied enterprise. Yet within hours of landing, the strength of the US 101st Division in the west was down to 38 percent, the US 82nd Division to less than 33 percent. In the east, dispersal had reduced the British 6th Airborne Division to approximately 40 percent. This in effect reduced the nucleus in each area to one single regiment or brigade. Although 20,000 men had dropped, their dispersal had reduced their measurable effect to one scattered weak division — not three — as the vanguard of the invasion of Europe.[3] Much of their heavy equipments had been lost. Reinforcements would continue into daylight, but would it suffice?[4]

# CHAPTER 7 ▬▬▬▬▬

# THE LONG NIGHT

*'Major, paratroops are dropping ...'*
*Adjutant Panzergrenadier Regiment 125*

## 'Condemned to inactivity' ... the Orne and the east.

Shortly after midnight on 5 June, the nightmare scenario feared, but never considered plausible, began to afflict the German Seventh Army garrisoning Normandy. Colonel Oelze, previously ridiculed by the staff of 84th Corps while attempting to provide early warning from radar scanners on Guernsey, received a further call. This time it was the Corps' Chief of Staff. He was agitated. 'You were right. Large airborne landings behind the whole front. Alarm!'[1]

Major Hans von Luck manning his regimental headquarters in Belengreville east of Caen 'heard the growing roar of aircraft which passed over us'. Not such an unusual event, as they normally bombed inland, or carried on to the Reich itself. But this time:

> *The machines appeared to be flying very low — because of the weather? I looked out the window and was wide awake; flares were hanging in the sky. At the same moment, my adjutant was on the telephone, "Major, paratroops are dropping. Gliders are landing in our section. I'm trying to make contact with Number II battalion. I'll come along to you at once".*

Panzergrenadier Regiment 125 was put on alert. 'First reports indicated that British paratroops had dropped over Troarn' where the 5th Company of his IInd Battalion were exercising with blank ammunition. Brandenberg, the company commander, had established his headquarters in a cellar, and was informed by telephone that the rest of the battalion would counter-attack toward him. 'Okay', he replied, 'I have the first prisoner here, a British Medical Officer of the 6th Airborne Division'.[2]

At half past midnight *Heeres* (Army) Coastal Artillery Battalion 1255 reported their beach sector 'was overflown by numerous low-flying aircraft towing gliders'. Moreover, 'at the same time paratroopers began jump-

ing from a height of 70 or 80 metres around Benerville, Auberville, Blonville and south of Champs Rabats'. This suggested an assault on the left flank of Fifteenth Army in the 711th Division sector. By 00.35 the Battalion alert state was raised to Level II, and units ordered to prepare for all-round defence. 'Numerous paratroopers who had landed directly next to battery positions were engaged with flak, machine guns and infantry weapons.' Detonations from air attacks could be heard around the Orne estuary; including the unit's 3rd Battery in Houlgate, which also received attention.[3]

Further along the coast to the west, Leutnant Raimund Steiner, commanding the 1st Battery of Artillery Regiment 1716 at Merville, saw outside his bunker on the beach at Franceville, that:

> *Bomber formations were flying overhead in unending numbers. They flew so low that one could see the exhausts flaming and glowing. They bombed mainly to the west of the Orne and only once to the east. Parachutists then landed to the south of Franceville and gliders came.*[4]

Waves of incident and contact reports began to assail Generalleutnant Wilhelm Richter's 716th Division Headquarters. 'They arrived at the Division in timed relays as the landings occurred' reported the headquarters, 'between 00.40 and 01.05'. Division raised the readiness state to Alarm Level II at 01.05. The Riva Bella sector commander in Ouistreham, manning coastal defences, had already done so 20 minutes earlier.

An aircraft carrying troops from 8 PARA, or 3 PARA Brigade Headquarters, dropped a stick of paratroopers across the 1st Company Command Post of Engineer Battalion 716 billeted in Hérouvillette. A fire-fight ensued immediately between the shocked adversaries of both sides. 'Those paratroopers that had penetrated the living accommodation were immediately wiped out; and following an immediate counter-attack, grievous losses inflicted on those who had landed outside.' But the small outpost of 20 men was to be besieged for the next 24 hours until finally relieved.[5]

Reports of landings continued to build up in 716th Division Headquarters, and continued throughout the

*Above:* 'Major, paratroopers are dropping.' Observing the parachute assault.

*Left:* A German 'Marder' SP from the Kampfgruppe 'Von Luck' in the Ranville area.

night and into the next day. There was a patchy response. Most units had been broken down into dispersed locations, penny-packeted on separate tasks or manning strong-points. Ost Battalion 642, for example, had units spread in company or platoon locations on both sides of the Orne river. The Battalion Headquarters in Amfreville, just south of the main British 5th Brigade drop zone, was quickly attacked, losing one dead and five wounded early on during the night. Nevertheless, five enemy prisoners were taken, including two severely wounded and three killed.[6]

The situation continued to deteriorate. *Schwerpunkt* or the main point of effort for the landings was reported by 716th Division as 'Parachute and glider troops set down east of the Orne estuary, in a zone encompassing Bénouville, Blainville, Hérouvillette and Bréville'. This was virtually astride the Seventh-Fifteenth Army Group boundary. Landing areas were pin-pointed according to observers by 'Christmas trees' or flares, launched by 'pilot aircraft' (pathfinders), easily visible from miles away. As Unteroffizier Hammel on guard duty with Panzer Reconnaissance Battalion 21, south of Caen, was to report:

*Suddenly at midnight on 5 to 6 June all hell broke loose. From my post I could see flares in the sky, followed by a concentrated air-raid on nearby Caen. "Now the fun begins" was my first thought.*[7]

Soldiers were cowed and impressed by this awesome demonstration of Allied air power. Leutnant Steiner, near the Merville battery, watching the terrifying fly-past exclaimed:

*They were vast. I did not understand how such things could fly! The bombers and other aircraft came in tight formations and made a great impression on me. The vibration in the air caused the sand in the dunes to crumble.*[8]

Division observed in its reports that the majority of the paratroopers appeared primarily to be securing the edges of the glider landing zones. 'The area between Ranville, Amfreville and Bréville seemed to be the logistic focal point for the air-landed elements.'[9] It became apparent that substantial measures would be required to counter this incursion, expanding inexorably in scale. Oberleutnant Rupert Grzimek also from Panzer Reconnaissance Battalion 21 was 'alerted that paratroops and gliders had landed in the sector of Panzergrenadier Regiment 125 under Major von Luck'. Within a very short time his unit was ready for action. 'Together with the bombing of Caen this suggested more than a commando operation.'[10]

Centralised direction was not immediately forthcoming from Headquarters 716th Division. 'Gradually we were becoming filled with anger', commented Major von Luck. 'The clearance for an immediate night attack, so as to take advantage of the initial confusion among our opponents, had still not come, although our reports via Division to the Corps and to Army Group B must long since have been on hand'.[11] Troops on the ground faced with the reality of the situation were incensed at the imposed inactivity. 'By now, we had a slightly better idea of and grip on the situation,' assessed von Luck. Division staff were, however, reluctant to act. Possessing — what they felt to be — the bigger picture, they ignored pressures to commit reserves prematurely, urged at local level, because they were uncertain of the extent of the landings. Major Forster, for example, the Division IC (Intelligence Officer) of Fifteenth Army had already warned Army Group B at 01.40 of substantial enemy overflights, including gliders. 'paratroopers had dropped near Mont Canisy [near Deauville]', he claimed, 'and near the 711th Division Command Post, where the noise of battle was discernible. Details, however, had yet to come.'[12] An objective was not yet clearly identifiable. Thirty-five minutes later, Army Group B was inclined to believe it was a diversionary manoeuvre, as the Supreme Naval Commander Channel had reported, 'The enemy had thrown out straw dummies on parachutes'. This interplay of fact and deception produced a command malaise, which had a crucial and cumulative effect upon immediate counter-measures. 'The hours passed', von Luck protested. 'We had set up a defensive front where we had been condemned to inactivity.'[14]

Generalleutnant Richter's move to Rennes to participate in the 84th Corps war games had been quickly cancelled; exercise had become reality. Counter-measures were, however, merely cosmetic. The credibility of what was unfolding lacked reality. Scant attention at this stage was paid to the possibility of that the Allies might follow up the airborne operations with sea-borne landings. Previous compromises in defence planning manifested themselves in the measures now taken. With the absence of a meaningful reserve directly behind the beaches, coastal defence units or their local reserves were poached to provide the necessary means to deal with the unexpected airborne incursion. A concentric strategy of applying pressure from all sides upon the identified airborne enclave began to haphazardly materialize. The process began at 01.40 when the third company of Ost Battalion 642 in Hermannville was placed under command of Infantry Regiment 736 and ordered to attack the paratroopers identified in Bréville. Twenty or so minutes later the dispersed companies belonging to Ost Battalion 642 on the west bank of the Orne (some five platoons of infantry) — together with two platoons of assault guns from Panzerjäger Company 716 — were ordered to move to Sallenelles on the east bank, to support an attack bearing down from north to south on the enemy concentration. Artillery was immediately to begin harassing the identified British drop zones.[15]

It was at this stage that Major Howard's côup de main assault on the Orne river crossing began to apply its initial drag upon the speed of the German response. Not until 02.10 did 716th Division Headquarters realise it did not possess this vital artery, so necessary to feed operations on both sides of the Orne. The whole of the local German mobile reserve was concentrated to resolve this sudden and critical development. Consequently, between 02.35 and 03.10 elements from 21st Panzer Division, which had been attached to 716th Division as a mobile reserve on the east bank of the Orne — a reinforced panzergrenadier battalion supplemented with heavy artillery and a company of assault guns — were ordered to force the Orne river bridges and attack enemy occupied Ranville.[16] Inevitably delays occurred as the tasked units attempted to regroup. 'During the interim period', Division reported, 'the enemy constantly reinforced, in particular the Bénouville area, with fresh parachute landings, so that the planned concentric attack upon the expanding enemy bridgehead, despite a penetration of Bénouville, did not succeed'.[17]

Major Howard had been relieved and taken under command of 7 PARA. The tempo of the fighting visibly increased as the German counter-attacks came in. Desperately, the under-strength battalion held onto its tenuous positions. One company cut off in Benouville for 17 hours, lost all its officers, killed or wounded. German assault guns and tanks disabled by PIATs or Gammon bombs added to the ruddy glow of conflagrations interspersed with blooming phosphorescent flowers as explosions lit up the night. Even the regimental aid post was overrun, and a gun boat attack on the Orne Canal was beaten off. Grimly the paratroopers held on. Their adversaries, confused and unable to apply their full combat power in the darkness, resolved to finish them off at dawn.

Generalleutnant Richter implemented his initial counter-moves, uncertain of the true situation. At 01.42 he requested 'the committal of reinforced task groups' from 21st Panzer Division, before releasing his only mobile reserve. Victim of the German compromise defence strategy, he could do little else. Under Richter's command were six battalions, four German and two Russo-Polish. These, spread over 40km were immobile, confined to manning static dispersed company strongpoints. He was totally reliant upon the operational reserve — 21st Panzer Division — located nearby, for reinforcement. Generalleutnant Richter's own mobile reserve committed within three hours or so of the landings amounted to one reinforced, but poorly equipped, mechanised infantry battalion with some artillery and a dozen or so assault guns. Facing them, albeit dispersed, was a force of six battalions of lightly equipped airborne infantry, soon to rise to nine, with some heavier (gliderborne) weapons. Attacking with local superiority, but at an overall inverse proportion of one against three

brigade or regimental groups, the German offensive impetus soon began to be diluted by further unexpected developments, as the British parachute battalions, despite their involuntary dispersal, began to achieve their primary missions. Three bridges across the river Dives were blown during the night at Troarn, Bûres and Robehomme, and a fourth over a tributary near Varaville. It gradually became accepted that Ranville was in British hands by 04.00. 'The airborne soldiers landed east of the Orne included the majority of the 6th Airborne Division' reported division headquarters; 'the break-down by units has yet to be determined'.[18]

Panzergrenadier Regiment 125 was ready to attack. Troops stood by armoured half-tracks, hands in pockets, stamping their feet, warding off the chill. Engines were intermittently turned over in the darkness, to keep them warmed up. 'We felt completely fit physically and able to cope with the situation' reported its commander, Major von Luck. Oberleutnant Grzimek nearby with Panzer Reconnaissance Battalion 21 'was ready for action' within a very short time. 'We knew the order: "To attack only on orders from the highest authority".' Reinforced by Major Becker's assault-gun battalion, von Luck was perfectly confident they would push the British off the two bridges at Bénouville. But the order never came. 'I concealed my anger and remained calm and matter-of-fact', although inwardly the regimental commander was seething.[19] His commanders, stymied by scant resources, assailed by alarming reports, were reluctant to commit themselves irrevocably until the full extent of the landings became clear. At 03.05 hours Army Group had been told of the 'assembly of four-engined bombers in England. Attacks in the early morning hours are anticipated'. Then 15 minutes later came a more reassuring report from 47th Panzer Corps, rapidly transmitted further onto the Seventh and Fifteenth Armies and Supreme Headquarters West: 'The enemy, concentrated around Bénouville in approximately regimental strength, has been thrown back from the Orne'.[20] The message was of course erroneous.

Major Friedrich Hayn the IC (Intelligence Officer) with 84th Corps was concerned. At 05.00 he reported 'there has been no contact with the Merville coastal battery on the east bank of the [Orne] estuary for half an hour'.[21] The reason, as observed by Oberfeldwebel Peter Timpf, a forward artillery observation officer (FOO) with 736th Infantry Regiment, was soon to become apparent. He ducked, as two gliders swooped low over the village of Merville. Moving with a group of 36 German infantrymen, they were en route to check and clear the southeast perimeter of the battery.

Less than 200 men from the 9th British Battalion of the Parachute Regiment were poised on the eastern perimeter of the battery waiting for this very moment. 'My attention', recalled Lieutenant Alan Jefferson, a platoon commander about to participate in this assault, 'and probably the attention of us all, was riveted on a glider that suddenly appeared silently and majestically out of the night, flying low over the guns'. There were two. The second, much lower, loomed up. 'Then the AA gun ... opened up, firing bursts of five rounds that appeared like glowing, red balls'. A flash lit up the surrounding area as the third burst hit the glider's tail, an aircraft that Jefferson recalled 'represented a container for 22 men, friends of ours, families and well-liked'.[22]

Bangelore torpedoes blew with resounding cracks, marking the ragged gaps in the wire with steadily rising smudges of greyish smoke. Whistles blew as the savage assault went in.

The Merville battery consisted of four casemates and other related command and logistic bunkers, containing 100mm Czech howitzers, a virtual World War 1 fieldpiece. Steel doors protecting some of the casemates had been left open to aid ventilation. The guns, due to the uncertainty of the situation, had just been man-handled inside. A furious battle ensued as the paratroopers stormed inside the perimeter. Tracer rounds flashed in all directions, Stens chattered interspersed with slow-firing Brens and the reverberating thud of rapid-firing German Spandau machine guns. Agonised cries and yells emerged with clouds of smoke from the doorways of casemates following muffled detonations within. The crew of No 4 gun were quickly overwhelmed and struck down by the violent assault, all the German gunners were killed. Unable to contain the assault, the defenders fled to the command and logistic bunkers, or simply lay low in weapon slits. Any resistance to the British was contained and annihilated.

Leutnant Steiner now outside the battery, had moved up from Franceville to find out what had happened. He discovered:

*The situation was chaotic. Nobody knew who was friend or foe. Houses and trees were on fire and the sky was red. Among this infernal din rang out the sound of small-arms, especially at the crossroads.*[23]

At the entrance to the battery he saw a large German AA gun mounted on a half-track firing into the perimeter. This reconnaissance detachment from an army flak unit commanded by Unteroffizier Windgassen,[24] now caught up in the engagement, originally had been seeking refuge inside the battery. Steiner found 'I could get no further, although I was in sight of my battery, because of the firing that was going on there'.[25] Inside, the 9 PARA raiding force continued to mop up the opposition. 'Close-quarter battle is unavoidable,' reported one defender, 'as the enemy gets closer, in a large semi-circle'. These blurred images were reported a few weeks after the engagement:

*Here a shadow jumps up and sinks into a crater. Over there crouches a dark shape as the earth swallows it.*

*They are now 200 metres away. They bring their machine guns and mortars into the battery position. We are outnumbered.*

*What use are rattling machine-gun salvoes, hand grenades and rifles when they are surrounded by attackers five times their number. The howitzers can fire no more, the hand grenades have been thrown, the machine-guns are silenced. The enemy breaks into the position.*

The position of the defenders was now hopeless. 'No-one has a proper field of fire. No one can see the enemy', lamented the report.[26]

Steiner, unable to enter the battery, returned to his bunker on Franceville beach, resolving to seek assistance by radio. Inside the perimeter the surviving gun crew and defenders, sheltering in unoccupied bunkers and underground chambers, were powerless to react as the British, using hastily improvised explosive charges of grenades and HE — designed for use against tanks — attempted to spike the guns before the arrival of a pre-planned air and naval bombardment. It had been an amazing achievement. Seventy of the raiding force were dead or wounded. Success, however, was to prove transitory; the guns could not be destroyed with the limited means available. Fearing the impending massive air-raid due upon the battery, the raiding party was obliged to hastily withdraw. The 716th Division felt that:

*The enemy managed to work their way onto and around the gun positions taking advantage of the earlier devastation wrought by the air attack, which had produced a shell-pitted landscape around the guns. The enemy were then obliged to vacate the 1/1716 Battery position due to the concentrated fire of the 3rd and 4th Batteries of the regiment placed upon it.*[27]

Steiner had directed the fire of his neighbouring batteries upon his own.

The sacking of the Merville battery, although not achieving the primary aim of destruction, did succeed in virtually shocking its defenders into a state of semi-paralytic inactivity. Unbeknown to the British, who feared the scattered nature of the drop may be jeopardising success, its very spread was distracting the German defence and eating up local reserves. Its presence began to have a negative impact upon coastal defences between the proposed landing areas at Sword and Juno. At 05.10 hours the IInd Battalion of Infantry Regiment 736 reported from its command post outside Taillerville, that following parachute descents to its front 'the enemy was assaulting northwards, and had penetrated Bernières'.[28] The southern edge of the town was engaged by artillery. Subsequent confusing reports led to the commitment of two reinforced infantry combat groups, one from each of the two Infantry Regiments — 726 and 736 — across whose regimental boundaries the activity was reported, and elements from Ost Battalion 441. The action momentarily tied up four distinct units,[29] until the muddle was sorted out, and a reinforced company from 736th Regiment, directed to locate and destroy the enemy; the others returned to their stand-to positions. Contact with the enemy was never confirmed. It is likely that this transitory battalion effort spent the early dawn hours searching for straw-dummies.[30]

## 'The situation in the Seine Estuary is probably worse than ours' … the West.

South west of Carentan, Oberleutnant Martin Pöppel, commander of 12th Company Fallschirmjäger Regiment 6, could not give his own commander a more precise report. Observation posts had been reporting detonations all night, more recent explosions sounded about eight kilometres away. It was after midnight.

*Now more aircraft, damned near this time. The loud explosions must be coming from Carentan itself. It's a restless night. Perhaps old Behne is right, and something is going to happen. As there seems to be no end to the formation of enemy aircraft, I order the company to be ready for action. Once more can't do any harm.*[1]

Further north on the coast Unteroffizier Hans-Rudolf Thiel could hear the familiar but distant sound of aircraft engines. 'There's more than a few', he noticed, 'I hope they're not going to drop their bombs on us'. Scanning the horizon with his binoculars, he suddenly froze 'when he saw masses of red and bright white lights in a north-westerly direction. To every soldier with any experience at all this could mean only one thing.' He grabbed the telephone connecting his high chair with the Regimental Command Post 'turned the handle like a madman', and blurted out his report:

*Mass of lights direction of the coast and Cherbourg. Enemy attacking. This is the invasion, Herr Major: should I sound the alarm?*[2]

The seemingly endless stream of aircraft passing overhead with a long drawn out pulsating roar could only mean one thing to Thiel, this had to be it — the Second Front.

The two American streams flew from west to east across the Contentin Peninsula, and began to spill their loads as they approached their drop zones. The 352nd Infantry Division had already raised the Alert state to Level II following a report at 01.00 that parachutists had jumped over its neighbouring Division 716. At 01.45 Infantry Regiment 914 reported '50 to 60 enemy parachutists have jumped around the Carentan Canal south of Brevands'. Fifteen minutes later '30 to 40 air-

craft were dropping more parachutists' in the same area. At 02.46 'eight aircraft towing gliders were observed flying north to south' by Artillery Regiment 352.[3] These were units landing from the US 101st Airborne Division.

In the town square of Ste Mère-Eglise a large house in Lattaule Park opposite the church was on fire, having been hit by a stray incendiary bomb. Townspeople were attempting to extinguish it when the pulsating sound of scores of aircraft began to approach from a westerly direction. Plane load after plane load dropped parachutists to the west of the town, where the majority of the American 505th Regiment achieved a concentrated drop. Some four sticks landed to the south of the built-up area; two among the buildings, two more just outside to the south east. A number of unfortunate paratroopers from these aircraft appeared over the light hue projected from the burning building.

Gazing upwards at these transparent mushroom shapes reflecting the light were startled German soldiers from a flak transport unit. They were Austrian and mainly old, commanded by Oberleutnant Zitt. Gunfire resounded around the square as they opened fire with all available weapons as the civilian inhabitants scattered for shelter. The church bell continued to toll throughout the ensuing apocalyptic scene. Howard Manoian a 19-year old private in the 505th Regiment confessed, 'I was scared out of my life, we all were'. There was little they could do; too low now to steer away, they drifted inexorably to the slaughter that occurred below:

*About 20 parachutists, no more, came straight into the sights of the Germans in the square, and they stood no chance.*[4]

Panicking, the Germans fired aimlessly into the air. It is virtually impossible to hit such a fleeting target; but once on the ground they were helpless, and cut down. At least one parachutist drifted into the burning building where plastic HE and grenades added muffled reports to the agonised screams. Few who survived would ever forget the shouts, yells, cries and moans which echoed around the town square. Manoian dropped into a field beside the cemetery on the eastern side of the square. Immediately he was grabbed from behind and dragged into a nearby house by a Frenchman, who made it clear despite the language barrier, there was little point in going into the square where the shooting had reached a crescendo. One paratrooper, hanging grotesquely from the church tower by his parachute appeared dead.[5]

Another American paratrooper landed squarely upon the shoulders of a local French veterinary surgeon, M. Mannier. A German officer named Werner, billeted in the town, woken by the commotion, was about to shoot the helpless American before Mannier courageously intervened. He took him prisoner instead. Meanwhile

*Above:* The Merville battery consisted of four casemates with 100mm Czech howitzers.

*Right:* 'About 20 parachutists, no more, come straight into the sights of the Germans in the square, and they stood no chance!' A dead US paratrooper entangled in a tree.

*Below:* 'Alarm!... In an instant we're wide awake and quickly ready.' Fallschirmjäger Regiment 6 went to immediate readiness.

the massive drop continued outside the town as stick after stick of the 505th Regiment descended, evident to the flak detachment aware of the huge number of aircraft, but unable to engage targets unless they were lit up by the eerie hue of the burning house. Isolated, and obviously in danger of being cut off, Oberleutnant Zitt ordered his unit to board their vehicles and then abandoned the town. They could well have been earmarked for a task elsewhere. Having overcome the immediate crisis, they used the opportunity to escape while they could. As a result, Werner surrendered himself in turn to his American captive. Lieutenant Colonel Krause of the 3rd Battalion 505th Regiment moved rapidly from the drop zone into the town with two weak companies, only a quarter of his strength. By 04.30 it was occupied.[6]

Further south the drops continued. Fourteen planeloads of the 101st Division and five of the 82nd — some 380 men — dropped into the assembly area of Fallschirmjäger Regiment 6. They were between eight and 20 miles off course.[7] Oberleutnant Pöppel having heard more aircraft fly over, 'this time very near and flying low' reported the outcome:

*02.00 hours. Alarm! The sentries roar the alarm signals through the night. All my observation posts are reporting enemy parachute landings. In an instant we're wide awake and quickly ready … Damn, our map exercise has suddenly turned into the real thing.[8]*

Major von der Heydte, the Regiment Commander, estimated '500 American paratroopers south west of Carentan in the area secured by his IIIrd Battalion, and another 100 to 150 paratroopers east of St Jores' held by his Ist Battalion.

*Counter-attacks and defensive fire from these named battalions accounted for the majority who were annihilated, taken prisoner or as stragglers driven out of the Regiment's area, apart from a few snipers who roamed about for a few days.[9]*

The first wounded prisoners began to appear, but revealed little on interrogation. Locating the enemy by night was difficult. Pöppel recalled 'the night is stormy and wild' and 'there are single cracks of rifle fire, but so far we have only detected the position of individual enemy soldiers and can't use our heavy guns yet'.[10]

Further reports flooded into the 352nd Division Headquarters throughout the night. At 02.55 Infantry Regiment 914 'estimated 70 paratroopers had jumped near Insigny, but not confirmed'. Fifteen minutes later a company of glider-borne troops were reportedly seen landing in meadows south of Carentan. At 03.20, artillery regiments along the coast were reporting 'strong formations of gliders flying into the south'. Infantry Division 709 indicated just after 04.00 that parachute landings had occurred near Morsalines, St Côme-du-

Mont and Ste Mère-Eglise. At the same time 84th Corps was monitoring the severity of the situation in 716th Division area, and further east, stating:

*The situation in the Seine estuary is probably worse than ours where there have been strong parachute and glider borne landings. Further details are not yet known, as the enemy is observing absolute radio silence.*

An American lieutenant captured by 916th Regiment 'said that dummies were also thrown out with paratroopers, which explode and cause a disturbance when they hit the ground'.[11]

As in the east, a sketchy picture emerged which generated only a patchy response, drawing in some local reserves. Following the first report of landings at 01.45 by 914th Regiment, 352nd Division felt 'despite the darkness, headquarters was of the opinion that the IInd Battalion 914th (without its heavy weapons support company) could move out of its assembly area and annihilate the reported enemy'. However intent did not match capability. American paratroopers proved adept at operating in the 'bocage' close-hedgerow terrain. 'Scattered widely in small groups, these paratroopers were to prove tough and capable snipers, who inflicted casualties upon our inexperienced soldiers'. Some prisoners 'had scarfs printed over with French maps, others had maps of the Vire estuary and west of that found on them, with sketch maps (air photographs) which showed the landing zones in every detail'.[12] It was however virtually impossible to estimate the true extent of the landings. At 04.00 Oberleutant Pöppel saw 'more parachutes come floating down' in the area south west of Carentan.

*It all happens so quickly that we scarcely have time to shoot. The 'chutes disappear rapidly in the thick underbrush of the Normandy hedgerows. We respond with machine gun fire, then sub-machine gun and carbine fire towards the enemy, although we aren't sure of his position.[13]*

A rough picture of the spread of the landings slowly began to emerge. Seventh Army at 02.15 reported 'it appears to be a substantial landing' and 'as the enemy landings are already very deep, the initial task is probably to cut off the Cherbourg Peninsula'.[14] It was requested that 91st Airlanding Division be placed under Army control, where later it was placed under command of 84th Corps. The southern part of the peninsula, and the Carentan region including the east coast were identified as threatened areas. By 04.30 Seventh Army had decided that 'the *schwerpunkt* or main point of effort for the enemy landings appears to be in the Ste Mère-Eglise region'.[15]

As in the case of the 716th Division, the scattered nature of the airborne landings, alarming in their extent

and depth, began to dilute local reserves that had originally been earmarked for counter-attacks to restore coastal defences. The 352nd Division provided the 84th Corps reserve. This force — the *Kampfgruppe Meyer* — consisted of three battalions: two from Infantry Regiment 915, and the 352nd Division Reconnaissance Battalion (Fusilier Battalion 352). At 03.25 it was ordered to begin a reconnaissance of enemy concentrations thought to be assembling in meadows south of Carentan. Eventually it was ordered as the result of further reports to move from the reserve assembly area south east of Bayeux to a threatened zone encompassing Isigny, Carentan and Mont Martin. Ste Mère-Eglise it appeared was cut off; the new force was to open up the roads around Carentan.[16] This was no easy task to coordinate, as the infantry rode on bicycles, while heavy weapons and ammunition were transported on requisitioned trucks driven by soldiers. They were not able to depart until 04.20. As they did so, they heard the grumble of artillery as 726th Regiment engaged suspected enemy parachutists south of Bernières. The estimated journey time was four hours. Because of poor communications and the nature of its ad hoc transport, the force was irrevocably committed. Gone was the flexibility to react against any sudden sea-borne incursion. The Corps reserve, ideally situated to counter-attack Omaha, Gold or Juno, moved steadily westward, drawn inexorably away from an even greater amphibious threat concentrating at sea, to the north. Turning back could not be a tactical option.

## 'A disturbed Beehive' … coordinating the response.

*…. At 01.11 hours — an unforgettable moment — the field telephone ran. Something important was coming through: while listening to it the General stood up stiffly, his hand gripping the edge of the table. With a nod he beckoned his Chief of Staff to listen in. "Enemy parachute troops dropped east of the Orne estuary. Main area Bréville-Ranville and the north edge of the Bavent forest. Counter measures are in progress".*

'This message', delivered personally to General Erich Marcks, the Commander of 84th Corps, 'struck like lightening' recalled his Intelligence Officer (IO) Major Friedrich Hayn. It was followed by a succession of others, all equally disturbing. By 01.45 it had been established there were 'three dropping zones near the front!' broadly conforming to the three Allied divisional objective areas.

*Two were clearly at important traffic junctions. The third was designed to hold the marshy meadows at the mouth of the Dives and the bridge across the canalised Orne near Ranville. It coincided with the Corps boundary, … it meant that a landing would soon take place and that they*

*were really in earnest!*

Hayn had the benefit of recording his impressions in hindsight. Nearly two hours after the first recorded sighting he had assessed 'that approximately 75 percent of the parachute and airborne troops which were known to us stationed in Southern England had been employed'.[1] This was certainly a landing of some magnitude, but whether or not it was a deception was not clear to German commanders. Rommel's Chief of Staff Speidel was to write after the war:

*One must have the nerve to wait. Continuous telephone calls to the Supreme Commander Wehrmacht (OKW) and West (OB West) show the nervousness evident in the higher chain of command.*[2]

Hayn's description of the impact of the landings on 84th Corps' Command Post, which 'resembled a disturbed beehive' is illustrative of the general command reaction throughout the long night of 5-6 June.

*At last the suspense was over, the constant round of "stand-to" and partial or full "state of readiness". Since the middle of April this had kept the troops in suspense, and they had in the end got so used to it that it wasn't taken seriously any more.*[3]

This induced state of sluggishness was compounded by the absence — to the war games at Rennes — of all the key division commanders. Priority messages were sent in all directions to recall them. All responded apart from the commanders of 91st and 709th Divisions. Even so, the commanders of 352nd and 716th may well have been unavailable as earlier decisions, particularly those linked to the employment of local reserves, were taken. General von Schieben, the commander of 709th Infantry Division, was actually in Rennes at 06.30 on 6 June when he received the message: 'The war games have been cancelled, all gentlemen are to return to their commands at once'.[4] Ahead lay a 160km journey before he could even begin to read himself into the threat that was to develop in his sector — the Utah Beachhead — and this was five hours after the invasion had begun.

General Falley, the commander of 91st Airlanding Division, already in a position to menace the scattered US 82nd Airborne Division, was even more unfortunate. Heavy air attacks, and the constant hum of aircraft overhead, had encouraged him to turn around and go back. Accompanied by his G4 (logistics/supply officer) Major Bartuzat, his staff car sped off the main road, to his chateau headquarters at Haut, north of Picauville and Valognes. Unbeknown to both men, was that three sticks of American paratroopers[5] from the 502nd and 508th Regiments had dropped 15 to 20 miles from their pre-planned drop zones. A group of these men had established themselves in the grounds of the headquarters. Falley and Bartuzat were cut down in a brief exchange of fire. They did not have the opportunity to issue a single order. The Command Post was left in turmoil. A subsequent counter-attack wiped out the small American enclave, but the damage had been done. As the headquarters reorganised, one of the regimental commanders, Oberst Konig, was summoned to take command of the Division.[6]

It is difficult to estimate the impact of the absence these divisional commanders had upon subsequent events. General Dollmann, the commander of Seventh Army, had ordered a series of moves designed to seal off the western air-head, once the extent of the landings became apparent. A concentric attack plan was developed requiring 709th Division with the 1058th Regiment (detached from 91st Division) to clear the area east of the Merderet. The 91st Division was likewise to counter-attack from the west with its own 1057th Regiment supported by Panzer *Ersatz* (training) Battalion 100, to wipe out the paratroopers who had landed west of the flooded area. Fallschirmjäger Regiment 6 was placed under command of 91st Division and ordered to attack northward through Carentan from the south. Seventh Army Sturm Battalion was ordered to attack toward Ste Mère-Eglise from Cherbourg in the north, as well as another regiment from 243rd Division ordered to move to Montebourg, also to bring pressure to bear onto the American bridgehead from this direction. These moves might well have contained the American enclave without the need for additional forces. But these were not ideal conditions, and subject to more difficulties than the Rennes 'war-game' may have anticipated. Communications had already been disrupted; and the Germans began to experience the same difficulties as the Americans — dispersed and out of contact — and fighting within the claustrophobic confines of darkened hedgerows. Key to any success in eliminating the American bridgehead would be the regrouping of substantial elements connected with 91st Division, whose commander had been killed and headquarters disrupted; and 709th Division, whose commander would not complete his return journey from Rennes until noon on 6 June. Not surprisingly the consequence of all this was to dilute the German response to the airborne incursion, characterised by a penny-packeting of resources. Units had already been dispersed garrisoning strong-points and villages. This resulted in a splintering of effort when parachute units descended in their midst. Unlike the Americans who had one, the German units were unaware of the overall plan. Psychologically they were at a disadvantage, prone to compromise or giving in to uncertainty when aggressive and decisive action was required. 91st Division's 1058th Regiment, for example, harassed by scattered American paratroopers, was unable to produce any momentum during its early attacks on Ste Mère-Eglise. Nor was its headquarters able to substitute any.

The lack of a comprehensive German defence strategy began to haunt the defence effort. Both forward divisions — 352nd and 716th — had already committed their local reserve to contain airborne landings, before any threat to the beaches even materialised. All was dependent upon the panzer divisions. The Allies were conscious that the race to dominate the invasion foreshore had already begun; the Germans were not. A response was coalescing, but it was fragmentary, disbelieving of the facts it faced. Seventh Army had appreciated by 02.15 'that according to reports from the troops and Luftwaffe, it appears to be a substantial landing'; Speidel, the Chief of Staff at Army Group, disagreed. He felt 'it is not the case of a large operation for the moment, airborne landings had only been successful in the area of 711th Division, south of the Seine'.[7] These differences of opinion concerning the significance of the landings continued at the higher formation level throughout the night. The troops on the ground had few doubts. Hesitantly, the extent of the crisis was being acknowledged. At 03.50 the Chief of Staff at Supreme Headquarters (OB West) commented that 'the width of the incursion should not rule out the possibility that this is more than a local operation'.[8]

Whatever the significance, substantial measures were required. Seventh Army was less doubtful about the seriousness of the predicament it was in. It formally requested at 02.45 that the 12th SS Panzer Division be placed on alert, and that it should commence reconnaissance operations in 711th Division area.

There had been unconfirmed reports shortly after midnight in the 12th SS 'Hitlerjugend' headquarters east of Falaise, that parachute landings had occurred in the 711th Divisional sector. It was of interest as an envisaged area of operations. The 'landings' turned out to be straw dummies. The 21st Panzer Division were contacted for information, but had nothing to report. Most of the staff returned to bed.

At 01.30, however, SS-Brigadeführer Fritz Witt awoke his Chief of Staff. 'Meyer, the invasion, seriously this time!'[9] Reports of paratroopers had been confirmed. Within one hour units began to be called out. SS-Obersturmführer Peter Hansman, a reconnaissance company commander was awakened by his sergeant major. 'Sir, the invasion has started. No practice alarm — the real thing! The Commander is on the telephone!' The whole experience seemed unreal. Hansman stood by an open window:

*From outside I could hear the company alarm bell, and the normal grumble of bomber squadrons, that for days now had been flying in unbroken formations against our communications and Homeland. But apart from that, all is quiet. The first tank drivers, already in tee-shirts, whisk down to their armoured vehicles to start them up. As I jump down the step into the orderly room, my thoughts oscillate between "a test inspection — Alarm — exercise," as so often in the last few weeks — or, are they really coming?*[10]

He was told to report to his battalion commander within 30 minutes, with 10 armoured cars and two squads of motor-cycle side-car troops.

SS-Sturmmann Oswald Beck, a signals platoon operator with Panzergrenadier Regiment 26 was awoken by SS-Unterscharführer Kleff. 'Away boys — up! The Tommies have landed!' Grumpily and reluctantly the crews stirred themselves into activity.

*Another night exercise, and Beck didn't tell us. Suddenly somebody said "Hey — Kleff was not in uniform, he was wearing his PT kit. Do you think something is really up? That doesn't normally happen; they certainly aren't dreaming".*

In virtually no time at all, the armoured half-tracks were loaded, and Beck recalled 'we sat and waited'. This was not normal exercise procedure, 'we had never waited so long for the order to march'. Once he had been relieved, the duty signaller joined them and confirmed that the British and Americans had landed. 'By 03.00', Beck calculated, 'we were all ready, and could have set off'. But they were sent back to their accommodation, and laid down, fully prepared for action, on their beds.

*Those who could, slept. The others conversed in low voices. With the grey light of morning, everyone sat up on the sides of the half-track, and all thought, "soon we'll be off".[11]*

Contrary to Allied expectation, the 'Hitlerjugend' Division was held impatiently within its assembly areas, and remained there for nearly 24 hours.

The 21st Panzer Division near the invasion coast was being similarly alarmed. Major Vierzig, commanding the IInd Battalion Panzer Regiment 22, recalled:

*Towards 01.00 hours I had moved my battalion into the scheduled exercise area 6 miles east of Falaise. Over Caen and the coast the sky was red with the glow of fire. We heard the ceaseless detonations of the Allied aerial bombardment. But this did not strike us as unusual since such attacks had become quite a regular feature.*

Vierzig, armed with blank ammunition, was recalled suddenly at 02.00 by despatch rider. At 04.30 Seventh Army, reacting to General Richter's call for assistance, formally requested Army Group to release 21st Panzer to operate east of the Orne. This was granted. Its commander, Feuchtinger, was ordered to contain the airborne landing areas in the area 'with the main point of effort east of the Orne'.[12] Complications in the chain of command were causing delays. Feuchtinger, as OKW reserve, felt bound by OKW approval before he would react. Before long, despite its non-appearance, he felt compelled to move. Long columns of tanks, shrouded in exhaust and the early morning mist began moving by daybreak in a north easterly direction — away from the proposed Allied beachheads.

That the eastern flank appeared to be the more threatened of the two by the airborne landings was reflected in Fifteenth Army's initial request at 05.30 to use the 12th SS in 711th Division's area to 'swiftly clean up the situation'. Twenty minutes later OB West agreed to a precautionary shift to a new assembly area near Lisieux, on the left flank of Fifteenth Army. The 12th SS 'were to immediately liaise with 81st Corps Headquarters and 711st Division, move, assemble, and immediately report'.[13] This did not ideally place the division to face the impending amphibious threat, tending like 21st Panzer Division to draw it away to the north east.

As dawn approached, reports suggest a contradiction of view between Seventh Army, rapidly appreciating it faced a serious situation, and Army Group B, its formation headquarters, which thought not. A geographical divide between Le Mans forward and La Roche Guyon to the rear was developing into a credibility gap. The race to dominate the fore-shore, to oppose the initial Allied seven to eight-division insertion, had yet to start.

German reserves were already being sapped away, diluted by an imperative to contain an, as yet, undefined airborne landing area, or simply misdirected. Both 21st Panzer and 12th SS 'Hitlerjugend' were beginning to mal-deploy east of the Orne, away from the proposed Allied sea-borne main point of effort west of the river. The 711th Infantry Division on the eastern flank of Fifteenth Army, far from being in a position to menace the flank of the future landings, was more concerned with its own. Two divisions expected to receive the full brunt of the Allied attack, 716th and 352nd, had already expended their local reserves, or at least committed them to move inland against airborne landings, rather than the vague menace now identifiable at sea. 91st and 719th Divisions had lost their commanders and were reacting sluggishly to the need to regroup and contain the immediate airborne threat. All these errors, based upon contradictory and often unreliable information, committed by night, would have to be corrected by day — under the nose of the Allied air forces. Vital junctions, cogs within the internal coastal road network, notably Ste Mère-Eglise and the Orne river bridges were already occupied by Allied airborne forces. It was an inauspicious beginning. Just how far removed Army Group B was from the situation is revealed by its optimistic telephoned assessment less than one hour before the Allied naval bombardment was to begin:

*The Seventh Army Chief of Staff has reported that until now, no landings from the sea have taken place. The situation east of the Orne appears to have been cleaned up. The enemy is still holding the bridge at Benouville. There appears to be only weak forces near Carentan, where enemy landings however have been very deep (at the moment 20 to 30kms), with additional concentrations still*

# The Long Night — The German Reaction to the Airborne Landings

The airborne landings on both the eastern and western flanks of the invasion succeeded in drawing off all the local reserves which might otherwise have been thrown against the amphibious landings. The 91st and 352nd Division reserves had been directed westward, away from the beaches, and the 716th and 21st Panzer focus of effort was on the wrong (eastern) side of the Orne. Complicated re-grouping was bedevilled by the crucial absence of division commanders at the Rennes war games.

To Cherbourg

Valognes

Lessay

x x
9 1

III
1057
P z2100

Montebourg
III
1058

+ Regt 243
x x

Périers

Ste Mère-Eglise
x x
8 2

x x
7 0 9

Carentan

x x
1 0 1

Fallschirm
Regt 6.

x x
Regt 275

II/914

Brevands

UTAH

Isigny

St Lô

x x
3 5 2

AMPHIBIOUS LANDINGS YET TO MATERIALISE

Kampfgruppe 'Meyer'
x x
Div Res 352
3 Bns moves
0420.

OMAHA

Bayeux

GOLD

Villers Bocage

Confusion
III  III
736/726

Bernières

JUNO

Pz Gren
Bn (21Pz)
II/192

Obj Ranville
(3/642 Ost)

x x
7 1 6

SWORD

Envisaged
counter-attack 21Pz
Div east of Orne

21 Pz

Caen
x x
6 (-)

Pz Gren 125
Von Luck

*hanging on in Contentin. The possibility of a bigger operation appears not to be manifesting itself.*[14]

This threat, yet to materialise, was standing off in the Channel mist, just beyond the horizon. Only slowly did it become apparent, and then it was too late.

## 'Look what's coming! …'

At 02.14 Naval Headquarters (*See Kommandant*) Normandy reported that 'enemy naval contacts have been located 11km north of Grandcamp'. This was off the proposed Omaha Beachhead. The 352nd Division Headquarters transmitted the warning to all sub-sector commanders. 'All OP locations were to constantly monitor sea approaches'.[1]

Naval radar at Port-en-Bessin reported further contacts nearly one hour later. 'Ten large ships were pinpointed — obviously unloading troops — they were still in the water' claims a naval staff officer, who personally passed on this information to Naval Command and Supreme Headquarters West. 'The size of the landing fleet was obviously apparent' to Konteradmiral Edward Wegener. 'The report: "hundreds of ships bearing south" gave a clear impression of the movement of a major landing fleet'. Wegener personally telephoned Oberst Zimmerman the Chief of Staff Seventh Army. There was no recorded response.[2]

Parachute landings and air attacks were distracting the attention of most headquarters who, overwhelmed by immediate crises having already committed reserves, had few resources or the composure to consider a multi-faceted threat. Despite the obvious link to the airborne activity, a sea-borne threat appears not to have been regarded with similar urgency at this stage. Staff officers, battling to establish a clearer picture of nocturnal chaos, vetted clues emerging, but remained focussed on the impact of the parachute landings. 'Engine noises were identifiable at sea' noted Seventh Army at 02.15. Ninety minutes later Fifteenth Army's 81st Corps observed 'sea contacts in the Orne estuary'.[3] Sightings in this region appear to be more frequent than observations further west, where the approaching fleet had been cloaked in mist. Army Coastal Regiment 1255 saw that:

*It was already possible by 03.40, despite low lying cloud, to detect the silhouettes of numerous naval elements in the moonlit night, just forward of the coast between Trouville and the Orne estuary.*[4]

These sightings on the left flank of Fifteenth Army were passed onto Army Group 10 minutes later.[5] The 1255th Regiment granted permission to commence firing 'from all barrels' once the ships came in range.

The 352nd Division to the west has scant information in its telephone log during the long night concerning the imminence of an amphibious landing. Staff had few illusions following the initial 02.15 naval warning that further sightings would be reported 'because an infantry division's capability to observe and report [on maritime activity] is unsatisfactory'.[6] In any case, it had already been realised by 03.50 that all their radar search installations had been either destroyed or damaged during bombing raids over the previous 24 hours. Kampfgruppe 'Meyer', the divisional reserve, was committed shortly after to counter the airborne threat to the west 'as contact with the naval activity has been lost for the moment'. Headquarters was further preoccupied with ensuing waves of air attacks throughout the divisional sector between 03.22 until 04.10. First of all artillery sites and then Infantry Regiment 726 were 'heavily bombed'. It proved a total distraction. The fact that the coastal sector — Le Guay, Pointe du Hoc and Grandcamp — was receiving particular attention elicited no comment from the Division telephone log. Despite the previous warnings and reminders, the FOOs from Artillery Regiment 352 spread along the coast insisted 'Landing boats are still not visible in front of Grandcamp'. The 352nd Division was alerted to a threat but was, as yet, unimpressed by its credibility. Between Utah, Omaha and Gold Beaches only air raids were reported and these, shortly after 05.00, escalated even further.[7]

Two miles inland of St Aubin, Feldwebel Karl Schieck sat on a latrine in the chateau grounds of a headquarters supporting one of the Infantry Regiment 736 strong-points. His somewhat incongruous perch offered a panoramic view of the Channel. 'We were at Alarm Stage II', he remembers.

*I was sitting on the latrine and able to look out to sea. It was out there, in the open, our latrine. Suddenly I saw — all over the place — spots on the horizon. Then along came our strong-point commander, and sat himself down beside me. I said to him "Oberfeldwebel — this is the invasion." He was amazed.*

*I said to him "Look — look what's coming!"*[8]

In a sector nearby, 22-year old Oberleutnant Fiebig, a forward artillery observer claimed 'as it became daylight, we were able to distinguish the silhouettes of very large ships on the sea'. His breath exhaled at the tension. 'There were so many that the sea appeared black.'[9] Galvanised by shouts of 'Alarm!' troops leapt to action stations.

Joseph Cassigneul, a Frenchman living in St Aubin, had risen at four o'clock that morning, and bumped abruptly into a German sergeant hurrying by, as soon as he had emerged onto his road.

*I was used to seeing him. He said to me: "Joseph, come*

*Above:* German reserves were sapped away, fragmented by an inability to focus-in on the threat. Skirmishing along a railway embankment.

*Right:* 'It was already possible by 03.40'...'to detect the silhouettes of numerous naval elements'. The invasion observed from a bunker at dawn.

*Below:* 'Lightning flashes briefly lit up the dark channel horizon.' The fleet opening fire in the dawn mist.

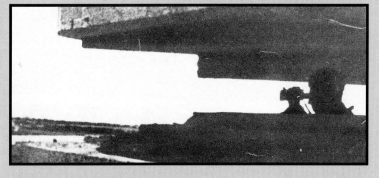

*and have a look. There are at least eleven hundred boats out on the sea."*

*I said "Don't be daft, eleven hundred boats?*

*So off we went down to the coast, and when we got there you couldn't see the sea any more. It was nothing but boats — it was black! He said to me: "That's it then, that's the invasion. We'll never see each other again".*[10]

Further to the west, Oberleutnant Frerking of the 1st Battery Artillery Regiment 352 facing Omaha Beach, gazing through binoculars from his bunker at *Widerstandsnest* (strong-point) WN62, inwardly sucked in his breath. 'My God, my God', he thought. 'Here they are!' he called to his NCO crew. 'But that's not possible', he muttered, 'not possible'.

At 05.02 the first electrifying message came in by telephone to divisional headquarters. It was from another artillery officer situated on the boundary between the central and eastern divisional sectors:

*One very large and four smaller warships sighted in front of Port-en-Bessin. Likewise in front of Grandcamp a number of lighter naval units have been reported.*

The divisional telephone reporting log itemises the build up as further silhouettes began to emerge from the early morning mist.

*Forward Artillery Observers of the 2nd and 4th Batteries of Artillery Regiment 352 report noises, probably naval units, some 24km away, moving towards the Vire Estuary. Further, 29 boats are on course for Le Guay and Pte du Hoc, of which four bigger ships (at least destroyer or cruiser class) have been seen at a range of between six to 10km.*

Within ten minutes came the anticipated yet foreboding news from Infantry Regiment 916, manning beach defences, that:

*Landing craft are approaching the beach in the Colleville-Vierville bay. Further substantial naval units are on a westerly course. One group with five battleships is on a heading of 0˚N. Small landing craft have set course for*

*land. It looks like the enemy is smoking himself off.*[11]

The storm was about to break on the western fore-shore.

To the east, a few kilometres inland south of Bernières, the 8th Company of Infantry Regiment 736 was cursing their luck. Sweating profusely, they were still seeking the airborne infantry who had been earlier engaged by artillery. As far as they were concerned, the night had been a catalogue of mishaps and confusion. Their more fortunate counterparts in Regiment 726 already had been returned to their strong-points. They, and a platoon from Ost Battalion 441, were still out looking for what was now emerging as a ruse. The phantom enemy paratroopers had yet to materialise. Moreover, working alongside trigger-happy Russo-Polish soldiers who could barely understand German and in darkness, was dangerous. Soldiers continued to dwell on the possibility of recapturing lost sleep at daybreak, particularly after so many false alarms, when a rippling crackling noise sounded in the night. Lightening flashes briefly lit up the dark Channel horizon, followed by an unearthly rasping screech that resembled an approaching express train.

Explosions tore the scattered groups of soldiers apart, as if they were dry leaves blown on the wind. Shell after shell lacerated hapless groups of infantry who, despite burrowing panic-stricken into the ground, were picked off one by one by flying shards of jagged metal, propelled by a succession of heat and blast waves the like of which they had never experienced before. Caught completely in the open they endured a barrage of shelling that continued long after the final man had his last breath snatched away. No 8 Company and its reinforcement platoon had ceased to exist. The 716th Division Headquarters was to report subsequently:

*They were caught in the fire of the heavy naval bombardment and annihilated. There were no eye-witness reports as all communications were broken, and of the units employed, not one man returned.*[12]

Their fellows who had already returned to their battle positions were perhaps not so lucky. The storm was now breaking on the eastern fore-shore. The long night was over.

# CHAPTER 8

# THE STORM BREAKS

*'When the enemy is firing at you, it is a case of killing or being killed.'*

*Director-Gunner, Battleship Warspite*

## 'The guns ... were too hot to be touched' ... the naval bombardment.

Breakfast aboard a number of the American transports was served at 03.00.

*The Mess boys of the USS* Chase *wore immaculate white jackets and served hot cakes, sausages, eggs, and coffee with unusual zest and politeness.*

But it was like the last meal for the condemned. War correspondent Robert Capa, soon to land at Omaha, observed 'the pre-invasion stomachs were pre-occupied, and most of the noble effort was left on the plate'.[1] There was a feeling akin to those about to 'go over the top' in the trenches of World War 1. Men were anxious. They were about to assault the much vaunted Atlantic Wall. Casualties were expected to be heavy. Private Ferrara of the US 29th Division said, 'all of the fellows went around shaking their friends' hands for we all knew that this would be it and it would be rough'.[2]

After 02.30 troops began assembling on the open decks. Sergeant Gilbert Gray of the 116th Regiment remembered, 'the hour came around and we all went up in single file to the upper deck and so out through the double blackout curtains on the main deck'. It was very dark and 'still no sound from the shore'.[3] This was both ominous and scary. The transports had anchored some 11 or so miles away from the coast so that landing craft could be loaded out of range of German coastal artillery. Everyone had been impressed with the need for secrecy, so much so that sailors on deck spoke in whispers, as if the Germans could overhear. Because of the offshore breeze and current that had built up off Utah Beach, it was impossible to prevent landing craft clanging against the steel sides of transports. 'That made an ungodly racket', recalled observers[4], and made the troops wince as they scrambled down cargo net laddering to reach the boats. 'A tricky moment,' commented Lieutenant John

Bentz Carroll of the 1st Infantry Division, 'because it was a 30ft drop, boarding in very choppy water'. That is, 'if you caught the boat at the bottom of a wave. If you caught it at the top, you could walk aboard'.[5]

The same process was repeated off the British beaches, where a similar feeling of insecurity reigned. Nineteen-year old Douglas Reeman, the No 1 of a Motor Torpedo Boat escorting landing craft convinced the Germans must have spotted the fleet by now, heard 'several angry cries of alarm as a torch splashed light on the superstructure of one of the bigger landing ships'. Somebody was immediately 'torn off a strip'. Nevertheless, 'I felt the shock of it around me, as if everyone expected swift attack from the darkness'.[6]

Cranes continued to lower boats as pensive soldiers stood patiently in line. Capa found himself reflecting like those around him.

*Waiting for the first ray of light, the 2,000 men stood in perfect silence; whatever they were thinking, it was some kind of prayer.*[7]

The inevitability of the traumas lying ahead gave the moment a certain poignancy. There was a desire to affirm friendships, perhaps for the last time. Sergeant Gray waiting now in the bow of his landing craft, bobbing queasily in the darkness listened. 'Voices could be heard all over, calling to friends in other boats.' He himself 'called goodbye to the third of our little triumvirate, Robert Bruce, who was in another boat' also bound for Omaha.[8] Lieutenant John Spaulding from the 16th Infantry Regiment observed, 'it took us much longer to load than it had during the practice landings, because of the rough water'.[9] Men continued to board boats. 'The ropes whined through the pulleys', recorded Brigadier General Theodore Roosevelt Jr bound for Utah, 'we landed on the water and cast off. It was rough and spray burst over us, soaking us to the skin and leaving us shivering with cold.'[10] There were four and a half hours yet to go.

Those still waiting to board were unaffected by delays. 'None of us', stated Capa, 'was at all impatient, and we wouldn't have minded standing in the darkness for a very long time'. It was like waiting for the dentist. Ominously it grew lighter, and with it, the prospect of their first baptism of fire.

*I too stood very quietly. I was thinking a little bit of everything; of green fields, pink clouds, grazing sheep, all the good times …*[11]

Idealistic reflection could easily be shattered. Members of the 1st Battalion 116th Infantry Regiment stuck in a landing craft, rising and falling directly beneath the sewage outlet of the British transport *Empire Javelin*, received a rude awakening to the vagaries of fate. 'During this half-hour, the bowels of the ship's company made the most of an opportunity that Englishmen have sought since 1776', recalled Major Tom Dallas, the battalion Executive Officer.

*Yells from the boat were unavailing. Streams, coloured everything from canary yellow to sienna brown and olive green, continued to flush into the command group, decorating every man aboard. We cursed, we cried, and we laughed, but it kept coming. When we started for shore, we were all covered with shit.*[12]

Landing craft began to head for a coastline so distant it had yet to be discerned on the horizon. 'It was a weird sight in the pre-dawn to see tiny lights bobbing in a broken line as far as one could see', said Lieutenant Carroll. Roosevelt saw 'in the darkness the boats circled in their rendezvous stations, coxswain calling to coxswain to gather the different waves and sort them out. Then began our long run to the beach'.[13] It was a long way to go, 14 miles; yet the defences were still ominously quiet. 'In no time', recalled Capa, 'the men started to puke'.

All along the invasion coast men at sea began to hear the comforting sound of bombers droning overhead. Hopeful eyes scanned the skies but there was nothing to see, their steady progress could, however, be heard. Douglas Reeman off the British beaches felt:

*The air seemed to cringe to the mounting roar of engines. There must have been hundreds and hundreds of them. It seemed to take no time at all for the bombers to reach their first objectives. You could faintly see the blur of land beneath the bombardment while the clouds overhead danced and reared up in vivid red and orange flashes.*[14]

Robin Duff, a BBC war reporter with the American Navy, also saw the comforting sight. 'The beaches shook and seemed to rise into the air, and ships well out at sea quivered with the shock.' The sights and sounds of the aerial bombardment put the men at ease. Duff glancing around said, 'as that weight of bombs fell some of the tenseness of expectation left the faces of the men who were going in to land and was replaced by a smile of the utmost relief'.[15] The landing craft of the initial assault

waves continued to plough their way remorselessly through heavy seas toward the beaches.

It was getting lighter by the minute. 'Someone gave a cheer', reported Douglas Reeman aboard an MTB and

*We saw the first of the heavy warships sweeping up from astern. The real Navy. From our low hull the cruisers looked enormous with their streaming battle flags and their turrets already swinging towards the land, high angled and ready to fire.*

Spread along the Normandy coast was the American Western Task Force off Utah and Omaha consisting respectively of Force U and O. Further along was the British Eastern Task Force, forming Force G opposite Gold, and J and S facing Juno and Sword Beaches. Each task force had a bombardment element, the Western made up of three American battleships, the British monitor *Erebus*, eight cruisers, a Dutch gunboat and 20 destroyers. The Eastern comprised two British battleships, the monitor *Roberts*, 11 cruisers, another Dutch gunboat and 37 destroyers. Reeman gazing among these ships and the mass of other craft closing the shore saw:

*Tall waterspouts shot towards the sky and then drifted down again very slowly.*

*The Germans were awake now all right. But the fall of shells seemed ineffectual and without menace.*

At 05.05 a shore battery fired on the US destroyers *Fitch* and *Corry* off Utah. Twenty minutes later the larger calibre battery at Ste Vaast began to engage minesweepers, and at 05.30 a light battery near Port-en-Bessin opened up on the US battleship *Arkansas*, lying between Gold and Omaha.[16] Between these times and 05.50 the bulk of the bombarding fleet opened fire along the whole of the Normandy coast from Barfleur on the Cherbourg peninsula in the west, to Villerville at the mouth of the Seine in the east. It was a dramatic spectacle. Few who witnessed the sudden outburst of fire would ever forget it.

*You could see the ripple of flashes along the grey horizon, and had to force yourself not to duck as the great shells tore overhead with the sound of tearing canvas. The shells were dropping on the enemy emplacements and supporting roads from each battleship at the rate of about ten tons a minute.*[17]

Each 15in broadside from the battleship HMS *Warspite* was able to propel a weight of 11,500lb out to ranges of six miles or more. It would have been heavier still if one of her turrets had not been knocked out by a German guided bomb off Salerno. The heaviest broadsides available were provided by the ten 14in gun main batteries of the USS *Nevada* and USS *Texas* that could deliver 12,750lb of steel and explosives each.[18]

*Above:* 'It was rough and spray burst over us soaking us to the skin.' American infantry scramble awkwardly down nets into waiting LCAs.

*Below:* 'You could see the ripple of flashes along the grey horizon.' The fleet opens fire.

The fire was so intimidating that sea-sick soldiers tossing their way to shore in fragile landing craft sought shelter lower in the boats. War correspondent Robert Capa with Company E of the 16th Infantry Regiment saw:

*The coast of Normandy was still miles away when the first unmistakeable popping sound reached our listening ears. We ducked down in the pukey water at the bottom of the barge and ceased to watch the approaching coast line.*[19]

Sergeant Gray of the 116th Regiment also heading toward Omaha Beach remembers passing the last coloured flare that amphibious engineers had placed in the water to mark the route, having been under way for almost two hours, when the battleship *Texas* fired.

*We could see the flash, then hear the roar of the shell overhead, then hear the report of it as it left the muzzle, then see the flash on the shore, and then hear the bursting shell explode. It all seemed weird as we were under this all the time.*[20]

The din was deafening. 'It made thought impossible,' declared Reeman, 'and when we shouted to each other our voices sounded strange, like divers talking under water'. Apart from the noise, the sheer spectacle of the scene unfolding mesmerised watching troops still at sea. 'There was too much for any one pair of eyes to see, however actively they moved,' remarked Lieutenant David Holbrook in an LST off Sword Beach. All over the ship, men climbed the rails to get a better view of the 'incredible sight'. As it grew lighter, the 'hugeness of the fleet' became increasingly apparent. There were ships everywhere.

*The larger ones lay strangely immobile, even looking commonplace. But then they would be enveloped suddenly in smoke … The squat grey mass of the largest battleship, the* Warspite, *flung swelling clouds of incandescence out of the long trunks of her fifteen-inch guns. The flames, as long as towers, unrolled into clouds of smoke as big as castles. A noise like an express train at full speed followed, as the projectile was thrust through the high air into France. One could see the missile, flying, at times; each shell weighed nearly a ton.*[21]

Conditions aboard these naval monoliths were far from comfortable. Each time 18-year old Able Seaman John Cooper pressed his foot on the trigger mechanism of 'B' turret in HMS *Warspite*, three tons of high explosive was launched with a terrible concussive effect towards the shore. 'The loading and firing cycle went on and on', he recalled, 'with some variations: one gun ranging salvoes, broadsides and lulls when I could hear other noises — our own 4in, other ships, and the rattle of splinters'.[22]

The pulverising bombardment continued. Turrets hummed and lifts brought up more of the big shells from the bowels of the ship. Ships' crews wearing flash masks crouched by turrets and braced in anticipation as scorched by heat and blast, the air was involuntarily sucked out of their lungs by the sudden vacuum of yet another broadside blasting out. The surface of the surrounding water was lashed up by the over pressure from each successive round, which seemed bodily to push the ship sideways, backward through the water.

*When the guns fired at once the great 35,000-ton battleship gave a tremendous shudder. Everything on board that can fall or break loose has to be fastened or battened down when the ship goes into action. Cabin doors in the bridge have to be removed or the blast that rushes from end to end of the ship when she fires would splinter the panelling. Ears have to be plugged with cotton-wool.*[23]

On the bridge, figures peering through binoculars wince at each flash report which momentarily envelops them in clouds of choking smoke, quickly dispersed by wind. All these blackened faces, obscured by binoculars, gaze shoreward. Those without have hands clamped firmly over ears. There is an involuntary crouching flinch at every detonation. Able Seaman Cooper in 'B' turret remarked 'the shock of discharge, hiss of air blasts, rattling of runners and banging about of the main and gun-loading cages began to deaden the senses'. His experience echoed that of Petty Officer Drake aboard HMS *Ramillies*, a 'Royal Sovereign' class battleship on station nearby with two of her four 15in turrets manned for action.

*By now we were causing damage to ourselves below decks, furniture was smashed and heavy pieces of equipment were shaken from bulkheads and thrown across the deck. The mess decks and spaces immediately below the 15in turrets were a shambles and there were even cracks appearing in the supporting steel stanchions, between the decks.*[24]

At 04.30 the 5th Torpedo Boat Flotilla out of Le Havre, moving east under command of Kapitänleutnant Heinrich Hoffmann, came up against a smoke screen. The *T28* leading the sortie — at 1,100 tons — was virtually equivalent to a small destroyer; she was accompanied by the *Möwe* and *Jaguar*, now old vessels. They had been under way for an hour, sweeping the area for 'targets located in the Channel'. Naval Group West Headquarters in Paris had instituted the search, having issued a preliminary alert at about 01.30. Bursting through the smoke screen, Hoffmann and his two skippers were taken aback at the panorama that lay before them. 'It's impossible', commented Heinrich Fromke, a rating aboard the *Jaguar*, 'there can't be that many ships in the world'. They had involuntarily rushed into the vision of the British Eastern Task Force bombarding Sword Beach. All three boats immediately started to zigzag as a precursor to attack runs.

Aboard the battleship *Warspite* Able Seaman Cooper in 'B' turret, totally preoccupied shelling the beach, recalled

*Then came an order which galvanized everybody. Practiced many times but still a surprise. "B Turret switch to Local, Local Control, Enemy in sight ..."*

*Ramillies* also joined the action. Cooper's turret swung steadily around. Faces were jammed into rubber telescope eyepieces, seeking out the enemy.

*There, in the haze against the coast, ships — possibly destroyers — at speed and in line ahead, came out into the open sea. Although still misty and with huge palls of gun smoke hanging heavily in the air, we were quickly "on" and fired a broadside over the heads of "A" turret (not much to their liking).*

Hoffmann's force, still zigzagging, began with gasps of compressed air to release torpedoes. It was a fearful target, exuding menace. 'Los! Los! Los!' the commands rang out, releasing one torpedo after another. With such a density of shipping they could not miss. Likewise they realised that only speed and evasion would enable them to survive the hurricane of fire that would inevitably respond. With 18 torpedoes launched, the terrifying and potentially suicidal foray was at an end. Frantically they sought to break off the action.

Reports from *Warspite* were contradictory. Cooper claimed

*The leading [German] ship disappeared into a smother of steam and smoke. The others reversed course and legged it for home, sensibly laying a smoke screen, and was soon lost to view.*

David Toms, the Director-Gunner observing the lead ship, 'saw two splashes but the third shell was bang on target and, within minutes, the German vessel was going down stern first'.[25]

Hoffmann and his boats disappeared back into the smoke screen, as ships on the eastern side of the task force, guided by look-outs, took evasive action. It was murky, blowing a fresh wind with 'a nasty top to the sea' remarked J.C. Turner, electrical officer aboard HMS *Largs,* the headquarters ship of Force 'S', and therefore difficult to trace a torpedo track. 'Suddenly away to port there was a flash and a heavy explosion.' The destroyer *Svenner* had been struck by a torpedo. A moment later, in company with the Chief Yeoman they saw a torpedo track on their port bow. 'What do we do, Sir?' Turnball realised with awful trepidation there was nothing he could do. 'I think we'll move over to the other [opposite] rail', he responded. Although the bridge had seen it and made a sharp alteration of course, it made little difference.[26] The torpedo missed them by yards.

Lieutenant P. Webber, an infantry officer on the Liberty Ship *Empire Cutlass* anxiously pondering his survival chances ashore, was up early on deck, 'feeling safer there than in the cavernous depths of the hull, which looked too vulnerable to a torpedo', when:

*Almost immediately, I saw a great flash in the distance on our port quarter. I could just distinguish the bow and stern of a destroyer standing out of the sea after being torpedoed amidships.*

It was not a reassuring sight. 'Soon twinkling lights appeared, from the life-jackets of the crew as they dived overboard.' At first nobody knew what had happened, until it transpired she was the victim of a German E-Boat attack, accentuating the feeling of vulnerability among soldiers awaiting the order to go ashore. 'It was not a very heartening beginning', confessed Webber.[27]

The hasty scattering of torpedoes among the invasion fleet was rather like a panic shot-gun blast by a hunter startled by the sudden emergence of his prey. Its impact was psychological rather than material. Only the Norwegian destroyer *Svenner* was lost. Hoffmann retired to Le Havre at speed, anticipating Allied air attacks the whole way. Within eight days both the *Möwe*, the *Jaguar* and the majority of the S-Boats that had so grievously wounded the 'Tiger' convoy six weeks before, were to be crippled smoking wrecks languishing beside the quays of Le Havre.[28]

The foray had little more than a nuisance effect upon the bombardment of the beaches, which continued unabated. The rate of fire was variable, but considerable. The American battleship *Nevada* expended 337 rounds of 14in and 2,693 rounds of 5in ammunition off Utah during the day. The *Tuscaloosa* , a cruiser nearby, made sixteen shoots firing 487 rounds of 8in and 115 of 5in ammunition.[29] On board HMS *Ramillies* in the Eastern Task Force, Petty Officer Drake was to comment, 'the guns themselves were too hot to be touched and the rifling was beginning to protrude from the muzzle as a result of the constant full-calibre firing'.[30] The crews could only imagine the impact this must be having on the Germans. 'You cannot help thinking that, in a few seconds, you may have killed men, women or children in the target area', said David Toms, director-gunner aboard *Warspite*. 'But when the enemy is firing at you, it is a case of killing or being killed.'[31]

## ... 'The Golden City'.

That Germans were being killed was axiomatic. From west to east they had been subjected to a storm of pulverising fire, from the air and sea. Headquarters 352nd Division in the west reported:

*Before first light (05.00) enemy naval artillery began with broadsides, outside the range of coastal batteries, to lay systematic barrages in the area both sides of Asnelles and*

*Vierville, and north of Grandcamp. The enemy smoked off parts of his fleet.*[1]

A storm of shot and shell drenched identified German positions. Few were prepared for the ferocity and violence of the assault that assailed them. It was a shocking psychological blow inflicted largely on unblooded troops. Most defenders, having observed the fleet, were in shelters. The remorseless 'drumming' of high explosive, reported by survivors on their positions disorientated individuals, who in time failed to respond to orders. Those in partially completed field positions stood no chance. Headquarters 352nd Division commented on the steady deterioration experienced, due to the punishment meted out on its occupied locations.

*Because of the impact of naval gunfire, one weapon after another in field positions was either destroyed or heavily damaged. The majority of earth constructed strong-points housing heavy calibre weapons belonging to the division were annihilated.*[2]

Conditions within concrete bunkers and trench systems became virtually untenable. The ground heaved with the concussive crack of each impact producing blast waves sufficient to collapse lungs. Clouds of dust and masonry scabs spewed into the interior of bunkers, lacerating and suffocating crews. Flying debris obscured all but sparks of red-hot shrapnel which whined through positions, plopping with a distinctive sizzle to earth. Dirt and dust penetrated every orifice of the body as crews were buried alive in bunkers and caved-in trenches. A mixture of air and ground burst remorselessly reduced spirits, until legs shook uncontrollably and men defecated or passed water in sheer terror. Air was constantly sucked out following the incoming whoosh of shells, producing a scorching flash, and then blast which shredded human frames, turning once familiar comrades into loathsome mutilated rag dolls. The stench of cordite and human debris caused survivors to retch and cough, struggling for air whilst constantly buffeted by high pressure impacts as salvo after salvo whooshed home. Nose, ear and even eye bleeding was caused by relentless high pressure hammer blows. A succession of such impacts could rob the mind of reason. The 352nd Division pointed out that 'reports reading strong-point (WN) "X" — only one machine gun operational, other weapons buried, majority of crew casualties — were being constantly raised'. Examination of the surviving divisional telephone log reveals a steady degrading of operational capability. At 05.50 the divisional commander recommended rescinding the original movement order directing the Kampfgruppe 'Meyer' — the divisional (and corps) reserve — to deal with the airborne threat inland. The change was to cause confusion. Infantry Regiment 916 reported its positions were under heavy fire at 06.04. As the bombardment reached a crescendo, its neighbouring Regiment 726 lamented 10 minutes later it was under 'particularly' heavy fire. Artillery Regiment 352, unable to fire back because the tormenting ships were out of range, complained that 'elements of the 1716th Battery positions had artillery pieces buried by bombing attacks. Three had since been dug out again and were under repair'. Telephone wires linking batteries inland to forward observers on the coast had been cut.[3]

What this meant for a particular strong-point is revealed by the fate of WN5, a strong-point measuring some 400 by 300yd, blocking one of the exits from Utah Beach. It was commanded by Leutnant Arthur Jahnke of Infantry Regiment 919. He had already lost his bet with his colleague Oberleutnant Ritter in neighbouring WN2. A crippling air raid had indeed confirmed 'something was up'. It had accounted for one 75mm gun and damaged an 88mm flak gun. Two ammunition bunkers had exploded and machine gun nests were buried in sand. A subsequent low level rocket-firing air attack knocked out two more 50mm bunkers. All that remained following the air raids was one 75mm gun, one damaged 88mm, some flamethrowers, 80mm mortars and machine guns. The naval bombardment shredded his barbed wire, levelled trenches, blew mines, buried further bunkers and knocked out the flamethrower control mechanism and 75mm gun. Jahnke was left to face the might of the US 4th Infantry Division with a damaged 88mm flak gun, some machine guns in armoured turrets and his surviving 80mm mortar emplacements. A number of his men had broken down under the pressure of the repeated barrages.[4]

It is difficult to assess the level of degradation achieved by the bombardment as its impact was so variable. In some areas it probably achieved 40-50 percent mortality of German direct-fire heavy weapons covering beaches. The larger and more prominent the weapon, the more liable it became for destruction. Many soldiers survived the shelling in shelters, but were initially dazed and concussed. Commanders desperately tried to re-establish control, switching resources to replace casualties.

This emasculation of defensive potential was being repeated further east in the 716th Division sector. One reinforced company from Infantry Regiment 736 had already been caught out in the open south of Bernières searching for paratroopers, and was annihilated. Shelling created gaps in minefields and beach obstacles. Following 'the heaviest air bombardment' the 716th Division Headquarters reported:

*The opening of naval fire along the coast at first light. Then at 07.00 a fresh aircraft assault began against the WN and strong-points throughout the Division area, with aeroplanes concentrating on subsequent landing areas.*[5]

As with the 352nd Division, contact with the troops on

*Above:* ' The din was deafening'. The sheer spectacle of the bombardment mesmerised watching troops still at sea.

*Below:* A storm of shot and shell drenched identified German positions. German observers view from the east bank of the Orne.

the coast was abruptly cut off by severed telephone connections. The bombardment of the coast here took on a sinister hue, as a grey all-enveloping smoke shroud rolled in from the sea. 'As soon as ships came into sight off the coast they were smoked off', commented the 716th Division report. 'A thick wall of smoke was also laid across the coastline.'[6] The ensuing battle was to be contested, invisible to supporting headquarters, behind this veil of smoke. Only a few troops would ever return.

Coastal batteries attempted to return fire, but were either overwhelmed by the response, or unable to bracket targets that zigzagged their escape into the protective smoke. *Heeresküsten* (Coastal) Regiment 1255 on the eastern flank of the invasion was luckier than most. Eleven dead and 48 wounded were lost to preparatory air attacks. Radio was substituted for telephones once the links were cut. As targets came into range, the guns opened fire. There were plenty to choose from.

> *36 units were identified, rising later to 80. This included battleships of the "Queen Elizabeth", "Nelson" and "Maryland" classes, as well as American battleships of unknown type.*[7]

The batteries, covering an area between the Orne estuary and Trouville, including Houlgate, began to engage ships on the eastern flank of the British Task Force. Forward observers noted:

> *Fire missions demonstrated excellent results. Direct hits were observed on several ships; one cruiser developed a heavy list after a succession of strikes.*

But it was difficult to capitalise on success. Targets were fleeting. 'All the ships engaged smoked themselves off immediately, following the initial salvoes, altered course or turned about and disappeared.'[8]

Damage to the batteries that day was slight. One of the three lost two of five guns (one temporarily), another battery lost a single gun, while some 37mm flak guns received direct hits. Casualties following counter-naval gunfire numbered 11 wounded and one killed. These official reports, written after the event, were attempting to gloss over failure. 'Despite effective enemy fire, the soldiers demonstrated excellent self control' and 'fulfilled duty'.[9] The truth, however, was that once the awesome power of the battleships offshore had been demonstrated, batteries were intimidated into a self-imposed paralysis. Generalmajor Hans Speidel, Rommel's Chief-of-Staff, was to later concur with this view of the bombardment. 'The intensity of it was such that German troops had never known the like'. Gunners soon became aware of the likely retribution if they took on a battleship. 'Without having actually been in it', emphasised Speidel, 'it was impossible to estimate the destructive effect on morale of this terrific combined bombardment'.[10] The German battery at Longues decided to

fight it out with four 155mm guns. Within 20 minutes the unit had received 114 6in rounds from HMS *Ajax*, shells actually entering the slits of two casemates. Some 115 spent shell cases were later found around the battery. More typical was the response elicited from Oberstabsfeldwebel Buskotte attempting to fire two battered guns from the Merville battery, directed by his battery commander Oberleutnant Steiner. Some desultory shooting was rewarded by a backlash of fire which churned over the battery position yet again. Buskotte's comment was

> *It's all very well for the Herr Lieutenant to give orders from down there [his OP on Franceville Plage], because it's here where we shall always catch it!*[11]

German outposts on the coast were beginning to appreciate the vast size of the Allied fleet, now becoming apparent to them all. Helmut Berndt, a German naval war correspondent among them, later described the impact of the sudden appearance of this sprawling conurbation off the beaches.

> *Most of the bigger ships lie at anchor; through the haze they resemble an imaginary city with winking towers in the mist — "The Golden City", as the troops called it.*[12]

This alien settlement had anchored itself off the coast of Normandy, and was now crackling and flashing with sinister portent. It already exuded an air of unsettling permanence. Those who observed it accepted in their hearts the war was probably lost.

## 'A Hollywood Show' ... Utah 06.30.

Soldiers aboard the landing craft ploughing through heavy seas toward Utah Beach had been enduring the queasy, wallowing journey for over four hours. 'It was sure rough', recalled Private Stanley Borok, an engineer battalion medic.

> *Everybody sits with a helmet between his knees, puking his guts out, so sick that he doesn't care what happens to him. But suddenly the boat starts moving in and somehow you stand up and swallow what you've got in your mouth and forget you're sick.*[1]

The first wave of 20 LCVPs each carried a 30-man assault team from the 8th Infantry Regiment of 4th Division. They were supported by four LCTs carrying 32 Sherman DD tanks. Just behind was the second wave with another 32 LCVPs bringing in the balance of the two assaulting battalions, combat engineers and naval demolition teams to clear underwater obstacles. Two more subsequent waves were to bring in more 'dozer tanks, combat armoured vehicles and further combat engineers. Some 90 landing craft were powering toward the coast carrying the first five waves all due to land within the space of 30 minutes.[2] 'For some three hours we jockeyed and pushed toward shore', wrote Brigadier General Roosevelt, 'and then the naval bombardment began. In the dusk flashes came from the big ships as the great guns were fired.'

It became lighter. As it did so, a navigation problem began to manifest itself. The nine-mile stretch of Contentin shore line designated as Utah is totally featureless. There were no steeples, buildings or distinctive hills visible to assist coxswains to orientate landing craft. Their objective was a gently sloping stretch of yellow sand, 300-400 metres wide, crossed by stream outlets and planted with several lines of anti-boat obstacles. Dry sand extended to a 100-150 metre wide belt of small sand dunes, covered with beach grass, with a low concrete beach wall on the seaward side. Exits from the beach consisted of gaps blocked by concrete emplacements and bunkered strong-points like WN5. Behind the beach, flooded pasture lands extended three to four kilometres inland. Causeways leading across these flooded areas from beach exits had been one of the prime objectives of the airborne assault. Landing craft coxswains who had set off in darkness, could not even view the beach until they were well over halfway. When they did, there were no visible landmarks to confirm the accuracy of their run-in. A number of control vessels had already been sunk by mines en route. Unbeknown to crews, the wind and a strong tidal current was steadily pushing them well south of their designated landing area.

Few in the wave-tossed landing craft were aware or indeed, because of sea-sickness, even interested in the error unfolding. 'Now we began to make out the low line of the shore', observed Roosevelt, 'revealed by the flash of the explosions as the naval shells landed'. Coxswains tended to steer toward the sights and sounds of the bombardment. Massive air attacks showed the way. 'Flight after flight', continued Roosevelt:

*dropped its bombs on the German emplacements. There'd be a ripple of thunder, blazes of light, clouds of dust, and the planes would pass us again on their way home. One fell by me, flaming like a meteor.*

The concentrated naval and air pounding raised a pall of obscuration which blotted out such few terrain features as there were. German gunners began responding. Inky black air-bursts suddenly blossomed over the advancing craft lashing the surface of the sea. 'German shells began landing among us', observed Roosevelt, 'sending up towers of spray'. Nothing but smoke and dust could be seen from the sea, and radar was unable to identify one beach from another. The boats ploughed on.

*We passed a capsized craft, some men clinging to it, others bobbing in the waves. The little boats were now going full speed, slapping the waves with their blunt prows. As we peered over the gunwale the shore seemed nearer, but veiled as it was in the smoke and dust of the bombardment it was hard to make it out.[3]*

Eye-witness reports refer constantly to the 'deafening racket' that had broken the silence of the early morning.

*Fire support ships "Belting away" at their designated targets raised an "almost continual wall of sound"; the enemy batteries were replying briskly; and overhead was the drumming of aircraft engines of the flights returning to Britain ...[4]*

Apparent to all was the spectacle of conflict. 'Well — it was just like a show', reminisced Sergeant William Clayton of the US 4th Infantry Division. 'The men were looking at the planes bombing just like it was a Hollywood show, saw the bombs falling, this and that ...'[5]

'Suddenly the beach appeared before us', recalled Roosevelt.

*...A long stretch of sand studded with wire and obstacles. Then with a crunch we grounded, the ramp was lowered and we jumped into water waist-deep and started for the shore.*

Twenty landing craft of the first wave touched down at H-Hour, 06.30, on schedule. But the strong current and tidal stream had swept them some two kilometres off course to the south. The noise was deafening. Men shouted as they waded ashore to a background orchestration of whooshing shells, stuttering machine guns, and the splash of surf as soldiers surged, as quickly as they were able, through chest deep water. Behind them could be heard the rising and falling bellowing of landing craft engines, changing to a high pitched whine as they negotiated obstacles or reversed out, having disgorged troops. 'We splashed and floundered through some hundred yards of water while the German salvoes fell,' wrote Roosevelt. 'Men dropped, some silent, some screaming.' There were about 400yds of open beach to run across. 'Grandfather puffed a bit'[6] he remembered, before reaching the sea wall and the comparative shelter offered by the sand dunes.

Sergeant Clayton was still affected by the unreality of the panorama unfolding before him. 'They dropped the ramps as we went in — the bombs ceased'. He declared:

*It was just like a big play, until they started shooting, you know — a few shells came and you realised it was not a play. But other than that, it was beautiful.*

Resistance was light. Men waved their rifles as they reached the dry beach and cried, 'Goddam we're on French soil', relieved and happy to have made it.[7]

*Above:* 'An imaginary city with winking towers in the mist.' A view of the sinister 'Golden City' observed from German positions in the Orne area.

*Below:* 'They dropped us in water up to my chest.' Wading ashore under fire at Utah.

Sergeant Clayton's landing craft wallowed to a halt just off the beach.

*They dropped us in water up to my chest and every man had at least one hundred and twenty-five pounds on him. I had a little fellow next to me, and he was down. So we picked him up — two of us — and we said, "now you walk and we'll get you in", with all the weight on him, and water up and over his head.*

Fortunately they were not under heavy fire. 'We walked in, and he was going "whoof!" — blowing water out — but we walked him in'. Men all along Utah Beach struggled ashore in a similar fashion, anticipating a storm of fire from the Atlantic Wall which failed to materialise. 'We couldn't come in any closer', explained Clayton, 'but we didn't lose a single man, actually, we got right in'.[8]

LSTs brought in DD tanks and self-propelled guns. Elliot Johnson, a battery commander in the 4th Division, realised their young navy officer 'wasn't gonna take us up that beach'. They would not get the SP ashore unless they moved in closer. So:

*I ended up taking my gun out on him. Shoved it in his mouth. Can you believe that? He wanted to get the hell out of there … He wanted to dump us.*

Managing to overcome this initial hurdle, the vehicle was manoeuvred into the water and driven toward the beach.

*Corporal Rackley was driving and watching me. I threw up my hand. He thought I meant stop. So I assaulted the beach of Normandy in the inglorious fashion of somersaulting through the air and landing on my back.*

He only 'just got out of the way' as the massive armoured vehicle careered past. His crew, who 'had never seen me move so fast' thought it hugely funny.[9]

Although the first assault wave had gained a foothold, Brigadier General Roosevelt, the Deputy Division Commander — responsible as such for co-ordinating the assault and initial move inland — was uneasy.

*The moment I arrived at the beach I knew something was wrong, for there was a house by the sea wall where none should have been were we in the right place. It was imperative that I should find out where we were in order to set the manoeuvre.*

Scrambling around the dunes he 'was lucky in finding a windmill which I recognized'. This confirmed his suspicion, they had been set ashore a mile too far to the south. He had now to brief the battalion commanders both left and right, and change some tasks. 'Fortunately it meant little change in plans.' His radio, however, was

out of action for nearly three hours. 'Most of our work', he recalled later, 'was done on foot.' Impromptu planning and co-ordination solved the problem. 'As the succeeding waves landed I pushed them inland if they halted, and redirected them when they started to go wrong'.[10] Ironically the error proved fortuitous. Not only were there not so many obstacles to the south, enemy shore defences were less formidable than those opposite the intended landing beaches.

German field fortifications were overwhelmed from the sides and rear by company-sized units. Against little opposition, houses parallel to the beach were rapidly cleaned out. The heavy preparatory bombardment appeared to have demoralised the defenders. Within two to three hours beach defences had been mopped up and units reorganized for the advance inland. The two assaulting battalions diverged. The first moved north and then inland in the direction of Ste Mère-Eglise using Exit 3, the second battalion along the coast toward Poupeville via Exit 1.

'Shells continually burst around us', wrote Roosevelt as German gunners inland, guided by the arrival of barrage balloons, began to find the range. Private Stanley Borok, the engineer medic, was soon at work.

*I took five steps and this 88 lands about 30 feet to my left. Then I run to the right and bang! another 88, and this time my buddy is staring at his hand because his thumb is shot off. Then two more, just like that, and I found some backbone and ribs and the back of a skull with the whole face cleaned out, all of it right near the pack next to me.[11]*

Lieutenant Elliot Johnson's first sight of the wounded 'continued my education recognizing our body as finite'. He saw:

*One young boy who was so badly hurt he was grey, like a piece of flannel. I thought he was dead. They gave him a transfusion and I could see his colour coming back. The relief I felt that this boy was gonna make it — I can't remember whether he was German or ours. It didn't matter. Isn't that interesting?[12]*

Casualties at Utah had, however, been astonishingly low. The 8th and 22nd Infantry Regiments were ashore by midday, losing only 118 casualties by the end of the day, 12 of whom were fatalities. The 4th Division in total suffered 197 casualties including 60 men missing through the loss at sea of part of an artillery battalion. Losses incurred during the disastrous E-Boat sortie against Exercise 'Tiger' six weeks before had been four times greater.

Twenty-six assault waves, the first 12 consisting almost entirely of landing craft and the remainder all beaching craft, were scheduled to land at 10 to 25-minute intervals until shortly after midday. There were delays, but transports were quickly unloaded. *The Empire Gauntlet* emptied by 08.30, *Dickman* and *Barnett* by 12.43. By midnight all three were back in Portland harbour to reload. By 18.00 that night 21,328 troops, 1,742 vehicles and 1,695 tons of supplies had passed across the Utah beaches.[13]

The US 4th Infantry Division penetrated inland, but had yet to establish a firm perimeter. Losses were slight, but merely a foretaste of appalling casualties to follow. Whatever the number, they dismayed troops on the ground. Injuries reminded soldiers of the frailty of human flesh, and that they may be next. The longer their exposure to the enemy, the correspondingly less their chances. Private Borok was already becoming conditioned to the transitory nature of life on the battlefield. His first patient on Utah 'was a guy who had his front tooth knocked out by a piece of shrapnel'. The second was buried in a trench up to his thighs.

*I didn't even notice it at first, but the blood was spurting from his chest. Two big holes. You can't plug up a guy's lungs, brother. We did all we could, though. I spotted this bottle of blood plasma we were giving some other guys and then I noticed this other one was dead, so I just took out the needle and put it in this guy's arm. But it didn't do much good. He died in my arms.*[14]

## '... A peaceful summer's day on the Wannsee'.

With most of his direct fire weapons destroyed by the paralysing preparatory bombardment, Leutnant Jahnke manning strong-point WN5, and the surviving members of the 3rd Company Infantry Regiment 919, fought on with machine guns and 80mm mortars. Green Verey lights were fired to bring down a planned artillery barrage arranged with Oberleutnant Schon who, with the 13th Heavy Weapons Company and a battery of 122mm guns from 1261st Artillery Regiment, were positioned in St Martin-de-Varreville, to the rear. However, the runner who had been despatched to initiate the fire plan was shot off his bicycle by a fighter-bomber. The battery position had in any case been traversed by a rolling serial of aerial carpet bombing. German artillery inland was firing blind. Only haphazard shell bursts were causing nuisance value on the beach. A transitory uplift of morale came with the metallic bark of the 88mm flak gun, which with a 'plunk' despatched a Sherman tank that had crawled up the beach. But the damaged gun in so firing, shot-out its barrel.

Gefreiter Friedrich who 'wore spectacles as thick as magnifying glasses' continued to engage enemy infantry with a heavy machine gun from within the protected confine of his French Renault tank turret, mounted on concrete. Despite an incongruous appearance 'everyone knew that what Friedrich aimed at he hit'. Methodically adjusting the beaten zone, he lashed the water around disembarking American troops, bowling over many unfortunates before they could struggle clear of the water. The remainder pressed on, powerless to react to the wispy fountains of spray that suddenly erupted around them, falling slowly to the surface. Overloaded with equipment and chest deep in water, they stoically pushed themselves through the surf as fast as they were able. Lacking cover, there was no alternative. When the Renault turret was hit 'it sounded as if a church bell had cracked', Friedrick miraculously survived; unlike the company reserve commanded by Oberleutnant Matz, fruitlessly attempting a counter-thrust from depth positions. Caught in the open by naval gunfire they were decimated and Matz killed before they could gather momentum.

By midday only a few single rifle reports rang out from the churned up trenches and dug-outs of strongpoint WN5 as it was mopped up. 'It looks as though God and the world have forsaken us', despaired Jahnke, facing defeat and capture. He was pulled out — suffocating, coughing and retching dirt — by the legs, from his half buried dug-out. His saviour was an American soldier. Feeling totally humiliated, he was marched down to the beach and assembled with a handful of other survivors. Dazed, he glanced around at the awesome display of military muscle unfolding about him. They were regarded with only passing interest by the streams of men and equipment coming ashore at Utah. Jahnke felt desperately in need of a cigarette. That night he was on a destroyer, England-bound.[1]

Headquarters 352nd Division, totally preoccupied with its own problems, heard the first unsettling news at 07.45. Fighting an assault to its front, the telephone call announced '15 landing craft are lying on the beach at Le Grand Vey in our left neighbour's sector — 709th Infantry Division'.[2] Reports were sketchy. Headquarters 84th Corps received its first indication between 07.00 and 07.30 of 'landings north east of Carentan'. Not until two hours later did confirmation come of enemy activity between WN2a to 10. The first attack had struck Oberleutnant Jahnke's 3rd Company of 919th Regiment — WN5 — 'whose garrison had been buried then dug out by the Americans'.[3] Infantry Regiment 914 on the south eastern side of the Vire estuary had seen '15 landing craft running into the estuary' at 08.22, and saw 'numerous landing craft' in front of strong-points opposite the Carentan canal at 09.12. Substantial landings were obviously in progress.[4]

At 09.45 the situation became critical. The 709th Division claimed 'tanks had landed between WN3 and 5', and earnestly requested anti-tank support 'because they had lost contact with higher command [84 Corps] headquarters'. Within 15 minutes the 709th Division telephoned again asking for 'fire from all available guns of the IInd Abteilung [Artillery task force] to engage the enemy between WN3 and 5, and harass his logistic sup-

*Above:* 'A succession of such impacts could rob the mind of reason.' A shell-shocked survivor.

*Above:* Friedrick engaged enemy infantry at the water's edge.

*Right:* Troops coming ashore are cut down by fire as seen through these cine-stills. A landing craft is approaching through the mist and obstacles behind.

port'. The situation between these two strong-points 'was critical. Even larger landing craft were standing off the coast, including a barrage balloon.'

Ninety minutes later it appeared the initiative was slipping ever further away. The 914th Regiment, able to see unfolding events, claimed 'the bridgehead by our left neighbour is expanding ... There are 22 ships with barrage balloons.' The 709th Division's contact with Carentan was lost soon after. At midday German artillery in depth began at last to lay a barrage of fire upon WN3 and WN5, where outposts were visibly crumbling. 'Numerous enemy companies had landed, and WN1 is surrounded' was the message from the Chief-of-Staff of the 914th Regiment at 12.05.[5]

Behind the coast off Utah, fighting continued with American paratroopers further diluting and distracting the defence effort. South west of Brevands, the IInd Battalion Infantry Regiment 914 was attempting a four-company sweep against scattered elements of the US 501st and 506th Parachute Regiments. Fighting surged back and forth throughout the morning. Progress could be measured from 07.08 when 'the attack could only slowly gain ground against bitter enemy resistance', to five hours later when only 'slow steps forward' were being claimed.[6]

Fallschirmjäger Regiment 6, south west of Carentan, better armed and trained than its Wehrmacht counterparts in the 914th Regiment, was having more success. 'More prisoners are brought in', wrote Oberleutnant Martin Pöppel optimistically in his diary, 'great hulking figures. Is this the American elite? They look as though they could be from Sing-Sing.' As daylight dawned, methodical company sweeps across their assembly area became more effective. Oberleutnant Prive of No 10 Company pushed across open countryside, driving stragglers and detachments toward Pöppel's company, forming a pincer movement. 'We use light signals to show the direction of the enemy', Pöppel observed until:

*They attack with hand grenades and sub-machine gun fire ripping into the hedgerows. Arms are raised aloft in the thick bushes as the enemy surrenders. A real triumph for Prive, who takes more than sixty American prisoners with a single platoon.*[7]

Major von der Heydte, the regimental commander, realising the focus of the American air-landings was to the north of Carentan, anticipated direction to move north to deal with them. At 08.00, the 84th Corps now vaguely aware of amphibious landings near the same area, directed the Regiment to 'advance across Carentan and St Côme-du-Mont, and attack air-landed enemy elements near Ste Mère-Eglise from the south, and fight clear the flanks and rear of the 709th Infantry Division standing on the coast'.[8] The true significance of this order was probably lost on both Corps headquarters — unaware of the amphibious breakthrough at Utah —

and von de Heydte, who believed he would only be opposing lightly armed airborne troops. By early afternoon the advanced elements of Fallschirmjäger Regiment 6 reached St Côme-du-Mont. The bulk of the follow-on elements were massed in assembly areas west and southwest of Carentan.

The regimental commander gathered his battalion commanders together at 14.00. There was to be a ground orientation for the attack conducted from the top of the church tower in St Côme-du-Mont. Glancing out to sea, they visibly paled at the spectacle unfolding before them. Von der Heydte described the scene:

*Thirty-six ships were peacefully unloading. The bustling shuttle of small boats between the transport ships and beaches reminded one of a peaceful summer's day on the Wannsee. [A popular boating lake near Berlin.]*

'German opposition was not in evidence', he scornfully observed. Long range artillery, if quickly brought up could capitalise on the vantage point offered by the church tower 'and cause heavy casualties among the enemy landings'.[9] Artillery appeared not to be available. Indeed, resistance seemed to have collapsed. He scanned the shore-line with binoculars.

*At every mile along the coast line was a German bunker and, of the three that I could see, only one was actually firing at the Americans. All the bunkers were manned, of course, but only one was firing. In my opinion, they feared for their lives.*

Cowed by the naval bombardment, cut off and lacking direction, strong-points were fearful 'they would easily be wiped out by the invading Americans'. Quite possibly viewing the final attacks on WN5, von der Heydte remarked 'only one bunker did its duty, forcing the Americans to spread out'.[10]

Aware now of the daunting task facing him, Fallschirmjäger Regiment 6 was issued a warning order, outlining the proposed counter-attack. Reinforced by the IIIrd (Wehrmacht) Battalion from Infantry Regiment 1058, von der Heydte disposed of a four-battalion task force directly supported by two batteries (8 and 4) from Artillery Regiment 191, and a flak battery from Regiment 243, setting up south of St Côme-du-Mont. The plan called for a two-pronged thrust to the north. One battalion — the Ist — toward Ste Mère-Eglise, with the immediate objective of capturing Hiesville; and a further — the IInd Battalion — toward Utah, to capture the high ground at St Marie-du-Mont, overlooking the coast. The Wehrmacht battalion was to protect his rear at St Côme-du-Mont, while his the IIIrd Fallschirmjäger Battalion would move up and secure the northern approaches to Carentan, after it had cleared its present assembly area of American paratroopers.

Von der Heydte had set himself a formidable task.

*Above:* 'He was pulled out suffocating, coughing and retching dirt.' A German soldier attempts to vainly dig himself out of a collapsed field position.

*Left:* Humiliated and shell-shocked, German prisoners wait pensively on the beach.

*Above:* 'Is this the American élite? They look as though they could be from Sing-Sing.' Captured POWs from the US 101st Airborne Division.

*Below:* That night he was on a destroyer, England-bound. German POWs are led out to a landing craft, and captivity across the Channel.

Ahead of him were isolated, yet menacing, pockets, of airborne infantry; some already in the objective area. Evidence of enemy activity was sparse. Driving him was evidence of German collapse which could only be reversed by vigorous countermeasures. On returning to his command post:

> *I came across a German battery which had been totally deserted … about six guns in the battery, totally unmanned, but all ready to fire, the ammunition boxes open on the left side of each gun. I don't know what had happened to the gunners, but it was my opinion that they had deserted, though it is possible that they had received a new order.*[11]

He was not to know that his proposed spearhead of two battalions was poised to drive into the flank of the entire US 4th Infantry Division, a force which would number 20,000 troops and 1,700 vehicles. As the time of his envisaged H-Hour advanced, odds were increasing to beyond 10 to 1.

General von Schieben commanding the 709th Division, having completed an unrewarding drive to and from Rennes, arrived back at his command post exhausted shortly after midday. He had been on the road throughout the night and morning, obliged by unexpected developments to undertake a totally pointless 320km round trip. Key decisions had already been taken during his absence. His staff outlined the measures that Corps had directed during the night to deal with the American airborne landings. Von Schieben's heart sank as he gazed at the map. A hole some seven kilometres wide had been ripped through his seaward defences. Reports suggested penetrations up to a similar depth. Now he was required to coordinate the activities of units and reinforcements he was not even certain existed.

Troops on the ground, even those fighting as part of shifting fronts had little idea what was going on. Seaborne landings were suspected to have taken place, but could not be confirmed. Oberleutnant Pöppel of Fallschirmjäger Regiment 6 was summoned by a messenger to report to battalion headquarters 'to discuss the new situation'. There appeared to have been more airborne landings and 'landing parties have landed in the Vire-Mundung [estuary] region'. With no idea of the extent of the Allied build-up, the coming counter-attack was viewed with equanimity. Counter-moves, like anticipated casualties, were only to be expected.

> *It turns out that this really is the Allies' big day — which unfortunately means that it's ours too.*[12]

# CHAPTER 9

# FIRST WAVE FOUNDERED

*'I didn't think I would make it you know. I didn't think that there was any way that you could get off that beach and survive.'*

*American Soldier*

## 'No sign of life or resistance' … approaching Omaha 06.15.

LCVPs are only 36ft long and 11ft across. Of the 48 in the first wave heading towards Omaha Beach, each contained about 30 men. There was not room for everyone to sit down. Most soldiers preferred to stand, as heavy backpacks made it difficult to pull oneself up from a sitting or kneeling position. They had been enduring these conditions, pitching and tossing through the water, for over three to four hours. Men standing in the centre could see little else but the backs of their friends. Only those at the side could see anything. Lieutenant Carroll from the 1st Division, forming part of an advanced headquarters for the 16th Regimental Combat Team (RCT), said:

*We could jump up and hold ourselves on the side and peer over, but there wasn't too much visible since there was a tremendous sea at this time. One only glimpsed a view of smoke, smog, spray and a shoreline to our front.[1]*

The 24 landing craft of the 16th RCT formed the left forward front of 1st Division, to their right were a further 24 boats carrying the 116th RCT, spearheading the 29th Infantry Division. The first wave was wallowing in on a front of three miles between Vierville and Le Grand Hameau. Behind them in successive waves, were a further 150 landing craft.

White caps smacked into the sides of the boats every few seconds. Spray soaked through clothing heavily impregnated to repel the effect of gas attack. High waves washed over the ships' sides drenching bodies made increasingly weak by a chill factor generated by strong winds. 'By this time', observed Sergeant Gilbert Gray of the 116th Regiment,

*Some of the guys were seasick and some were arguing over little things that didn't count. Some guys, like myself, were just standing there in the boat thinking and shivering. By this time there was a cold fine spray, like rain … and the boat was beginning to ship water.[2]*

Ten boats carrying infantry were swamped and sank on the way in. Gray, like the rest of 'A' Company was overloaded. They were wearing especially thick 'impregnite' OD uniforms, covered by special assault jackets with four huge pockets in front and two to the rear. Riflemen carried 60 rounds plus three bandoliers around the neck, five grenades of various types, a quarter-pound of TNT, 'K' rations for one day, a raincoat, and a small self-contained medical pack — as there were no medics in the first wave. Blanks for propelling anti-tank grenades were carried in pockets, and Sergeant Gray carried a webbing bag full of anti-tank grenades under his left arm. Equipment weights could vary between 40 to 60lb or more, depending on weapons. Cramped conditions added to sea-sickness. Unable to move, Lieutenant Carroll remembered:

*People were throwing up all over the boat, trying to avoid each other. Some just stood stoically and said not a word the whole way in. It took us a long time to cover those six miles, a long time![3]*

Sea-sick pills did not help. 'In fact', recalled Gray, 'one guy took half a bottle of the darn things. He was practically walking in his sleep when we went off the craft.'[4]

It was becoming lighter. Lieutenant John Spaulding of the 16th RCT could now 'see the outlines of other boats around us and overhead we could hear a few planes'. Shortly before 06.00 they noticed the first flashes from the shore. 'We didn't know whether they were our planes bombing, as we had been told to expect, or whether the flashes were from German artillery'. Most soldiers, steeped in misery, sea sick, lashed by the elements, paid no attention at all. 'We caught sight of the shore about 06.15' said Spaulding, but the coast obscured by dust and debris, and an early morning mist, was difficult to see. Unbeknown to coxswains, craft were drifting eastwards, some by only a few hundred yards, others by as much as 1,000. Unit cohesion was already

*Above:* 'Some guys like myself were just standing there in the boat thinking and shivering.' Fear is reflected on the faces of these infantry Omaha-bound.

*Above:* 'We could jump up and hold ourselves on the side and peer over.' Approaching Omaha Beach, some attempt has been made to waterproof weapons.

*Left:* 'Two hundred yards out we took a direct hit.' Landing craft on fire running into the beach.

involuntarily loosening.

There was no sign of activity on shore.

*As we went in toward the beach, there was no sign of life or resistance. Approaching closer, the concrete wall just to the east of Dog Green became plainly visible. There appeared to be openings along its length. Some structures which appeared to be pillboxes, a few houses, and the church steeple of Vierville were sighted. There was an intense quiet, so quiet it was suspicious.*[5]

One officer's impression was 'it looked like another big tactical scheme off Slapton Sands, and I couldn't get the feeling out of my head that it was going to be another miserable two-day job with a hot shower at the end'.[6] Another Ranger Lieutenant claimed 'I seriously believed that the Jerries had abandoned their coastal defences and had pulled back further inland to make their stand'.[7] 'As we came in', remarked Spaulding, 'there was considerable noise from the shore and sea'. Men were spotted in the water. 'We passed several yellow, rubber boats. They had personnel in them, but we didn't know what they were.'

Companies 'B' and 'C' of the 741st Tank Battalion had launched 32 DD tanks more than 50 minutes earlier, five to six kilometres out from the eastern sector of Omaha Beach. They were in difficulties as soon as they entered the choppy water. Nightmare fears were realised as canvas screens split and struts buckled under the impact of waves. Some tanks floundered soon after engine compartments flooded. Left broadside-on to the mercy of the elements, they broached and went to the bottom like stones. Anguished cries from crew compartments were abruptly silenced by the sudden convergence of slapping waves. Men pinned half in and out of driver compartments were snatched beneath the water. 'It was pitiful to see them disappear one after another,' reported observers.[8] Within two to three minutes 27 tanks launched had gone under. Few of the 135 men struggling in the water were saved. Two tanks managed to swim to the beach; three colliding while attempting to exit remained on board their LCT. It was a disaster. Spaulding and the assault wave drove on through them, ignoring pleas for assistance; leaving them for control boats. All eyes were now on the beach, which still gave no indication of an enemy.

Taking advantage of the apparent lull in shelling, German soldiers poured out of their dug-outs and shelters, and half-crouching trotted toward their stand-to positions. Furious activity ensued at points where caved-in trenches showed tell-tale signs of life, or protruding limbs. Only the sobbing of the wounded and crackling brush fires consuming dune tufts broke the silence, punctuated here and there by the odd shouted command and clattering of equipment, broken up by the wind. Frantic digging occurred to clear bunker slits masked by sand drifts bordering shell craters. Machine gunners unclipped bipods with purposeful set faces and began to pile boxes of linked ammunition nearby. Their tormentors would soon be in range. Number twos began clipping belts of machine gun link together, ensuring a clear passage to feed trays. Smoke from grass fires billowed across the dunes, obscuring the sea view, smelling strongly of burnt wood interspersed occasionally with cordite fumes. Riflemen laid grenades on the edge of parapets, slowly exhaling breath when ready, tersely observing the dark rectangular shapes ploughing through the surf before them. The landing craft had yet to reach the line of outermost obstacles. It was low tide.

The batteries of 1352nd and 1726th Artillery Regiments stood waiting, crews tensed up in anticipation of the frenzied action that was about to ensue, to feed the guns. Mortar crews made final adjustments to their sights. All along the beach weapons were cocked, breeches of heavy weapons opened and clanged shut. Attempts were still made to dig out anti-tank guns from collapsed field positions. Commanders peered through binoculars, estimating and re-checking the range to the outer-most obstacle belt. Nervous fingers played with trigger guards. They were still out of range, reported observers from Artillery Regiment 352:

*Something like 60 to 80 fast landing craft are approaching the coast near Colleville. These boats cannot be reached by our own artillery ... the battleships in the foreground are too far away for our own artillery to reach.*[9]

Damage from the bombardment had been considerable, but the veteran officers and NCOs of the 352nd Division had experienced similar on the Russian Front. Fortunately, the majority of the bombers had off-loaded their lethal baggage to the rear. They had felt, but not seen the massive rolling blanket of impacts that had hit the rear areas. In broad terms their positions were intact. Their commanders were confident and in control. Only elements of the awesome fleet facing them could be made out through the brush fires. Infantry Regiment 916 telephoned through to Division headquarters at 06.20 claiming: 'tank landing craft can be clearly seen in the Vierville inlet'.[10]

The section of beach between Vierville-sur-Mer, stretching almost six and a half kilometres to Ste-Honorine, was probably one of the more densely defended sectors of coastline held by the 352nd Division. Elements of three to four battalions from the 916th Regiment on the left and the 726th Regiment to the right, defended five ravines that cut their way through the sand-dune covered bluffs that overlooked the beach. In depth were elements of the 914th Regiment directly supported by at least three artillery batteries, numerous mortars, and well sited heavier calibre 75mm, 88mm and 50mm anti-tank and field pieces. Each ravine could produce a diverging cone of fire, based upon a series of bunkers and trenches situated on either side. Heavy calibre weapons swept the beach from both west and east. Bluffs, rising like primitive earthworks, 50 to 60 metres high, in between, provided blind spots for attackers, but were impassable to vehicles. They could be climbed with some exertion, but were mined.

The beach was a broad expanse of flat sand, stretching 300 to 400 metres beyond the waterline. There were two broad obstacle belts, one sited at the low water mark, the other at high tide. Sand at high tide gave way to a slight shingle embankment bordering a wire-covered sea wall, which ran along half the length of the beach. Gun emplacements were sited in the cliffs bordering the eastern and western sides of the beach. Inland lay the villages of Vierville, St Laurent and Colleville, situated at the head of the five various ravines exiting the beach.

The defence was almost medieval in its simplicity. Attacking troops had to cross a moat of water strewn with mined obstacles, until facing a high earth rampart, 150ft high, with cliffs either side. There were only five exits through this rampart, well secured by a miniature 'keep' of bunkers and trenches. Mines and wire either side channelled approaches into these virtual arrow slits facing the beaches, simplifying the task of repelling boarders, as half the beach was visible from any one of these vantage points.

Manning strong-point WN62 beyond Colleville was a platoon of 17 soldiers from 726 Regiment under Unterfeldwebel Pieh, protecting the artillery OP of the 1st Battery Artillery Regiment 352nd, commanded by Oberleutnant Frerking. They could clearly see the approaching landing craft. Orders for opening fire were clear: not until the enemy had reached the waterline. To their right, the sound of revving engines signified landing craft were attempting to negotiate the first line of low water obstacles. Infantry Regiment 726 telephoned the result through to the 352nd Division Headquarters at 06.37.

*The first landing boats have beached on the coast in front of WN65 and 69. There are tank landing craft among them.*[11]

Unteroffizier Hein Severloh in WN62 had been carefully tracking an approaching landing craft, which he estimated to be at 400 metres range. It was about to beach. His finger had already taken the first slack of the trigger pressure. Oberleutnant Frerking linked to his inland battery, shouted into the telephone: 'Target "Dora" — Fire!' Severloh squeezed absorbing the recoil in his right shoulder, controlling the lashing pattern evident in the water with his left hand, adjusting the stock of his MG42.

## 'Entire First Wave Foundered' …

*The first man, a Sergeant, raised up to see how much further it was to land — and fell back dead.*[1]

'Gee fellows!' exclaimed Sergeant Golas from the 2nd Ranger Battalion approaching 'Charlie' sector, 'they are shooting back at us!'[2] Any hope that the preparatory bombardment had neutralised beach strong-points died 400 metres from the shore. As the 16th RCT approached between 'Charlie', 'Dog' and 'Easy Green', the Germans commenced firing mortars and artillery. Initially inaccurate, fire became increasingly effective as landing craft neared the beach. Artillery shells and mortar bombs beat a splashing pattern among the boats. Geysers spurted up around them, blown abruptly into a fine wind-dispersed spray.

'A' Company of 116th RCT and 'C' Company 2nd Rangers were assailed by a vortex of fire from bunkers at beach level, shooting defilade to their front, while cliff emplacements high to the right fired down, hitting them in enfilade. They were conducting a bruising frontal assault upon an unassailable position. 'The first ramps were dropped at 06.36', recalled Private Howard Gresser, 'in water that was waist deep to cover a man's head'. Disembarking troops became enmeshed in this moat.

*As if this had been the signal for which the enemy waited, the ramps were instantly enveloped in a crossing automatic fire which was accurate and in great volume. It came at the boats from both ends of the beach. Company "A" had planned to move in three files from each boat, centre file going first, then flank files peeling off to the right and left. The first men tried it. They crumpled as they sprang from the ship, forward into the water. Then order was lost. It seemed to the men that the only way to get ashore with a chance of safety was to dive head-first into the water.*[3]

One of 'A' Company's six boats had swamped 1,000 metres off the beach. *LCA 1015* nosing through the outer obstacles staggered under the impact of a direct hit, and following the flash, belched flame and smoke. It drifted, dead in the water, broadside on, burning furiously as waves pushed the wreck inshore. What happened to the occupants was never known. 'Every man was killed, and most of the bodies were found along the beach.'[4] The four remaining 'A' Company boats ploughed on through the barrage, dropping ramps in waist deep to overhead water. 'We saw landing craft with men we had known so well disappear under a mortar explosion', said Lieutenant Kenneth Sewell, a British LCA captain. 'We watched a mortar bomb bounce off a wave and slowly spin overhead.' Soldiers had scrambled over the sides of the boats, 'and had gone down into water over their heads' noticed Private Gilbert Murdock. 'They were around the boat now, struggling with

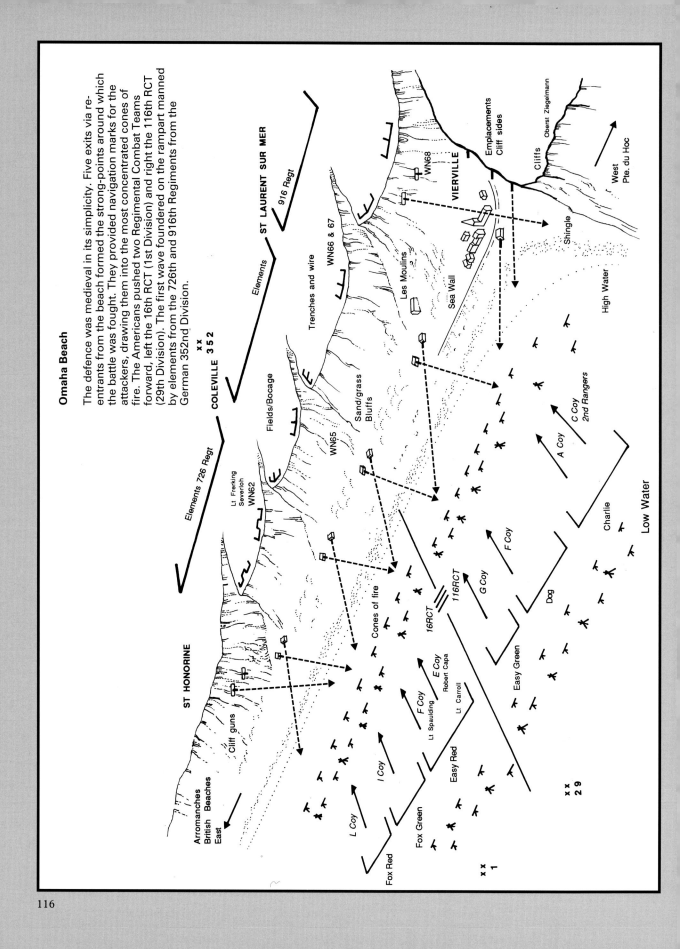

## Omaha Beach

The defence was medieval in its simplicity. Five exits via re-entrants from the beach formed the strong-points around which the battle was fought. They provided navigation marks for the attackers, drawing them into the most concentrated cones of fire. The Americans pushed two Regimental Combat Teams forward, left the 16th RCT (1st Division) and right the 116th RCT (29th Division). The first wave foundered on the rampart manned by elements from the 726th and 916th Regiments from the German 352nd Division.

COLEVILLE
xx
352

ST LAURENT SUR MER

916 Regt

Elements

Elements 726 Regt

ST HONORINE

Aromanches
British Beaches
East

VIERVILLE

WN68

Emplacements
Cliff sides

Oberst Ziegelmann

Cliffs

Cliffs

West
Pte. du Hoc

Les Moulins

Sea Wall

Shingle

High Water

WN66 & 67

Trenches and wire

Fields/Bocage

Sand/grass
Bluffs

WN65

WN62

Lt Frerking
Severloh

Cliff guns

Cones of fire

C Coy
2nd Rangers

A Coy

Charlie

Low Water

F Coy

G Coy

116RCT

16RCT

Dog

Easy Green

xx
29

F Coy

E Coy
Robert Capa

Lt Spaulding

Lt Carroll

Easy Red

I Coy

L Coy

Fox Green

Fox Red

xx
1

their equipment and trying to keep afloat'. Lieutenant Sewell realised 'something had gone badly wrong'.[5]

*Others wounded, dragged themselves ashore and upon finding the sand, lay quiet and gave themselves shots [injections of morphine], only to be caught and drowned within a few minutes by the on-racing tide.*[6]

Within a minute the second wave had piled-in on top of the first. 'About 75yds from the beach the ramp was dropped, and the enemy automatic fire then beat a tattoo all over the boat front', reported one 'B' Company boat. Captain Zappacosta the company commander, first out, yelled 'I'm hit!' Private Kenser surging through the water after him called 'try to make it in!' But he was shot. Zappacosta went down and nobody saw him come up again. The third man out, Lieutenant Tom Dallas reached the sand, where he was immediately killed. Private Sales, fourth in line, sprawled on the ramp and fell headlong into the water. It probably saved his life. Each man leaving the ramp behind him was either killed or wounded. One American soldier animatedly recalled:

*I didn't think that I would make it you know. I didn't think there was any way that you could get off that beach and survive. You know I really thought it was my last day.*[7]

Sales was the only one to get as far as the beach. It took him two hours. He was later joined by Private Mack L Smith, who had been hit three times in the face, and Kemper, a man shot three times in the leg. They lay there listlessly as the fighting raged around them.

*The dead washed up to where they lay and then washed back again. They pulled the bodies of their own men onto the sand.*[8]

It was an immense physical effort for those still able to move, to even cross the beach, soaked as they were on landing. Adrenalin propelled limbs stiffened by the hours of enforced, cramped and spray-drenched inactivity that had preceded the assault. Captain Goranson, a Ranger on 'Charlie' sector, recalled 'going across the beach was just like a dream with all the movement of the body and mind just automatic motion'.[9]

Problems were compounded by the inability of combat engineers to clear obstacles. Casualties for the Army-Navy Special Engineer Task Force ran to 41 percent on D-Day, most suffered during the first 30 minutes. Men burdened with equipment and explosives were excellent targets for enemy fire as they unloaded in water often several feet deep. Of 16 'dozers only six got to the beach in working condition, three immediately disabled by artillery strikes. Eight navy personnel of Team 11 dragging a pre-loaded rubber boat off their LCM were scattered when an artillery air burst touched off their primacord. Only one man survived. Another shell hit the Team 14 LCM, detonating explosives on deck, killing all the navy personnel. Team 15 wading through the surf pushing a rubber dinghy loaded with explosives received a direct hit from a mortar round. Three men died and four were wounded.

Six complete and three partial gaps were blown through the obstacle belt on Omaha, the majority (four) in the 'Easy Red' sector. The cost, however, was horrific. All teams were handicapped by the rising tide, landing craft crashing through their obstacles as they worked, infantry taking cover behind their prepared demolitions and enemy fire. Team 12 having completed preparations for a 30yd gap were enveloped by a premature explosion when a mortar bomb struck primacord as they dispersed to take cover. Nineteen engineers and nearby infantry were killed and wounded.[10] One engineer wading ashore with a team of 28 due to blow gaps in one of the concrete walls blocking beach exits related how:

*I was coming out of the water when this guy exploded right in front of me. There just wasn't anything left of him except some of his skin, which splattered all over my arm. I remember dipping my arm in the water to wash it off. I guess I was too excited to be scared.*[11]

Further east the 16th RCT was coming ashore between 'Easy Red' and 'Fox'. Casualties were heavy, but not as fearful as those on 'Dog Green', possibly the worst on Omaha. Losses were proportional to the number of boats drifting into the carefully surveyed German arcs of fire emanating from the ravines. Strong-points were, ironically, the very navigational indicators guiding boats in. Coxswains steered toward these tell-tale gaps in the dune-covered bluffs overlooking the beach, incongruously baiting boat-loads toward destruction. Off 'Easy Red', Lieutenant Carroll's LCM strayed into just such a fire zone, its momentum checked by the staggering impact of a heavy calibre projectile.

*Two hundred yards out we took a direct hit. It knocked out an ensign and a sailor beside him who were steering the craft in rear. They disappeared along with the rest of the controls. The boat started to get out of control, to weave and wobble.*

Sudden catastrophe — the inversion of the norm to abject terror — accompanied by horrific sights to uninitiated 'green' troops, was often the precursor to battle shock. Carroll recalled the heavy automatic fire that now enveloped the boat.

*It was shooting a rat—tat—tat on the front of the boat. Somehow or other, the ramp door opened up, probably due to the loss of the controls, and the men in the front were being struck by machine gun fire. Everyone started to*

*Above:* Their tormentors would soon be in range. German infantry observe the approaching landing craft.

*Left:* 'I didn't think that I would make it you know.' First wave ashore on 'Easy Red'. They are protected by smoke from grass fires shielding them from German fire on the high ground ahead.

*Right:* 'No leaders were there to give orders, and none was given. Each man made his own decision.' Survivors shelter under the cliffs.

*jump off into the water. They were being hit as they jumped, the machine gun fire was so heavy.*

Men previously unblooded in battle had no conception of the scything impact of heavy machine gun fire. Red-hot shards of tracer rushed up suddenly into the centre of vision, accompanied by deafening multiple 'cracks' as projectiles broke the sound barrier, displacing air at tremendous velocity as they went by. The whip-lash sound is followed by the 'thumping' report of the weapon firing, the time taken for the sound to reach the human ear. Veterans are able to differentiate the pause between 'crack' and 'thump',thereby giving an indication of the range and direction of the threatening weapon. But few had the presence of mind to do this; bursting impacts and whining ricochets from several weapons drove men over the side of boats. 'Every man acted for himself, on his own instinct' said Carroll.[12]

More distressing was the impact of this high velocity punishment on the human body, on friends and colleagues. To be under machine gun fire is a brutalising experience, the results quite horrible. Private Irwin Spandau, also on 'Easy Red', saw a GI 'raked with bullets across his neck. The blood came gushing out, and his head all but fell off his shoulders'. It was 'the worst thing I had ever seen', and reduced him to a condition 'of terrible fright, and of unspeakable terror with a deep, cold, shaking feeling going all through me, as though a large piece of ice had passed completely through my body'.[13] On 'Dog Green', Private Nash of 'A' Company 116th RCT saw his platoon commander Lieutenant Tidrick collapse, shot through the throat. The officer rolled over, and while futilely enjoining him to advance, momentarily exposed himself. Nash horrified, watched 'machine gun bullets cleave him from head to pelvis'.[14]

Sights such as these were having a debilitative effect on advancing troops who thought now, less of objectives, and increasingly more of survival. 'A' Company on 'Dog Green' had abandoned arms and helmets to avoid drowning. 'The Company's combat effectiveness was almost zero', recorded an official account.

*All thought of moving forward was abandoned. Only a few men were still armed, and only a few of these weapons; clogged with wet sand, could fire. No leaders were there to give orders, and none was given. Each man made his own decision.*[15]

At 06.41 Patrol Craft *552* observing the beaches reported back to the USS *Chase* — 'entire first wave foundered'.[16]

## Assaulting the 'Jib' ... Pointe du Hoc 07.10.

The line of approaching cliffs seemed featureless as Lieutenant Colonel James Rudder's 2nd Ranger Battalion task force bobbed and tossed its way toward the French coast. Twelve miles of rough seas had already exacted a toll. *LCA 914*, a supply craft transporting clothes and ammunition soon sank, leaving only one survivor. Captain Slater the 'D' Company Commander was next to be swamped in *LCA 860* with 20 men. The remainder of the flotilla — nine surviving LCAs and four DUKWs — carrying companies 'E', 'D' and 'F', chilled by menacing spray-blown waves, began baling with helmets.

The force, some 225 men, faced a formidable objective: a 155mm coastal defence battery with concrete observation and range-finding stations atop the cliffs at Pointe du Hoc. Two of the six guns were casemated, and all were able to reach transport shipping areas feeding Omaha and Utah Beaches. It was a priority objective, held by an estimated force of 125 men from Infantry Regiment 726 and 85 artillery men from the 2nd Battery Coastal Artillery Regiment 1260.[1] Pointe du Hoc is a blunt, triangular cape rising a sheer 117 feet from the rocky shore seven kilometres west of Omaha. This conspicuous knife edged outcrop derives its name from the old French for 'jib', whose shape it resembles. Rudder's Rangers had planned a three-company assault to scale the cliffs, supported by a further company, 'Charlie', securing its left flank, landing at Vierville. 'A' and 'B' companies would land on the Hoc, if the initial assault was successful, or alternatively across Omaha. 'They said it was a futile attempt', recalled Sergeant Lou Lisco of the 2nd Rangers. Arguably the batteries might have been attacked from the landward side, like the Merville battery, following an airborne assault. One Naval Task Force intelligence officer certainly had misgivings. 'It can't be done', he remonstrated, 'three old women with brooms could keep the Rangers from climbing that cliff'.[2] For whatever reason, Rudder's indirect assault became the proposed solution.

This conspicuous knife-edged outcrop was not the feature Lieutenant Colonel Rudder could observe through binoculars coming up ahead. The escorting British Fairmile, *ML 304*, had taken them short of Pointe et Raz de la Percée, some four kilometres to the east — a significant error. Turning into wind and tide the flotilla was obliged now to plough on for an additional 35 minutes westwards, parallel to the cliffs, running a gauntlet of enemy fire. One DUKW was hit by 20mm cannon fire which sank the craft, killing or maiming five of the nine crew. *LCS 91*, a support craft, broached in the heavy seas, 'her stern rose so that her propellers churned the air',[3] whereupon she too was holed by machine gun fire. The vessel was abandoned and sank. Omens were not good. Headquarters US 1st Infantry Division aboard the command ship USS *Ancon* reported 'a brilliant white flare seen near Pointe du Hoc'.[4] The Germans had guessed the likely objective. 'We were supposed to land five minutes after the bomb-

## The Ranger Assault on Pointe du Hoc

Lieutenant-Colonel Rudder's 2nd Ranger Battalion assault force mistook Pointe et Raz de la Percée west of Omaha, as the objective. Surprise and two boats were lost in the resulting change of course against wind, tide and German fire. A desperate medieval attack was conducted against the east side of the feature, late and contrary to the plan, from one direction. German defences were sited to withstand an assault from the landward side. A precarious hold was wrested from the enemy, but the gun emplacements were found to be empty.

A + B did not receive success signal and continued to Omaha

A + B to Omaha

C To Vierville (Omaha)

Wrong direction lined up on Pte et Raz de la Percée

Two boats sunk

Pointe et Raz de la Percée

Planned Approach to include A + B if successful

Against wind/tide and parallel to German cliff emplacements

2 RANGERS (-)

D Coy (-)

E Coy

F Coy

D Coy (plan)

OP

861
862
888
722
668
858
887
884
883

Mines

To Grandcamp-Vierville road

**Key:**

| | |
|---|---|
| Gun emplacements | |
| Machine Gun | |
| AA Gun | |
| Trenches | |
| Wire | |
| Strong-pts | |

ing and shelling ceased', said Sergeant Lou Lisco. 'So we were half an hour late and the Germans were waiting for us, so all hell broke loose'.[5]

A bizarre medieval scene was now enacted as German soldiers appeared on the cliff edge, preparing to 'repel boarders'. One Ranger standing on the ramp peering through the smoke exclaimed 'my God, they are up there waiting for us!'[6] Two destroyers, HMS *Talybont* and USS *Satterlee*, raked the cliff-top with fire, silencing one small gun and dispersing many of the German infantry. Due to the revised direction of approach, all nine of Rudder's LCAs touched down, one after the other, on the east side of the Pointe at 07.10 along a 500-metre front. There was now no hope of dividing the defence by assaulting from both sides.

Some 200 Rangers struggled ashore onto a narrow pebble beach pock-marked with craters. Stumbling into the water-filled holes, they swarmed to the base of the sticky clay-covered cliff, assailed by machine gun fire and German infantry lobbing 'potato-masher' grenades from above. A series of rasping 'coughs' heralded flights of grappling hooks powered by rocket projectiles, that flung up web-like strands attaching to the cliff edge. Ropes soaked during the run-in to the beach, caused a large number to fall short. None of those fired from *LCA 888* reached the top. Rangers began free climbing. Further ropes snaked up the cliff face, propelled by rockets in twos and threes, and began to hold. Over zealous German infantry, leaning out to shoot were tumbled down from the cliffs by fire below. Grenades were rolled down instead. The preparatory bombardment aided the climb by collapsing sections of the cliff edge. This formed a 40ft mound in front of Colonel Rudder's craft which enabled Rangers to scramble up and negotiate the remainder of the cliff, section by section, using a 16ft ladder and toggle rope. Further cliff edges blasted out, reduced the slope and height of the climb at other points, giving cover from enfilade fire. Free climbing Rangers struggled upward using a combination of bayonet and toggle rope. Sticky-wet clay reduced the friction grip on ropes, causing soldiers to slide down uncontrollably, impeding the progress of those clawing their way upward. Rangers were blasted from tenuous fly-holds by the concussive impact from grenades, spun off by small-arms fire or cut ropes.

The German defenders were surprised by this battalion strong 'commando operation', as their defence positions had been configured for a landward defence. Assaulting the cliffs had not seemed a viable proposition. Headquarters 352nd Division, having difficulty explaining the loss of this seemingly impregnable position, claimed: 'the enemy had gained the cliffs by shooting projectiles which released, in each case on detonation, a rope ladder which dropped free'.[7] Desperately trying to contain the inexorable creeping fingers of Rangers inching up the cliff, German infantry were increasingly obliged to expose themselves to fire, to get at them. Both sides fought with the certainty that failure would mean extinction.

Ingenuity led to the employment of any means, however bizarre, to reach the cliff top. Three surviving DUKWs waddled up onto the narrow stony beach, but were prevented by craters from moving close in to the cliff edge. With grotesque deliberation, fire ladders began to slowly extend before the startled gaze of the Germans. The first, resting at an acute angle below the cliff top was made further untenable by the wave motion on the rocking DUKW. A furious response greeted the appearance of the second, which was steadily raised to full height with Staff Sergeant William Stivison raking the opposition with twin Lewis guns. Stivison, struggling to prevent himself pitching from the ladder now 80ft high, weaved and bobbed with the motion of the tossing craft by as much as 20ft from side to side. Tracer rounds could clearly be seen flashing all around him, but none found their target. Private John Gilhooly, gazing up from the DUKW below, marvelled that he still lived, thinking his Sergeant 'looked very much like a circus performer at the time'.[8]

Within 15 to 30 minutes the Rangers had gained the cliff edge. Below were some 15 Rangers lying dead or wounded on the beach, or hanging grotesquely from the web-like laddering and toggle ropes adorning the cliff face. All the attacking force numbering 140 men, except for the injured, headquarters and mortarmen, were on the top. The pitted lunar landscape confronting them momentarily confused navigation. But as planned, small groups gaining the top moved off at once toward objectives, without waiting for the rest of the boat group, or forming into sections and platoons. With at least 20 such groups fanning out as soon as they reached the end of the web, it was almost impossible for the Germans to distinguish the line of attack and organise to meet it. A series of vicious small-unit actions now developed. The massive undamaged concrete observation post on the edge of the escarpment was despatched by bazooka. The first round fired by Sergeant Yardley, who had landed from *LCA 861*, struck the edge of the slit, blasting scabs of concrete in all directions. The second entered the chamber and despatched the opposition with a deep resonant hollow ring. Fighting in this surreal landscape was so confusing, that 12 Rangers, late-comers, diverted by the command group to deal with an anti-aircraft gun to the west of the position, were overwhelmed and captured by a German counter-attack without anyone realising. So torn up was the ground that the Ranger command post in a crater only 100yds away was unaware what had happened until a survivor returned. Casualties began to mount as the Rangers pushed inland. Fifteen were killed and wounded before elements of 'D' and 'E' Company reached the main road at Le Guay shortly after 08.00. 'F' Company moved up on the left. Casemates and open gun emplacements were penetrated during the contested advance and found to be empty.

German infantry were increasingly obliged to expose themselves to fire to get at the Rangers.

Pointe du Hoc is a conspicuous knife-edged outcrop. The 'Jib' observed from the German-occupied cliff positions. *US Army*

Free-climbing Rangers struggled upward using a combination of bayonet and toggle rope.

'Further ropes snaked up the cliff-face propelled by rockets in twos and threes, and began to hold.' Pre-assault training.

The whole point of the mission appeared negated.

Sergeant Len Lommell, well appreciating why, later explained:

*They were being bombed silly with thousands and thousands of bombs from aerial bombardment and ships also, so they moved their guns in anticipation, maybe weeks before D-Day — and to an alternate position.*

By 09.00 patrols were being despatched to make doubly sure they were not still in the area. 'It was just pure luck that we happened upon the guns in a little valley', continued Lommell, 'and incidently there were no shell or bomb craters around their alternate positions. So you see, they had wisely moved them.' It was a tantalising sight, giving at last some point to their steadily mounting losses. Lommel and his men could hardly believe their good fortune.

*And there they all were, in camouflaged positions pointing towards Utah beach, with all their shells and everything in readiness to be fired, and their men, about one hundred or so Germans in a field, being reorganized by their leaders and listening to their officers. I went down into the emplacement and took my Thermite grenades and laid them in the hinges and traversing mechanism, anything that could be melted by a thermite grenade, to make it inoperable.[9]*

The guns were finally despatched.

Within an hour of the assault, Infantry Regiment 916, responsible for the defence of this sector of the coast, telephoned Headquarters 352nd Division, advising that 'weak enemy units had penetrated Pointe du Hoc. A platoon from the 9th Company 726th Regiment had been despatched to counter-attack.' Two hours later came the realisation that the enemy occupation force was two companies strong. There was still some wonderment from the IIIrd Battalion 726th Regiment, the reserve force tasked to contain the incursion, over the 'special shells' that had produced the rope laddering enabling the cliffs to be climbed. 'Available reserves have been despatched to Pointe du Hoc to restore the situation.' By 12.25 counter-attacks were under way. 'The strong-point garrison ... is surrounded by two companies'.[10] The *Stossreserve* from the IIIrd Battalion 726th Regiment were confident, as they moved up toward Le Guay that they would 'clean up' the situation.

Lieutenant Colonel Rudder sent out a plea for assistance at the same time, by radio and pigeon.

*Located Pointe du Hoc — Mission accomplished — Need ammunition and reinforcements — Many casualties.*

They had been beset by communications difficulties throughout the day. Not until 15.00 did the 116th Regiment respond from Omaha, stating its inability to deci-pher the message; which was repeated. The USS *Satterlee* standing off Pointe du Hoc was able to respond with a brief message from General Heubner, commanding the 1st Division — 'no reinforcements available'.[11] By last light Rudder's position was critical. One third of his force was dead or wounded and ammunition low. He was dependent on relief from Omaha.

## Coming ashore on 'Easy Red' ... Omaha 06.30 - 08.30.

Press photographer Robert Capa[1] approaching 'Easy Red' with 'E' Company from the 16th RCT had no conception of what lay ahead. 'The first empty barge, which had already unloaded its troops on the beach, passed us on the way back to the *Chase* and the negro boatswain gave us a happy grin and the "V" sign.' France 'looked sordid and uninviting'. His remarkable series of photographs taken from the ramp of his landing craft, to the beach, are snapshots of the same field of vision American soldiers had, coming ashore at Omaha.

*The boatswain lowered the steel-covered barge front, and there between the grotesque designs of steel obstacles sticking out of the water, was a thin line of sand covered with smoke — our Europe, the "Easy Red" beach.*

All that is missing from the pictures is the deafening 'cracking' of machine gun fire, explosions, screams, bellowing landing craft engines and the sobbing of the wounded interspersed with the sound of surf. The pervading smell was that of diesel from crippled landing craft, cordite and oily smoke, and the tang of the sea. The first blurred image [Photo 1] taken from the ramp shows a glimpse of heavily laden infantrymen scrambling — thigh-deep — through the surf, toward the vague outline of three DD tanks distinguishable in the distance. Capa recalled 'a German machine gun spitting bullets around the barge'. One man is down, already wounded, and starts to crawl toward the Czech 'hedgehog' beach obstacle to his front. 'The water was cold', Capa wrote, 'and the beach was still more than a hundred yards away'.

The next image [Photo 2] reveals the substantial number of men who have reached the nearest DD tank, crowding its left side. Fire is coming from WN65, the German strong-point blocking the St Laurent ravine to the right. 'Bullets tore holes in the water around me', relates Capa, 'and I made for the nearest steel obstacle'. Running back toward him to the right of his field of vision is a combat engineer, carrying explosives, engaged in obstacle clearing. The troops on exiting his boat are ankle deep in water, a radio operator among them, the man in the immediate foreground has a full sling bag — probably anti-tank grenades — over his left shoulder, others carry satchel charges. Nearing the DD tanks,

Photo 3: Nearing the DD tanks. *Magnum Photos Inc*

Photo 1: 'The first blurred image.' *Magnum Photos Inc*

Photo 2: Crossing the sand bar. *Magnum Photos Inc*

Photo 4: Pause before running for tank '10' extrem left. *Magnum Photos Inc*

which now number four, the third frame [Photo 3] reveals the infantry, cowering from the fire to the right, are waist deep in the deepening water beyond the sandbank. Capa reached his steel obstacle in the shallow water. He was intent on taking good pictures. 'It was still very early and very grey for good pictures', he decided, 'but the grey water and grey sky made the little men, dodging under the surrealistic designs of Hitler's anti-invasion ... [obstacles] very effective'. Capa joined a soldier who fired his rifle 'without much aiming at the smoke-ridden beach' before he moved forward 'and left the obstacle to me'.

Lieutenant John Spaulding landed from another boat nearby. 'We headed ashore and the small arms fire became noticeable', he recalled.[2] Although he could see craft to his left, there were none to the right. They were the right forward element of the 1st Division. Spaulding said 'we had seen some tanks coming in, but didn't know what they were'. His men spread out in 'V' formation about 50yds wide. 'There was soon a noticeable decline of sand beneath our feet and we were soon over our heads, so we tried to swim.' Sand bars caused difficulties. Spaulding lost his rifle and began to be swept leftward by a strong undercurrent. 'We lost none of our men, but only because they helped each other or because they got rid of their equipment', he said. His Sergeant, Streczyk, and a medic, were struggling through the water nearby with an 18ft extension ladder. Spaulding having trouble staying afloat grabbed for it. 'Lieutenant we don't need any help', shouted Streczyk, but the officer's reaction was, 'hell I was busy trying to get help not to give it'. The ladder was abandoned. Now able to touch the bottom, the water reached mouth height. 'I had swallowed about half of the ocean and felt like I was going to choke.' The wade ashore had cost them all their heavy weapons, 'we lost our mortar, most of the mortar ammunition, one of our two bazookas, [and] much of the bazooka ammunition'. Finally gaining the beach 'they were too waterlogged to run, but they went as fast as they could'. They were almost overwhelmed by fatigue. Finding a blind spot to enemy fire, they pushed on to the shale, looking 'as if they were walking in the face of a real strong wind.'[3]

Capa behind his obstacle 'finished my pictures' and became distracted again by his surroundings, the sea he noticed 'was cold in my trousers'. Peering at the scene he had already recorded [Photos 2, 3 and 4], he could see there were at least two platoons (50 or more men) sheltering on the lee side of now five identifiable DD tanks. Turrets are facing half-right towards the direction of enemy fire. Forward of the tanks, clusters of men are visibly taking shelter behind the dark grey incline of the shingle strip bordering the beach. There are further ragged lines of men, above and beyond them, behind the sea wall. Injured soldiers are floating in the surf, and in some cases being pulled into cover by half-submerged soldiers sheltering behind Czech hedgehogs in the fore-

ground. Capa himself is filming from the prone horizontal. Clearly visible in the background are the German-held bluffs, their outline broken by small copses of trees.

The tanks ahead had apparently been disabled by enemy fire. Capa, anxious to secure better cover, reluctantly 'tried to move away from my steel pole, but the bullets chased me back every time'. Fifty yards ahead 'one of our half-burnt out amphibious tanks [number 10] stuck out of the water and offered me my next cover'. Abandoning his 'elegant raincoat' he made a run for it, and 'between floating bodies I reached it' and 'paused for a few more pictures'.

German fire intensified as Capa 'gathered my guts for the last jump to the beach'. Any prospect of success seemed increasingly remote as 'now the Germans played on all their instruments and I could not find any hole between the shells and bullets that blocked the last twenty-five yards to the beach'. He reached it, but conditions did not improve; a view shared by a Lieutenant with whom he had played Poker the night before on the USS *Chase*. Nothing could be seen ahead, although the young officer whispered cryptically 'I see my ma on the front porch, waving my insurance policy'. Capa saw the irony of taking cover on a beach which doubtless had been a 'cheap resort' for vacationing holiday-makers, but now 'it was the ugliest beach in the whole world'. Their situation appeared untenable.

*Exhausted from the water and the fear, we lay flat on a small strip of wet sand between the sea and the barbed wire. The slant of the beach gave us some protection, so long as we lay flat, from the machine gun and rifle bullets, but the tide pushed us against the barbed wire, where the guns were enjoying open season.*

He took out his second Contax camera and began to take more photographs, just above the surface of the water 'without raising my head'. Wavering shots show a fresh perspective [Photos 5 and 6] to his left flank. Behind a phalanx of stake landing craft obstacles interspersed with Czech scrap-iron 'hedgehogs', troops are lying prostrate in a foot of water. They resemble a khaki slurry being washed ashore by the surf. The stakes follow the line of the sand bar. Fire appears to be coming across Capa's right shoulder. Men are attempting to move forward in rushes. Two may be seen [Photo 6] to rise, stagger a few paces forward, before splashing back into the water.

Lieutenant Carroll, having survived the ordeal of his sunken landing craft had reached this line of obstacles. 'The tide was moving us so rapidly', he said ...

*We would grab out at some of those underwater obstructions and mines built on telephone poles and girders, and hang on. We'd take cover, then make a dash through the surf to the next one, fifty feet beyond.*

They offered paltry cover, so they had to move on. This scene, encapsulated in Capa's photographs, was described by Carroll.

*The men would line up behind those poles. They'd say, "You go — you go — you go," and then it got so bad that everybody just had to go anyway, because the waves were hitting with such intensity on these things.[4]*

Capa filmed the 16th RCT crawling ashore like mud-coloured prehistoric amphibians. Men weighted down by packs are sprawled full length, crawling through freezing water. Intermixed within this flotsam are human remains, wreckage, helmets and hundreds of discarded life jackets, all piling up into a disturbing scum on the water's edge. The stench of diesel fumes and smoke is all pervading. Behind the amphibians lurking in the water are the shadowy outlines of more landing craft, ramps lowered, running in. These can be discerned in the background murk, drifting left to right. Capa commented:

*Shooting from the sardine's angle, the foreground of my pictures was filled with wet boots and green faces. Above the boots and faces, my picture frames were filled with shrapnel smoke; burnt tanks and sinking barges formed my background.*

The water level was steadily rising with the tide. A sudden surge of water caused him to turn and freeze the blurred image [Photo 7] of a helmeted soldier, anxiously kicking himself through the water, supported by a section of shrapnel-torn rubber dinghy. He holds a life jacket to his front. The picture, hastily snapped, is indistinct. Capa was under pressure. 'The next mortar shell fell between the barbed wire and the sea, and every piece of shrapnel found a man's body.' Increasingly unnerved, the heavy fire was affecting his concentration. 'The next shell fell even closer. I didn't dare to take my eyes off the finder of my Contax and frantically shot frame after frame.'

Looking behind, his pictures pan from the blurred image of the half-submerged soldier struggling by, to record the arrival of yet another wave of landing craft. [Photo 8] Their labouring engines attempting to negotiate the outer obstacles has attracted his attention. In the foreground, behind two Czech hedgehogs, is an officer and a group of infantrymen under cover. Around them, discarded life jackets, packs, equipment and other flotsam is being washed toward the beach. Capa zooms to this pathetic party struggling for survival. [Photo 9] One lies face down in the water. Behind both obstacles are three to four men sheltering in its fragile lee. Seven landing craft are now in view; and troops are disembarking in water over their heads, struggling ashore neck-deep in water.

*Half a minute later, my camera jammed — my roll was finished. I reached in my bag for a new roll, and my wet,*

shaking hands ruined the roll before I could insert it in the camera. I paused for a moment .... and then I had it bad.

Capa's nerves were at breaking point. He simply had to get off the beach.[5]

## 'When, and from whom will the counter-attack ... come?'

Directly opposite Capa, the German defenders of Infantry Regiment 726 were beginning to feel the pressure. Strong-points held on grimly, aware they would only survive an assault of this scale if planned counter-attacks materialised. Oberst Fritz Ziegelman, the Chief of Staff of 352nd Division, had seen the extent of the landings from strong-point WN76, atop the cliffs at Pointe et Raz de la Percée at the western end of Omaha. 'The view ... will remain in my memory forever', he later wrote, 'the sea was like a picture of the "Kiel review of the fleet".'[1] The telephone log at Headquarters 352nd Division dramatically recorded the ebb and flow of battle.

The 916th Regiment opposite the 116th RCT on the western side of Omaha had checked the initial assault waves. It reported at 07.05 'that a 50-strong enemy force had landed next to WN68 east of Vierville'.[2] Their achievement was the blazing, smoking flotsam strewn along this side of the beach. The commander of WN76 observing the low water mark near St Laurent and Vierville, could see right across 'Charlie', 'Dog' and 'Easy Green' in the distance.

*The enemy is in search of cover behind the coastal obstacles. A great many vehicles — among them ten tanks — stand burning at the beach. The obstacle demolition squads have given up their activity. Debarkation from the landing boats has ceased, the boats keep further seawards. The fire of our strong points and artillery was well-placed and has inflicted considerable casualties among the enemy. A great many wounded and dead lie on the beach.[3]*

The situation opposite the 726th Regiment covering 'Easy Red' and 'Fox Green' was similar. 'WN60 was engaging 40 men and a tank which had landed north east of Colleville.' By 07.20 landings were coming ashore along the whole eastern sector, reported by Oberleutnant Frerking in strong-point WN61 and engaged by artillery. Even at this stage, one hour into the assault, German troops manning strong-points were being attrited by successive enemy waves dashing against them. Telephone contact was intermittent. Shouted messages were barely discernible over the background distorted metallic sounds of battle. The 726th Regiment on the east side of Omaha was in difficulties, as the log reveals:

*07.20: Between WN61 and WN62 enemy in company*

*Photo 5:* Phalanx of stakes. *Magnum Photos Inc*

*Photo 6:* Men attempting to move forward in rushes. *Magnum Photos Inc*

*Photo 7:* Helmeted soldier kicking himself through the water. *Magnum Photos Inc*

*Photo 8:* Another landing craft wave.*Magnum Photos Inc*

*Photo 9:* Final zoom image.*Magnum Photos Inc*

*Right:* 'Debarkation from the landing boats has ceased.'

*Below:* 'Something like 35 tanks are attacking...towards Arromanches.' Allied DD tanks ashore and advancing.

*strength are on the beach, being engaged by our own artillery. The 88mm flak in WN61 has been knocked out by a direct hit.*

*07.25: One company is attacking in front of WN60 and 62. Four further boats have landed in front of WN61. One boat has been shot in flames by the 50mm gun. The enemy has penetrated WN62 and at the same time WN61 is being attacked from the beach in front and the rear. Telephone connection with the Ist Battalion 726th Regiment in Port-en-Bessin has been destroyed.[4]*

Headquarters 352nd Division, acutely aware of the grumbling, crackling conflict beneath the columns of smoke rising above the general obscuration forward on the beaches, pushed and remonstrated with despairing regimental commanders; willing success, but lacking the local reserves to create it. Oberst Ziegelman's response to the 726th Regiment's difficulties was simply to grip the commander.

*Question — Chief-of-Staff to Grenadier Regiment 726: when, and from whom will the counter-attack that will throw back the enemy between WN61 and 62 come?[5]*

Rhetoric alone would not win this battle. Ziegelman was obliged to report to Corps, that between the two strong-points 'north east of Colleville, 100 to 200 enemy had achieved a penetration. The enemy was not yet through in the Vierville inlet, but an even larger number of landing craft were approaching the coast at speed.' He asked for permission to detach one battalion, (IInd Battalion 915th Regiment), from the corps reserve, the Kampfgruppe 'Meyer', already confusingly diverted from its original anti-airborne sweep, to counter-attack the developing gap between WN60 and 62.

Infantry Regiment 916 covering 'Charlie' and 'Dog' was also under threat. Ten minutes later Ziegelman heard:

*Three tanks had climbed up onto the flat ground north east of Vierville near WN70; three tanks had penetrated WN66, and we have heard from WN62 that the upper gun casemate has been taken out by a direct hit.[6]*

Inside WN62 Unteroffizier Severloh by now had fired thousands of rounds. When the shell entered the bunker, shrapnel and concrete struck him in the face, and tore off the fore-sight of his MG42. Wiping the blood from his face, he carried on, estimating the strike with tracer. There would be an eventual retribution once his red-hot flashing signature was spotted. Frerking the 352nd Artillery OP officer had been warned 'to go steady with the ammunition' by his supporting Ist Battery inland. One lorry-load of fresh ammunition had already disintegrated approaching the gun emplacement, struck by a 16in naval shell.[7]

Problems were piling up when Oberst Ziegelman, scraping resources together for his proposed local counter-attack, received an electrifying message from Infantry Regiment 726. His immediate difficulties paled into insignificance as the content of the report became clear. It was 07.57.

*Between strong-points WN35 and 36 with our right neighbour 716 Infantry Division, there are already 30 tanks ashore.*

Fifteen minutes later came the confirmation. 'Something like 35 tanks are attacking over WN35 and 36 towards Arromanches.'[8] A breakthrough had occurred.

# CHAPTER 10

# TANKS FROM THE SEA

*'As it rolled forward the tracks kept coming higher; and then as it got to the edge of the water, down came the screen and there was the gun. This was a terrific surprise and shock.'*

*Canadian Tank Lieutenant*

## 'Out Ramps!' ... Sword 07.30.

Stephen Sykes in an LCT off Sword Beach noticed:

*The Normandy coast was slowly changing from a dim line on the horizon into recognisable features, the undulations of the country behind the beaches visible at first, then blocks of woodland, and finally the villas, the Ouistreham lighthouse and church tower all began to appear as they looked on the wave-top photographs.*

The noise from the naval bombardment was deafening as the DD tanks from 'A' and 'B' Squadrons 13/18th Hussars were launched into choppy water, in the dreary light of a grey morning. Lance Corporal Patrick Hennessey heard the metallic cue over the ship's tannoy: 'Down door, No 1'. Tank engines started. The bizarre looking rectangular shaped vehicles nosed into the heaving swell, and slipped suddenly from the ramps. 'As we righted in the water I could just see the shoreline some 5,000yd away'; Hennessey recalled, 'it seemed a very long distance and in a DD tank, in that sea, it certainly was!'[2] Sergeant Howard Clewlow of the same unit said 'you pulled a lever and it turned these two propellers and you went around 5kts an hour and when you got heavy seas you really rocked'.[3] Crews anxiously remained on deck, apart from drivers who crouched nervously in driving compartments. The driver was the key man. Should the engine stop, they stood no chance of survival. They made slow headway towards the beach.

'The noise seemed to increase' noticed Hennessey, 'and the sea appeared even rougher from this low point of view, with only a flimsy canvas screen between us and the waves'. Water slopped over the edge of the screens, keeping co-drivers manning bilge pumps hard at work. Everybody's fear was the assault craft coming up rapidly behind. 'Anything that faltered just had to be run

down', was Trooper Mawson's experience,[4] echoed by Sergeant Clewlow. 'The real panic came when the other stuff started to back up on us.' Lance Corporal Hennessey observed the large bulk of an LCT bearing down on the Squadron's second-in-command, who had just cleared the ramp. Struck by the bows the DD tank was forced under the surface, disappearing beneath the hull. Only one head was seen bobbing in the water. Captain Denny survived. Thirty-four tanks launched, and 32 rectangular screens could just be discerned, looking like black driftwood, bucking and tossing their way towards the beach. Hennessey, very much on edge described how:

*We battled on towards the shore through the rough sea. We were buffeted about unmercifully, plunging into the troughs of the waves and somehow wallowing up again to the crests. The wind, fortunately was behind us, and this helped a little.*

They were under way for an hour. 'It was a struggle to keep the tank on course, but gradually the shoreline became more distinct and before long we could see the line of houses which were our targets.' Every wave slapping the canvas screens, taunted and reminded crews of their precarious situation. Tracks gained contact with shelving sand, and the strange shapes began to rise out of the water, before the startled gaze of open-mouthed German gunners. Struts were broken and screens collapsed one by one as soon as the bases emerged clear of the water. German defenders had not anticipated tanks until well after an initial infantry assault. They did not have the resources to meet them. The squat grey shapes lurching crab-like ashore along the beaches, with guns traversing in support, were harbingers of doom. Infantry landing craft were soon among them.

DD tanks were to engage enemy pill boxes, while ahead of the infantry, further specialist support armour — Crab Flail tanks — were to advance up beaches in echelon, clearing mines. On reaching sea walls, AVREs would lay bridges up them, providing a plank to enable accompanying DD tanks to climb up. These having mounted the wall would continue to engage pill boxes at

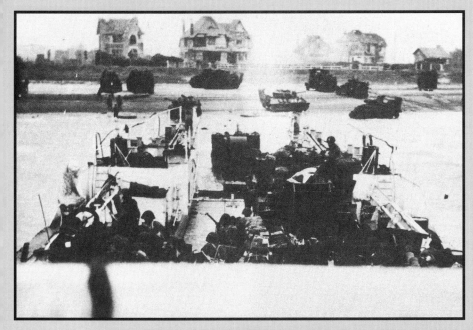

*Left:* The sudden arrival of tanks on the British beaches was the key to eventual success. Tanks and armoured vehicles disembarking near La Brèche.

*Centre:* They were approaching the 'Atlantic Wall', an edifice they imagined would instantly spew out death and destruction. An LCI prepares for the command 'Out Ramps' moments before touchdown.

*Below:* 'Some of the men were talking, some smoking, some vomiting...the slow wallowing motion of the craft eased' as they came into shallow water. An LCA just off the beach.

131

close range. Other AVREs were to follow with fascines, to fill anti-tank ditches. Those AVREs which had working Petard mortars would then advance, lobbing high explosive demolition charges through bunker embrasures to destroy any remaining pill boxes. A sequential arrival of these equipments in the appropriate order was rarely achieved. On Sword rough seas slowed LCTs, so that many landed together with the infantry, or shortly after. But armoured support was quickly in place.

> *"75, HE, Action — Traverse right, steady, on. 300 — white fronted house — first floor window, centre."*
> *"On."*
> *"Fire!"*

'Within a minute of dropping our screen', Hennessey reported, 'we had fired our first shot in anger.'[5]

The sudden arrival of tanks on the British beaches was the key to eventual success. The engine deck of Lance Corporal Hennessey's tank was engulfed by a wave, and the engine spluttered and cut out. The guns were fought on for as long as they were able before, finally flooded, Hennessey and his crew baled out, and reached the beach after launching a dinghy. By this time the 22nd Dragoons had arrived on LCTs. These and further specialist armour poured ashore. Major Tim Wheway recorded his touchdown at 07.25, churning into the beach at such a speed 'the impact nearly shoots the tanks through the doors'. Thereupon:

> *The flails stream out in 3 feet of water, followed by the AVREs. We are met by terrific shell, mortar and 88 and 75 AP and small arms fire at 300 yards range … several tanks are hit as the landing craft doors go down.*

The tanks surged forward through the water and began engaging concrete gun emplacements. 'Tanks are brewing up right and left' Wheway observed as the Crab tanks began flailing. Marine George Foster just off the beach in *LCF 36* providing supporting fire watched the tanks progressing up the beach.

> *About two minutes later a tank was hit by shell fire, the turret blew off from the caterpillars leaving just the wheels tearing along the beach.*[6]

Three and a half hours after the landings, only 11 of 26 Flail tanks were left in Wheway's unit. It was a determined assault, checked by bitter resistance.

> *The AVREs follow the flails and the bridging AVREs dropped their bridges, but the crews jump out to make them fast and in doing so are killed or wounded and the tanks receive direct hits and are brewed up. German soldiers rush from the houses shouting and firing as they come and soon the beach is strewn with the dead and wounded of our own and enemy troops.*[7]

At 07.30 infantry landing craft deposited the leading companies of the 1st South Lancashire Regiment on the right, and the 2nd East Yorks on the left of the beach between La Brèche and Lion-sur-Mer. These men were enduring perhaps the most traumatic experience of their lives. They were approaching the vaunted Atlantic Wall, an edifice they imagined would instantly spew out death and destruction. German fire was at first sporadic. Marine Neale, a deck-hand aboard a Landing Craft Assault (LCA), recalled the impact this had upon the Army men about to disembark.

> *I heard someone in the craft say "O God". Many of the lads had been sick during the journey and the stench in the craft was fairly high. It is strange how emotions transfer themselves. I heard someone sobbing and felt the urge to do the same, but just then, machine guns started to fire and you could hear the bullets whipping by.*[8]

Men were keyed up, praying it would be 'all right', desperately trying to control their natural emotions, hoping they would not appear foolish in front of their fellows. 'Everybody had butterflies in their stomach' recalled one soldier during the run-in to the beach.

> *Everyone was quiet, not their usual jovial selves and I suppose everyone had their own anxieties — as you normally did; realising what a great Armada it was and if we should fail, what a chaos it would be.*[9]

The build-up of tension palpably increased the nearer the craft approached the shore. In one infantry unit:

> *Some of the men were talking, some smoking, some vomiting quietly into brown bags of grease-proof paper. The wind was bringing to them now the sounds of shells bursting ashore. Each man could feel each thudding detonation somewhere inside him. The talking stopped. Men took up their rifles and machine carbines; there was the click of bolts being drawn and rammed home. The slow wallowing motion of the craft eased; they were coming into shallower water.*[10]

There was already a mass of floating rubbish interspersed with bodies inshore. Marine Neale saw the ramp door drop. German fire had now intensified. There was about 20-30 yds of water-covered beach to negotiate:

> *The lads left the craft knee deep in water holding their rifles above their heads. I saw several stagger and fall and can remember thinking "God help you poor bastards …"*[11]

All along Sword the initial infantry assault waves of the 8th Brigade 3rd Division poured ashore. German artillery fire intensified still further. Private Jim Cartwright of the South Lancs Regiment said:

*Well — the shells were dropping in the water, and I don't think you can imagine the whiplash, the shock wave coming through the water. As soon as I hit the beach I wanted to go. I wanted to move, get away from that water. I don't know — I think I went across that beach like a hare.*

The intensity of fire was variable. Further along the beach, another assaulting soldier claimed 'it was much less than we expected', because the air and sea bombardment had 'really done a job, and rather stunned the Germans to begin with. It only hotted up when we got close to the beach'.[12] Marine Neale's LCA had difficulty extricating itself from the sand. They were momentarily grounded. 'There was an explosion in front of us and the bow of the craft reared up in the air and the boat began swinging broadside on to the beach.' Helpless, 'I began to feel panic as fear welled up inside me', but another explosion floated the boat off again. They were damaged beneath the water-line. The crew tried desperately to get the craft out into open water again, baling and pumping out an in-rush of water as they tried to get under way.

*This was it, I thought. This is where it is all going to end. I felt the tears rolling down my face and was weeping quite unashamedly working in an automatic fashion. I felt totally isolated from my companions and completely resigned myself to the fact I was going to die.*

As they passed a control boat, they were instructed by loud-hailer to return to the beach. 'Get ...ed, you stupid bastard' responded his sergeant. This completely relaxed the tension. Neale 'was laughing and crying hysterically, in fact we all became a little unhinged, forgetting completely our plight'.[13]

The brutal reality of suffering casualties close-in was a distant, albeit dramatic spectacle to subsequent waves well able to see much of the activity occurring ahead. 'The first ones in, especially, were taking heavy punishment', remarked one soldier, 'and were being blown to pieces, but as there were such a lot of them, obviously quite a few were getting through'.[14] Naval officer Douglas Reeman, observing off Sword in an MTB, likened the sea-borne assault to a dramatic cavalry charge.

*All the while the lines of landing-ships sailed on, some breaking away in smaller formations to head for their allotted beaches. Shell-bursts hurled towering columns of water all around them. It was heart stopping to see them moving steadily through the smoke and falling spray. Nothing it seemed, could stop them.*[15]

Cruising in depth to the initial assault waves came Royal Marine Commandos from the 1st Special Service (Commando) Brigade. They were in LCIs (Landing Craft Infantry) unlike the initial assault waves in LCAs. The vessels were larger, more cumbersome — some 20ft above the water-line — and slower to unload. This should have made little difference as they were follow-on troops. As they approached the beach, however, the German strong-points at La Brèche and Hermanville were still firing, and formidably intact.

Combat photographer Sergeant Ian Grant was on board with Lord Lovat's 45 Commando, already filming landing craft on the run-in to the beach. Under a grey overcast sky, with ensigns and halyards flapping in the strong wind, the LCIs broke line and in clouds of spray, began to buffet their way in towards the beach in extended line. [Photo 1 and 2] Grant recalled the impact of the metallic announcement over the tannoy that the South Lancs and East Yorks had made a successful landing. 'Everybody cheered and laughed, but this gradually subsided as we realised we now had about 45 minutes to beaching.' There was no sign of nervousness 'although one or two hastily knelt with heads bent and murmured their private prayers'.[16]

Commanding *LCI(S)516* was Lieutenant Commander Denis Glover carrying 104 men of the same Commando on board. He was gazing anxiously ahead, checking constantly for navigation fixing points. 'Hello, splashes,' he remarked. 'Not all ours then. That destroyer is firing as if it's had a fit, yes, and someone's been badly knocked about over there'. It was as apparent to him as Douglas Reeman that these landings, follow-on or not, would be under fire. Reeman observed 'lines of red and green tracer ripped across the water, and were answered immediately by the destroyers and gunboats'. Landing craft were still being engaged by pill boxes at the water's edge. Reeman was mesmerised by the images.

*Another, and then another of them was hit, vivid blobs of tracer licking out from the shore, the shells shrieking low over the surface in straight lethal lines. Flat trajectory cannon fire, probably from some anti-tank guns close to the shore.*

Glover felt vulnerable. 'There were 4,000 gallons of high-octane petrol under my deck.' Sergeant Grant, alarmed by reports of flamethrowers on the beach, trying to judge distance, could clearly see the coastline ahead, perhaps one mile away. 'At the speed we were moving' he thought apprehensively, 'they were only a few minutes away'. Lieutenant Commander Glover was lining up for the beach run, and conferring with a Marine Lieutenant Colonel on board:

*That's surely the chateau, Colonel, through the smoke. A cable to starboard of it is our limit. Can you see the modern villa? Not there. That should be it, Sir, that white ruin, what do you think?*

*Above:* All along Sword Beach the initial infantry assault waves of the 8th Brigade 3rd Division poured ashore, under fire. The soldier bottom left has been hit in the face.

*Photo 1:* The LCI squadron carrying 45 Commando. Lord Lovat's craft is in the foreground. *IWM*

*Photo 2:* With ensigns flapping the LCIs broke line in clouds of spray and began to buffet their way toward the beach in extended line. Note the overcast sky. *IWM*

Grant was filming everything that was going on around him. A tense silence prevailed on board. Two naval ratings moved into position behind the port and starboard Oerlikon guns — one had earlier brought him a bacon sandwich. Turning his camera to the in board starboard side of the craft, he began to film the waiting Commandos. 'Their faces registered complete calm and a latent toughness, and I wished I could feel the same way.' The Oerlikon gunner and soldiers stare at the beach coming up ahead, screwing eyes into the wind, trying to see through the smoke. [Photo 3] Soldiers are nervous, breathing heavily, trying to control their emotions. Staring eyes flicker from side to side, taking in the breathtaking spectacle.[17] [Photo 4] Nearby were a group of LCAs, belonging to 4 Commando, also running into the beach. Lieutenant Murdoch McDougall commanding 'F' Troop, looked round the boat:

*Thirty-two pairs of eyes seemed to be fixed upon me. Panic seized me. My mouth was dry. God don't let me do anything idiotic. Please let me seem normal.*

Private McVeigh his Bren gunner turned a green face toward him and said 'for Chrissake get me ashore!' which made him feel better for 'someone was in worse shape than myself'.[18]

With 10 minutes to go Grant recalled the 'hellish thunder' of broadside after broadside belching out from escorting destroyers. 'It seemed like every gun the Royal Navy possessed opened up at once.' Glover steering LCI(S)516 had 'eyes for everything, eyes for nothing'. He was totally intent on identifying the correct beach, which 'looms close, maybe a mile'. Before him stretched a series of threatening surreal images. 'Wrecked landing craft everywhere, a flurry of propellers in the savage surf and among those wicked obstructions.' They were under fire. Grant 'knew that somebody was taking umbrage. Whining salvoes were passing overhead and gouging the water nearby.' The nearest LCI was suddenly hit, caught by his camera, retiring from the beach as their own LCI(S) sped onward in the foreground. [Photo 5] 'Diesel fuel burns black' commented Glover as the orange flowering bloom of oily destruction rose into the sky.

Grant now filming over the ramp recorded the final run into La Brèche. There were already troops on shore. A bridge-layer has raised its scissor bridge into the air, beckoning like a huge finger. [Photo 6] Salvo after salvo of rockets were screeching their way to shore. [Photo 7] 'The noise was terrific', recalled Private Farnborough with 4 Commando. 'We were crouched in our landing craft when a voice suddenly said, "a bloody racket out there and we've all got to keep quiet!" This made everyone laugh and eased the tension.' 'Christ, what'll they think of next?' remarked a Commando to Sergeant Grant, made nervous by this awesome display of fire

power. 'The next sound was the weirdest of them all' remembered Grant. 'Lovat's personal piper began playing his bagpipes!'[19]

Glover was concentrating on avoiding the anti-ship obstacles, 'lines of bristling stakes', as they came in, stretched before them in rows. 'The mines on them look as big as planets', he recalled. They began a series of erratic manoeuvres to get them through the obstacles, all the time under steadily escalating German fire.

*Whang, here it comes — those whizzing ones will be mortars — and the stuff is falling all round us. Can't avoid them, but the mines and collisions I can avoid. Speed more speed. Put them off by speed, weave in and out of these bloody spikes, avoid the mines, avoid our friends, avoid the wrecked craft and vehicles in the rising water, and get these troops ashore.*

It was a difficult operation, fraught with a whole host of conflicting pressures. 'Don't jump, you fool', Glover chided himself. 'It was near, but you're not hit. Straddled. All right, keep on.'

Lieutenant McDougall with 4 Commando checked with the naval coxswain: 50yds to go. 'Any time now', he shouted, 'prepare to land!' They were also in among the obstacles. Glover meanwhile discovered precisely the zone he was seeking: 'and here's where I go in, that little bit of clear beach'. He began to issue the executive commands:

*Slow ahead together. Slow down to steady the ship, point her as you want her, then half ahead together and on to the beach with a gathering rush. Put her ashore and be damned! She's touched down. One more good shove ahead to wedge her firm. Out ramps!*[20]

Grant looking — and filming intermittently — ahead, remarked 'it was obvious from the speed we were travelling, when we hit that beach our LCI would not be on a return ticket'. As in the case of many landing craft, the shock of impact broke one of the ramps from its stanchions. The bow was 15ft above the water level, 'we would all have to crowd down the remaining one — or jump!' He carried on taking pictures of the chaotic scene. Troops began to scramble, steel-capped boots skidding uncontrollably, down the ramps to the water's edge. [Photo 8] Some with heavy weapons abruptly fell on their backs, while others made their way carefully down, gripping the single rope balustrade with knuckles whitening under the intense grip required to hang on. Groups of soldiers tried to steady the ramps at the bottom, but still the heavy swell pitched soldiers into the water. [Photo 9] Grant panned the camera forward and left, as the rest of the Commando struggled ashore, wading through waist-deep water, pausing behind tanks knocked out at the water's edge. [Photo 10]. He scanned the surf line, obscured by the smoke of a burn-

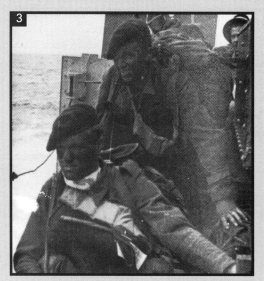

*Photo 3:* The Oerlikon gunner and soldiers stare at the beach coming up ahead, screwing eyes into the wind, trying to see through the smoke. The gunner has only minutes to live.

*Photo 4::* Another still from the same cine film. Soldiers are nervous. ...staring eyes flicker from side to side taking in the breathtaking spectacle of the terrifying final run-in to the beach.

*Photo 5:* An LCI is hit as balancing on his 'Bergen', Grant films the orange flowering bloom of oily destruction rising into the sky.

*Photo 6:* A bridge-layer has raised it scissor bridge in the air. Only metres to go before breaching at La Brèche.

*Photo 7:* 'The noise was terrific' as salvo after salvo of rockets screeched their way ashore.

*Photo 8:* Troops began to scramble, steel-capped boots skidding uncontrollably down the ramps. Some with heavy weapons fall.

*Photo 9:* Groups of soldiers try to steady ramps but still the heavy swell pitches soldiers into the water.

137

ing tank, which had hot flickering flames licking hungrily around the open turret hatch. [Photo 11] Troops ashore were spreading out. [Photo 12] Eventually he stopped filming, draped the camera around his neck and joined the queue 'cramming' its way down the ramps. Looking backwards, he was horrified to see the young rating he had filmed earlier, who had provided him a bacon sandwich, 'slumped over his Oerlikon gun, his face and arms covered in blood'. There was little time for sentiment, 'I got a hefty push from the Commando behind me and I was on my backside, thumping down the ramp into about two foot of water'.

Glover observing and anxiously waiting for his craft to empty, saw:

> *How efficiently, how quickly, they run down the accustomed ramps, not a man hit that I can see, and there they go splashing through a hundred yards of water, up over more of the flat beach than that, and out of sight among the deadly dunes. The Colonel turns to wave, and is gone with them.* [21]

Casualties on Sword were variable. Troops of the first assault wave ran into a wall of fire in certain areas. The Commanding Officer of the South Lancs was killed alongside five officers and six wounded. In all 96 other ranks were killed or wounded. The 2nd East Yorks lost nearly 200 men in the first few minutes, while initially the Lancs were relatively unscathed. By contrast, 20 other landing craft bearing the assault waves of 8th Brigade successfully landed, avoiding all obstacles without a single casualty. [22] Soldiers in earlier waves speak of 'mostly small-arms fire, light machine guns and sniper fire'. One commented:

> *The fellow behind me on the Landing Craft was hit in the groin. The fellow on the port side was killed outright. I remember seeing his blood spurting out.* [23]

As the Commandos came ashore they were subjected to mainly indirect fire, as batteries inland had yet to be silenced. Private Sidney Dann of 6 Commando recalled seeing the East Yorks on landing. They had been tasked to hold the coast road and let them through. But they were still on the water's edge, digging in behind knocked-out vehicles. No 6 Commando pushed on, but were shocked at the cost of the initial attack. 'Most of us', said Dann, 'had never seen a dead body before, so it was somewhat of a shock to see bodies floating in the water, and others, minus head, limbs etc, lying on the beach'. [24]

Lieutenant Murdoch McDougall storming ashore with 4 Commando was very aware of the rising crescendo of sound. Thigh-deep in water, he recognised their landing craft were attracting 'counter-fire'. 'The water on my left', he later wrote, 'seemed an odd colour; it was swirling round a threshing red stump, which was

all that was left of an arm, the body attached to it was invisible under the churning water'. They pressed on, assailed by 'peculiar whines and whizzing' of rounds speeding past, displacing air.

> *As I splashed out of the water, I found one of the men from Peter's section lying just above the water-line. He saw me, and I could see that he was calling to me. I bent over him. He had been caught by a burst of machine gun fire, which had slashed across his thighs, and his legs were almost severed. I tried to undo the harness of his rucksack, whose weight was holding him to the ground, but he had fixed it somehow to his belt and equipment. I had to leave him.*

'Stop a minute, Sir, for Christ's sake ...' came the poignant appeal; but the Commando had to push on to its objective — the Ouistreham battery and Casino. [25]

Back on the water's edge, the destruction continued. *LCI(S) 516* had all but extricated itself, still under fire. Glover was going to be required for yet another run-in to the beach. Oerlikon gunners were engaging German-occupied houses. Sub-Lieutenant Leslie observed one lone sailor left on board a stranded LCT on the beach, engaging enemy riflemen concealed in the roofs and what was left of the upper storeys of shattered houses. 'We could see him changing magazines all by himself and he was such a "shorty" he had difficulty doing this, but we couldn't help him. I hope he survived'. [26] Commander M.O.W. Miller bringing in an LCT squadron carrying elements of 185th Brigade recalled the confused fighting around these beach villas, where care had to be taken, despite sniper fire, not to hit their own men. But 'eventually someone lost his temper and opened fire'. Within seconds every Oerlikon within the Squadron, some 36 in all, opened fire 'and the line of villas folded up like a house of cards'. [27] German artillery fire was still lethal, as Glover saw:

> *Hell! What an explosion! And, my God, it's one of ours! "Fitz, who is it, who is it?" Must have been hit in the tanks. God, oh God, poor bastards! "No we're too far away. Others are going in." There won't be a man alive when the smoke clears.* [28]

Five LCI(S)s were lost during the Sword landings. One blew up two miles off the beach after coming under heavy cross-fire. Only her commander and three ratings were saved. Another mined on the beach had 54 bodies taken from the wreck, a sister craft attempting a rescue was sunk with several casualties. Two others were sunk just off the beaches and many others damaged. [29] Marine Neale's crippled craft eventually reached his mother ship. 'Once back on board I was overcome with exhaustion and can recall that things were happening around me as if in a dream.' Some images would endure for the rest of his life. 'I saw several limbs and feet in buckets being thrown over the side of the ship and thought to

*Photo 10:* Commandos from Lord Lovat's command group wade waist-deep through water and pause behind tanks knocked out at the water's edge.

*Photo 11:* Hot flickering flames lick hungrily around the open turret hatch of the abandoned tank.

*Photo 12:* Troops ashore at La Brèche are spreading out.

myself how pink and clean they looked without any feelings of repugnance.'[30] Lieutenant Sidney Henry commanding *LCI 300* buried his dead at sea. They had to use sections of the galley stove which was dismantled to provide weights. 'Young matelots, who had been considerably shaken by the day's events, thought it all very callous.' They were not aware that landing craft commanders had been expressly forbidden to bring any bodies back to the UK, so as to avoid choking the embarkation ports.[31]

The landings on Sword were a success. No 41 Commando was able to turn westward and begin penetrating Lion-sur-Mer. The East Yorks moved east, followed by 4 Commando into Ouistreham. By 09.00 the South Lancs had occupied Hermanville-sur-Mer. The strongpoint at La Brèche was eventually overwhelmed after nearly three hours fighting by 10.00. Beaches narrowed by the tide were still under fire when the 1st Suffolks, 8th Brigade's third battalion, later achieved a troublesome landing. 'It was all very confused', said Private Richard Harris of the Suffolks.

*Between the crunch of mortar bombs and the whizzing sounds of shells and chunks of metal flying about I remember hearing cries of "stretcher bearer" and then breaking off into shuddering sobs. I never saw this lad nor do I know what happened to him, but his plea for aid was one of my most poignant memories of the beaches.*[32]

The rest of the 3rd Division, the 185th and 9th Brigades and the 1st Special Service (Commando) Brigade came ashore during the morning and early afternoon. By then Lieutenant Commander Denis Glover aboard *LCI(S)516* was attempting to rendezvous off Sword with the rest of his flotilla. He said:

*I say, Number One, we're two miles out and still being shelled. Persistent sods, aren't they?*[33]

## 'The appalling number of church spires' … Juno 07.15.

Lieutenant Blois-Brooke aboard the LSI *Queen Emma* approaching Juno, remarked:

*My abiding impression of the whole day was, as soon as it grew light, the appalling number of church spires there was on the French shore. I had already encircled the churches I would use to fix our position, but daylight revealed so many I couldn't pick out my selected ones!*[1]

The group of villages Courseulles, Bernières-sur-Mer, St Aubin and Langrune lay along the low-lying coast, 7-10km west of La Brèche. They formed the focal point for the landings of the 3rd Canadian Division Group off Juno. Like parts of Sword, houses lay beyond a substan-

tial sea wall along the water's edge. Lieutenant Reginald Edwards commanding *LCT 2436* powering-in towards the beach was similarly perplexed by the spires. He was due to land at Bernières where there was one. There was another at St Aubin to his left, and a third at Courseulles, with its small harbour on their right. He had been assured by 'some bright US Air Force General' during D-Day briefings 'that three squadrons of Fortresses flying on each village would erase these objects from the face of the earth'. But when the French coast came into sight, 'the first majestic items we were able to recognize', through binoculars, 'were those three church spires, erect and intact — so much intact that the Germans had a machine-gun nest in each one'.[2] Beach obstructions had been thickened and the water front fortified. Behind mined areas and barbed wire, houses had been strengthened for defence, and concrete bunkers sited to fire in defilade, both east and west, along the shore. Despite the bombardment, the defences were intact. Nevertheless, the invaders were reasonably confident. Major R.B. Forbes of the North Shore Regiment had been briefed:

*It was going to be a push-over actually. We were told approximately 20 to 25 men would be in the position. No big weapons of any kind, or artillery pieces or anything like that; a machine gun, but probably mostly rifle fire.*[3]

'Above the noise of the engines, strange train-like noises rushed overhead', recalled Lieutenant Ian Hammerton, a flail tank troop commander. His LCT was buffeting its way toward the beach, beneath the flight path of heavy navy shells. 'Explosions could be discerned on the land, while a pall of smoke from burning grass and buildings blotted out some of the landmarks.' The intention — as on Sword — was for tanks to land ahead of infantry. DD tanks had been launched, but as yet, the infantry were ahead in the race to the shore. Boats were perilously close to each other. Hammerton heading for Bernières could see 'we were on target' and the LCTs were given the order 'to go flat out for the beaches'. As they surged forward they were suddenly confronted by a higher, larger vessel that had slipped down the swell into their path. With a metallic grind, they 'managed just to scrape alongside'. As they did so, 'There was a sound as of tearing calico, a belch of flame and smoke over our heads' as a salvo of hundreds of rockets launched from the deck of the LCR 'Hedgehog' launcher they had bumped alongside. He observed the spiralling mass of dots arch majestically into the sky and begin to disappear over the beach. 'At that moment a Spitfire flying along the beach dissolved silently into a puff of black smoke',[4] having inadvertently flown into the rocket salvo. Almost immediately the LCT grounded on the shore. The ramp came down. It was 07.15; 'H-Hour'. Very few tanks had reached the beach.

One Canadian film cameraman recorded images of

heavily-laden infantry approaching the sea wall — possibly Bernières — from within an LCA. A naval rating is shouting details of the beach ahead to the infantry, cautiously waiting, crouched down, wearing camouflage-festooned helmets, beneath the ramp below. [Photo 1] The rise and fall of the surf, some four to five feet, is discernible by the rocking line of houses beyond. They flinch as a ricochet whines overhead. The ramp door is cautiously lowered, and with a sharp gesticulation of the hand, the naval rating motions them through the door — out! — as he observes the beach ahead. [Photos 2, 3 and 4] Struggling with heavy equipments, a scaling ladder for the sea-wall, the heavily laden assault troops pour clumsily and jerkily through the restricted LCA exit. Immediately they are waist deep in surf, pushing their legs as fast as they are able through the foaming water, in between twisted-girder hedgehog obstacles. Still the craft rises and falls on the swell as more men climb out. One soldier [Photo 5] turns back. He seems to seek a little moral support. 'Will it be all right?' he appears to enquire. A hand with a wedding ring, probably a more mature soldier, pats him reassuringly on the shoulder. 'Go ahead', it seems to say.

Beyond the ramp is a totally alien environment, replacing the stench of vomit and diesel they have just endured in the landing craft. There is noise, a stiff sea breeze, violent surf, the pungent smell of cordite and the staccato crack and thump of machine gun fire, and in the background the even sharper and louder report of bunkered anti-tank guns. 'There were so many men on the beaches, I think it was like shooting at a flock of birds', said Major J. Anderson of the Canadian North Shore Regiment. 'You think you can't miss and you fire both barrels and nothing happens', he recalled. 'This was the impression I got; and I thought it was like that as I came ashore.'[5] Lacking support from tanks the infantry streamed across ramps thigh-deep in water, and waded toward beaches ominously overlooked by sea walls, resembling medieval castle parapets.

The 7th Canadian Brigade Group had been tasked to capture Courseulles and Graye. Over a kilometre further east, the 8th Canadian Brigade group was landing at Bernières and St Aubin-sur-Mer. All road exits from the beaches had been blocked by concrete walls. They had to be surmounted by a virtual medieval assault. The first task was to cross the moat, the obstacle strewn sea from landing craft ramp to sea wall. For many it was an appalling experience, one that even now visibly draws upon emotional reserve to describe. 'I saw this fellow out a little further in the water', said Corporal Harold Brasier of the Queens Own Rifles of Canada, 'and he had been hit — along with a lot of others — but he was screaming'. He felt impelled, despite being part of the assault himself, to help. 'As I tried to point him towards the shore, I couldn't help him much, I was dragging my own leg, he was hit.' Brasier paused in his description, reliving the horror. 'He was just ... something came over

my shoulder — something really big — and he was just obliterated in front of me'.[6] They were under fire from heavy calibre weapons.

Desperately, Canadian infantry came to close grips with the German bunkered positions. Quarter was neither offered, or anticipated. Major Charles Dalton of the Queens Own Rifles of Canada reached the sea wall, and 'saw that the pill box was shooting our men that were lying on the beach'. He proceeded to tackle it.

> I had a sten gun, and got back a little from the pill box and fired back through the aperture, and the machine gun stopped firing. All of a sudden I just blacked out. It was the man in the pill box, who got up and fired through the ventilator, and the bullet went through my helmet and back of my head and scalped me, and came out the other side.[7]

Some specialist support began to land, able to deal with the pill boxes. 'The thing I hated', recalled one Canadian soldier 'was when they'd call up a carrier with a flame-thrower to burn out one of their pill boxes'. There is no defence against flame, which normally asphyxiates before it does its gruesome work. 'I can still turn sort of green when I think of it', said the witness.

> I remember once there was this pill box, and we could hear the guys inside yelling. We didn't know what they were yelling and I told the Sergeant maybe they wanted to surrender but the door was jammed. I said it might have taken a hit and buckled and they couldn't get out. He said, "Fuck 'em", and yelled at the guy with the flame-thrower to turn on the heat, and you should have heard those Germans in that pill box screaming. God it was awful.[8]

Opposite Bernières, Lieutenant Ian Hammerton's Flail tanks began to exit the LCT. 'When the first Flail went out, the lightened craft surged forward a few feet'. This happened twice, until Hammerton's Flail exited, lurching as the landing craft ramp struck a submerged mine. The immediate problem was to assist with the primitive, assault of the sea wall and get into the village, where German strong-points could be engaged at point-blank range. They began flailing a pathway clear of mines up the beach to the sea wall. Up ahead were infantry, and 'I can see the Bridge AVRE moving through the beach obstacles behind them, when there is an explosion on the turret and the bridge falls uselessly'. They were momentarily stuck. 'The AVRE tries petarding the sea wall for some time but without success.' Resorting to an alternative plan, the armoured vehicles attempted to blow their way up a concrete ramp leading to the top of the sea wall. Shooting an 'Element C' railway-steel gate blowing it to pieces, an AVRE climbed the ramp but tipped over on its side when one track slipped off, trying to push the wreckage away. Another AVRE successfully

*Photo 1:* 'Prepare to beach' — the final minute approaching Juno captured on cine-film.

*Photo 2:* 'Doors open — stand-by.'

*Photo 3:* 'Out!' The naval rating motions the infantry through the door, some with assault laddering to scale the sea wall.

Photo 4: Troops continue to scramble awkwardly out. The surf-line is rising and falling in motion with the craft.

Photo 5: 'Go ahead' the reassuring hand seems to say.

*Left:* Opposite Bernières, Lieutenant Ian Hammerton's Flail tanks begin to exit their LCT. One has been hit.

*Right:* 'There is an explosion on the turret and the bridge falls uselessly.' A continuation frame on cine film, the smoke is the exhaust of a tank exiting the water.

forced the wreckage to one side, but in so doing set off a mine, marooning it at the top of the wall. Hammerton's tank attached a tow rope to the disabled hulk and dragged it down, reversing backwards into the rising tide; whereupon the engine deck, swamped by a wave, caused the tank to stall. Hammerton and his crew were obliged to bale out. They struggled through water up to their necks, bumping grotesquely into bodies and debris, as they made their way to the beach.[9]

It took time to clear the strong-points. Courseulles and Graye-sur-Mer were stubbornly held against the Canadian 7th Brigade. Bitter street fighting was to continue into the afternoon. Hold-ups resulted in delays securing exits, keeping nearby beaches under prolonged fire. Some tanks gradually crawled to the top of the sea wall in front of Bernières, while intense fighting continued for a further three hours in and around St Aubin. Meanwhile the tide was rising, causing congestion as more and more wrecked equipments piled up on the ever narrowing beaches. Sergeant John Shineton, a swamped DD tank commander of the Fort Garry Horse, commented on its macabre appearance as he 'eventually floated in on the tide' opposite St Aubin.

*As the battle went along in the morning, bodies started to appear on the sand, in the distance between the sea wall and the tide coming in. And with the ones already getting killed on the beach in the machine gun fire, it was a pretty horrible sight.*[10]

One by one bunkers were overwhelmed. 'They fixed bayonets and we just assaulted', said Major Edward Morrison of the Irish Battalion The Kings Regiment, having spotted a machine gun post on their flank. 'It wasn't too far to go, so we could go like the clappers really, which we did ... no question about it.' Defences which had appeared unassailable fell to assaults conducted by soldiers who knew they had to succeed to survive.

*They didn't put up any real fight. But I must say we killed about a good 20 or 30 chaps when we swept over the gun post ... I remember going behind one and thought, gosh, if I were in this defensive position I could have held that for a week.*[11]

There was little opportunity for tactical flair. The invasion was a blunt instrument, a frontal assault, bludgeoning the German opposition into submission. It was a bloody business. Bill Williams, an RASC soldier seconded to the Canadian 3rd Division said:

*My first shock was spotting the first dead body. I'd never seen a dead body in my life before. This particular corpse was so immaculate — just as though he had been stood to attention, with his small pack and his webbing all beautifully blanco-ed. There he was, and we had to stop*

*for a moment right beside him. It was as if he had been standing then just gone flat on his face. It absolutely shattered me — I couldn't take my eyes off him.*[12]

Even pastoral support was overwhelmed. 'You lost all sense of time', recalled Captain R. M. Hicky, a padre with the North Shore Regiment.

*You were just there and you did what you could, and when you came to a fellow dying, I'd tell him that he was dying. You'd get a nod of the head from him. If he were an RC, I'd anoint him. This was all done automatically, with a second for each, you see.*[13]

Ministerial support is important to the infantry, it is they who invariably receive the most, and often, earliest casualties. One Canadian soldier running-in to Juno on a landing craft recalled the comfort he felt on learning there was a chaplain aboard.

*He was in the wheelhouse, I guess, and after our Colonel said, "Good Luck" — and as I remember he came ashore six hours later, big hero — this Chaplain came on the loudspeaker and we're getting pretty close, maybe only a mile away from the beach, and he says there, "Not much time, men" but he would leave us with words from Exodus.*

The soldier, suitably impressed, and a believer, took out his pocket Bible and map marking pencil, prepared to mark the passage about to be quoted; when 'a shell from a shore battery comes zooming down and starts skipping at us and runs alongside, making one big skip the length of half the ship and disappears, and that's all from the Chaplain'. The boat began taking machine gun fire from the shore, but the Chaplain is 'probably too scared to read the verse for us, although I'm waiting for it'. He subsequently looked up the missing verse from Exodus (23/20) where 'if ye hearken attentively to His voice, and do all that I say, then I will be an enemy to your enemies, and an adversary to your adversary'. With a soldier's typical propensity to generalise, the trooper realised 'God was on our side and was going to kick the living be-Jasus out of Jerry'. But the message did not quite materialise that way. 'That Chaplain' should have 'given us some real old-time religion, you know ... an eye for an eye and a tooth for a tooth. That's what we bloody well needed that day!'[14]

Even some 90 minutes into the landings, it was still not apparent to follow-on waves, how successful the initial assaults had been. On the left of the 9th Canadian Brigade, the LCI(S)s of 48 Commando were off St Aubin at about 09.00. Lieutenant-Colonel Moulton, the CO, and Timmermans, the naval LCI Squadron Commander, examined the beach with binoculars 'trying to make out how things were going and what sort of conditions we should meet'. On the beach was confused firing, one or two stranded landing craft and 'a dark line under the sea wall and low sand cliff which might be men'. This was of some concern to the CO as it could mean the Canadians had been pinned down, 'but everything else seemed what one would expect'. Moulton had reason to be concerned. His landing craft (LCI(S)) were unarmoured; indeed, made of wood they were vulnerable even to small arms fire. This ought to have been of little consequence as they were a follow-on wave. The beach was to have been secured by the Canadians. A number of the Commandos were, nevertheless, unimpressed with their choice of transport, preferring instead the lower profile, faster LCA, which could be cleared by troops in a fraction of the time it took to exit the cumbersome LCI(s)s. Corporal Len Wakefield of 48 Commando was explicit.

*Well the boats were diabolical. They should have been Landing Craft Assault instead of Landing Craft Infantry (Small) … We used to clear those in about seven seconds. That wasn't bad going. But the Landing Craft Infantry stood about twenty feet off the level of the sea. You had two ramps off the front of them. Obviously when you dropped the ramp, and with the ramp soaring around [the waves] it was at an angle. A diabolical way to assault.[15]*

Moulton, undecided what to expect on the beaches, had no flexibility in the interpretation of his orders in any case. 'May as well beach, Timmy', he ordered. The wallowing grey hulls came to life as they increased speed, and the squadron changed formation into line abreast as it bore down onto the beach. Moulton observed 'everywhere men were fastening their equipment with their bulky packs, inflating their life-belts, picking up their weapons and going to beaching stations'. There was little sign of life from the beach. 'No one seemed to be shooting at us' noticed Moulton with some relief. 'It was probably all right.'

Captain Dan Flunder, Royal Marines was bemused at the obvious tension among the LCI naval crew. 'The young sub-lieutenant and the rating who were to run the two ramps down, were very flat on the deck indeed, and looking really — I thought rightly or wrongly — over impressed by the occasion.' Contrary to this over-dramatic behaviour, he wished to demonstrate a more relaxed poise to his men. 'So I was walking up and down the fore-deck, and it honestly wasn't until I saw some people fall overboard from the next craft, that I realised we were actually being shot at.'[16] Moulton's worst fears were being realised. Some landing craft snagged on beach obstacles, their forward motion suddenly arrested and began to swing broadside on to the beach. The surf caught Moulton's stern and carried the craft forward, beaching it, rolling, at an awkward angle. 'As we struck the obstacle', Moulton recalled, 'the enemy opened fire with mortars and machine guns from the esplanade, a little more than a 100yds away'. They

were in a mess. Four craft were reasonably close-in to the beach, but two others were hung up, helpless on obstacles, well out from the beach. 'No question now of our smoke upsetting the Canadians' battle or interfering with the work on the beach — that had all too clearly gone very wrong.' In the noise, din and confusion of battle, his men were being hit. Moulton 'realised with a sinking heart that the Commando was meeting something like disaster'.[17]

They had to vacate the boats quickly. Smoke was laid down by mortars and before long the Germans were firing blind. 'And then of course', said Sergeant Jack Ward, 'as the boats gradually went in, and the sailors on the boat I was on put the landing plank over the side for us to get out, the sea was so rough, it just floated away'. A vicious lateral tidal stream swept some men off their feet and drowned them, as they paused in the water, seeking to steady the ramps. Captain Flunder was flung from the bows of the cork-screwing landing craft by gyrating waves, and then terrifyingly run down by his landing craft, which propelled by the surf washed over him. Barely conscious he struggled to the beach, where he found the blow had ripped his pistol from its shoulder lanyard. There, 'he was violently sick from the salt water he had swallowed and from the thick white smoke, which now filled the air'. Moulton described the difficulties experienced by his own craft, which although closer to the beach:

*Still rolled, and her bow swung each time a wave hit her stern. Up in the bows, seamen and marines struggled to get the second brow out and at last managed it, although it tilted, lifted and threatened to drop off the roller at each wave. The men, under their loads, tried to hurry down this crazy gangway, plunged waist deep into the sea, and waded ashore.[18]*

The process could not be reasonably speeded up despite all the previous practices. That it was not working well was evident to RSM Colin Travers, who having launched himself from the ramp 'sank, and my head was covered with water, and I came up to the surface and could see the ship, because I turned on my back, and I couldn't see any of the others following'. These crazy antics were carried out under fire, which added to the unreality of the disaster unfolding in slow motion. 'I didn't really think they were drowning', admitted Lieutenant Square, also of 48 Commando, observing some of his men in the water. 'I wasn't sure about that.'

*Later in hindsight of course I knew perfectly well they were. In fact one chap, I actually waved to as a sort of thumbs-up sign; and by the time a reply was due the ship had veered round and I lost sight of him.*

The Germans were still mortaring and shooting at the water's edge. 'One thing that always stands out in my

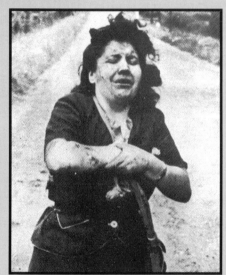

*Left:* Moulton 'realised with a sinking heart that the Commando was meeting something like a disaster'. Commandos struggle through the surf from LCI(S) waist-deep in water.

*Centre left:* 231 Cine-Film Shot. It now became apparent 'what that black line on the beach was' - 48 Commando 'Nan-Red'.

*Right:* Just beyond another 48 Commando LCI(S) is burning.
The incoming tide was shrinking the beach surface area to an ever narrowing strip of sand and pebble. The banners are markers for incoming craft. *IWM*

*Centre right:* 'It's almost inevitable that many of them lost their lives.' Injured French civilians.

mind', said Sergeant Jack Ward, was 'towards the right of me, underneath a jetty which was there, was a heap, or a pile, of bodies stacked on top of each other'. He continued:

*And sitting very near the top of them was a young chap with a mop of ginger hair. Well, I remember him as having ginger hair; and his left arm had been blown off ... It always stuck in my mind how pure white the bone was showing. I had never sort of seen a human bone before, I don't suppose, and I never expected it to look so gleaming white.*[20]

Things were going badly. The Commandos had to rush the sea wall, under fire all the way. 'One should not stop to help wounded men in battle', admitted Moulton, 'but I passed close to one lying in the shallow water, and rather than let him drown, got my hands under his shoulders and dragged him a little way up the beach; he seemed terribly heavy and helpless, and I could not take him far; but he was calm and brave and thanked me for what I had been able to do'. It now became apparent 'what that black line on the beach was' observed earlier from out to sea; it was 'the human debris of the assault; some dead, many wounded, some bewildered, some, like the stretcher bearers, with work to do'.[21]

An incoming tide was shrinking the beach surface area to an ever narrowing strip of sand and pebble. No 48 Commando became enmeshed with the Canadians, similarly trying to extricate themselves from difficulty. Control appeared to be slipping away. A squadron of tank landing craft wallowed in to an untidy beaching, hampered by beach obstacles and the stranded wooden LCI(S)s. Captain Dan Flunder watched, dismayed from the shelter of the sea wall.

*Looking back down the beach there were some tanks coming out of the water. They had their lids closed which tanks should never do in action — and never do if they are experienced — and they were in fact running over some of the wounded. I don't know whether they were ours or North Shore.*

Aghast, Flunder tried to prevent it.

*I went back down the beach. Hammered on the side of one of the tanks, the nearest one to me, with a Verey pistol, I had borrowed to arm myself for something. Couldn't make anyone hear. I put a grenade into his track which blew the track off and that opened the lid. Then I suggested, it might be better if they looked where they were going.*

Grim as it appeared, there was little option. Tank crews hyped-up by the terror of the moment, negotiating their way around fiercely burning tank hulks, with restricted vision, desired only to exit the beach. 'It's quite possible this was true', agreed Sergeant John Shineton of the

Fort Garry Horse, 'that we did run over bodies in the manoeuvring up and down the beach'.[22] Few wished to admit to themselves that, overwhelmed by the situation, they drove on. John Leopard commanding a troop of Centaur tanks of the Royal Marine Armoured Support Group 'ordered all tank crews to dismount', during a lull, 'to clear the bodies which had washed up against our tracks. I could not move the tanks further up the beach while they were still there, in case any were still alive.'[23]

The crushing of the helpless wounded was not the only tragedy of the day. Most of the villages, including Bernières, St Aubin and Courseulles and others off the British beaches were still occupied by French civilians. 'It was so horrifying that there were French people there', admitted one British soldier. 'Our own allies, we had to go on and bombard them; and with the best will in the world, it's almost inevitable that many of them lost their lives.'[24] Monsieur Serge Constant driven into cover by the ferocious naval bombardment that descended upon St Aubin, described how:

*My wife was frightened and she left the house. There was a little alleyway and a garden at the end of it, and everybody went down into the garden. And we were all down there by the wall. And then suddenly, one of those — you know — torpedo rocket things exploded. Oh my God! My wife was wounded and two aunts were killed right by me.*

Madame Constant recalled the agony, 'I suffered terribly. I felt a great burning on my leg.' She quickly descended into shock.

*I didn't think at that time I would have to have it amputated. But I felt terribly heavy elsewhere. I couldn't get up at all of course, and my shoulder was giving me agony.*

The Canadians fighting their way through the village were not to take it for a further three hours. They became aware of the misery of the inhabitants at the moment of success. 'What I felt sorry for after the thing was over', admitted Major J. Anderson of the North Shore Regiment, 'when we came out and started to walk up the road, towards Langrune, was the civilians, poor souls'. It made them feel empty.

*Houses were wrecked and so forth. Little children. This is what hurt you, but I guess, that's warring.*[25]

Lieutenant Colonel Moulton was desperately trying to salvage some semblance of order from the catastrophe his battalion-size group had undergone. Large elements of 48 Commando were missing. Craft were still marooned at sea. Casualties had been heavy. The Canadians were still trying to battle their way into the St

Aubin esplanade strong-point. The landing plan in his opinion had been too inflexible, 'too much of a bull charge', unintelligently handled and further hampered by tide and weather. Moulton realised now he 'should have cast aside all advice and orders and loaded the men much more lightly'. As he tried to rally the disparate elements of the Commando he was suddenly hit by a mortar bomb blast, which took him off his feet. Lightly wounded, he felt even more depressed. 'I was glad to be knocked out and not have to go on with this impossible struggle to make some sort of sense of what was happening to the Commando.'[26]

But the landings on Juno were breaking through the crust of the German defence, even though isolated strong-points continued to resist. The carnage on the beach, evident to incoming waves, seemed to belie this impression. Of 306 landing craft of various types used on Juno, 90 were lost or damaged smashing their way through obstacles to get in or when withdrawing after discharging their loads. Like Sword, major gaps were torn in the German defences. Courseulles and Graye fell during the afternoon. The sea wall at Bernières was breached at 09.15, when the first tanks crawled on top. St Aubin took three hours to fight through, enabling the reserve battalion of the North Shore Regiment to advance on Tailleville, three kilometres inland. By 11.30, the Division's third brigade — the Canadian 9th — was coming ashore. By 14.00 the whole of the Canadian Division was moving rapidly inland, together with four regiments of field artillery and a third regiment of armour. No 48 Commando meanwhile turned eastward from St Aubin to attack Langrune-sur-Mer.

Lieutenant Colonel Moulton typified the grim determination required of the assaulting troops. Despite the psychological shock of casualties, and with nearly half the Commando out of action, the CO had 'somehow to contrive a means of getting on with the job'. There were only five of 15 officers left in the rifle troops, and 'Y' Troop was missing. Only 223 all ranks appeared left of 500 who had embarked at Warsash. 'Altogether we had something over 40 killed and a lot more wounded. This included many of our best NCOs and Marines, whose loss we were to feel for many months to come as we tried to rebuild the Commando.'[27]

One of the dead was Lieutenant Raith Rigby whose wife Peggy, pregnant, was justifiably concerned at the prospect of the then coming invasion. 'I knew from my husband's letters', she confided, 'that the "Second Front" was imminent, and I really began to worry.' Like many civilians she 'had a feeling this was going to be some kind of suicide squad, they could not land off those beaches without a terrible loss of life'. Her experience was to encapsulate the poignant moments later felt by many families fearfully waiting at home.

*Each soldier, officer, or Marine or whatever had been*

*given this small brown card, which was to be posted when they reached France. My card never came, and as the days sort of dragged on I felt something was amiss. And then it was the 15th of June and I had a bland telegram, telling me that my husband was killed. I was not at home, I was working in fact, in the office. My sister brought down this — well, came to tell me the news. It didn't register really. I couldn't believe it, I was completely stunned. It just said: "Regret your husband killed in action. Letter following."*

Three weeks later Peggy Rigby lost her baby.[28]

## Tanks from the sea ... Gold 07.25.

'Can you see your beach marks? — OK, beach at full speed. Good luck', intoned the metallic voice of the LCT commander, Lieutenant R.B. Davies commanding *LCT 647*. He was running-in to Gold Beach with armour.

*The last mile coming up — no opposition yet noticeable — then suddenly hundreds of flashes right along the sand dunes. "Here it comes", I thought, "coast batteries opening up at the last moment". But nothing came and I realised that the flashes were rocket explosions.*

But 'something was flying around — my tin hat registered a "ping". Plumes of water were shooting up here and there, but they were not under heavy fire. We were due to beach at 7.23am; ahead stretched the last few hundred yards of choppy water. "Stand-by Kedge!"'[1]

The British 50th Division, leading XXXth Corps, was assaulting Gold Beach east of Arromanches-les-Bains and Ver-sur-Mer, four kilometres west of the Canadian Juno objective at Courseulles. They were the right forward British division. Omaha lay 16km to the west. Assault Force 'G' was attacking with two brigade groups up front. The 231st Brigade was to capture 'Jig' Sector to the right, and the 69th 'King' on the left. The coastline was low-lying and sandy. To the west lay the bluffs and a rock-bound shore stretching from Arromanches to Port-en-Bessin. 'Jig' Sector was covered by fire from strongly defended positions at Le Hamel and Asnelles-sur-Mer, and a smaller strong-point near Les Roquettes. 'King' Sector was protected by defences at La Rivière and Hable de Heurtot on the coast, and on higher ground inland at Mont Fleury and Ver-sur-Mer.

As with all the British beaches, success hinged on the speed with which tanks could be placed ashore. Lieutenant Davies aboard *LCT 647* ordered: 'Down Ramp'.

*Then the exodus of a mechanised Noah's Ark began — Flail tanks, armoured trucks with impossible gadgets, metal monstrosities of all types — pride of the REME designed to clear beach mines and other defences for the infantry coming in behind us.*[2]

To the right Lieutenant H.M. Irwin observed the first Flail tanks come ashore on 'King' Sector.

*The first tank moved out. Amazing, unbelievable, not a shot fired! All was quiet for a minute or two — nobody on the beach but one tank. An explosion as the waterproofing was disposed of. Her flails started. Then black smoke came from the tank as she was hit and it caught fire. This was H-1 minute.*[3]

The 231st Brigade was attacking on a two-battalion front, with the 1st Hampshires on the right and the 1st Dorsets left. Le Hamel presented a formidable target for the Hampshires. The beach was flat and sandy, bounded by a belt of low sand dunes. A gentle slope led up to a sea wall and inland plateau. At the eastern end of Le Hamel was a concealed battery of German 75mm guns. These were to enfilade the entire beach. Machine gunners and riflemen were stationed in every building overlooking the shore. The decision on DD tanks had already been taken. Lieutenant Jim Ruffell commanding an LCT carrying DD tanks of the 4th/7th Royal Dragoon Guards was convinced it was too rough. 'There was no doubt in my mind that to launch these crack troops would have had even worse results than the charge of the Light Brigade at Balaclava.'[4] It was decided to put the tanks ashore dry. The men of the Hampshires were thus temporarily without the support of heavy weapons.

'One of the main snags', recalled Major Mott, 'B' Company 1st Hampshires, 'was the weight the men had to carry'. Every rifleman had 50 rounds of small arms ammunition, Bren magazines, four grenades, 2in mortar bombs as well as special equipment. There was in addition the helmet, Mae West, weapon, entrenching tool, and small packs with further equipment. Mott waded in knee-deep in water some 100yds out. His was not an auspicious beginning. 'My GS watch stopped at 7.48, my map case had floated away, my binoculars were misty and for all I knew my sten would not work.' Some tanks had appeared on the beach attracting company HQ who moved behind one. 'I heard a bang, and a steel helmet flew up in the air and I think that was Dosser who died of his wounds'.[5]

Fear was all-pervasive. 'Except for fools and liars I believe that everyone is afraid when going into action', admitted Captain J. Triggs, wallowing toward the beach in an LCA off Le Hamel. 'I certainly was, although it is pretty easy to conceal it when you are sharing the experience with a mass of other people.' Fear affected people in different ways. To the left was a Canadian, Lieutenant H. Foster serving with the Dorsets. 'You had the feeling of "what am I doing here?" Of all the thousands in uniform, how come I'm right at the front of what we knew was the biggest assault in history?' There was another misgiving 'more or less general' that 'we would not return'. Foster confessed this produced 'a deep calm', something he observed in others. 'It just seemed

impossible that we would make it — and we were more or less resigned.' Triggs was blown into the sea when his craft exploded a mine a few yards out. He was convinced 'death or capture was to be our fate', an emotion echoed by his Cumbrian batman Lewis, who being very small in stature was up to his shoulders in water. 'This is a rum go, Sir' he said.[6]

An officer from the Hertfordshire Regiment approaching the beach 30 minutes after H-Hour observing the fate of those ahead 'the stutter of machine gun fire, the first falling figures', exhibited all the classic symptoms of a healthy terror of the unknown. 'My feelings changed to those one had before a vital race on sports day — the wet palms (you kept your hands in your pockets in case it showed), a chalk-dry throat and that overwhelming desire to yawn.' The assault craft powered on through the turbulent waves, bringing retribution ever nearer.

*… and as we first came under fire I saw a shaking hand and found it was my own. I bravely gave my cigarettes to Wheeler, with instructions to pass them round to the lads — it wouldn't matter quite so much if they noticed that his hand was shaking too.*

With an 'almighty crash' the bows of the landing craft fell open at a drunken angle 50 yards before they were to order 'Ramp down'. They had hit a mined underwater obstacle. As they were jammed fast, there was no option but to disembark there and then. 'No words of martial exhortation came to my lips, no "Charge" or "Berlin or bust!" only a mild conversational (as I was later told) "I think we'll go in now".' At a reluctant trot, the officer and his men slithered down the ramp into six feet of water.[7]

The infantry assaults desperately sought the succour of the sea wall, under fire all the way. Lieutenant Irwin commanding an LCA assault group watched the East Yorks land and rush up the beach. 'We were 150yds away and saw it all. One man was wounded. Just like a rabbit, up, down, up and crawled to the sea wall.' On arrival it had to be stormed like a Middle-Age fortress. 'The Germans on top of the sea wall were chucking hand grenades over the wall onto the soldiers (ours) below.' Another officer recalled the speed at which the Dorsets had to move across the sand, so that the 'Deballikers', mines designed to pierce between the legs, only hit 'one in the fleshy bum.'

*Most of us had seen men shot before but nothing like the damage done by Spandau fire and 88s. Men were blown apart and in the case of machine gun fire, men were hit a dozen times at once — not a chance for them to live. We had been trained in most all aspects and actually pretty well knew what to expect. However, it was not enough to bolster you for this kind of carnage. It took a few minutes on the beach to comprehend, adjust and move forward. Some did not.*[8]

*Above:* 'Then black smoke came from the tank as she was hit and caught fire.' A Flail tank shortly after being struck by an 88mm.

*Right:* 'It just seemed impossible that we would make it — and we were more or less resigned.' The nervous approach to the beach. Wallowing craft in this cine-still can be made out in the smoke behind on a heavy swell.

*Left:* 'Just like a rabbit, up, down, up and crawled to the sea wall.' Another cine-still of troops swarming by vehicles under fire on the beach.

C and D Companies of the Royal Hampshires having reached the sea wall east of Le Hamel, managed to exploit a gap in the coastal wire and minefield belt. They pushed inland in depth and managed to outflank and capture Asnelles. By 08.00 this movement was under way.

Four of the first five Flail tanks that had crawled onto the beach at Le Hamel were burning furiously. Bulbous clouds of black smoke enveloped the leading troops and obscured the beach. More tanks disembarked from LCTs, including 'Funnies'. Flail tanks whipped the sand detonating mines, while 'Bobbins' laid matting over patches of treacherous soft blue clay. Bridging tanks laboured across the beach, straddling craters and anti-tank barriers with narrow box girders. Tanks and technology were unhinging the defence, but at some cost. 'There was quite a shambles on the beach' admitted Major Peter Selerie of the Sherwood Rangers Yeomanry. 'Out of the Squadron's 19 original tanks, only five were still mobile.'[9] Corporal Herbert-Smith arriving on the beach, summed up the situation with typical soldierly directness:

*And do you know, one of the first things I saw was a Sherman tank with three bloody great holes through it. Crikey, I thought, so old Monty was having us on. He told us at Alemain that the gun hadn't been invented that could pierce a Sherman — well it certainly had now, as we could clearly see.[10]*

But the sheer number of tanks gaining access to the beach was overwhelming the German defence. 'We bottomed in about six feet of water' said R.J. Mellen a Churchill AVRE operator, 'which meant my only way of seeing, via the periscope, was blocked by the sea water'. He had to drive under water until 'suddenly my periscope began to clear and I could see a sandy beach dotted with gun emplacements and tank traps'. He was carrying a bridge and set to work. 'The roar of engines and the sound of exploding shells seemed insignificant now we were on dry land. There was a babble of shouts from the crew ... We had arrived'.[11] Now armoured vehicles began ponderously to roll down the road to Le Hamel.

Sergeant Bert Scaife was on this road in a Churchill AVRE tank. 'I was fortunate', he said, a survivor from an Engineer Assault Squadron, he was 'the only armoured vehicle at the particular time'. Up ahead, Major Selerie had paused on the outskirts of the village with his five remaining Sherman tanks when 'we were overtaken by one of the AVRE Churchill tanks armed with a petard that looked like a short and very wicked piece of drainpipe sticking out of the turret'. The gun was a 290mm mortar which fired a 40lb projectile. It appeared the sergeant commanding it was 'the sole survivor of his troop'. His vehicle was tasked to join the five tanks. Selerie echoing the Duke of Wellington said: 'I don't know what effect you will have on the enemy, but

by God you terrify me!'.

Sergeant Scaife explained 'the crucial thing was to get into Le Hamel behind the defences'. The target was 'the back of a pill box which was housing an 88mm gun firing along the beach'. They found it, and 'my gunner — he dropped a petard through the back door, blew the place up, and eliminated that'. Major Selerie, noticing on entry into Le Hamel that a stream of enemy fire was coming from a large tall multi-storeyed house, ordered the AVRE to deal with it. His five tanks provided a storm of covering fire.

*The petard fired and something like a small dust-bin hit the house, just above the front door. It collapsed like a pack of cards, spilling the defenders with their machine-guns, anti-tank weapons and an avalanche of bricks into the courtyard.[12]*

By 08.15, the 231st Brigade Group's third battalion, the 2nd Devons, began landing as planned close to Le Hamel. By-passing the battle for the strong-point, except for one company which joined in, the rest of the battalion moved around Asnelles to the south and pressed westwards towards Ryes, three kilometres south of Arromanches.

Close behind the Devonshire battalion was 47 Royal Marine Commando. As with many other troops that day, watching the battle at a distance, 'the loud cracking of machine-gun bullets immediately overhead' transformed the journey 'from mere observation to participation in the battle itself'. Marine Frank Wright in the leading troop observed 'heads tucked in noticeably lower', but despite this, as the landing craft drew nearer to the beach 'one caught glimpses of the shore as the boat's stern lifted on the swell'. The yellowish-coloured sand was now clearly identifiable, and 'black looking tanks crawled along it like squat stag beetles'. They appeared to be still under fire. 'One tank was standing still and burning with a hot transparent red flame'. Soldiers, 'scurrying figures' were running to and fro with equipment. 'These images branded themselves on my brain' said Wright, 'and I shall never be free of them'. Since H-Hour the tide had risen considerably, submerging obstacles before the engineers could clear them. The inevitable happened. Three of five landing craft bringing in the Commando were damaged and sunk by the attached explosives:

*Boo-o-o-oom — there came a terrible roaring explosion on the starboard side and I felt the shock of it through my boots. A great pillar of smoke and debris shot high into the air on our starboard bow until it became a great spreading tree over 100ft high. Two irregular black shapes rocketed straight upwards through the smoke, they turned slowly over and over, slowed, hung stationary for a moment and began to plummet downwards.*

Wright 'wrenched my gaze away, feeling sick and cold'. One of their LCAs had disintegrated only 50yds away.

It was a shallow landing, and presently the Commando began to stream up the beach, seeking the shelter of the sea wall. Wright ran, 'looking neither to right nor left'. He was mortally afraid. 'For a few yards I ran through an imaginary tunnel of safety which shut out all the terrors.' But there was much to remind him of the all pervading reality around.

*A khaki-clad figure lay almost across my path, curled up on the sands on his left side in an attitude of sleep. His knees were drawn up and his arms folded across his chest. His head was bent forward so that his face was turned towards me, but where his face should have been was a featureless red mask.*

No 47 Commando lost 43 men, but some 300 men concentrated at the back of the beach.[13] They set off toward Port-en-Bessin on the inter-allied boundary.

No 69 Brigade Group made swift progress. The Green Howards landing to the west of La Rivière quickly cleared the strong-point at Hable de Heurtot, followed by a German battery position near Mont Fleury inland. The East Yorkshires overcame La Rivière and moved on towards Ver-sur-Mer. By 08.20 both assault brigades of the 50th Division were ashore and fighting their way inland. They were followed by the 151st and 56th Brigades between 11.00 to 11.30, so that by early afternoon all four brigades of the 50th Division were ashore.

Follow-on supporting troops landed with the brigades. There was still much to see as recounted by Private Leslie Kershaw, coming ashore with a tracked light anti-air regiment at about 08.00. 'The place was full of Military Police directing traffic, less concerned with casualties than with getting lorries out of the way.' Truck drivers had laid sand bags on the floor of driving compartments but this did not prevent some unfortunates being blasted through cab roofs on hitting mines. 'I had never seen anything like it' remarked the young gunner, 'the wheel flew absolutely vertical, spinning in the air' before bouncing back to ground. Kershaw was not worried. 'You look around, see these things, note what happened and remain watchful what you are doing.' Casualties from accidents appeared as numerous as those resulting from enemy fire. He watched as a DUKW, revving up prior to coming up a sandy slope out of the sea 'zoomed up out of the water catching a poor officer on the head — I don't know if he survived'. There was also, inevitably, the bizarre, 'like 'Tubby' Barnes, who was flung up in the air, with one leg entangled in the cable of a barrage balloon'. The grisly evidence of the assault was all too apparent. Up the side of a building 'was a splash of blood, as if done by a big red paint brush'. Next to the crater that produced it was 'all that was left, brains in a helmet'. Kershaw's impression of the beach was one of 'the smell of diesel fuel', a constant background 'noise of flak' and the sweet pungent 'smell of death'. The Padre was already hard at work, next to the wounded and alongside lines of dead, who 'already had a brown shiny look about them'. The gunner's experience was perhaps more typical of those who endured D-Day. Assault troops were in the minority. Few were to survive the coming battles in any case. Most soldiers were employed with supporting arms, often viewing the aftermath. 'People don't seem to realise what a machine gun can do to the body', he said. 'Like a blunt knife, it can cut you in half'. Kershaw was manning a triple-Oerlikon mounted on a Cromwell tank chassis, scanning the skies for enemy aircraft. He was not particularly afraid. 'At barely 19 I was only a kid — really interested in what was going on, rather than being frightened — except when shrapnel was whizzing around.' He felt secure because just on the other side of the road, beyond barbed wire entanglements and dead cows, were dozens of infantry 'with small-packs' lying on the ground; he assumed awaiting the order to move on. But the following day they were still there, prostrate, lying in the minefield that had claimed their lives.[14]

Most private soldiers, like John White of 200 Field Ambulance recall mainly confusion. He was blown over by a Flail tank exploding mines. The tank lurched to a halt, and a head appeared in the turret and asked him what he was doing. White explained he was looking for the Regimental Aid Post (RAP) of the Dorsets. 'There's nobody in front of me but b... Jerries' came the caustic response. He was further ignored by the Bren gun team in a ditch nearby who 'did not take kindly to my enquiries' because he was giving their position away. 'But help was at hand!' when he bumped into the CO of the Devons. 'RAP of the Dorsets', he exclaimed. 'I can't even find my own b..... regiment!'

*It seemed we had all landed on the wrong beaches, but I don't know much about that, and the Hampshires had the Dorsets' objectives and vice-versa. However, I can't be sure of this, being but a private soldier.[15]*

50th Division by midday had achieved an appreciable breakthrough. Le Hamel was to take almost eight hours to subdue, but Bayeux appeared within their grasp. Infantry, as Lieutenant Nicholas Somerville of the South Wales Borderers recalled, were making good time on bicycles. Tanks were up ahead. 'I set off straight through the smoke and things like a cycling club'. It was in such incongruous circumstances they lost their first casualty.

*There was a German 88mm firing from up on the Meuvaines ridge down at us, and we just pedalled on, because our job was not to stop but to get through somehow or other. And I looked round and found this thing had fired solid shot behind me, and found a chap pedalling a bicycle without a head on — which was rather worrying — and he crashed into a ditch. He was the first casualty I saw, and I had a sick feeling about it. But the obvious thing to do was to get on as fast as we could.[16]*

Squadrons of Allied tanks were streaming ahead, doing just that.

CHAPTER 11

# A BRUTAL DEFENCE

*'Beach defences were good and it was brutal cracking them.'*

*Chief of Staff (US) 1st Division.*

## Stalemate on Omaha …

The battle on Omaha was entering a decisive phase. As Sergeant Francis Murray came ashore with the 1st Division:

*I had a decided feeling that this was it, I wasn't going to make it any way. I remember not even dropping to the side or anything when the mortar rounds came in. I just thought this was the end of the world so why bother.*

The sudden trauma of seeing 'twisted bodies rolling back and forth in the surf' was 'the worst thing'; made more poignant because 'we just didn't know who they were, but they had American uniforms, so they were ours'.[1] Soldiers in the first assault waves had been traumatised by the initial storm of shot and shell that greeted their appearance. Later waves fared better. Some were shielded from fire by the smoke of burning grass that continued to smoulder across the bluffs. As landings increased in volume, enemy fire was less concentrated, dispersed and distracted by the multiplicity of targets offered. Although crippling damage was inflicted on craft, often as they tried to retract through obstacles after disembarking, few were actually destroyed. Those that were, however, made a vivid and discouraging impression on the men watching from the shelter of embankments. Lieutenant Spaulding off Easy Red saw 'back in the water boats were in flames', not a reassuring sight. 'After a couple of looks back, we decided we wouldn't look back any more'. Staff Sergeant Popkin Krekorian 'saw nine boats. He counted them; seven were ablaze and sinking.'[2] Another soldier admitted:

*It was the most heartrending experience that I ever had. I hope I never have another like it … looking back and see the remains of a crack battalion, strewn all over the beach. Men floating in the water, face up.[3]*

By 07.30 Regimental Combat Team (RCT) headquarters began to arrive. The initial problem for the commanders was even to begin to get men moving, surrounded as they were by those who would never again. 'Two of the men from my section', said Private John Amendola, 'got down behind a tetrahedron [beach obstacle] to escape the bullets'. But these offered only dubious cover.

*An artillery shell hit the tetrahedron and drove the steel back into their bodies. I tried to pry the steel loose from the men but couldn't do it. Then I figured they were dead anyway.*

Blow after psychological blow disorientated inexperienced troops unable to relate to or cope with the horrors confronting them. The tide at high point was washing bodies up on the sand. They lay parallel with the beach, almost in straight lines, 'like Madame Tussaud's, like wax' Amendola observed.

*None of it seemed real. I felt like I was seeing some kind of show. I felt this really can't be happening.[4]*

*LCI 91* approaching 'Dog White' at about 07.40, transporting the alternative headquarters of the 116th RCT exploded into a voluminous orange-tinged slurry of oily flame, just as the ramp was dropped. Captain Robert Walker, a member of the Intelligence (S2) section recalled:

*Flamethrowers on our landing craft were hit. Flames burst all around the deck, scorching us and setting some of the men on fire. I saw one man with a six inch fire blister on his face. Another man had his hair burning. He dragged himself to the rail and lowered himself head first into the water and drowned. Others jumped over the side of the boat and tried to swim in 150yds to land. Those who made it to shore had swallowed lots of water and were sick there, vomiting on the beach.[5]*

Conditions could hardly have been worse for landing vehicles, now beginning to arrive. Wherever they landed, engine failures and artillery strikes produced

153

'I had a decided feeling that this was it, I wasn't going to make it anyway.' Troops storming ashore at 'Easy Red'. A disabled DD tank is distinguishable ahead, and engineer dinghies to the left.

*Below:* Omaha, the aftermath: 'The remains of the crack battalion strewn all over the beach.'

*Below:* 'Those who made it to shore had swallowed lots of water and were sick there, vomiting on the beach'. Rescuing survivors on Omaha Beach. *US Signal Corps*

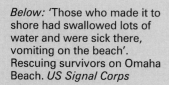

hopeless traffic jams. Immobilised vehicle concentrations, piling up, fell easy prey to enemy mortars. Just as well, was the view held by Sergeant Paul Kiska, because the situation was already 'harrowing' enough.

*Because I tell you, I was quite thankful our vehicles did get sunk, because we would have had to drive on dead bodies - that's how many there were on the beach at the time. No question about it - we would have had to drive over dead bodies.*[6]

As arriving headquarters took stock of the situation, it became apparent that apart from a few isolated groups, many elements of the assault force were immobilised in what seemed a hopeless confusion. Bunched landings and an eastward moving current had mixed up companies on crowded sectors such as 'Dog White', 'Easy Green' and 'Fox Green'. Engineers and navy personnel from wrecked craft, naval shore control parties and other support units intermingled with infantry. Disorganisation was the inevitable consequence, as remarked by Lieutenant Carroll on 'Easy Red'. Unit cohesion was:

*Terrible, terrible. I really think it took somewhere between 72 and 98 hours to get the companies straightened out again. You'd find an "E" Company man in "I" or something like that, or an "F" in "C" and so forth, and we didn't have time to sort them out on the beach.*

A command party could only influence a narrow sector of beach. The 16th RCT contained a seasoned cadre of the 1st Division's veteran element, unlike the 116th RCT to their right. 'What really got us going', said Carroll, 'was the hard core of young lieutenants who had experienced Sicily and Africa, and the older regular noncoms they had with them'. Left to solve their own problems of morale and organisation, 'that combination' noted Carroll, 'attracted to them the remnants of their companies, and anyone else nearby'.[7] That there was 'a problem of morale' is admitted by official accounts.[8] It bedevilled the reorganisation process.

*I remember distinctly taking my trench knife and pressing it into people's backs to see if they were alive. If they were alive I'd kick them and say "let's go!". Later it dawned on me after I'd checked a few that some of them were alive, but they wouldn't turn around - just absolute terror!*[9]

Commanders slowly but surely got men moving. By 07.25 German reports reveal that at one or two locations, American troops were already penetrating the thin crust of the beach defences. 'The officers and NCOs just gathered men by bodies, maybe 25 or 50 together', Carroll said, 'and began operating all along the beach like that. It was that 'gang' leadership that I think saved the day at Omaha'.[10] But something more tangible was required to supplement it.

At about 08.00 individual destroyers began closing the beach to fire on opportunity targets on their own responsibility. Commander James Semmes aboard the destroyer *Frankford* decided:

*With a sick feeling in my stomach that we were facing a total fiasco, I left my assigned sea area and moved in as close to shore as I could without bumping the bottom. This gave us an extra mile to improve vision ... My gunnery officer in the gun director found pill boxes, machine gun nests, and other targets by telescope ... We began to bang away.*

The USS *Harding* moved in so close that she banged her sonar dome - which extended two feet below the keel — on the bottom.[11]

The main problem was ship to shore communication. 'It was most galling and depressing', wrote Commander Marshall of the USS *Satterlee*, 'to lie idly a few hundred yards off the beaches and watch our troops, tanks, landing boats and motor vehicles being heavily shelled and not be able to fire a shot to help them'. Commander Robert Beer aboard *Cormick* lost contact with his naval gunfire team ashore, because the transmitter key of their radio had been mistakenly left on permanent 'send'. Although the team was consequently unable to receive messages, conversations from the beach were clearly audible aboard *Cormick*.

*Their remarks were quite detailed and to the point. We could also hear the whine of enemy machine gun bullets over their foxhole, which they were rapidly digging deeper ... but unfortunately there was nothing we could do to help them.*[12]

As a result, only about 20 percent of the destroyers' fire support capabilities were used.

Nevertheless, the 20 percent that did get through was lethal and brought instant respite. Lieutenant Carroll, cowering from fire directed from cliff emplacements, was beginning to suspect 'we were never going to get off the beach'. He suddenly noticed the sleek grey saviours slipping inshore, just beyond the line of obstacles. 'Then the cruisers and destroyers opened up' he said:

*They were 600yds offshore and firing flat trajectory at the German gun emplacements above us with 8 to 12in shells. The emplacements were being completely destroyed, and chunks of cement as big as a foot square were falling all around us and on us. The shells were coming in no higher than 100ft over our heads. They hit and blew that cliff right out.*[13]

Corporal William Preston, who had managed to drive ashore with the 743rd Tank Battalion was elated. 'Whenever any of us fired a burst of tracer at a target, the destroyers, standing in so close they were almost ashore, fired a shot immediately after us each time hitting what we were firing at on the nose the first shot.'[14]

The supporting fire could also be a two-edged weapon. One battalion command group from the 116th RCT was pinned down from late morning to late afternoon by a destroyer. Smoke was released to signify 'Allied troops here!' When the fire continued handkerchiefs were adapted to wave a flag signal 'We are Americans! Cease firing!' Back came the stoic blinkered-light response: 'Surrender to the Americans!'[15]

The German bunkers had no chance. Colonel S.B. Mason, the Chief-of-Staff of the 1st Division, was later to point out this 'was one element of the attack they could not parry'. Naval support was decisive. 'Without that gunfire we positively could not have crossed the beaches.'[16]

Part of the problem was that RCT artillery units had suffered difficulties getting ashore. The 111th Howitzer Battery supporting the 116th RCT was scheduled to land 12 guns on DUKWs between 08.00 to 09.00. They were afloat by 03.30 and wallowed laboriously to a rendezvous area 400 to 800yds from their LSTs. Each DUKW carried 14 men, the howitzer, 50 rounds of 105mm ammunition and all their ancillary equipments. The craft were barely manoeuvrable. Three DUKWs had engine failures before getting there, cutting off the bilge pumps. They gradually settled in the water before slowly slipping under the surface. Two others were swamped and sunk by large waves while travelling cross wind. Four more DUKWs broached and foundered attempting to circle in the rendezvous area. The four surviving DUKWs departed for the shore, a battery commander, Captain Jack Wilson, rationalising the move by saying 'we figured that if we got four guns in, we'd have a battery and that would help some'.

For a while, the four were able to take advantage of the protected sea aisle provided by large transports and LCTs flanking either side. Eventually they had to turn right-side on to the waves and leave the protected water to reach the beach. The change in direction caused one DUKW to turn-turtle. The remainder carried on for a further five miles, groping around now for the correct landing point, having lost their guide boat. Another DUKW got mixed in with the wrong unit which in error took it to within 500yds of the beach, where its motor cut out. Now quite literally a sitting duck, it was lashed with machine gun fire while the crew tried to get it going. It sank.

The two surviving DUKWs belonged to the two battery commanders, even more determined to get at least one gun ashore. On approaching the beach at 09.00 it was obvious the infantry was pinned down, and they would have no firm base. The two officers lashed their craft together to discuss the apparent impasse. Wilson called across to Captain Shuford 'if we can get one gun in we might be able to destroy one pillbox'. But machine gun bursts severed the ties holding the two craft

together and holed Wilson's engine. The latter drifted helplessly until the first incoming shell smashed the howitzer breech block and killed one of the crew. Geysers erupted intermittently around the vulnerable craft until a bright flash transformed into a dirty smudge of smoke signified the end. Burning fiercely Wilson's DUKW slipped beneath the waves, only the officer and four others were saved. Shuford, turning away, was engaged 11 times by the persistent gun, but each report splashed wide. He sought guidance away from the beach. 'Where do I come in?' he radioed. 'Beach not clear; go to Fox' was the response, then 'Don't come to Fox. Go to Easy Green'. Now confused, Shuford sought advice from a navy ship who 'told him they hadn't the slightest idea what he should do'. Eventually he tied up alongside a Rhino Ferry, where it was discovered the craft was about to sink. Fortuitously they managed to off-load the last surviving howitzer with a crane, before the crippled DUKW settled lower and lower in the water before finally slipping under.[17]

The 111th Battalion had suffered a total catastrophe. Several other artillery units fared equally badly. The 7th Field Artillery Battalion supporting the 16th RCT lost six 105mm howitzers, all of which swamped en route to the beaches. Losses in personnel and half-tracks were considerable.

There was nevertheless movement at three or four places inland, off the seven-kilometre long beach. It remained to be seen whether the few limited penetrations beginning to open up, could be exploited.

## Success or Failure? ...

At virtually every point where an advance was attempted, penetrations were achieved in company strength. They were invariably mixed sections from several units, or groups of 20 to 30 men, often acting in isolation. The first break-ins to the west of Omaha occurred either side of Les Moulins. By 08.30 C Company 116th RCT and the 5th Rangers had created a penetration 300 metres wide. Infantry began to move up from behind the sea wall. To the east, elements of the 16th RCT had scaled the bluffs, and were groping their way inland to the west of Colleville. Lieutenant Carroll observed movement 'about 8 or 9 o'clock'. Sergeant Francis Murray clearing the route up to the escarpment explained:

*The guys would go single file, and there was about four men lying there with their foot blown off from mines. We could not walk on either side, just step over them. There were mines either side of ya, more or less. They would go as far as they could, they would step on a mine and another guy would take over marking them. He would then step on one ...*[1]

Virtually all the enemy strong-points blocking exit

*Left:* 'We began to bang away' – close-in naval fire support.

*Right:* 11.37: 'Germans reported leaving positions and surrendering to American soldiers.' A cine-still records the round-up.

*Left:* Strong-point WN65 ('Easy Red') shortly after capture. A naval shell has hit the top and entered the aperture holing the gun shield. The bunker is still in place today.

ravines were still in action. The assault moved forward slowly and not to plan. Breakthroughs were on the lightly held stretches of grass covered high ground between ravines. On gaining the escarpment, enemy fire would often die away as troops emerged onto the fields at the edge of the plateau overlooking the beach. Some reorganisation was attempted here. Lieutenant Carroll recalled 'it was sometime between 9 o'clock and 10 o'clock, I believe, that we pushed up the slope' with the advanced headquarters. Inland, the battle behind Omaha developed into three generally unconnected and largely uncoordinated actions around Vierville, St Laurent and Colleville. 'Keep in mind', Lieutenant Carroll emphasised:

*That they had gone through a tremendous ordeal getting up there, and the whole unit was shot through with confusion. It was operating like groups of Commandos until some semblance of regimental control began to assert itself, which I would say wasn't until around 4 to 5pm at the earliest.[2]*

Sergeant Francis Murray, having reached the top of the bluffs looked down. He was to comment in later years, 'now you think of it, it's rather awesome when I look down from here, of the German's view of us'. With a wry chuckle he mused 'I don't know, I don't think I would want to do it again'.[3]

Aboard the USS *Ancon*, the 1st Division command ship, reports were fragmentary and discouraging. Major Kenneth Lord, the assistant G3 (Operations) officer remarked 'we simply were not getting enough messages to know what was going on'.[4] At 08.09 a control craft reported 'all DD tanks for Fox Green beach sank between disembarkation point and line of departure'.[5] The Vth Corps reported at 08.43:

*Wave Claude and Eric touched down at 07.20. Obstacles not breached. Four tanks held up by enemy fire, heavy this area. Wave E and C forced to withdraw. Casualties appeared heavy.[6]*

General Bradley, commanding the US First Army aboard the USS *Augusta* was later to admit:

*As the morning lengthened, my worries deepened over the alarming and fragmentary reports we picked up on the navy net. From these messages we could piece together only an incoherent account of sinkings, swampings, heavy enemy fire, and chaos on the beaches.[7]*

It had been anticipated that by 08.30 both the 16th and 116th RCTs should have penetrated the beach defences, and have reached the road running parallel to the coast one mile inland. Yet at 08.49 the 1st Battalion 116th RCT reported 'held up by enemy MG fire. Request fire sp'. Almost one hour later a report read 'firing on Beach

"Easy Red" is keeping LCIs from landing', and nine minutes after, on 'Dog Red', 'many LCTs standing by buoy, but cannot unload because of heavy shellfire on beach'.[8] Aboard the *Ancon*, both the division and corps commanders - Heubner and Gerow - Bradley recalled 'clung to their radios as helplessly as I. There was little else they could do'. Events were out of their control. 'Though we could see it dimly through the haze and hear the echo of its guns, the battle belonged that morning to the thin, wet line of khaki that dragged itself ashore.'[9] A PT-Boat was sent inshore with liaison officers to find out what was happening.

Reports from boats off-shore were discouraging. Lieutenant Robert Loveless, No 1 of the British *LCT 921* said:

*The beach was a shambles when we arrived. The instructions from a frantic beach officer were, "For God's sake lie off somewhere - there is no room for you among this goddarned wreckage!"*

Leading wire-man J. Ray Allmark aboard *LCT 2130* off Omaha:

*Saw craft going up in smoke, fully laden, without getting within striking distance of the shore. The whole beach area was a mass of destroyed vehicles, tanks, bodies, and shell after shell was being pumped onto it from either end and from gun emplacements built into the cliffs at the end of the beach.*

Fortunately, they were bound for the British beaches. 'On we went, feeling glad not to be involved in that holocaust and hoping that by now Sword beaches had been captured.'[10]

The PT-Boat returned with a 'discouraging report' for Bradley. The Vth Corps was still reporting a 'critical' situation on the beach exits at noon. Bradley later wrote: 'I reluctantly contemplated the diversion of the Omaha follow-up forces to Utah and the British beaches'. Scanty reports from both those sectors indicated the landings there had gained a foothold. But unbeknown to Bradley, and typical of the general confusion emanating from Omaha, were the tentative suggestions of success being radioed to 1st Division, reported in its operations journal. These belied Bradley's apparent dilemma. As early as 10.40 the beach-master on 'Easy Red' was radioing 'send in H+195 wave at once'. Another message at 11.15 read 'Inf advancing send reinforcements. Also Dog Green needs inf'. At 11.37 a turning point appeared to have been reached: 'Germans reported leaving positions and surrendering to American soldiers'. By 13.20 the 16th Infantry were reportedly in Colleville, while 'other units progress in slowly – beaches not yet clear of fire'. Within 20 minutes the Navy were announcing:

*Beaches DOG GREEN WHITE RED are entirely clear of opposition and ready for landing trs. No opposition on beach. EASY GREEN AND RED tps ashore apparently waiting infantry reinforcements. All fire support ships are waiting on Army for target assignments.*[11]

Bradley's discouraging assessment was shared by many soldiers who had survived the landings. Private Irwin Spandau 'felt that a chunk had been taken out of his life that would never be returned'. Sergeant R. Slaughter of 'D' Company 1st Battalion 116th RCT later said:

*We hit the eye of the storm. The battalion was decimated. Hell, after that we didn't have enough to whip a cat with.*

Losses in 'A' Company 116th Regiment were particularly poignant. Twenty-three of the soldiers killed came from the small town of Bedford USA, which had a population of only 3,000. The figures included three sets of brothers, of which five were killed and one wounded.[12]

Moreover, soldiers were aware they had only achieved a tenuous foothold. Captain Goranson, who had scaled the cliffs at Pointe et Raz de la Percée with the 2nd Rangers thought 'we were to be stranded, alone, for quite some time'. Lieutenant Saloman, with him, 'thought the invasion was a failure and I wondered if we could make a successful withdrawal and try the invasion sometime again in the near future'. There were fears and rumours they may be cut off from the beach in rear. Staff Sergeant Charles Semchuck 'was worried as all hell on top of the cliff', captured by the 2nd Rangers, 'just waiting for the Jerries to push us back into the channel'.[13] Tank crew-men from the 743rd Battalion 'sweating it out on the beach', unable to clear the exits were waiting for engineers. Corporal Preston 'expected a counter-attack all the time we sat there like ducks unable to move forward or backward'. He echoed the suspicions of many when he wrote a few days later:

*We know something wasn't going right. We were never supposed to be on the beach so long, yet I never considered the fact that we could fail, that we wouldn't soon get off that terrible strip of sand. Time flew by, before I realised it the tide had risen, fallen, and risen again. Night was approaching.*[14]

Landing schedules were thrown totally off balance. A force of 25,000 troops and 4,400 vehicles were due to land on the second tide, but only a portion of the 34,000 assault troops and 3,300 vehicles had reached the beach. 'From where I was', remarked one soldier succinctly, 'it seemed a failure'. Colonel Mason, the 1st Division Chief of Staff, was frank in his assessment of the difficulties they had faced. 'Beach defences were good', he admitted, 'and it was brutal cracking them.'[15] Penetration inland was continuing, but at a cost.

*When we finally cut through the wire and everything like that, a shell hit close, so that the brush went on fire. They told us to use a gas mask, which was no good, it just pooled all that smoke into our faces – the ones that put it on – and I didn't. I saw these guys suffering, coughing and everything, and I thought "Jesus – what are they using on us now!"*[16]

## 'They stick tight' … the German defence Omaha.

American soldiers closing with their tormentors began to make physical contact with German soldiers, accessible in bunkers. It now became apparent what they were up against. 'We hit all of the 352nd German Division plus part of another' assessed Colonel Mason. 'Heinies have to be rooted out of every strong-point', he reported, 'they stick tight'. Experiences were varied. Lieutenant Spaulding on Easy Red had already captured a Pole:

*He said that there were 16 Germans in the area; that they had been alerted that morning and were told they had to hold the beach. They had taken a vote on whether to fight and preferred not to, but the German noncoms made them.*[1]

Resistance on the water-line was bitter. Colonel Mason identified 'mostly very young boys' and a 'few scattered older men'. In his opinion the German defence had been 'pretty much on the alert for our arrival'. Little quarter was expected, and rarely was it given. Many of these troops had already fought in Russia; to Lieutenant Carroll 'they looked like seasoned, rough men, 30-45 years old'.[2] Moulded by their experience on the Eastern Front they fought on. Lieutenant Jack Shea moving with the 2IC 29th Division on the beach road next to the ruined village of Hamel au Prêtre off 'Dog', saw two of a group of five German prisoners felled by a burst of machine gun fire from their own troops, as they were being led away by their American captors. The survivors sank to their knees in the open. 'They seemed to be pleading with the operator of the machine gun, situated on the bluffs to the east, not to shoot them', recalled Lieutenant Shea. 'The next burst caught the first kneeling German full in the chest, and as he crumpled the remaining two took to the cover of the sea wall with their captor.'[3] There were no compromises. Colonel Mason summed up in his immediate note-form impressions:

*Still dogged and bitter fighters. Automatons only and seemed satisfied with capture. They are falling back little by little.*[4]

The German headquarters of the 352nd Division was aware of the gravity of the crumbling situation. Initial success on Omaha was slipping away. The 916th Regiment to the west had identified tanks in front of its strong-points, and had sent in its local reserve, an anti-tank platoon. Oberst Goth the regimental commander managed a fleeting report to General Kraiss his superior. Off shore destroyers were causing a major problem. 'Naval guns are smashing up our strong-points. We are running short of ammunition. We urgently need supplies, Herr General.'[5] His only response was the metallic click on the line as it was cut off. Artillery observers still in contact at 08.46, echoed this message of a disintegrating defence between 'Charlie', 'Dog' and 'Easy':

*It appears that WN65, 66 and 70 north of St Laurent have been taken by the enemy. In front of WN68 there are landings from bigger boats carrying some 150 men.*[6]

Nearly 20 minutes later, Infantry Regiment 726 facing the 16th RCT onslaught reported the situation, was becoming critical:

*WN61 north east of Colleville is in enemy hands. WN62 is still firing with one machine gun and WN60 is still fully intact. Enemy forces are penetrating forward between 61 and 62 up to 63. Further, stronger landings are occurring near WN62 from about 50 boats. Company reserves from the 1st and 4th companies have been put in there.*[7]

Lieutenant Frerking in WN62 ordered his battery to bracket the new approaching wave of landing craft. 'Sorry, Herr Oberleutnant', responded his gun position officer, 'order from the commander. Because of a shortage of ammunition individual rounds only are to be fired.' Unteroffizier Peesel on the battery cursed the decision to relocate stocks in depth, only a fortnight before. The intention had been to ensure their safety. One lorry load had already exploded approaching the battery position. By 10.00 Artillery Regiment 352 reported to the Chief of Staff that the 'ammunition situation of the 4th Heavy Battery is critical'. In any case there been only a sufficient out-loading for one day's supplies. Corps could only guarantee a response in 36 hour's time.[8]

Enemy intercepts in clear speech confirmed Headquarters 352nd Division's realisation the battle was turning against them. 'To all unit commanders', it read, 'everything proceeding to plan, only a little late - Alaska'. Hopefully this referred to artillery fire, or the obvious reinforcement in progress. General Kraiss was dependent now upon the success of local counter-attacks that had been set in motion after 07.30. There were two. One agreed at 07.35 extracted the IInd Battalion 915th Regiment from the Kampfgruppe 'Meyer' from Blay, west of Bayeux, to an immediate counter-attack towards Colleville 'in order that the enemy that had penetrated between WN60 and 62 be thrown back into the sea again'.[9] It was anticipated it would take one

and a half hours to get there. A further battalion, the 916th Regiment reserve – II/916 – was ordered at 09.30 to counter-attack the enemy penetrations north of St Laurent between WN65 and 69. It was to be supported by 14 assault guns from the 1st Company Panzerjäger Battalion 352; these, however, were in Engreville seven to eight kilometres to the south. Not surprisingly their committal to battle became separated and uncoordinated. In addition the majority of Flak Regiment 32, being hounded by air attacks and naval artillery south east of Maisy was re-located to Formigny, four kilometres south of Omaha, and set up in grand defence. This represented little more than a piece-meal committal of reserves: two separated infantry battalions and some self-propelled assault guns; all moving by day, on foot, trucks and by bicycle, under constant harassing air strikes. Odds by this time were already in the region of 1:10 favouring the Allies. Despite set-backs five American regiments, (15 battalions) were to be ashore by nightfall. The German response was two one-battalion pin-pricks on an eight-kilometre front.[10]

Two hours after the initial order, 'the enemy were sitting on the escarpment of the high coast-line north of St Laurent'. The division commander repeated his order to the 916th Regiment to get his reserve moving and 'throw them back in the sea'. Although by midday the battalion was in contact with the enemy, the assault guns had not arrived. Confusingly it was found, 'contrary to earlier reports' that WN66 and 68 north of the village 'are still in our hands'. The situation however was inexorably slipping out of control.

Four hours after the Colleville counter-attack had been set, there was still no result. The 726th Regiment was desperate. 'The situation on our left is critical, the enemy are already around the Colleville church. WN60 and 62 are still gamely holding out.' By 11.40 the 'enemy had occupied the south western exit' of the village. These were elements of 'G' Company of the 16th RCT which had moved up from 'Easy Red'. They clashed with the advanced elements of the IInd Battalion 915th Regiment, detached from the Kampfgruppe 'Meyer', attempting to reach their comrades stranded between WN60 and 62. Infantry Regiment 726 triumphantly proclaimed at 12.35 that 'Colleville has been snatched back again from the enemy.' WN60, 62 and 62b were still grimly held by their own troops, but '61 is occupied by the enemy, with one tank standing by it'.[11]

The American 'G' Company, unable to progress felt increasingly isolated. German groups were now moving back from the outflanked bluff positions, appearing unexpectedly in supposedly cleared areas. Lieutenant Spaulding nearby 'saw several squads of Germans coming toward us' but 'we had no contact with the battalion'. A 'G' Company runner just reached the edge of their defences when he was cut down by the approaching Germans.

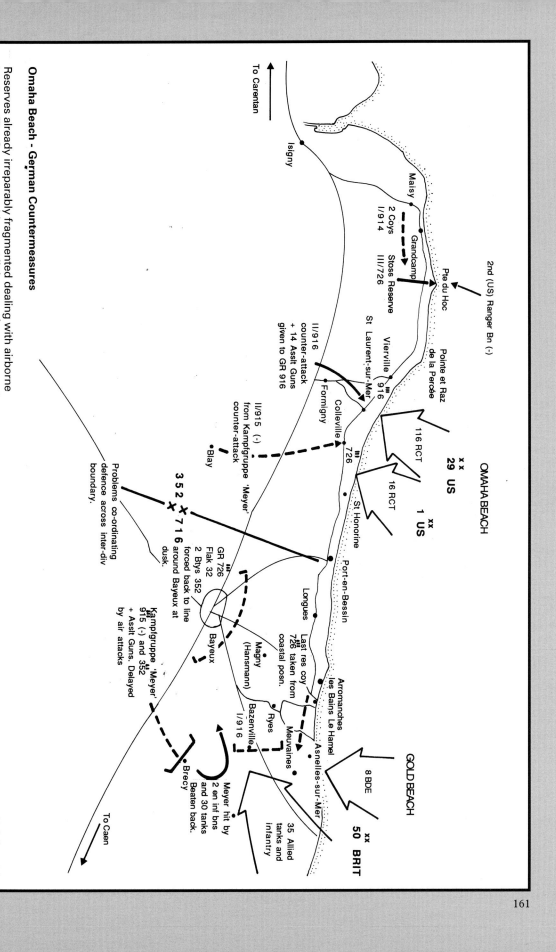

## Omaha Beach - German Countermeasures

Reserves already irreparably fragmented dealing with airborne landings. The Germans could mount little more than company to battalion size counter-attacks. These were merely soaked up by the violence and scale of the Allied assault. Transitory success was to be outflanked by British armour landing at Gold. The 352nd Division had been brought to a standstill by dusk.

To Carentan

Isigny

Maisy

2 Coys
I/914

Grandcamp

Stoss Reserve
III/726

Pte du Hoc

2nd (US) Ranger Bn (-)

Pointe et Raz
de la Percée

St Laurent-sur-Mer
Vierville
iii
916

II/916
counter-attack
+ 14 Asslt Guns
given to GR 916

Formigny
Colleville
iii
726

II/915 (-)
from Kampfgruppe
'Meyer'
counter-attack

Blay

116 RCT

xx
29 US

16 RCT

xx
1 US

OMAHA BEACH

St Honorine

Port-en-Bessin

Longues

Last res coy
726 taken from
coastal posn.

Magny
(Hansmann)

Ryes

Arromanches
les Bains Le Hamel

Meuvaines

Asnelles-sur-Mer

8 BDE

xx
50 BRIT

GOLD BEACH

35 Allied
tanks and
infantry

Meyer hit by
2 en inf bns
and 30 tanks
Beaten back.

Bazenville

I/916

Brecy

Kampfgruppe 'Meyer'
915 (-) and 352
+ Asslt Guns. Delayed
by air attacks

To Caen

Bayeux

GR 726
Flak 32
2 Btys 352
forced back to line
around Bayeux at
dusk.

3 5 2
X
X 7 1 6

Problems co-ordinating
defence across inter-div
boundary.

161

*Above:* The field of fire from WN65 (gun barrel to left). It totally dominated the waterline, evidenced also by the wreckage to its front. *National Archive*

*Right:* Stragglers moving back from strong-points, such as walking wounded shown here, fell easy victims to vengeful American ambushes.

162

*After he fell they fired at least 100 rounds of MG
ammunition into him. It was terrible but we do the same
thing when we want to stop a runner from taking
information. Of course, we didn't find out what he was
coming to tell us.*

They were surrounded just outside Colleville. Presently
Spaulding was down to six rounds of carbine ammunition. 'Some of the fellows were down to their last clip.'[12]
Confusion reigned as elements of five American battalions fought in an area some two kilometres square
between Coleville and St Laurent, containing only scattered pockets of enemy resistance, supplemented around
the two villages by local counter-attacks. Eighteen German casualties sprawled amongst the buildings and
tracks leading into Colleville marked the extent of the
failed German counter-attack.

Colleville exchanged hands several times. The 1st
Battery 352nd Artillery Regiment reported it lost again
at 13.58. This coincided with a pessimistic report from
the 916th Regiment to the west, as it committed its last
company (the 5th), attempting to block the enemy that
had penetrated between strong-points north of St Laurent. This 'was the final thrust from the II/916 counter-
attack'. Success had not been anticipated. It, like the
other doomed piece-meal attacks on Colleville, petered
out with no result. Lieutenant Frerking's detachment in
WN62 had no chance of relief now. The Regiment
reported:

*Our own attack struck bitter enemy resistance, thereby
suffering heavy casualties. WN62 is still holding, WN62b
has run out of heavy calibre ammunition. The enemy in
the Colleville church and chateau is infiltrating southward.
A counter-attack has been initiated.*

Oberst Ziegelman, the 352nd Division Chief of Staff,
was unsympathetic. His uncompromising and immediate response was that 'enemy in the chateau is to be
thrown out, by hook or by crook, WN60 and 62 must
remain firmly in our hands'.[13]

Tanks were now engaging WN62. Oberleutnant
Frerking's position was untenable. He did not know the
Americans had already occupied the dunes on either
flank. A last message was relayed to the battery inland.
'Gunfire barrage on the beach. Every shell a certain hit.
We are getting out'. The response was a few desultory
explosions among the equipments piling up on the sand.
Only two guns had shells left. Frerking ordered the
detachment survivors to withdraw in intermittent leaps
and bounds. The reserve counter-attack fought its way
once again into Colleville, knowing full well they had no
chance of success. Division lost contact with it until
17.10, when it announced:

*The battalion has been by-passed to the rear by enemy. He
is pushing southward from the Colleville Chateau.
Wounded can no longer be brought back out.*[14]

Stragglers moving back from the strong-points, unaware
they had already been outflanked, fell easy victim to
vengeful American ambushes. Oberleutnant Frerking
and Unterfeldwebel Pieh were early victims, perishing
en route. Only Gefreiter Hein Severloh and one signaller
made it back from WN62. Moving along sunken farm
tracks and crawling through ditches, they eventually
reached the command post of the 1st Battalion the
726th Regiment, situated between Colleville and the
coast. They had their wounds dressed and reported
what they had seen. Resistance was continuing strongly,
but crumbling under the sheer attrition being meted out
by the invasion force. Everybody accepted they had
done all that could reasonably be expected of them. It
was up to the panzers now.

# BREAK-IN

*'I wish I could call on all the Generals up to Adolf Hitler and say "Get here quickly - before it's too late. Anything that can still fight, get it here!"'*

SS -Obersturmfuhrer

## *Einbruchsraum West.* Break-in Point West ... Gold.

Richard Dimbleby, a BBC war correspondent flying along the Normandy beaches, eagerly sought out the enemy. As is often the case, apart from points of contact – the preserve of assaulting troops – few soldiers could actually see Germans. He recorded his impressions, live on board the aircraft for subsequent broadcast.

*Of enemy troop movements there was, until noon today, little or no sign from the air, even close to the immediate battle area. Long stretches of empty roads shining with rain, deserted dripping woods and damp fields – static, quiet – perhaps uncannily quiet – and possibly not to remain quiet. But here and there a movement catches the eye, as three German soldiers running like mad across the main road to fling themselves into cover. And nearer the battle area, much nearer the battle area than they, a solitary peasant harrowing his field, up and down behind the horses, looking nowhere but before him and at the soil.[1]*

The first panzer reconnaissance was, however, under way. SS-Obersturmführer Peter Hansmann command-ing a recce company of the 12th SS Division 'Hitlerju-gend' had been tasked to find out 'what was on the coastal strip north of us between the Seine estuary and Bayeux'. Specifically: what type of enemy troops had landed, how far they had penetrated, and what their likely future intentions were. At 04.00 five patrols were despatched to provide the answers.

Hansmann set off himself with two eight-wheeled armoured cars armed with 20mm cannon, heavily fes-tooned with foliage for camouflage. They sped along the most direct route between Broglie and Lisieux towards Caen at 40kmh. Ahead lay a two-hour journey. Hans-mann's observations provide a unique insight of what was happening behind the invasion front, as the German Seventh Army sluggishly prepared itself for unexpected action. Within an hour they were driving through Lisieux.

*Here one could already see solitary pedestrians, workers and farmers whose day had just begun, like every other day before. Several windows in the houses were lit up.*

They were greeted with waves by despatch riders and single military Volkswagens going about their business. Reaching the bridge at Touques he questioned the NCO security detachment commander who said that 'he was at a higher state of readiness, but apart from unbroken swarms of bombers to the west nothing appeared to be happening'. They drove on towards Caen, with some 60km still to go. 'Visibility began to improve, and soon', Hansmann remarked, 'the sun would come through the fog and cloud. My eyes were streaming from the cold wet morning mist.'

More Wehrmacht vehicles were in evidence as they approached Caen, but the roads were still clear. At the entrance to the city there was a 'bustling to-ing and fro-ing of vehicles of all types', where also a Wehrmacht pla-toon was digging in. Its commander enquired where he had come from, and if he had experienced 'enemy inter-ference' en route. The local commander briefed Hans-mann on the latest alert status. 'Enemy paratroopers had attacked the Orne bridges some 10 km to the north, and the battle was still going on.' The SS-Obersturm-führer now realised the reason for all the activity in the street, and the gathering infantry on the edge of the town. 'They were panzergrenadiers from the 21st Panzer Division.' He was warned British paratroopers had landed on both sides of the Orne estuary. Bridges were probably occupied by the enemy and telephone links with Ranville had been cut. 'The noises of battle, clearly audible, came from there.' Even as they spoke fighters strafed the area. 'French civilians, panic-stricken, vacated their houses and began to pour out of the city.'

Driving onward to the western outskirts of Caen, he came across a similar scene. 'The streets were practically jammed, primarily by anti-aircraft gunners, with and without vehicles.' They were coming from the direction of Carpiquet airfield. 'A thick cloud of smoke rolled toward the south east, probably a success from the fighters.' The clearing sky added to his unease. He would now be vulnerable to the increasing fighter activity. 'More light – Ja – even the sun was threatening to appear, which made me wish for more of the mist which appeared to be coming from the coast to the right of the road.' Nevertheless, the road leading to Bayeux, although 'dead-straight' was lined with trees, and a number of villages which could provide cover from the air.

The reconnaissance detachment accelerated along this final dangerous 20km stretch at 80kmh. 'Heavy on-coming traffic' confirmed his suspicion that so far 'no Tommies could have landed here'. Bayeux and its approaches were buzzing with activity. Hansmann observed as they drove onward:

*The first houses on the road, running civilians. Soldiers, old enough to have been our fathers, stood by garden fences chatting with civilians. The nearer we came to the market place – the city centre – the greater the number of people. There were baggage vehicles, Volkswagen cars, motorcyclists and uniforms from all arms of the services, only the Navy were not represented. A platoon of military police was trying to create some order.*

Bayeux, according to the Garrison Commander, had already been under artillery fire. There was further disturbing news of 'heavy fighting in the Arromanches inlet, and the English were disembarking from hundreds of ships off the coast'. They could clearly hear sounds of battle 'which must have been pretty intense, because one could discern the boom of artillery – we must see this! Not only airborne landings but amphibious ones too!' They turned north east in order to approach the coast some seven kilometres away. Driving carefully from cover to cover, the two vehicles traversed rising meadowland dotted with farm houses.

On reaching the village of St Sulpice they saw 'burning houses and erupting fountains of earth' to their left, near Tracy on the coast. Unable to view the sea from here they drove on, tactically, covering each other, moving behind stone walls and hedges until arriving on the high ground at Magny-en-Bessin. From the farmhouse and barn there it was possible to view the whole Arromanches inlet. Hansmann felt reasonably secure studying the terrain from his armoured cars, 'which looked like huge overhanging bushes'.

*Over there heavy artillery fire was coming down. Fountains of earth as big as houses rose up and collapsed in on themselves. To the east stretched a seemingly limitless dark grey mass – the sea – endlessly to the horizon, but slightly lighter than the water. I looked through binoculars – and now I could make out the individual silhouettes of ships. In the foreground and beyond, up to the horizon – ships, masts and command bridges. In the background flashes blinked at irregular intervals, but incessantly –*

*naval artillery! Between the beach and the dark grey ship armada was a murky grey sea. White stripes were apparent within this shadowy mass of water, stretching along an endless front of ships, extending from the cliffs at Arromanches to the horizon east of the Orne estuary – all coming towards us!* [2]

Gold Beach lay astride the boundary of the German 352nd and 716th Divisions. Four companies of infantry covered the nine-kilometre sector of coast assaulted by two brigade groups, especially supported by armour and engineers. Odds were in the region of 10:1 in favour of assaulting troops, not even including the overwhelming support provided by the air and sea bombardment. There were six German anti-tank guns in the sector. In depth and scattered over the same frontage, behind the coast at distances varying from two to five kilometres, were a further seven companies, with perhaps four to seven batteries of artillery of various calibres and types. 50th British Division, the vanguard of XXXth Corps, could immediately bring four brigade groups with tanks and artillery to bear against this mixture of Russian auxiliary and German infantry companies. Odds were overwhelming. Local counter-attacks, due to dispersion, could rarely be beyond company strength. The companies from 726th and 736th Regiment moreover were controlled by two different division headquarters. Coordination was never effectively achieved.

At 06.32 the 726th Infantry Regiment reported to its parent 352nd Division headquarters that landing craft could be seen off Asnelles. By 07.20 the strong-point at Le Hamel observed 'enemy landing craft approaching the coast', and that 'landings were imminent'.[3] At the same time, Grenadier Robert Vogt, an infantryman from 726th Regiment, was working his way forward to the coast 'to try and make contact with the other platoons in our company', as tasked by his platoon commander. He was pinned down en route by ferocious Allied 'carpet-bombing' but managed to reach the company position atop the Arromanches cliffs. As he approached, he could already pick out the sound of cannon and machine gun-fire; at which point he gained sight of the Allied Fleet.

*Somewhere I heard a voice calling "Enemy landing craft approaching!" I had a good view from the top of the cliffs and looked out at the ocean. What I saw scared the devil out of me. Even though the weather was so bad, we could see a huge number of ships. Ships as far as the eye could see, an entire fleet, and I thought, "Oh God, we're finished! We're done for now!"* [4]

The strong-points held out, but in between British forces immediately began to trickle through a thin defensive crust, that had no chance of withstanding the troop densities swiftly run ashore. By 08.12 Oberst Ziegelmann the 352nd Division Chief of Staff was relaying disturbing news to his opposite number at 84th Corps, of a tank break through on his right, apparently

*Left:* 'I looked through binoculars - and now I could make out the individual silhouettes of ships.' SS Reconnaissance.

*Centre:* 'Ships as far as the eye could see.' The sea was black with shipping. The invasion fleet.

*Below:* 'At first one saw the cupola, and then they surfaced like some monster from the deep.' DD tanks in difficulties.

in the 716th Division sector. 'About 35 tanks had passed through WN35 and 36 heading towards Arromanches'; probably the Notts Yeomanry. It was confirmed nine minutes later they were attacking Meuvaines. Artillery Regiment 352's third battalion, monitoring continued resistance by the Le Hamel strong-point observed: 'Of the tanks that have landed near WN35, already several (about six) have been shot in flames by anti-tank guns and artillery pieces'. Artillery reported further that two neighbouring strong-points in the 716th Division's sector (WN35 and 36) had been 'overrun', and that the Russian auxiliary infantry battalion – Ost 642 – had been committed to the heights east of Meuvaines to contain the 35-tank breakthrough. Le Hamel was fighting on. Moreover its neighbouring strong-point WN40, possibly Les Roquettes, 'had shot-up three or four tanks' and could see 'two to three landing craft burning'.[5]

Headquarters 352nd Division resolved to check this crisis developing on its eastern flank. General Kraiss, the Division Commander accepted by 08.35 that the 'situation on the right wing near Meuvaines and Asnelles was serious'. Meuvaines was occupied by the enemy. It was decided to commit the bulk of the Kampfgruppe 'Meyer', which had already committed a battalion to bolster the Omaha defences, to restore the break-through. Permission was sought from Corps for a counter-attack reinforced by the bulk of Panzerjäger (Assault Gun) Battalion 352, against the enemy infantry and armour break through on the right flank, 'and throw them back in the sea'. It was granted. However, the Kampfgruppe 'Meyer' was still strung out on the roads west of Bayeux, already having been committed against airborne landings inland, and further had one battalion and assault guns also had been detached one hour before to go northwest to Omaha. Lacking sufficient radio sets and true mobility, as it was reliant upon bicycles and commandeered lorries for transport, these new directives would not be easy to enact.[6]

SS-Obersturmführer Peter Hansmann, observing the assault on Gold from the high ground above, would have advised it was already too little, too late. He saw:

*Fast boats with high white foaming bow waves, landing boats which spat out brown balls of soldiers onto the beach. I also see fountains of white water rise up in the landing sectors, probably from our coastal batteries. Then I clearly see and hear the muzzle flash of German MG42s. This meant therefore our coastal defences had not been completely overrun!*

The troops coming ashore wore 'flat-helmets'. They were British. 'Whole companies were slowly tramping ashore through the dunes in our direction, apparently encountering no resistance.' He gazed toward Arromanches through his binoculars, where a number of houses were burning. 'The smoke passed over us, and at times covered the entire bay.'

Of particular significance was the large number of tanks, 'one – two – three – a complete troop', making their way through the dunes, 'without even pausing to fire'. Among them were strange armoured vehicles, he had never seen before.

*I clearly saw tanks which were pushing long dozer buckets ahead of them. Were they building a coastal road already, or burying mines? Unflinchingly further tanks surfaced directly from the sea. Is there such a thing? At first one saw the cupola, and then they surfaced like some monster from the deep. And nothing appeared to hinder them. Is there no 88mm flak there?*

There was not.

Allied tanks appeared to be spearheading the advance. It was tanks, reported first of all by the 726th Regiment at 07.35, that were by-passing Asnelles and le Hamel to the east. Hansmann was not at all surprised tanks were leading. He appreciated the fatigue the Allied infantry must be experiencing, noting the distance they had to wade from landing craft to the shore line. 'And today with the wind – Ja – one could practically label it a storm, whipping up the sea beneath!' It was impeding the landings, and 'certainly no stroll'. The enemy infantry looked exhausted, 'Tommies moved tiredly and sluggishly forwards'. Only the vehicles were 'flitting here and there', and 'were attacking the villages from the rear with machine gun fire'.[7]

The 716th Division reported the heights east of Meuvaines were stormed at about 08.00, having been subjected to 'heavy fire' and soon surrounded. The strong-point holding the feature – 35a – was held by Russian auxiliaries from 1st Company Ost Battalion 441, who 'fled rearwards'. Thereupon, 'the enemy moved east of Asnelles with very strong armoured forces and attacked both to the south east and south west'. By now the 716th Division was labelling this fast deteriorating situation 'Einbruchsraum west', the western break-in point. Four kilometres further east, at Ver-sur-Mer, the junction between Gold and Juno, resistance was broken by 10.32, tearing open the western gap even further.[8]

The 7th Company 736th Regiment was overwhelmed by the 5th East Yorks Battalion on King Sector. There was a substantial breakthrough according to the 716th Division both sides of Vaux, between Ver-sur-Mer and Courseulles. The company from Ost Battalion 441 providing the guard force 'fled to the rear in small groups'. An immediate counter-attack by three companies of the IInd Battalion 726th Regiment retook the heights to the south, but they exchanged hands again following a Canadian tank-infantry attack. Major Lehman who had led the attack clung to part of the heights at Sainte-Croix but 'apart from some *Panzerfaust* (bazooka) rounds, had no anti-tank weapons'. Trying to restore an untenable situation, Lehman's battalion was overrun. Survivors held out around the battalion CP at the northern edge of the village, where the battalion commander was later killed. Division reported 'a small group resisted until nightfall, but with no anti-tank weapons available, pulled back'.[9]

SS-Obersturmführer Hansmann watching this dramatic, yet unequal, contest from afar, was feeling increasingly vulnerable. Allied fighters, completely unmolested were strafing the area behind the Arromanches cliffs. Watching rockets directly penetrate bunker embrasures caused him to glance in alarm at his own lightly protected armoured vehicles. 'Were they sufficiently camouflaged?' he considered. He had few illusions about the lethality of these aircraft. 'Once they have located us, we would be finished. Even our "Tigers" were powerless against these "deadly blowflies".'[10] Grenadier Vogt was similarly dismayed by the awesome display of might parading off Gold Beach. 'I think we were used as cannon fodder' he complained.

*You know, it was the fifth year of the war, and we just didn't have the means. The Allies could afford to spare their troops, what with their superiority in equipment. They said, "why should we sacrifice a single GI against German infantry fire; the Germans outfight us there anyway. No, we'll just carpet bomb them. We'll just use our flyers to drop the sky on their heads. We'll just make use of our superior artillery."*[11]

SS-Obersturmführer Hansmann radioed his division from Magny at 07.45:

*Over 400 ships with a wall of barrage balloons along the whole 30 km stretch towards the Orne estuary. British are streaming ashore, unhindered, including heavy equipment. 11 heavy tanks identified. Coastal defences knocked out and overrun. Infantry in battalion strength moving south toward Bayeux. Enemy naval gunfire is engaging Bayeux and approach roads. Fighters are strafing cliff strong-points. I will recce towards Creully – out.*

Suddenly coming under naval shellfire, Hansmann's two armoured cars broke cover and began to recce further eastwards. Depressingly, 'everywhere it was the same picture, troops were disembarking without pause along the beaches from the never ending line of ships stretching to the east.' He could see the situation was fast deteriorating. 'It now appeared that bunkers in sight had been shot out of action by engaging battleships. Return fire could not be discerned.' Prospects for a successful defence of Bayeux with the forces in place did not appear plausible. Hansmann had already seen earlier that morning that 'there were more Pioneers [*Arbeitsdienstmänner* – construction workers] and office clerks than soldiers'. His own division – the 12th SS – he realised 'with considerable horror' was still 100 kilometres away and 'it would take two days before they could attack here'. He had no idea what the situation further along the coast in Caen, Cabourg, Houlgate and Deauville might be like. 'But surely the 21st Panzer

Division could manage to attack here today?'[12] There seemed little chance of forming a local reserve between himself and Bayeux, some four kilometres to the rear. The only possibility might be the Kampfgruppe 'Meyer'.

Oberstleutnant Meyer's battle group was jointly the 352nd Division and 84th Corps reserve. Meyer had been up all night dealing with a succession of orders and counter-orders that had steadily diluted the coherence of his Kampfgruppe. His soldiers were mounted on bicycles, his heavy weapons and ammunition on lorries. He had been given three conflicting tasks since 03.13, all of which involved regrouping and the further dispersal of his already scarce radio assets. He was required to provide two headquarters, one for the Omaha task and the other, now primary mission to counter-attack north eastwards towards Meuvaines and restore the breakthrough in *Einbruchsraum west*. Once on the move, because of the lack of radios, he was difficult to contact. Furthermore, it was almost impossible for him effectively to command and control such a wide range of disparate units, ranging from bicycle infantry, lorried heavy weapons and now assault guns from Panzerjäger Abteilung 352 – who had yet to join him. Meyer had an unenviable task; and now Allied 'Jabos' – fighter bombers – were beginning to appear. Hansmann already on reconnaissance in his area remarked how 'despite low clouds they would dive like lightning and bang away in the villages south of Cruelly'.[13] The very area through which Meyer had been directed to clear.

By 11.00 the situation was getting worse, and nobody knew for certain where Meyer was. Headquarters 352nd Division appealed for information by radio. 'When will you arrive? From what attack direction?' The 716th Division reported the British were 'attacking Ryes with 40 heavy tanks' at 13.17. This was about five kilometres northeast of Bayeux. Still no news from Meyer. The 1st Battalion from Infantry Regiment 916 was pulled out of its coastal positions and ordered to strike eastwards to St Côme to relieve the pressure on Meuvaines. It was a futile gesture.[14]

Meyer's progress, however, could be discerned by the columns of inky black smoke that boiled up from the lanes and by-roads north east of Bayeux. Vehicles drove into ditches and infantry dropped their bicycles and ran for cover into fields, following each sudden fighter attack.

Heralded by the throaty growl of engines, these became a screaming howl as aircraft dived, dissolving into chattering cannon fire as each attack came in. Sortie after sortie left its pathetic cluster of dead and wounded by the road side. It was virtually impossible, under these conditions, to advance and maintain unit integrity. In desperation 352nd Division despatched a liaison officer as 'there was no contact with the Kampfgruppe while it was on the move'. The reasons soon became apparent. After finding the battle group during the afternoon, information began to flow again after 15.30. 'Due to ceaseless fighter attacks (Jabos) along roads and lanes, the battle group has been able to progress only slowly forwards, losing both personnel and material.' It was estimated 'an attack H-Hour of 16.00 may be possible'. Assault guns began to arrive 20 minutes later.[15]

At H-Hour the Kampfgruppe began to move forward, conducting a two-pronged advance, with Fusilier Battalion 352 on the right, from Villiers- le-Sec, and the 1st Battalion 915th Regiment left, in Bazenville. 'Enemy tanks' were just ahead 'near Creully, attacking southward'. Meyer's Kampfgruppe, some two battalions with assault guns, was assaulting enemy forces around Meuvaines which according to German radio intercepts 'were already estimated to be one division strong'.[16] The outcome was predictable.

By 17.30 the attack had collapsed, in the face of an 'overwhelming enemy'. Both assault wings were pushed back, 'the assault guns could not penetrate the superiority of heavy tanks'. Contact was lost with the left prong, the IInd Battalion 915th Regiment. 'The commander', according to one report, 'Oberstleutnant Meyer, appeared to have been badly wounded and taken prisoner'. Misfortune piled upon misfortune. The 716th Division reported at 18.00 'a particularly deep penetration' on the right. Finally at 21.00 the missing left attacking battalion reported in by radio 'that it was surrounded in Bazenville, although it had captured an English Brigadier'. Nearly two hours later Meyer's Kampfgruppe headquarters with the 352nd Fusilier Battalion radioed 'the battalion is 40-strong, there are still 50 men remaining from I/915 [the left wing] and additionally six intact assault guns. Enemy pressure had obliged the battle group to retreat to Ducy' two kilometres south of the Bayeux-Caen Route Nationale 13. Meyer was dead.[17]

Contact with the coastal strong-points in the break-through area was now lost. At 16.12 the 726th Regiment heard the signature of the final collapse through telephone reports, which were relayed to Division headquarters.

*WN39 is occupied by enemy, WN38 surrounded, similarly WN40 is being attacked by six tanks and a company of infantry. Further seven tanks are standing before WN42 and several tanks in front of WN44. Considerable enemy landings in front of WN62.*

Ryes was reported overcome 26 minutes later. Schnelle Brigade 30, a reinforcement infantry-bicycle unit, arrived at 16.00, 'but because of a lack of heavy weapons is suited only for defence operations'. Forces were frantically scraped together to defend Bayeux. Flak Regiment 32, which had been hastily moved from Maisy, was located east and west of the city. The 352nd Division's training battalion was recalled from the rear. It appeared that the Allied spearhead, within two kilometres of Bayeux at the end of the day, would not be contained. General Kraiss, realising he had insufficient

strength to restore the situation on his eastern flank, admitted late that night 'what I could commit as reserves for the division had been done already. Every strip of ground is to be defended and made as expensive as possible until further reserves are committed.' The 716th Division on the other side of the chasm, with its western flank in the air similarly despaired. In addition to the Kampfgruppe 'Meyer', it had pinned its hopes upon Panzerjäger Battalion 200, two flak platoons and another assault engineer platoon. Measured against assaulting enemy divisions, not surprisingly, little was achieved by these hastily committed companies and platoons. The 716th Division was to later report 'the tasked units were struck by the enemy, who had already broken through to the south, before they could reach their ordered locations'. No details could be given about their fate. They were swallowed up without trace by the Allied advance.[18]

The German defence on Gold Beach, as the soldiers were well aware, stood no chance against the overwhelming echeloned assault to which they were subjected. 'I was scared stiff the entire time', admitted Grenadier Robert Vogt, 'but at the same time, I was incredibly angry that we were even being used against such odds'. Oberleutnant Werner Fiebig was equally despondent.

*I saw hundreds of English tanks but not one of our own German tanks. Because of all these things it became very clear to us that we were up against an irresistible force we could not hold back.[19]*

Coastal defences before Gold had collapsed. The road to Bayeux was open.

## *Einbruchsraum Mitte.* Break-in Point Centre ... Juno.

Lance Corporal Ernest Foster aboard an LCA had been visibly impressed by the power of the Allied bombardment on Juno.

*We thought there'd be nobody left alive on that beach, and yet when we got there, landing craft were being blown up, on the mines. The Germans were still there. They must have been like us, felt exactly the same as we did, absolutely shit scared ... they must have been, and so were we. We knew that when we landed, we had to get in, we had to take that beach; and if we had been driven back into the sea it would have been the end of us – but it wasn't.[1]*

The three villages with prominent church spires seemingly beckoning the Allied advance toward Juno, at Courseulles, Bernières and St Aubin were held by two companies of the 736th Infantry Regiment. They were covering an eight-kilometre frontage, normally a task for three times their number. The likelihood of a successful defence appeared daunting. 'I looked towards the sea'

*Above:* Coastal defences before Gold had collapsed. An exhausted German soldier. The road to Bayeux was open.

*Above:* Behind the wall of smoke that came rolling in from the sea the 736th Regiment's 9th and 10th Companies fought an anonymous battle, counter-attacking beach exits.

Above: On shore desperate fighting continued on the shoulders of the break-in point. A German infantryman hurls a stick grenade, recorded in a German newsreel.

*Left:* The collapse at *Einbruchsraum Mitte*, or Juno, began at about 10.32. A cine-still of defenders being led away. Half-submerged and wrecked LCAs are in the background.

commented Lieutenant Gustav Pflocksch manning a bunker off 'Nan-Red' Beach at St Aubin, and 'the sea was black, full of ships, I couldn't even count them'. They were going to be overrun. There was no doubt about it. The panzers were unlikely to arrive within the time they predicted they could hold out, and Pflocksch was aware of the paucity of local reserves compared to the panorama of naval might unfolding before him. 'I immediately thought', he reflected, 'this is the beginning of the end'.[2]

Elements of three companies held the beaches on the nine-kilometre Juno sector. In depth, covering a similar frontage were a further one Russian auxiliary, and two German companies, all dispersed. Four to five artillery batteries were in positions able to fire within sector and six anti-tank guns. They faced the Canadian 3rd Division spearheaded by two assaulting brigade groups, which were to beach with a local superiority in excess of 15 to 1, supported by tanks and specialist equipments. The 8th Company of the 736th Regiment had already been annihilated, caught in the open by naval gunfire, searching for bogus paratroopers south of Bernieres. German strong-points were merely stones that would produce a momentary wash as this irresistible tide poured in. Lieutenant Werner Fiebig, observing nearby, saw the force gathering momentum before crashing ashore. 'As it grew light, landing craft and assault boats left the assault craft, trying to reach the beach.'[3]

A short distance to the east SS-Obersturmführer Peter Hansmann, having by-passed burning houses in Creully, made intermittent observation halts until he was in a position to view Juno. 'Despite the bad weather and clouds of smoke that obscured the coastal road, now and again it was possible to get a good view of the wide sandy beaches west of Courseulles.' He was staggered at the awesome display unfolding beneath.

*Along the complete width of about 20km of coast, unbroken light coloured wavelets of fast landing craft advanced to the beach. Hundreds of boats were already unloading in shallow water. Vehicles were diving into the sea and wading on land.*

He was observing the 3rd Canadian Division coming ashore, immediately penetrating and fighting a headway into Courseulles and Bernieres.

*Our own artillery must be in Creully "plastering" this sector of the coast. Strikes both in water and on land were showing good results. The beach is overflowing with much equipment and the Tommies are trying to quickly get into the first houses on the beach. Among several houses pockets of men are assembling in company strength. The front must still be holding here.*[4]

But the collapse began at about 10.32 as recorded by Headquarters 716th Division. *Einbruchsraum Mitte* or the central break-in point occurred when 'strong armoured forces landed at St Aubin, Bernières and broke through to the south'.[5] Hansmann remarked 'tanks are already driving on the coastal road, the short outline of the Sherman is quickly identifiable as an enemy tank'. They were well supported by artillery 'which methodically ploughed up the hinterland and roads which led across the heights beyond to Caen'. Hansmann decided after 11.00, following a further radio contact report to headquarters, to return to the division 'to report personally' what he had seen 'otherwise nobody would believe it'.

Three kilometres south of the break-in point lay the village of Taillerville on the high ground overlooking the coast. During the course of the day the battalion command post (CP) of the IInd Battalion 736th Regiment was completely surrounded by the Canadian North Shore Regiment, but managed temporarily to fight itself free. The last message came from the CP at 15.48. 'Hand-to-hand fighting inside the command post.' Surrounded once again, the remnants held on, 'hemmed into a closely confined area, but still holding out'.[6]

'The strong-point was overrun by the British', said Oberleutnant Werner Fiebig, but he was 'luckily separated' with his forward artillery observation team. Unfortunately their rations had been left behind in the strong-point. The small group 'waited until dusk, and once darkness had fallen tried to get past English positions, patrols and bivouacs, and break through to our lines'. Four days later, 'laying in a coma, exhausted, having had hardly anything to eat or drink in the meantime, we were discovered and taken prisoner'.[7] Oberleutnant Pflocksch's bunker in St Aubin was by-passed and subsequently overrun. He survived and was also taken prisoner. 'I asked myself whether I should be happy or unhappy about the invasion', he said, 'and I found out there was every reason to be somewhat happy. Now the war will very soon come to an end.'[8]

The Canadian advance continued south and southeast, recoiling from the shoulder of the Luftwaffe strong-point situated between Juno and Sword, three to four kilometres inland at Douvres-la-Délivrande. The strong-point commanded by Oberleutnant Igle was to prove a tough nut to crack. Igle had at his disposal 238 men, three 50mm anti-tank guns, three 50mm pieces originally designed for use in Mark III tanks, six 20mm flak, 20 machine guns, mortars and 12 flamethrowers. Initial Allied attacks bounced off the bitter resistance offered by the defenders. It was an imposing objective, described later by Frank Gillard, an Allied warcorrespondent as 'that colossal strong-point'.

*That's a place to see. Somebody this morning called it an inverted sky scraper. That's not an unreasonable description. Fifty feet and more into the ground it goes - four stories deep.*

It was to hold out for 10 days, providing the German defence effort with important information, as the telephone lines remained intact. The 716th Division commented how 'headquarters was kept constantly informed on Allied progress that could be monitored within sight of its observation area, providing useful material for further operations'. As Gillard remarked 'the Germans who were standing here on this ground ... certainly must have felt that they had little to fear'.[9] Igle and his men held on, secure in the knowledge the panzers would come.

Other observers did not share his optimism. SS-Obersturmführer Hansmann having decided to pull back and rejoin the 12th SS Division, was well aware the initiative was fast slipping away, having witnessed the steady degradation of the forward coastal defences. It appeared to continue.

*Despite the noise of our own engines I heard the loud throbbing of aircraft engines. They must be directly above us in the clouds. What is going to happen now? ... I'm already looking for a protective building wall in the village coming up. There – I can see flashes of lightning. The distance is 20 kilometres to the south east, which can only be Caen. The black clouds of smoke are ever bigger and widening, lit up by flames. Then the sound of booms reached us!*

Only hours before they had driven through the city. 'Or has a day already passed by?' Hansmann voiced the frustrations of many who, having seen the fleet, had no illusion that this was the invasion, and had to be met head on, quickly.

*I wish I could call all the Generals up to Adolf Hitler and say: "Get here quickly – before it's too late. Anything that can still fight, get it here! The fastest, strongest divisions – here! The Air Force – where are you now? Get here! The Navy ... where are they? They must get here!"*[10]

The Canadians advancing south from Juno were to achieve a penetration of almost 12km by nightfall.

## *Einbruchsraum Ost*. Break-in Point East ... Sword.

Hauptmann Schimpf, commanding the IIIrd Battery of Artillery Regiment 1716, screwed up his eyes and tried once again, peering through the binoculars, to focus on what was happening at La Brèche. It was virtually impossible to see. He could only discern intermittent views of fighting which, as Headquarters 716th Division later commented, 'lay behind a thick wall of smoke'. In between clouds of smoke he could pick out scores of landing craft approaching the beaches. Some were burning. Tracer rounds suddenly flashed from a bunker and seemingly passed through the dark shapes silhouetted on the sea. Single anti-tank rounds flashed horizontally across the water, the glowing tracer base occasionally skipping with a splash and arcing into the air. Dark bee-

tle-like shapes, possibly tanks, crawled onto the beach; and then the smoke rolled back again, blotting out the scene. What was going on? A later report commented:

*Only sparse and fragmentary reports are available over the actual conduct of the landings, because observation due to the extensive smoke screen was hardly possible. Communication to the coastal defences had been interrupted during the bombardment, and only a few troops ever returned.*[1]

Schimpf suspected it was not going their way.

Only three German infantry companies from the 736th Regiment defended the eight-kilometre frontage on Sword. A fourth company defended Franceville on the other side of the Orne estuary. They were concentrated around three strong-points at Luc-sur-Mer, La Brèche and Lion, and Ouistreham. Inland were further dispersed elements of another three companies roughly two to three kilometres from the coast. Four batteries of artillery could provide direct support, with another two east of the Orne. Allied troops were observed coming ashore between Colleville and Luc. In essence, a two-brigade echeloned assault, spearheading two divisions, struck only two companies able to engage with direct fire. There were few anti-tank weapons sited in this area, apart from medium guns enclosed in bunkers. 'The coast here was only held by field positions, or troop constructed and reinforced trench positions', remarked Headquarters 716th Division. Beach barriers were, moreover, sparse on the western side of the beach 'due to the rocky ground beneath the surface which presented difficulties erecting obstacles'.[2]

Behind the wall of smoke that came rolling in from the sea, obscuring them from support, the 9th and 10th Companies of the 736th Regiment fought an anonymous battle. The troop-constructed earthworks were overcome by 'assault groups, who broke their way in with explosive charges and flame-throwers'. As with all the landings, the sudden appearance of tanks unhinged the defence. 'Shortly after the first landings of specialist troops and infantry', the 716th Division reported, 'it appeared that already, at the same landing points, tanks were on land'. Eight tanks were reported to the west of Riva Bella by 09.10.[3]

A misty shroud cloaked everything. The German strong-point and battery at Riva Bella, Ouistreham, was smoked off and neutralised by naval gunfire as the landings continued. Oberleutnant Steiner manning a bunker at water level at Franceville was unable, due to the protrusion of the Ouistreham harbour mouth, to see what was going on around the corner from Riva Bella. Consequently his Ist Battery of the 1716th Regiment at Merville, crippled by the ground parachute assault, but with two to three guns still in action, was unable to bring accurate fire to bear. At La Brèche however, artillery observers holding on with the 10th Company of the 736th Regiment could direct fire. The enemy had broken in among the buildings fronting the beach. Fire from four batteries, including the Merville, were brought down. This was a mixture of coastal and heavy artillery and Army batteries inland. The result according to the 716th Division was:

*Two large boats were sunk, and two smaller ones set on fire. Enemy losses according to observers and prisoner of war reports, were very high.*[4]

But as Stabsfeldwebel Johannes Buskotte directing fire in the Merville battery position was to remark, 'for every round we fired, we got anything between 20 and a 100 back'.[5]

At 08.21 'it appeared', according to the 716th Division, 'that the enemy had broken through between Riva-Bella and Lion-sur-Mer'. *Einbruchsraum Ost* – Break-in Point East had been torn apart. Within two and a half hours it was reported enemy infantry had stormed Colleville and the heights at Point 61. Both the IInd and IVth Batteries of Artillery Regiment 1716 'are surrounded'. At 11.50 Riva Bella was 'encircled', the Infantry Regiment 736 command post was by-passed, so that both it and the Ist Battery 1716th Regiment command post was cut off. The defence line before Caen was teetering. Enemy cyclists had already been spotted advancing from Ouistreham south west towards St Aubin d'Arquenay at 12.15. This was the vanguard of the British Special Service (Commando) Brigade advance on Bénouville. Penetrations of up to four kilometres had already been achieved, only five or six kilometres from the outskirts of Caen. The 716th Division hurriedly scraped together resources to shield the city. At this point, only Flak Abteilung (Battalion) 996 and a Pioneer (Construction) Battalion 803 were available. They were committed to a 'second position' being formed north of Caen.[6]

On the shore desperate fighting continued on the shoulders of the break-in point. At 10.00 the IIIrd Battalion 736th Regiment was moved out of its defence positions and attacked from Plumetot north eastwards into Lion-sur-Mer. Its aim was to reach the 10th Company, marooned and now fast disintegrating in its defence of La Brèche. Directly supported by the 13th Heavy Field Howitzer Battery – '*Grafwaldersee*' – with 150mm self-propelled guns, it penetrated 'as far as the high point of the church in Lion'. They were, however, abruptly struck in the rear and flanks by British troops coming from the west. Temporarily cut off, the battalion fought its way back to the western outskirts of Lion.

The situation by 16.00 in *Einbruchsraum Ost* was critical. The 716th Division reported that while these events were continuing 'the enemy continued to land further forces at several points on the coast within the divisional sector throughout the entire period. The landing places were engaged ceaselessly by those batteries still able to shoot.'[7] The IIIrd Battalion 736th Regiment held grimly on to its positions along the coast on the western side of Lion, holding the left shoulder of Break-in Point East. Meanwhile to the right, in Ouistreham and Riva Bella, the British methodically reduced all resistance.

Hauptmann Schimpf had been following the progress of the battle off La Brèche and Riva Bella from his bunker on the eastern bank of the Orne throughout the day. He could only fleetingly glimpse developments, because of the rolling clouds of smoke that constantly obscured his view. Two landing craft had certainly been hit and gone down. He had been able to make out the scores of dots of survivors' heads in the water. It had given him grim satisfaction to see the reddish orange hue reflecting through the smoke screen as two more burned furiously, clouds of bulbous inky black smoke rose majestically into the sky. But now at 16.00 he could see that British soldiers were behind Riva Bella, having penetrated Ouistreham 'and were attacking from the landward side'. Likewise, 'the strong-point's flank had been turned in the west'. Helplessly he watched the final resistance of comrades he would have spent happy hours drinking with, in regimental messes along the coast, being mopped up. The muffled thump and outpouring of smoke from bunkers surrounded by British infantry signified the end. More disturbing were the sudden jets of oily flame which seemed to extinguish all signs of resistance. He reported to the 716th Division:

*It could be seen from Franceville how assault groups worked their way from bunker to bunker, breaking into dug-outs and embrasures with flame throwers and explosive charges.*[8]

It was all over for them.

In Lion-sur-Mer, along the beach, in houses now beginning to show the shabby signs of conflict, the IIIrd Battalion of the 736th Regiment was pondering its ever diminishing chances for a renewal of the counter-attack. Their comrades at La Brèche had clearly succumbed to the assault some hours before, but all was not completely lost. They had only to hold onto these coastal positions until the panzers arrived, and they would be in a position to turn the British flank. At about 19.00 the first armoured half-track churned into the western outskirts of Lion with a clattering of tracks and the whine of Maybach six-cylinder engines, and stopped. A second and third followed and pulled up, dust and exhaust gently rolling beyond the vehicles as even more clattered into side streets and halted. Soldiers wiped the grime from their faces and slapped the dust from their uniforms, and smiled, they had reached the coast. 'Bravo!' came the shouts from houses nearby, when the tired defenders realised these were panzergrenadiers. Kampfgruppe 'Rauch' had arrived. This was Panzergrenadier Regiment 192 of the 21st Panzer Division. The panzers were coming.

# CHAPTER 13

# COUNTER-ATTACK

*'Oppeln, if you don't succeed in throwing the British into the sea, we shall have lost the war.'*
General Marcks Comd. 84 Corps

## 21st Panzer attacks ...

By 09.00 the bulk of the armoured forces of 21st Panzer Division were moving steadily north east of Caen, away from the landings, to destroy the paratroopers that had landed east of the Orne. Oberleutnant Rupprecht Grzimek of the reconnaissance battalion remembered a liaison officer reporting 'not only had an airborne division landed east of the Orne, but the enemy had brought up a vast armada off the coast and was preparing a landing from the sea'.[1] Yet Panzer Regiment 22, the nucleus of the tank strength of the division, continued to drive north eastwards away from the threatened sector, which even as their original order was issued, was under naval gun fire. Behind them 'we saw Caen at the horizon as a burning smoking town' said Unteroffizier Werner Kortenhaus, a tank commander in the IVth Abteilung (battalion). 'The march was slow and difficult, the roads choked by other units moving up and by refugees fleeing from Caen.'[2] At 10.30 Seventh Army, under whose command the 21st Panzer had been placed, announced that the division, due to the change of situation was to be committed <u>west</u> of the Orne. The 'axis of advance was to be Lion'[3] against the amphibious landings. What followed mirrored the parallel difficulties already experienced by the 352nd Division reserve, obliged to check, and turn in mid-stride.

By early afternoon, as the implication of the counter-order became apparent, forward units had already closed with the airborne enemy. 'East of Caen lay the first British paratroopers to be killed' recalled Unteroffizier Hammel of the 21st Panzer Reconnaissance Battalion. 'From their parachute silk we cut ourselves scarfs as protection against the dust'.[4] The 8th Company of Panzergrenadier Regiment 192 was fighting in Benouville on the west bank of the Orne. It had now to cross to the east bank. Assault Gun Battalion 200 now moving through Caen to the west, was ordered to turn about to the east. The Ist Battery of Panzer Artillery Regiment

155 (SP guns) was already fighting in the Mathieu area on the west bank, and had suffered heavy losses from naval and air bombardment. Panzerjäger Abteilung 200 with 24 88mm self-propelled guns was already in position north east of Caen. All these units were now required to change location.

At 13.00 General Feuchtinger the Division Commander ordered the tank force to be split. Three tank battalions (Abteilung I to III) were to attack the sea-borne landings, the fourth battalion of Panzer Regiment 22 was to combine with Major von Luck's Panzergrenadier Regiment 125, together with some divisional artillery, mortar and reconnaissance elements, and continue the attack on the parachutists. Three battle groups or 'Kampfgruppen' were thereby formed; two for operations west of the Orne and one for the east. The Panzer Kampfgruppe 'Oppeln' – with two tank battalions, one panzergrenadier, one engineer and an armoured artillery battalion; and the Panzergrenadier Kampfgruppe 'Rauch' – with two armoured infantry battalions with armoured engineers and artillery – were to be committed against the sea-borne landings. The third Kampfgruppe, 'von Luck' – with two panzergrenadier battalions, one tank, panzer reconnaissance and assault gun battalions – was to attack the paratroopers on the other side of the Orne.

The main implication of the countermanded order was that the one panzer division actually able to menace the invasion at the point of landing, chose to dilute its combat power at the main point of effort, instead of concentrating it. Only two thirds of the division would attack the amphibious landings west of the Orne. Major von Luck commanding the third battle group was to later comment:

*The regrouping of the division took hours. Most of the units, from the area east of Caen and the Orne had to squeeze through the eye of the needle at Caen and over the only bridges available in this sector. Caen was under virtually constant bombardment from the navy and fighter bombers of the RAF.*[5]

The tank force was abruptly recalled and turned around

174

just as it was beginning to give orders and form for the originally conceived attack east of the river. The vanguard became the rearguard, and the former rearguard became the spearhead. Colonel von Oppeln-Bronikowski, the regimental commander, now found himself at the rear of the column. As the bridges at Bénouville were held by British paratroopers, a detour through Caen was unavoidable. Allied air attacks at 13.30 had partially blocked the streets with rubble and enveloped the city in rolling clouds of smoke. Detours and additional bridges could not be made ready in time. Refugees choked the streets. This obliged the majority of units frustratingly to move south and cross the Orne via the Route Nationale 158 road bridge. Part of Panzer Regiment 22 used the bridge at Colombelles accepting time delays diverting through the industrial area. Advance parties and military police hurriedly drove ahead to man checkpoints and junctions, waving on dust shrouded clattering convoys as they sped through narrow streets. Eight rocket-firing Typhoons attacked the columns as they emerged on the western outskirts of the city. Six tanks were damaged. Two were left in flames while four others belched smoke by the roadside.[6] Shortly before 16.00 the Ist and IInd Battalions of 'Oppeln's' group began shaking out into a tactical formation near the small town of Lebisey north of Caen.

General Marcks, the 84th Corps Commander, was already there. Apprehensively, He had been looking for the unit ever since it had come under his command. Assembly was subject to delays as platoons and companies clattered into position on arrival and sat motionless, menacing silhouettes in the long corn awaiting the order to attack. There were coordination problems as five command vehicles had fallen out on the line of march.[7] Some six to eight hours had already been squandered in delays while Allied troops poured ashore. The General himself guided the Kampfgruppe 'Rauch' from the 192nd Regiment into position, anxious to save time and get the advance moving. The force disposed of about 90 tanks for the coming attack, a reduced panzer and panzergrenadier regiment supported by engineers and artillery. Ahead lay the gently sloping Périers ridge — the only physical barrier, apart from dispersed villages, before the coast — incorporating the villages of Périers and Beuville. It was key ground, thought to be German held, by flak and assault guns. Oberst von Oppeln-Bronikowski had little idea what lay beyond, but felt confident he had sufficient force to reach the sea. After all, the panzers had traditionally swept all before them, when used en masse. General Marck's closing comment, however, left him feeling extremely uneasy.

*Oppeln, if you don't succeed in throwing the British into the sea we shall have lost the war.*[8]

At the command 'Panzer - Marsch!' engines fired, and tell-tale smudges of grey exhaust rose from the dark menacing shapes dispersed in the fields. With a lurch and squeal of tracks the two panzer battle groups 'Oppeln' and 'Rauch' began steadily to drone northward. The time was 16.20. The leading elements of the 3rd British Division's 185th Brigade had by this time occupied Beuville seven kilometres inland, and was also moving down the west bank of the Orne canal in parallel. The 8th Brigade in depth, was well established in Hermanville, Colleville-sur-Orne and Ouistreham, mopping up a faltering German resistance. The 9th Brigade was assembling just clear of the beach, preparing to advance into, and close the five to six-kilometre gap to the Canadian sector further west. Traffic jams around beach exits were slowing operations. Nevertheless, a battalion of the Shropshire Light Infantry had pushed on ahead toward Caen, and after some skirmishing occupied the Périers ridge. The German assault guns and flak previously in occupation had been relocated to deal with the breakthrough threatening in the west south of Gold. Beuville and Biéville on the road to Caen had also been occupied by the spearhead of the British advance. The infantry's 6pdr anti-tank guns had caught up, and were disposed along the ridge and villages to cover the advance to Caen. They had been thickened up by 17pdr SP guns from the 20th Anti-Tank Regiment. One squadron of the Staffordshire Yeomanry was with them on the ridge and another around Beuville and Biéville with a third on the way. Unbeknown to the Germans, the key ground overlooking their advance to the sea was occupied by an effective anti-tank screen, able to both block and fire in defilade. Soon after 16.00 a troop of the Staffordshire Yeomanry spotted approaching armour. Observers in Beuville watched with bated breath as up to 40 squat menacing shapes moved at speed left to right, northwards, towards the Périers ridge. The scene encapsulated the greatest fear of invasion planners - the panzers were sweeping down on the beaches.

Bad news travelled quickly. The attack produced a scare, spawning numerous rumours. Only those occupying the villages and ridge could see the enemy. Lieutenant Paul Holbrook, a troop commander in the Yeomanry Regiment, waiting in depth saw only that 'bursts of shot swung now and then their way, red lights soaring in dotted lines overhead'. But he could make out what was going on as 'confused voices came over the air'.

*"Hallo Able one Hallo Able one. Enemy hornet is attacking my Able three."*

*"Fire at the bastard", an angry scream.*

*"Hallo Able two … Fire! Fire!"*

*Meanwhile a dull dogged voice here and there would be checking a net.*

*"Hallo Dog two, Hallo Dog two."*

*"For Christ's sake get off the air, Dog two. There's a hornet attacking Able three … I want to keep through to Sunray. Where's Able three?"*

*"Hallo Able three, Hallo Able three … report my signals. Over?"*

There was no reply. 'Nor was there ever to be', recounted Holbrook.

*Sergeant Toynbee lay in the high corn with his legs shattered, while his turret companions, having scrambled free from the tank with their clothes on fire, ran for a stretcher under a hail of spandau fire. The driver and co-driver were dead in their seats.*

This particular duel with a German assault gun was lost, even though the victor was reduced to a 'burning pyre' by the remainder of the troop.[9]

Dust and the eye-watering rush of air blowing in the faces of panzer commanders travelling at speed, made forward observation difficult from their bumping and lurching turret cupolas. Nevertheless, the ridge line and the villages of Biéville and Beuville to their right were an obvious navigational aide. Hauptmann Herr commanded the phalanx of 25 Panzer Mk IVs to the right. There was still no opposition as, with a distinctive change in engine pitch, tanks began to change down in gear to climb the higher ground bordering the ridge line. The first 'crack' and distinctive 'plunk' of armoured shot was not at first apparent, but the flash and immediate oily conflagration that followed was. A Mk IV tank had burst into flames, followed quickly by another. Clunk after clunk followed as two more tanks shuddered, bursting into flame and smoke as they lost momentum and trickled to a halt. Burning figures could be discerned around turret hatches, slapping frantically at smouldering overalls, as they leapt and rolled over and over in the corn. 'The first Mk IV was blazing before a single German tank had the chance to fire a shot', reported one of the survivors. There was little they could do, the enemy had them cold. 'Their position was tactically well-chosen and their fire both heavy and accurate.' They tried 'firing at where the enemy were thought to be; but the English weapons were well concealed'. The impetus of the attack swung eastwards, to the left. Tanks sought cover among small woods, but were still being picked off. Six tanks were spluttering and crackling, dispersed oily-black columns of smoke began arcing into the sky. The advance here had to be broken off.

To the west, the Ist Abteilung under Hauptmann von Gottberg pushed steadily northward, through Epron past Cambes and began detouring around Mathieu when he too was struck by a storm of armoured shot from the Périers ridge. One tank after another was picked off as with a resounding 'plunk' armour-piercing shells plummeted home, ricocheting about inside and mutilating tank crew-men within. Ammunition fires blew turrets with a resounding hollow report into the air. Burnt crew-men sought cover or dragged their wounded toward rescue vehicles that attempted to recover them. One British anti-tank gun was knocked out, but with a further half-dozen tanks burning, von Gottberg attempted again to envelop the ridge from the western side. Three more tanks were crippled, adding even more spitting, spluttering smoking pyres to the scene. It was hopeless. The group had been repelled. One survivor expressed the scale of the set-back, in this, their first action:

*The fire of the English, from their outstandingly well-sited defence positions, was murderous … within a brief space of time, the armoured regiment of 21st Panzer Division had lost a total of 16 tanks, a decisive defeat, from which, especially in morale, it never recovered.[10]*

In contrast to the sounds of battle to his right, Oberst Rauch and his panzergrenadier half-track battle group punched, virtually unscathed, directly through to the coast. He had found the gap between the 3rd Canadian and 3rd British Divisions. Slipping through via Mathieu, Plumetot and Cresserons, they were able, with the SP artillery battery 'Grafwaldersee' to re-establish contact with the IIIrd Battalion Infantry Regiment 736, still holding the coastline west of Lion-sur-Mer. A tenuous wedge had been driven between Juno and Sword. It would require further armoured leverage to force a gap.

Meanwhile, the third prong of the 21st Panzer's trident-like thrust at the coast struck the paratroopers east of the Orne. Spearheading the Kampfgruppe 'von Luck' assault was Panzer Reconnaissance Battalion 21. Von Luck, bedevilled by the re-grouping problems attendant upon the change in the divisional attack plan, had to delay the advance until tanks from the IVth Abteilung (battalion) of the panzer regiment arrived. Major Becker's Assault Gun Battalion 200 did not, 'so I had to start without them' said von Luck. His IInd Battalion 125th Regiment was already engaged in heavy defensive fighting against paratroopers. Therefore 'I could free only limited elements of the battalion for the attack'. They could not delay the advance any longer. 'Our goal: to push through via Escoville-Hérouvillette to Ranville and the two Orne bridges.'[11]

'We went into the attack practically from the march', recalled Gefreiter Hammel of the reconnaissance battalion. They were supported by Mk IV panzers of the IVth Abteilung. 'Further west we could hear the sounds of battle', as the Kampfgruppe 'Oppeln' struck the Périers ridge.

*That, we heard, was where our armoured group was*

*Left:* Caen. Allied air attacks blocked the streets with rubble and enveloped the city in smoke. It could not easily be by-passed. *IWM*

*Right:* The panzers were sweeping down on the beaches. Panzer Mk IVs in the attack.

*Left:* Tanks sought cover among small woods, but were still being picked off. *Wochenshau* German newreel frame of Mark IVs in Normandy counter-attack.

*Right:* 'The fire of the English from their outstandingly well-sited defence positions, was murderous.' German cine-still of a tank battle in Normandy.

*supposed to attack. The enemy was apparently concentrating his naval fire against this, for him, dangerous thrust. His air force was also in action there. So we made good progress as far as the outskirts of Escoville.[12]*

Ranville, and the two important bridges across the Orne, lay just a few kilometres ahead. Von Luck, sensing he had achieved surprise pushed hard, his objective was a mere 10-minute drive away.

*Then all hell broke loose. The heaviest naval guns, up to 38cm in calibre, artillery, and fighter bombers plastered us without pause. Radio contacts were lost, wounded came back, and the men of the reconnaissance battalion were forced to take cover.*

Von Luck moving just behind the advance 'saw the disaster'. The attack was broken off. Such densities of artillery fire had never been experienced before. The reconnaissance battalion fell back to the southern edge of Escoville where it was ordered to dig in and contain any enemy advance. The assault guns and armour would be brought up to provide support. Division was informed of the impasse. The situation was not totally clear. It appeared that the armoured group to their west, across the Orne, may have reached the sea. Much air activity could be seen in that direction.

The psychological impact of the 21st Panzer attack outweighed its achievement on the ground. General Montgomery decided since it appeared 'likely that 21 Pz Div intends to hold Caen', it would be better to capture the city by envelopment.[13] This meant of course its collapse must come later. Members of the 3rd British Division, in depth, unable to observe the outcome of the battle, prepared for the worse. Major Tim Wheway moving up from the beach with his sadly depleted squadron of Flail tanks from the 22nd Dragoons, was held in check at the 27th Armoured Brigade assembly area. His mission to move onto the 'Ouistreham Canal' to assist the 6th Airborne 'was not possible', he confided in his diary, 'as fierce fighting was taking place around Hermanville and we were told to take up positions and be prepared to fight to the last'.[14] Similarly Private Richard Harris an infantryman in the 8th Brigade from the Suffolk Regiment described how 'we were warned to stand by for a counter-attack by German tanks advancing quickly north of Caen'. Infantrymen felt particularly vulnerable to the panzer threat. 'Even though Harry and I had dug a good protective slit trench we nevertheless felt, with only a rifle apiece, somewhat inadequately equipped to take on what was later identified as part of the 21st Panzer Division.' Although he learned some armour had been knocked out, ominously some of it had 'actually reached the coast at Lion-sur-Mer between the Canadians and our division'.[15]

No 48 Commando, having already suffered heavy losses on Juno, was on the eastern edge of the Canadian sector, engaged in clearing through the Langrune strong point. The intention was to link up with the British enclave further east. Lieutenant Colonel Moulton was suddenly ordered to call off the attack and 'organise the rest of the village for defence; German armour was moving up towards the coast, and Langrune was on its axis'. This added to already considerable difficulties. 'I was not sorry to be told to stop the attack', he recalled, 'as I was feeling at a loss what to do about it'. Lieutenant P.C. Webber of the 2nd Middlesex Regiment on the other side of the gap, having landed at Sword was worried, because 'it was rumoured that German tanks were mounting a counter-attack, which was all too true, for they had reached the coast just behind me'.[16] Exhaustion was sapping their spirit. There was little they could do in any case. They were tired. The events of the day, storming the beaches, the move inland – and now the panzers – were physically and mentally draining. 'I wondered what the morning would bring', speculated Moulton, 'we hardly seemed to be in shape to stand up to a panzer attack for long. We could but try.'[17]

That tanks were the panacea for panzers was the general Allied view. This was why indeed armoured brigades had been given priority on landing. Their crews however did not exude confidence. 'During the day I passed the survivors of tanks of the Staffordshire Yeomanry who had been blown up on a hill outside Hermanville', said R. Cadogan a DD tank crew-man who had landed at Sword. The sight did little to engender confidence, it instead emphasised their fragile mortality:

*They passed us like zombies with burnt uniforms and staring eyes, oblivious to their surroundings. At that time I had never seen anyone badly shocked before, and their appearance and burnt hands and faces frightened me when I thought of the days ahead, going into action and perhaps suffering as they were.[18]*

Lance Corporal Patrick Hennessey of the 13/18th Hussars like many other tank crew-men could identify with the horrors they had endured. 'Our friends, the Staffordshire Yeomanry had come up against elements of the 21st Panzer in the area of Biéville', he said, 'and had suffered severe casualties'. This was in subsequent fighting. 'When the remnants of their knocked out tanks were recovered and brought back, we saw for ourselves just what a Tiger could do to a Sherman, and it was a sobering sight.'[19]

The situation of the Kampfgruppe 'Rauch', the kern of Panzergrenadier Regiment 192 in Lion-sur-Mer, was precarious. They had driven a thin wedge between massive invasion forces, but there was nothing available to develop the breakthrough. Equally the Allies, who had seen or heard that panzers had punched through to the coast were feeling vulnerable. Dusk was approaching, and would likely stymie counter-measures by both sides.

At about 21.00 a vast low hum came in from the sea,

## 21st Panzer Division Counter-Attack

The main focus of effort by the 21st Panzer Division on D-Day morning was due to be directed east of the Orne against airborne insertions, ignoring impending amphibious landings to the west. The effort eventually fragmented into three battle groups, only two of which assaulted west of the Orne, one reaching the coast at Lion. The arrival of the airlanding elements of the 6th Airborne Division led to the collapse of this operation that had forced a German wedge between Juno and Sword. It was a case of too little, too late.

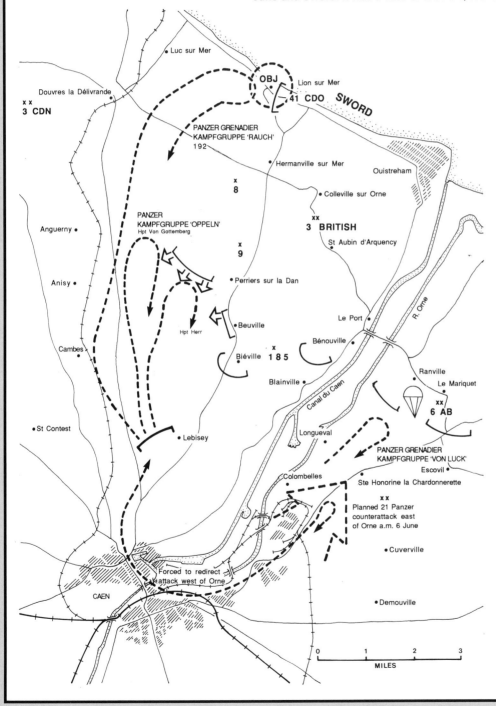

Luc sur Mer
OBJ
Lion sur Mer
41 CDO
SWORD
Douvres la Délivrande
xx
3 CDN
PANZER GRENADIER
KAMPFGRUPPE 'RAUCH'
192
Hermanville sur Mer
Ouistreham
x
8
Colleville sur Orne
PANZER
KAMPFGRUPPE 'OPPELN'
Hpt Von Gottemberg
Anguerny
xx
3 BRITISH
St Aubin d'Arquency
x
9
Anisy
Perriers sur la Dan
Le Port
R. Orne
Hpt Herr
Beuville
Bénouville
Cambes
x
Biéville 185
Ranville
Le Mariquet
Blainville
xx
6 AB
Canal du Caen
St Contest
Longueval
Lebisey
PANZER GRENADIER
KAMPFGRUPPE 'VON LUCK'
Escovil
Colombelles
Ste Honorine la Chardonnerette
xx
Planned 21 Panzer
counterattack east
of Orne a.m. 6 June
Cuverville
Forced to redirect
attack west of Orne
CAEN
Demouville
0 1 2 3
MILES

179

rising to a deep multiple growl. Eyes turned toward the source of the sound coming from the north, across the sea. Light was waning into evening, and clouds were growing darker. A weak sun partially obscured by cloud radiated its presence, bathing grey areas of sea with a silky iridescence. Waves of sound pulsating across the water heralded the arrival of a long column of black aircraft – four engined bombers Stirlings and Halifaxes, and Dakota and Albemarle twin-engined transport planes. The procession was endless. The Stirlings and Halifaxes were towing black gliders, Horsas and Hamilcars, clumsy looking long square boxes with wings. The long steady line of black aeroplanes stretched from the coastline over which they flew, far out to sea, into the horizon. To the Allies, the sight generated triumphant elation. It made them feel irresistible. For the Germans, it was a harbinger of doom. Unteroffizier Werner Kortenhaus of Panzer Regiment 22 declared 'no one who saw it will ever forget it'. They were taken completely by surprise. 'Suddenly, the hollow roaring of countless aeroplanes, and then we saw them, hundreds of them, towing great gliders, filling the sky.'

The air flotilla came over like a vast destructive cloud. It was carrying the rest of the British 6th Airborne Division's air-landing elements. The column, on arrival, bulged into a vast swarm as over the Orne estuary, wooden gliders were released. At the same time, just inland, thousands of red parachutes burst into blossom, most bearing ammunition. 'The sky was full of colour, flame and falling objects', described one witness, 'and it was impossible to know where to look'. Black and white gliders began to steeply swoop down towards the fields by the bridges over the Orne. The panzergrenadiers of the Kampfgruppe 'Rauch' dismally looked at each other with tired resignation on drawn faces. A number shook their heads in dismay. They were going to be cut off.[20]

## Assault towards Utah ...

H-Hour for von der Heydte's attack by Fallschirmjäger Regiment 6 toward Ste Marie-du-Mont, overlooking the American Utah Beach, was set for 19.30. This was to be the only substantial counter-attack mounted towards the Utah sector on D-Day. It did not get off to an auspicious start. As the columns trailed through Carentan en route to forward assembly areas, they were struck by an Allied bombing raid. Casualties were light, but the episode epitomised the unequal nature of the battle they were to fight. 'Not a single German aircraft had been spotted that day' commented Oberleutnant Pöppel in his diary.

*Where the hell are they? Every day is absolutely critical. Every day and every night – in fact every hour – the enemy is bringing his reinforcements ashore. Only by destroying the landing craft, the enemy fleet involved in the whole operation, can we destroy the enemy's supplies*

*and give ourselves a chance to drive him back into the sea.*[1]

The form-up points for the attack were reached at 17.30. Two hours later the two-pronged battalion assaults began. By this time the majority of the US 4th Division Regimental Combat Teams were pushing westward toward Ste Mère-Eglise. Fallschirmjäger Regiment 6 attacking north eastward came across scattered elements from the American 501st and 506th Parachute Regiments, part of the 101st Division. Both the 4th Division and the counter-attackers were assaulting blind, seeking each other in the dark. Neither side managed to grip his opponent sufficiently firmly to force a decision. In the close terrain of the 'bocage' or 'hedgerow' country, units feinted past each other in the gloom, without being aware of the other's presence. Von der Heydte reported 'the advance reached the tasked objectives – Ste Marie-du-Mont and Hiesville – by about midnight, following occasional costly and bitterly fought actions'.[2] The IInd Battalion well supported by the 8th Battery of Artillery Regiment 191 successfully penetrated Hiesville, but the Ist Battalion relying on the 4th Battery found its support, at best, intermittent following the onset of darkness. It too, however, pushed on through the night fighting occasional bloody hedgerow skirmishes until it reached Ste Marie-du-Mont. By then its commander, Hauptmann Preikschat, realised his battalion was in serious trouble.

At about 20.00 the drone of approaching aircraft developed into a pervasive humming sound that ominously grew in volume. Columns of black aircraft hove into view, breaking up into a swirling bird-storm as glider after glider was released, to swoop down into the darkening landscape. Taut wing-spans produced an eerie strumming sound as they skimmed across hedgerows and bellied in clouds of billowing dust and scattered foliage. Some driving into hedge-banks at speeds of up to 90mph disintegrated in splintering crashes. Casualties within such aircraft were fearful. Whimpering moans began to emanate from broken bodies within the surreal wrecks, often a maze of disjointed spars held loosely together by canvas.

The two leading battalions of Fallschirmjäger Regiment 6 attacked those gliders unfortunate enough to land between their objectives. 'They were', declared von der Heydte, 'immediately overwhelmed by concentrated fire from the 8th Battery and the heavy weapons of the IInd Battalion, and then annihilated by rapid reacting assault forays despatched by the latter'.[3] The regiment, he assessed was enveloped by a force of '146 gliders, including 45 giant gliders; concurrently paratroopers from 321 American transport aircraft jumped into the same area, Angoville, north of Carentan'. There was some dismay as the mass of air-landed troops had 'driven a wedge' into his flank, cutting off the Ist Battalion from the 'hedgehog' position already established to

*Left:* 'Thousands of red parachutes burst into blossom, most bearing ammunition.' Allied resupply on D-Day.

*Left:* 'The writing was already on the wall for our proud 6th Regiment' wrote Pöppel. Fallschirmjäger in the attack.

*Right:* 'Whimpering moans began to emanate from the surreal wrecks of American gliders, often only a maze of disjointed spars held loosely together by canvas.' Casualties as shown here, could be heavy.

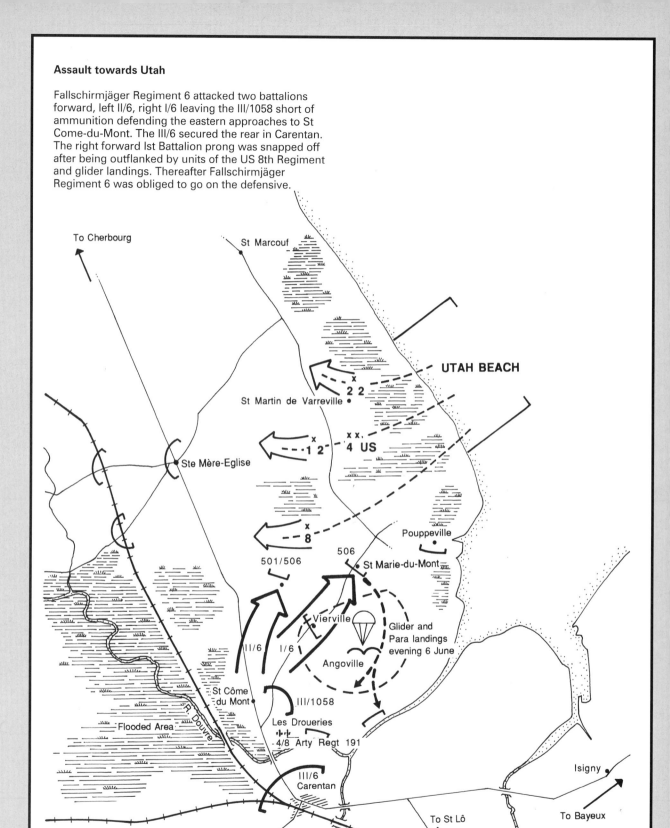

## Assault towards Utah

Fallschirmjäger Regiment 6 attacked two battalions
forward, left II/6, right I/6 leaving the III/1058 short of
ammunition defending the eastern approaches to St
Come-du-Mont. The III/6 secured the rear in Carentan.
The right forward Ist Battalion prong was snapped off
after being outflanked by units of the US 8th Regiment
and glider landings. Thereafter Fallschirmjäger
Regiment 6 was obliged to go on the defensive.

To Cherbourg

St Marcouf

UTAH BEACH

x
2 2

St Martin de Varreville

x
1 2

x x
4 US

Ste Mère-Eglise

x
8

Pouppeville

501/506

506

St Marie-du-Mont

Vierville

Glider and
Para landings
evening 6 June

II/6    I/6

Angoville

St Côme
du Mont

III/1058

Les Droueries

Flooded Area

-4/8  Arty Regt 191

R. Douve

III/6
Carentan

Isigny

To St Lô

To Bayeux

his rear at St Come-du-Mont by the IIIrd (Wehrmacht) Battalion of the 1058th Regiment.

Preikschat's battalion began to disintegrate. Spread between Vierville and Ste Marie-du-Mont, it was now cut off. At about 23.00 misfortune struck again. A sudden concentration of naval shellfire bracketed his supporting artillery battery. Pandemonium ensued: 27 men had been cut down by the swathe of high explosive that enveloped the gun positions. Von der Heydte indignantly complained that 'prompted by one of the battery officers, the crews fled without permission or direction from the regiment'. They remained missing until located in a village near Graignes the following afternoon. The Ist Battalion, now without fire support was subjected to 'heavy harassing naval and artillery gun fire throughout the night'. Further parachute landings came into the Angoville area at first light 'from about 100 machines', and a further 150 gliders were reported landing around the same area between 06.00 and 07.00. Von der Heydte, accepting the impasse, ordered the encircled battalion to break off the attack and fight its way back at 06.30. But the opportunity to escape had long since passed. The rest of the regiment suspected the likely outcome. Oberleutnant Pöppel bleakly confided to his diary:

*We all reckon that I Battalion has been thrown into battle alone with no prospects of success. It must have already have suffered considerable casualties if it hasn't been wiped out completely - and my friend and comrade Eugen Scherer is with them.[4]*

Unbeknown to the regimental commander, the US 8th Infantry Regiment having advanced inland from Utah, had already cut off Preikschat's battalion, not the paratroopers.

'The last radio message from the Ist Battalion reported the destruction of five enemy tanks', stated von der Heydte. Breaking down into small groups led by officers or NCOs, the battalion attempted to fight its way back. Regimental headquarters was powerless to do anything other than monitor progress. 'During the last decisive engagements that led to the battalion's destruction', it reported, '24 fighter-bombers attacked one after the other in rolling sorties with bombs and machine guns'. Some 300 stragglers began to disperse in a southwesterly direction toward the Douvre river. They moved directly towards previously entrenched elements of the 101st Airborne Division. Enmeshed in marshy terrain and largely leaderless, they fell easy prey to units of the 501st and 506th Regiments who, although outnumbered, mercilessly flailed the stragglers with fire until they surrendered. Oberleutnant Pöppel manning his position north of Carentan with the IIIrd Battalion tried to discern what was going on.

*Enormous explosions can be heard in the north and north east, which must be coming from the enemy's naval heavy artillery. We can also hear the noise of battle from that direction.[5]*

Von der Heydte's pitchfork-like thrust toward the coast was blunted. Indeed one prong had been snapped off. It was the only counter-attack mounted towards Utah on D-Day. From now on the regiment would be on the defensive. Only 25 soldiers led by Oberleutnant Stenzel managed to exfiltrate the hapless Ist Battalion lodgement in small patrols. Fallschirmjäger Regiment 6 had lost one-third of its strength in its first action. It now began to prepare for the defence of St Côme-du-Mont, the gateway to the causeway leading to Carentan, which would have to be taken if the American beachhead at Utah was to link with Omaha. Pöppel had few illusions about what lay ahead. 'On the first day', he wrote in his diary, 'the writing was already on the wall for our proud 6th Regiment'.[6] This, the second of the two substantial German counter-attacks on D-Day, had failed also.

# CHAPTER 14

# A TENUOUS FOOTHOLD

*'There were Germans ahead of us and Germans in back of us ... There was no straight line. It was a mess.'*
*American Artillery Officer*

## ... Reinforcement.

B.A. Tomblin, a glider pilot, admitted that despite the excitement of the invasion, in which he was about to participate, 'thoughts of my pregnant wife remained uppermost'.

*Would I survive another three months to see my first son, or would he say "I never knew my father".*

He was piloting a Horsa glider towed by a Dakota transport aircraft. Climbing into the June evening sky on D-Day, the heavy glider 'just missing as always, the spire of the Cricklade village church and flying over the local pub where the Airborne had devoured many a pint', he mused 'would we ever return to this small part of rural England, or was this the beginning of the end ...?'[1] The heavy lift and airlanding elements of the British 6th Airborne Division were en route for landing zones around Ranville. Group Captain Desmond Scott observing the armada from a Typhoon fighter-bomber overhead described it as a 'sky train' – 'a stream of tugs and gliders that reached out southwards from Selsey Bill as far as the eye could see'.[2] Tomblin glanced down as they crossed the English coast at Littlehampton, the sea towards France stretched out before them.

*This was it – no turning back now – what turmoil would we land ourselves in? Thoughts raced through our minds, and it was with a feeling of sadness that we watched the English countryside disappear behind us.*

The flight across the sea was largely uneventful. All aboard were impressed by the spectacle and size of the invasion fleet as it came into sight. The blast from battleship guns could be felt within the gliders. Rhino rafts carrying as many as 50 lorries attracted Tomblin's attention. 'It seemed uncanny seeing large numbers of lorries apparently parked on the Channel waiting to go on the beaches.' Warrant Officer Parslow, a navigator in an

Albemarle towing a Horsa, saw a Hamilcar – capable of carrying the light Tetrarch tank – 'about one mile in front of us' in difficulty after casting off its tow cable. 'Suddenly the tank broke through the front of the glider plummeting to the sea, followed by the glider.'[3] It was about 21.00 as the vast armada crossed the Normandy coast, northeast of Caen. 'Pretty lights floated up to us', said Tomblin, 'and it was not until something hit our starboard that we realised it was anti-aircraft fire'. The formations roared onward, unperturbed, seemingly invincible. 'Black puffs of smoke formed around us, but did not give us any impression of being dangerous.'

'They were an amazing sight', declared 18 year-old Midshipman Godfrey Joly aboard the destroyer HMS *Scourge* four kilometres off the beach near Ouistreham. 'At one time the unbroken stream of aircraft stretched as far as the eye could see in both directions while the returning "tugs" formed a second stream which also stretched almost as far as the eye could see back in the direction of England.' David Thoms, director-gunner aboard the battleship HMS *Warspite*, remembered 'there was a fantastic sight when the airborne troops went over - the sky was full of aircraft and gliders'.[4] Tomblin's tug pilot's voice announced over the intercom 'Tug to glider: we are on our run-in. Pull off in your own time.' Tomblin could see his target field and pulled the tow release lever, releasing the twin grapples which fell downwards and away from the wing roots. The Dakota banked and began to turn away. Pulling back the stick the glider pilot found himself being distracted by 'the Army padre standing in the cockpit doorway praying loudly'. He was now committed like dozens of other similar aircraft to an irrevocable descent to the objective, within a swirling swarm of like minded pilots. Group Captain Scott observing from above saw:

*One glider was shot down by flak, but the rest ploughed on down into fields alongside the Orne like a flock of exhausted black swans. Some skimmed along the ground and finished up in a cloud of yellow dust. Others hit the ground at too steep an angle and burst open like paper bags.*[5]

Tomblin coming in to land made a slow descending half turn, lining up on his intended landing track. 'This was the great moment. What was waiting for us? Was it the right field?' It was the correct spot, but it had been festooned 'with poles about 15ft in height, inviting us to crash amongst them'. He was powerless to do anything about it, 'a glider can't go up again'. His only recourse was to try and steer the nose through the poles as best he could. The starboard wing struck a pole with a splintering crack, which immediately slewed the glider round in a half circle to a gut-wrenching stop. 'Relief must have shown on all our faces, but was short-lived — there was a crash somewhere behind, a sound of rending wood, and on looking back we saw that another glider had collided with our tail, wrenching it almost off.' This was to simplify unloading the jeep.

Desmond Scott, still viewing the spectacular traffic jam from above, marvelled at the ability of pilots to escape seemingly unavoidable collisions. 'Some gliders seemed to have no place to go. But they just dropped into the smallest of spaces and elbowed their way in among the dust, splinters and torn fabric.'[6] Scott at several thousand feet could view the scene with a detached equanimity that was impossible for those on the ground. 'The German gunners were quick to size up the situation and began shelling the gliders from across the nearby [Orne] canal. Several burst into flames.' Tomblin at ground level 'greeted by bullets whining past us' ducked down into the corn, and for a moment stared 'at the incoming black cloud of gliders and tug aircraft'. He was later to learn the tail of the glider stream was just leaving England as he arrived over the French coast.

The huge Hamilcar gliders faced particular difficulties, restricted as they were by the weight of light tanks within, from taking any violent evasive action. Tomblin saw a heavy Hamilcar come in so steeply, the tank shot out of the nose followed by the glider 'helplessly out of control'. It crashed, killing the pilot 'a man who lived two streets away from me in my native Northampton'. He continued:

*A few of the gliders were burning, and their ammunition stores were exploding. So much was happening one could not absorb everything, except to carry out your own orders and ignore the seemingly chaotic background to it all.*

Staff Sergeant Heaton piloting a Hamilcar loaded with 17,500lb of petrol and ammunition for re-supplying Tetrarch tanks carried in most of the other 30 Hamilcars, struck one of the tanks, which suddenly clattered across his committed landing path. 'The tank commander, who was standing in his little turret, took one look, mouthed imprecations and leaped from the tank a second or two before we hit it at a speed of 90 to 100mph.' The tank was knocked upside down beneath the aircraft, 'with grenades and cannon shells dropping like ripe plums from their containers into the field, and a strong smell of petrol'. Two gliders were burning fiercely nearby, having been mortared by the Germans. Miraculously all survived. They managed to extricate the unfor-

tunate driver and gunner from the upturned tank alive, 'but not very pleased and somewhat shaken'. Heaton's philosophy as a result of this experience was 'I have felt ever since that each day I have lived is a bonus'.[7]

The massive airlanded reinforcement at the end of D-Day provided the Allied armies with a much needed fillip to their morale. Lance-bombardier K. Hollis, a sapper NCO felt 'we had the feeling that with a sight like this we must be making headway. These air armadas were terrific morale boosters.' Another sapper driver, A.O. Palser, confessed after a long and tense day 'my confidence was restored'.[8] The sight was as unnerving to the Germans as it was reassuring to the Allies.

The 21st Panzer Division was convinced the airlanding operation was specially mounted to cut them off in the rear. Elements landed behind the western Kampfgruppe 'Rauch' and 'Oppeln's' panzer group. Rauch's panzergrenadier battle group broke off its action in Lion, menaced as it was from behind also by a British tank advance on Cresserons, and withdrew from the coast to Anguerny six kilometres inland. It was subsequently to pull back to Epron north of Caen on order from 84th Corps. Wounded and prisoners were taken with them. One company of Panzergrenadier Regiment 192 fought its way to Douvres, where it was included within the defence of the encircled German bastion. Similarly the panzer battle group 'Oppeln' fell back to its start point, and was later placed in line to the right of the Kampfgruppe 'Rauch' north of Caen. West of Epron, there remained only surviving elements of the 716th Division, including the IInd Battalion Regiment 736 with the self-propelled guns of the 'Grafwaldersee' battery. The opportunity to split the British and Canadian beachheads had been irretrievably lost.

The D-Day landings had been broadly successful. However, the foothold gained was tenuous. The Allied situation as dusk fell on D-Day was not entirely clear to either commanders, or soldiers on the ground. The glider reinforcement to the 6th Airborne Division was a welcome addition to an effective strength that barely measured 40 percent. Montgomery had achieved his aim of getting five to six divisions ashore on D-Day. Elements of 10 divisions were now in Normandy, but only five to six of these were in any way complete. The American airborne divisions were both below 40 percent of their effective strengths.[9] Accurate D-Day figures are difficult to confirm, but a reasonable estimate is that British formation out-loading times over the subsequent three days were to fall behind by 48 hours.[10] Similarly on D+1 no more than one quarter of a planned American logistic tonnage of 14,500 tons was to be unloaded across the western beachheads. An envisaged troop total of 107,000 to be achieved within two days was 20,000 short. Little more than 50 percent of 14,000 vehicles planned, were ashore in the American sector.[11] Nevertheless the achievement overall was impressive. The Atlantic Wall had been breached and 156,000 troops were already ashore.[12] But in reality, this was an insub-

*Above:* 'One glider was shot down by flak but the rest ploughed on down into fields alongside the Orne like a flock of exhausted black swans.' Glider reinforcement at Ranville on D-Day. The dots are glider stakes; discarded parachutes may be clearly seen.

*Below:* The Atlantic Wall had been breached and 156,000 troops were already ashore. British Commandos move inland off Sword Beach.

*Above:* 'Even at the very beginning of the campaign it seemed that the odds were very heavily stacked against survival!' Allied casualties were rising. Picking over British dead.

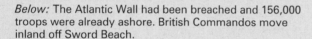

stantial lodgement. Montgomery predicted when planning the invasion, the first critical point would come within 48 hours, when 12 Allied divisions could be matched by 12 German. Elements of 10 Allied divisions would be ashore by D+1. Of five German divisions facing them, two had already been dealt crippling blows. But some 60 German divisions had been identified in France. The race to dominate the fore-shore was now on. The Allies held a local initiative. It remained to be seen whether the Germans could match the enemy troop densities pouring ashore.

## Beyond D-Day … dusk 6 June.

In order to profit from the shock of their successful assault, the Allies needed to advance inland quickly, to secure a lodgement able to repel the anticipated German counter-stroke, and large enough from which to launch an offensive to break out. Initially Allied tanks forged ahead in the centre towards Caen and Bayeux. Lieutenant W.D. Little advancing out of St Aubin on Juno managed to cut off 100 retreating Germans from the 736th Regiment fleeing the coast.

*The excitement was just fantastic, and I called my other tank and pointed out the target and said "let them have it!" It was a real bird-shoot. We caught them in the open, with all the guns. The exhilaration after all the years of training, the tremendous feeling of lift, excitement, exhilaration, of doing this! It was like the first time you had gone deer hunting, and the deer had come out. You quivered with excitement.[1]*

The initial momentum could not be maintained. Neither was Little's enthusiasm shared by all troops coming ashore. The adrenalin flow that had energised the assault waves burned out in time. As the realisation of heavy casualties became apparent, depression set in, and impetus was lost. Much planning and training had been directed to the primary objective of scaling the Atlantic Wall. Once this had been achieved, a psychological vacuum set in. The amphibious landings like the earlier parachute assaults surprised both sides. Whereas the Germans were shocked by the suddenness and ferocity of the attack, the Allies were similarly disorientated operating on unfamiliar terrain requiring a tactical decisiveness which did not come easily to those fighting their first campaign. The onslaught had been a rapid success. Few in the assaulting waves had thought beyond this, assuming they were unlikely to survive it. Infantry units on attaining their objectives tended to dig in and await developments, rather than immediately press on and exploit surprise.

Fatigue also played a role. The lead troops had been confined to camps and ships for many days - in some cases, weeks – before the assault. Physically inactive, and denied sleep during the mounting and preparation phase, soldiers were called upon suddenly to push themselves to the limit. Waiting had blunted some of the training edge. Lieutenant P.C. Webber who came ashore with the 2nd Middlesex Regiment at Sword explained prior to landing 'it was quite impossible to project one's thoughts beyond the first twenty-four hours. The thought of facing a whole campaign scarcely occurred to me.'[2] The catalyst of the amphibious assault, losses and fatigue all took their toll:

*At last one had to think beyond D-Day, and the thoughts were not optimistic. I felt a deep gloom, not only for comrades to whom one had become attached, but over one's future which seemed likely to be brief and brutish.*

The imperative had always been to crack the beach defences. 'We had screwed our emotions up to a pitch for the assault landing', declared Webber, 'which was probably as eventful as most of us had ever imagined'. Now, 'everything after D-Day was anti-climax, because most of us were going into action for the first time, and the type of fighting was quite unlike anything else we experienced subsequently'.[3] This, combined with the shock of seeing comrades die in large numbers produced a lethargy that only firm command and control could overcome. It was to be gripped, but fatefully, the process took time. As one Canadian soldier expressed it:

*Honestly, I guess you might say my mind didn't like what was going on and just turned off, but my body just kept going. Crazy eh?[4]*

The first night was a psychological low point for many in the Allied armies who had never seen action before, as they took stock of their individual circumstances and began to come to terms with their fears. Even the veterans had their difficulties. Thomas Dalby manning an artillery observation post with infantry from the 50th Division recalled, 'after the North African Desert and the open hills around the Volturno, the Bocage country crowded in on us. I didn't like it.' Seasoned soldiers, who recognised fear, could be compassionate with those unable to come to terms with it. Alexander Baron described the inner turmoil of a veteran infantry sergeant during the first night ashore:

*His day in battle was catching up on him, and living in retrospect the hours through which he had shown no signs of fear, he huddled shivering against the earth wall of the trench, feeling his stomach muscles contract and his lungs freeze with the physical sensation of fear until the pain became unbearable.*

He was violently and noisily sick.[5] Dalby, meanwhile, in the forward line with the infantry, settled down in his damp ditch, and although still under intermittent fire, tried to snatch some sleep.

*Amidst the noise and growing tension, I still remember a quiet sobbing from one of the infantrymen: maybe some of his friends had died earlier, or the layers of fear gathered in Africa and Italy were becoming too heavy for him to bear. I never knew what happened to him.*[6]

Newcomers had to be quick to identify new dangers, already known to the veterans, secreted under 'layers of fear'. Lieutenant David Holbrook, a tank officer, rapidly assimilated 'that compelled lesson of war, that one must always listen'. A basic tenet within the animal kingdom.

*But as yet all the languages were foreign, and so every great sound was a menace. To listen for every predatory sound anew was too intolerable, and so their minds began to learn to distinguish, between machine-gun fire which was coming in your direction and that which was going for somebody else … Already, they had taken in that the nearer the missile is coming, the less you can do about it: you'd not hear a direct hit.*[7]

Another tank officer, Lieutenant Stuart Hills, declared 'one learned as one went along — if one was lucky enough to survive — but, in becoming more canny, perhaps one's edge was dulled and it was then that one needed to be brave!' An infantryman, Private J Garner of the 1st South Lancs commented 'after a while one could read the shell fire' but mortar bombs were very different; 'the pop of the weapon could be heard and sometimes the swish as they landed close to you. Nasty …' The mortar was universally condemned by both sides as the artful killer. R. Cadogan, a DD tank crew-man, in particular feared 'sneak mortar attacks which would come without warning and kill or badly wound one's friends'. It was depressing 'even then at the very beginning of the campaign it seemed that the odds were very heavily stacked against survival'.[8] The span of life for tank crew-men in Normandy depended very much upon their ability rapidly to identify a target, lay-on, fire and reload. Norman Smith, a Cromwell tank soldier in 22nd Armoured brigade emphasised:

*Truly it is said that there are the quick and the dead. To anyone whose life has never hung upon split second decisions, this is probably difficult to comprehend … The faster and more accurate you were the longer you tended to live but the German tank crews and anti-tank gunners were no slouches, there is no doubt about that.*[9]

Private N. Mason of the 2nd Battalion East Yorkshire Regiment summed up his feelings at the end of D-Day

*The mood of the men prior to D-Day was of frustration and everything that goes with it. On the word go it was elation and buoyancy of spirit, wanting to get the job over with as quickly as possible.*

Now on landing 'everyone lived on their nerves as it was a case of hunting and being hunted. To me it was all like a bad dream.'[10]

If anything, the mood in the American sector, particularly around Omaha was even more sombre. More than 500 men of the US 29th Division and its attachments had died since morning in the shallow beachhead. In the 116th Regiment alone 341 officers and men were killed. Casualties by D+1 including wounded and missing reached 797.[11] As with the British the situation was unclear. Corporal William Preston of the 743rd Tank Battalion bivouacked 'about a mile in' from Omaha on the night of 6 June, was 'still not feeling quite secure, as there were not visible an over abundance of troops'.[12] Inland from Utah, the most successful American landing, was confusion. Private Vincent Angeloni of the 4th Infantry Division offered a typical observation:

*In the evening I kept thinking, well, we're in this field now. I wonder where the Germans are? We had them surrounded, maybe they had us surrounded. My thought was, Gee, I hope it gets to become daylight again. We all felt that way. I think we prayed for daylight, and we prayed for night-time. And when night time came we thought, Gee, I wish it were daylight so we could get outta here and move somewhere else.*[13]

Four days later, Lieutenant Elliot Johnson, an artillery battery commander described a situation that had not much improved.

*There were Germans ahead of us and Germans in back of us. Americans over there ahead of these Germans. The infantry and the artillery were side by side. There was no infantry out in front. When the infantry moved, we moved. There was no straight line. It was a mess.*[14]

D-Day had been a success. The assault had secured a lodgement. It was, however, a tenuous foothold. The British beaches had yet to link between Juno and Sword, while Utah and Omaha were also separate enclaves. Lieutenant Carroll, manning an advanced headquarters of the 16th RCT just inland from Omaha, recalled 'the English and Canadians were so far off I don't know when we finally got in touch with them'. Contact was finally established with 47 Commando on the night of 7th June. 'The Germans could have driven right straight down to the beach if they had known about that', Carroll said, 'but their communications were shot to hell'.[15] Lance Corporal Hennessey just inland from Sword Beach in the British sector, recalled 'there was a feeling of considerable tension in the air'.

*It was true we had arrived on the shores of Europe, but our bridge-head was still fairly shallow. We could not imagine that the Germans would delay a massive counter attack for long, and the priority, as we saw it, was to push ahead as fast as possible to establish ourselves in depth before the expected blow fell.*[16]

The anticipated blow was on its way.

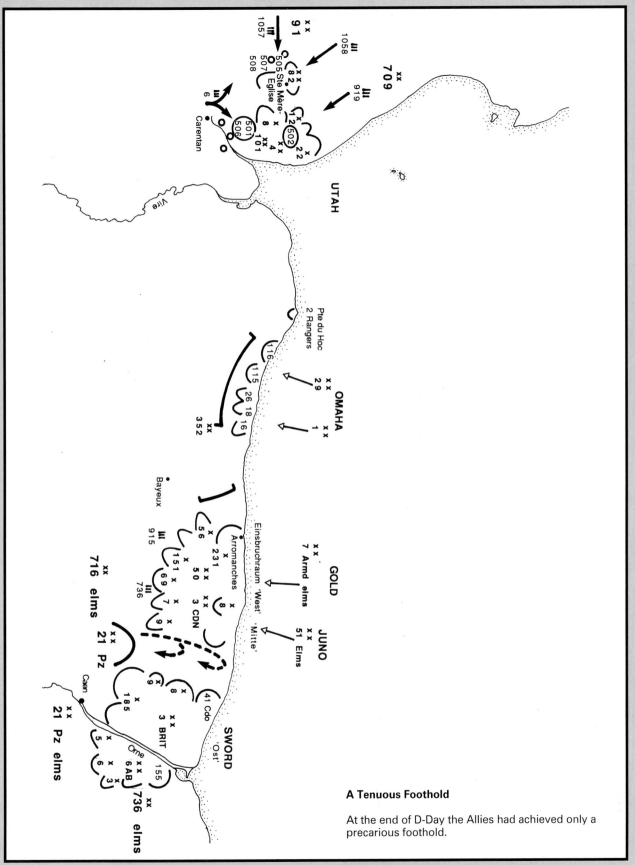

**A Tenuous Foothold**

At the end of D-Day the Allies had achieved only a precarious foothold.

# CHAPTER 15

# PANZER-MARSCH!

*'Make certain, all of you, that you either move on or next to the roads as fast as possible - and don't get fleeced on the way.'*

*Commander Panzer Lehr Division*

## Where are the panzers? ...

Where were the panzers? Pierre Clostermann flying a Free French Air Force Typhoon along the Contentin Peninsula, inland from Utah, reported: 'we couldn't see much'. There was six-tenths cloud over Normandy at 2,000ft, which had impeded much bombing support. Near Ste Mère-Eglise there were a few houses in flames. 'A few jeeps on the roads. On the German side, to all intents and purposes nothing.' His second patrol that day was over Omaha.

*It was a nightmare. The night was dark, with low cloud. In the gloom hundreds of aircraft were stooging about without being able to see each other, blinded by the fires raging from Vierville to Isigny.[1]*

Over the British beaches it was much the same. Group Captain Desmond Scott flying another Typhoon recorded his impression of the Orne estuary.

*All along the fringe of the bay, as far as visibility would permit, I could see smoke, fire and explosions. Inland some areas were completely smudged out by evil clouds of smoke. Underneath it great flashes of fire would erupt and burst like bolts of orange lightning. Normandy was like a huge fire rimmed boiling cauldron.[2]*

Air Chief Marshal Sir Trafford Leigh-Mallory commanding the AEAF was concerned at the density of the cloud cover, which he felt might impede his plan of creating 'choke points' so as to 'redress the balance which is against us, in so far as the problem of building up is concerned'.[3] He was well aware of the tenuous nature of the Allied foothold. Progress was not yet entirely clear. Group Captain Scott felt 'in view of the confused state of the bridgehead, it was impossible to learn, exactly what was happening'. Several pilots had already been shot down by flak, but his squadrons 'had destroyed

their first tanks in an attack on two enemy road columns southwest of Caen, many thin-skinned vehicles had been destroyed'. He himself had seen little action:

*Two motorcycles and what appeared to be a staff car were racing along a road near Cagny, and I swept down and raked them with cannon fire. All three came to a sudden and dusty stop.[4]*

Allied fighter-bombers dominated the area behind the beaches. Numerous sweeps were made in search of more substantial prey, but the panzers had yet to appear in force.

At 09.40 on 6 June Generalleutnant Gunther Blumetritt, the Chief of Staff of OB West (Supreme Command West), telephoned Generalmajor Speidel, Rommel's Chief of Staff at La Roche Guyon with bad news. Contrary to expectation, both the 12th SS and Panzer Lehr Panzer Divisions had not been released from the OKW (Supreme Command Wehrmacht) reserve. Speidel was warned 'that care was to be taken that the 12th SS was not involuntarily committed'. There was no scope for innovatory meddling, the 'Hitlerjugend' was not to be released. Clearance to move up the Panzer Lehr near the coast toward Flers had been requested, 'but the Führer's decision was still pending'.[5] Generalfeldmarschall Rommel received his first indication of landings by telephone at 10.15 at his home in Herrlingen in Swabia. Understandably shaken, he said he would immediately return.

Generalfeldmarschall von Rundstedt at OB West had initially reacted to the invasion reports by ordering both Panzer Lehr and the 12th SS nearer the coast, assuming OKW would confirm this necessary initiative. The call at 09.40 indicated otherwise. Its impact upon the troops involved was predictably confusing. Reconnaissance activity had been begun by the 12th SS, and elements of the division were already reaching the initially identified assembly area east of Lisieux, by early afternoon. It now became apparent that the likely new deployment area to check the enemy amphibious thrust might be west of Caen. Whatever the tactical plan, the divisions order of march was already set to occupy the Lisieux assembly area. A degree of reorganisation would therefore be required once reconnaissance activity and liaison with front units confirmed the requirement.

Similarly the Panzer Lehr Division near Chartres had been notified at 04.15 by signal: 'British landings likely at dawn – code word Blucher!' A warning order from von Rundstedt instructed them to prepare to occupy an assembly area near Bayeux and Caen. Precise notification would follow,[6] but throughout the morning of D-Day they waited. General Bayerlein, the division commander, telephoned constantly for clearance to move, but the division remained motionless in its march form-up points. The unit official historian recalled:

*The sun burned down from a June sky. The men sitting at readiness in their tanks grumbled. The uncertain situation played on their nerves. The sky was constantly scanned as fighters scoured the area overhead. But no German fighters.*

Panzer Lehr, like the 12th SS, had its organisational problems. Bayerlein, its commander, had always objected that his fast units were located too near the coast, while his Mk IV Panzers – the slowest – were positioned the furthest away, on the southern extremity of his assembly area near Chartres. It was too late to change now.[7]

Myth has propagated a view that Adolf Hitler delayed the committal of the OKW panzer reserve because he was not woken sufficiently early during the night, to be warned of the naval activity assembling off the Normandy coast. SS-Hauptsturmführer Otto Gunsche, his personal adjutant, alleges the contrary, claiming Hitler once declared: 'I would rather be needlessly awoken a hundred times rather than miss the one important occasion requiring an important measure or decision'. During the night of 5-6 June the Fuhrer had retired to bed at 02.00. He was reawakened 'in the early morning hours' by his head servant Linge on direction from Oberleutnant General Schmundt, following a conversation with Hitler's Chief of Operations, Generaloberst Jodl, and informed about 'air and sea landings on the Cherbourg Peninsula. Gunsche states that contrary to normal practice, Hitler appeared in the great hall in the Berghof earlier - at 08.00' and spoke with Generalfeldmarschall Keitel, the Chief of OKW, and Jodl, announcing: 'Gentlemen, that is the invasion. I have always said it would come there.'[8] Whether this allegation is as simplistic as the earlier suggestion that Hitler slept on because the news was withheld is irrelevant. Examination of contemporary documentary evidence implies that senior staffs were uncertain at this early stage whether the Normandy landings were indeed significant. Hesitation was influenced largely by a belief, encouraged by Allied intelligence, that Normandy was a diversion. Further substantial landings were anticipated opposite the Pas-de-Calais.

Even Marck's 84th Corps, near the frontline at St Lô was uncertain, but increasingly convinced, diversion or not, that there was substance to these landings. At 10.20 Generaloberst Dollman the commander of Seventh Army, convinced this was a 'major attack' felt it 'necessary to immediately move the 12th SS Panzer Division and additionally Panzer Lehr to the coast'.[9] There was an understandable desire to sit tight and wait for the situation to clarify before committing reserves. Major Hayn, the Ic (G2 - Intelligence Officer) described how following the landings:

*… the minutes dragged by. One individual report followed another; they confirmed or contradicted each other. Army or Army group HQ were constantly telephoning. But all the Corps staff could do was to wait - wait until the confused overall picture had been clarified, until the main centres of the dropping and landing zones had become apparent.*

A particular complication was that all reports were from the Army. Luftwaffe support 'was nonexistent from the very first minute'. Consequently they lacked an 'overall picture'; so much so that Major Hayn felt obliged to drive forward to the coast and see for himself.[10]

Another telephone request by Army Group B at 13.00 to release the two divisions was rejected;[11] 45 minutes later it was 'still being considered'. A Seventh Army report at 14.05 that 'the situation in the 352nd Division area' opposite Omaha 'had been cleaned up', likely complicated the assessment process. Not until 14.30 was a decision 'pending', when two minutes later tension broke with the announcement that the 1st SS Corps – both the 12th SS 'Hitlerjugend' and Panzer Lehr Divisions – would be committed, with Corps troops.[12]

A plan began to emerge. Both divisions under the command of SS-Oberstgruppenführer Sepp Dietrich (the 1st SS Corps Commander), alongside the 716th Infantry Division and 21st Panzer, were to interdict the Allied advance, contain it, and drive it back into the sea. Both panzer divisions were to deploy west of Caen, 12th SS right, Panzer Lehr left.[13] A panzer counter-stroke was beginning to develop in embryo.

At 15.00 the 'Hitlerjugend' received notification from Army Group B to assemble west of Caen in order to prepare for a counter-attack. 'Now we're off', announced SS-Standartenführer Kurt Meyer, commanding Panzergrenadier Regiment 25 on receipt of the operation order one hour later, '16 hours after the first reported contact with the enemy'. Armoured infantry mounted their half-tracks, motor-cycle combinations sped off, engines roared into life. Meyer, a veteran, reflected how often he had previously experienced such momentous departures 'in Poland, in France, against the Balkans, Russia and now again in the West'. It was an unsettling moment for the seasoned grenadiers.

*We older soldiers considered the future with some apprehension. We could foresee what lay ahead. The fine young grenadiers by contrast glanced smiling at us. They had no fear, full of confidence, trusting in their strength and innate aggression. How willing will these youngsters be to stand the test?[14]*

Units were on the move by about 17.00.

The weather throughout the morning of 6 June had been blustery, with low cloud and occasional drizzle. It had added to the frustration of the wait, because these were ideal conditions for a forward deployment. Now the weather began to change. During the afternoon it began to clear. Army Group B discussed a Panzer Lehr request at 15.50 to postpone its march call forward until 20.00, following dusk, to avoid the hostile air threat. Generaloberst Bayerlein, an African veteran, was well aware of its potential lethality. He was over-ruled. Commander Seventh Army wanted Panzer Lehr south of Caen by early the next morning. Bayerlein argued he would be unable to cover the 160km journey in time. Air attacks he assessed would slow his columns to an average 8kmh. Dollmann facing an imminent British break-through north of Caen felt too much time had been wasted already. Panzer Lehr was to march now. Bayerlein had no alternative but to brief his assembled regimental commanders on the outcome at his command post at Nogent-le-Rotrou. His three regiments would follow separate routes, one through Vire and Villers Bocage, another via Alençon and Flers and a third over Falaise to Caen. Although they were taking the most direct route, there was no hope of meeting their envisaged H-hour near Caen. 'Make certain, all of you', urged the division commander, 'that you move either on or next to the roads as fast as possible - and don't get fleeced on the way'. At 17.00 the order was given: 'Panzer - Marsch!'

The division moved off with 229 tanks and assault guns and 658 armoured half-track infantry carriers, probably over 2,000 vehicles in all, along three routes.[15] It was fully motorised — a show-piece — the best equipped armoured division in the Wehrmacht. Exuding lethality, its soldiers impressed by the spectacle of hundreds of exhaust wreathed vehicles on the march, anticipated victory. Within an hour, the sun broke through, shining intermittently between fast moving broken cloud. With the sun came the 'Jabos'.

## Delays ... the 12th SS 'Hitlerjugend'.

'We'll soon give it to Tommy!' was the enthusiastic banter among the troopers of Panzer Regiment 12 of the 'Hitlerjugend'. SS-Sturmmann Helmuth Pock remembers the order 'make ready' was given. Drivers serviced their tanks once again, examining equipments to ensure everything was in order 'but that was more a sign of nerves, than a technical necessity'. They awaited the command to 'mount-up'. Individual belongings had long since been stowed 'and there seemed no necessity in my opinion to hang around here any longer'. Time

dragged on. Eventually the soldiers began to fear they might even miss the heavy fighting that would inevitably drive the Allies into the sea.

*One felt the prevailing tension under which men laboured. The jokes tailed off. After the first rush of confidence the anxiety of facing the unknown took possession of us. We all knew that waiting was the worse thing for all troops. Rather get on with it!*

'Are we to be off, or aren't we needed any more?' asked one irresolute soldier kicking his heels. Pock noticed men smoking to steady their nerves 'but today it had no effect'.[1] Finally the order arrived 'mount-up, advance!' It was early afternoon.

There was confidence that the German Army would blunt the invasion; a feeling more pronounced among those inland, who had yet to view the fleet, or feel the impact of Allied air power. Grenadier Willi Tagte, east of Paris in the Nancy area, unimpressed by the invasion news, simply wrote in his diary on 6 June: 'Invasion starts, and we're not there yet'.[2] Another 18-year old infantryman, Kurt Maier, training in Besserabia wrote to his mother: 'the training will soon be at an end, and one day we'll get the opportunity to prove ourselves against the enemy'. He was a committed National Socialist. 'Right now I would like to be in France. It would definitely be better there than in this lousy land.'[3] The announcement released tension; the long awaited invasion had arrived and at last there was a chance to do something about it. A staff officer in the 17th SS Division declared 'everyone was in a good and eager mood to see action again – happy that the pre-invasion spell of uncertainty and waiting was snapped at last'.[4]

Helmuth Pock driving towards the coast with Panzer Mk IVs of Panzer Regiment 12 presently came across traffic jams as the 12th SS hurried northward. 'Mainly Grenadiers' he observed, driving heavily camouflaged vehicles 'like moving bushes' liberally coated with the dust of several hours driving. Both he and his comrades were inspired by the spectacle of a panzergrenadier regiment on the move.

*They passed us by as they had priority, an interminable queue of vehicle after vehicle - unstoppable - armoured half-tracks, radio vehicles, platoon vehicles with mounted infantry, anti-tank weapons, motor-cycle infantry and despatch riders, command vehicles and many more, all fully motorised. Wherever a route seemed even remotely negotiable, as far as the eye could see, troops were moving in the direction of the coast.*

Pock, filled with optimism, was enjoying the glorious weather and not an enemy aircraft in sight. 'We assumed our fighters were responsible for this.' The troops were elated 'victory is ours!'. Pock enthusiastically reflected 'it could go no other way'. They called to each other as they drove by – 'Good luck boys!' 'Even

*Above:* 'Panzer-Marsch!' Panzer Lehr begins its march to the sea.

*Right:* 'They passed us by as they had priority, an interminable queue of vehicle after vehicle – unstoppable.' The 12th SS on the march.

*Left:* 'Burned-out transports in their typical rust-red colour.' The incidence of wreckage increased as the march progressed.

better for you!' was the cheery response. Once the panz-ergrenadier unit had passed the tanks continued on their way. Visibility was improving all the time.

Further on 'the number of our vehicles shot up by the enemy became even greater'. Tanks nosed past burned-out transports 'in their typical rust-red colour'. Presently there was a need to negotiate the wreckage of what had likely been a supply convoy 'caught-out' by the aircraft. Pock commented 'for the most part one could only imagine what these objects had once been, now fall-out from dreadful explosions'. All around lay the detritus of war, shells, cartridges, various types of ammunition and dispersed among the rubbish – bodies. The frequency of such sightings began to dilute the earlier bravado.

*Next to one of the bomb craters was a shot-up armoured personnel carrier. The hatch to the rear of the vehicle was open, and from it protruded the leg and lower torso of a soldier, and what looked like a knee. Driving slowly past it became apparent that the top half of the corpse had been completely roasted. Perhaps he had already been mercifully despatched by a bullet.*

The tank crews began to feel increasingly vulnerable. Their daylight move was deteriorating into a dangerous situation. Meadows and fields around the road had been pock-marked by craters. 'We began to gradually wonder if we would ever get there' reflected Pock. 'What the enemy had by way of material superiority was becoming increasingly apparent, as was also the doubts about our capability to match it.'[5]

High above the Normandy countryside, Allied fighter bombers sought their ever more numerous prey. 'On any operations' said Flying Officer Phillip Murton of No 183 Squadron RAF 'there would be say, a section of four going out looking for anything – anything German'. Flights of Typhoon fighter-bombers worked beyond a 'bomb-line' indicated on their maps, 'so anything beyond that which was moving – guns, artillery, despatch riders – was fair game'. Once the enemy was located, 'depending on what it was, the leader decided whether to use cannon or rockets, or whether it warranted a second attack'. Until an accurate picture of the German build-up developed, fighter-bomber sweeps were conducted on an opportunity basis:

*This was simply free-lance stuff; anything you found you just attacked it. The leader tried to make a note of where it was so he could report the exact position when he got back.*[6]

A panzer battalion column, to which SS-Sturmmann Pock belonged, might number some 120 vehicles spread over 10km. On the move, it was not too difficult to pick out from the air. 'We had just driven through a small village', recalled Pock, 'when those in front of us suddenly baled out and got into cover'. Puzzled, 'I was just about to ask what was going on, when I saw it for myself'. Jabos! – enemy fighter-bombers.

*Like we were taught, I took up my weapon, loaded it, and began to track the daring fighters' flight from cover. Now they have disappeared into the sun, one cannot locate them. But in came the first, engines howling, at great speed – "Brrt, drrt, brrt" – the cone of fire detonated on the road, a low-level strafing! I took aim, just like in the training manuals, and – "brtschsch" – the burst is away. Meanwhile all around, the others have opened fire on the fighter. "Not one of these buggers is smoking at all!" exclaimed one fellow near me. And he seemed to be right, for although our fire was generally accurate, we were not able to shoot a single one down!*

The depressing absence of any smoke signatures confirmed their initial suspicion that 'our noble 98K rifles were seemingly useless against enemy planes'. They were probably right. Flying Officer Murton RAF admitted:

*A lot of time it was cheating in a way, because there was nothing firing back at us. It was almost like a practice, though obviously the tanks and troops on the ground would fire back.*[7]

Flak did, however, thicken up on the following day, when Group Captain Desmond Scott reported 17 Typhoons shot down attacking enemy columns.[8] Murton noticed an increased effectiveness, combined with lethal guile when the Germans:

*…increased their flak everywhere. You could be attacking something and there would be no flak at all. Then as soon as you got in a dive, they would open up and you would have to go through the lot.*

The 12th SS pressed on toward Caen and the coast. As frightening as the air attacks were, the troops adapted to changed conditions. Helmuth Pock observed that 'the initial repeated dismount – then – mount procedure rarely lasted for long'. Soldiers became more canny. 'After a few hours of this we remained on board even when aircraft were suspected in the vicinity. We sat tight, leaping off only when we thought we had been located, and then like lightning.'

The attacks were fearful, but losses were not excessive. The division escort company lost 16 vehicles, but the majority of those falling out were technical breakdowns, and could follow on later. There were no casualties on the first day. Casualties in the Ist Battalion Panzergrenadier Regiment 25 were also light: four men were killed, 12 wounded and one missing. Three vehicles were destroyed, three damaged – mainly light-skinned – and one anti-tank gun was lost. By contrast, the engineer bridging column was caught on the road and badly mauled. But overall, at the close of the first day the 'Hitlerjugend' lost 22 killed, 60 wounded and one missing.

*Right:* 'Next to one of the bomb craters was a shot-up armoured personnel carrier.' The columns began to feel increasingly vulnerable.

*Left:* The tanks, self-propelled guns and armoured half-tracks of the Panzer Lehr resembled a moving wood as they set off along three main, and two subsidiary routes towards the coast.

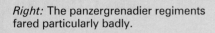

*Right:* The panzergrenadier regiments fared particularly badly.

Of more importance in terms of the build-up to dominate the invasion fore-shore, were delays. Some of this was self-inflicted due to the switch of assembly area from Lisieux to south west Caen. Delay in releasing the division meant that even in a benign air environment, the 12th SS according to its previous Chief of Staff, could not have been operational around Caen before the early hours of 7 June.[9] In the event only one panzergrenadier regiment, the 25th, with a battalion of armour and another of artillery arrived during the late evening of D-Day, reaching Missy 15km south west of Caen. Even more time was lost regrouping in the dark, over unfamiliar ground. Practical difficulties had been immense. March distances varied from 70km for one battalion in the 25th Regiment, to 190km for another battalion in the 26th. Averages lay between this.

An examination of the march implications for one panzergrenadier battalion from SS-Standartenführer Meyer's 25th Regiment is illustrative of the problems affecting all unit moves to the invasion front. The unit consisted of about 100 vehicles. These moving at 30kph with traffic driving 100 metres apart formed a column 10km long, which would take 20 minutes to pass. Air-raids apart, the 70km journey would require 3 hours 20 minutes to cover, including halts. Tanks took longer, moving an average 15kmh. Panzer battalions needed 8 hours 40 minutes to complete the journey, with additional time for regrouping, refuelling, finding accommodation on arrival and so on. Air attacks reduced the speed of the I/25 Panzergrenadier Battalion to 3kph over a three-hour period.[10] The cumulative effect of all this was to spread the division along the line of march so that just over one-third of its fighting strength was to reach its assembly area south west of Caen on 6 June. The second panzergrenadier regiment, another missing panzer battalion and two other artillery battalions would continue to travel throughout the night, well behind. SS-Sturmmann Pock's panzers, obliged to halt again, hiding within the confines of yet another village along the interminable route, summed up the situation:

*The fighters are about again, cleaning up the roads. We are among the houses, partially protected and camouflaged. We're waiting under an archway … Outside the village a few vehicles must have been surprised by the aircraft, because the machines dive down without pause, and badly aimed bursts are smacking into the walls and streets as far back as us here.[11]*

## A Nightmare Trek … Panzer Lehr.

The tanks, self-propelled guns and armoured half-tracks of the Panzer Lehr Division resembled a moving wood as they set off along three main, and two subsidiary routes toward the coast. They sneaked from cover to cover to escape air reconnaissance, but even the best camouflage could not disguise the huge clouds of exhaust and dust that billowed out from behind vehicles. This rose majestically into the air, clearly indicating progress along the primary march routes. 'Suddenly they were there', declared one observer riding with the Panzer Mk IV (II) Battalion of Panzer Regiment 130. 'Nobody knew where they came from.'

*Roaring the Jabos approached at low level, flitting over bushes and hedgerows. An accompanying Vierlings [quadruple 20mm] flak opened fire.*

Distracted by the cone of tracer the aircraft changed course.

*The first detonation thundered, forward in the column. The thought was registered on everyone's face. Is it one of ours?[1]*

Generaloberst Bayerlein the Division Commander drove with two staff cars and a pair of radio vans along the central route taken by Panzergrenadier Regiment 901, along the Alençon-Argentan-Falaise road. The first fighter-bomber attack forced him off the road near Beaumont-sur-Sarthe. He was lucky. Nevertheless, Bayerlein had cause for concern:

*The columns were getting further apart all the time. Since Army Group had ordered radio silence we had to maintain contact by despatch riders. As if radio silence could have stopped the fighter bombers and reconnaissance planes from spotting us! All it did was prevent the division staff from forming a picture of the state of the advance – if it was moving smoothly or whether there were hold ups and losses, and how far the spearheads had got. I was for ever sending off officers or else seeking out my units myself.[2]*

Group Captain Scott, RAF described the system that soon evolved around the fighter-bomber attacks on enemy columns. 'When the reconnaissance squadron sighted a road convoy it radioed immediately to its own operations room stating the nature of their find and the size of the required reinforcements – one, two or even three squadrons. One squadron would attack the column and remain until the next arrived.'[3]

To the Germans on the ground, it appeared as if they were being assailed by swarms of aircraft, which attacked, turned away, came in again or called in others. 'Even today', testify survivors, 'many years after the event, memories of this march can still conjure up nightmares to those who took part'.[4] Each attack halted the columns which split apart to seek cover. The destruction of bridges and cratered village streets slowed progress even further. 'Before long', remarked Bayerlein, 'bombers were hovering above the roads, smashing cross roads, villages, and towns along our line of advance, and pouncing on the long columns of vehicles'. As in the case of the 12th SS, anti-aircraft fire consisted of some machine guns and light flak. 'But little fire was returned with few hits', recounted survivors; 'and what was the point, with a sky full of Jabos', complained many bitterly, 'if one was shot down'.[5] They were helpless in the face of a seemingly dispassionate adversary, who showed no mercy. Attacking pilots were clinically removed from the carnage they wrought on the ground. As one admitted:

*When we went in on an attack I honestly don't think we had any feelings about it. We were young, and you tended to enjoy things. Over the years you tended to forget the horrible things, and shooting up a whole lot of troops on the ground was a lot of fun. It was very impersonal.*[6]

Panzer Lehr lost some 30 vehicles on the line of march during the first day.

The central column drove through Sées at about 23.00. At first the night had been quieter, but after incendiaries were dropped, detonations began to sound again in the darkness. By about 02.00 the same column was in Argentan. 'The scene was as bright as day', said Bayerlein, 'what with fires and explosions'. The whole town was burning. He continued:

*We were in a witch's cauldron. Behind us the road was blocked too. We were trapped in a blazing town. Dust and smoke reduced visibility to nil. Sparks were flying about our vehicles ... We could hardly breathe with the pungent smoke. We had to reconnoitre a way out on foot.*

Engineers worked on the heavily damaged bridge over the Orne, so that by 03.00 'we succeeded in escaping this fiery cage across the fields in the direction of Flers'.[7] The division had trained extensively to cope with a hostile air situation, but they were shocked by the extent and strength of the enemy's air power, which had surpassed everyone's imagination. 'A feeling of helplessness descended upon the troops' commented one observer.[8]

Progress was painfully slow. The Panzer Mk IV battalion having already experienced three air attacks by dusk had only reached the wood north of Alençon by the morning of 7 June. Having completed half its 160km journey, it was obliged to stop and refuel. Despite being well camouflaged, they were pounced from the air, and a number of tanks and wheeled vehicles were shot in flames. Generaloberst Bayerlein had meanwhile reached Flers by 04.00 and Condé-sur-Noireau one hour later. But 'as for the vehicle columns of the division, there was not a sign of them anywhere'. The 901st Regiment was stuck either side of the destroyed bridge in Condé. Bayerlein, acutely aware of the continued attrition of his division, appealed to Army Group to delay his march. 'At daylight', he said, 'Generaloberst Dollman, commander of Seventh Army, gave me a direct order to proceed and there was nothing else to do'.[9]

In an attempt to avoid further losses from rolling our attacks by day, vehicle spacing was increased, and formations reorganised into small groups. The nightmare trek continued into its second day. Panzergrenadier

Regiment 902 commanded by Oberst Gutmann, on the southerly Domfront-Vire-Villers-Bocage route, was attacked again by Thunderbolts at dawn. As one observer recounted 'the grenadiers in their open half-tracks were constantly surprised by overflights and shot-up in neat lines'.[10] The first battalion suffered particularly heavy casualties, so much so, it was eventually obliged to hide in a wooded area to await the onset of darkness. The division was to suffer greatly from a shortage of infantry in the coming weeks. Panzergrenadier Regiment 901 was attacked again near Falaise.

Group Captain Scott flying at dawn across the forest of Bretteville towards Falaise fell upon just such a column after crossing the railway north west of the town.

*As I sped to the head of this mile-long column, hundreds of German troops began spilling out into the road to sprint for the open fields and hedgerows. I zoomed up sharply over a ploughed field where 20 or 30 Germans in close array were running hard for a clump of trees. They were promptly scythed down in spurts of dust by a lone Mustang which appeared from nowhere.*

On the same route Hauptmann Alexander Hartdegen, Bayerlein's orderly officer, a veteran officer of Africa was enduring similar punishment nearby.

*Unless a man has been through these fighter-bomber attacks he cannot know what the invasion meant. You lie there, helpless, in a roadside ditch, in a furrow on a field, or under a hedge, pressed into the ground, your face in the dirt – and there it comes towards you, roaring. There it is. Diving at you. Now you hear the whine of the bullets. Now you are for it.*

But for Scott, cocooned in his Typhoon cockpit, the scene before him was playing itself out like a fast-forwarding video game. He, like all combat pilots in action, was solely concentrating on the task in hand.

*The convoy's lead vehicle was a large half-track. In my haste to cripple it and seal off the road, I let fly all eight rockets in a single salvo; I missed but hit the truck that was following. It was thrown into the air along with several bodies, and fell back on its side. Two other trucks in close attendance piled into it. There was no escape. Typhoons were already attacking in deadly swoops at the other end of the column and within seconds the whole stretch of road was bursting and blazing under streams of rocket and cannon fire. Ammunition wagons exploded like multi-coloured volcanoes. A large long-barrelled tank standing in a field just off the road was hit by a rocket and overturned into a ditch. Several teams of horses stampeded and careered wildly across the fields, dragging their broken wagons behind them. Others fell in tangled kicking heaps, or were caught up in the fences and hedges. It was an awesome sight: flames, smoke, bursting rockets and showers of coloured tracer.*[11]

*Right:* An Allied pilot declared 'I know you were killing people, but it wasn't like the army who went in hand-to-hand fighting.' Aftermath of a 'Jabo' air-raid.

*Left:* 'As I sped to the head of this mile-long column, hundreds of German troops began spilling out into the road to sprint for the open fields and hedgerows.' Cockpit-eye view of an Allied strafing run on a German road convoy.

Hartdegen recalled the sheer terror of such an assault:

*You feel like crawling under the ground. Then the bird has gone. But it comes back. Twice. Three times. Not till they've wiped out everything do they leave. Even if you survive it's no more than temporary a reprieve. Ten such attacks in succession are a real fore-taste of hell.[12]*

One eye-witness described how the forward units of the Panzer Lehr were hit by 'an air parade' of concentrated squadrons during the early hours of 7 June. The expression [Nazi] 'Party-Day Squadrons' began to be used by troops to describe reams of attacking aircraft pouncing down, reminding them of prewar Nuremberg Rally days. The 9th Company's mule-drawn ammunition train belonging to Panzergrenadier Regiment 901 was annihilated. Even the baggage lorry was shot up. Inside, Gefreiter Griethe, pinioned within the burning vehicle by the smashed cab, could not be extricated.[13] Agonised screams echoed along the column as his comrades, unable to focus on a scene distorted by a shimmering heat haze of flames, turned away in despair. The first of many vital petrol lorries were blazing fiercely within the column.

Flying Officer Phillip Murton, RAF confessed:

*I know you were killing people, but it wasn't like the army who went in hand-to-hand fighting. You were just letting loose at a whole lot of people on the ground and you would see them fall over like nine-pins and not think an awful lot about it.[14]*

The aim of the Allied Tactical Air Force was to redress the imbalance between the landed amphibious force, and the German counter-measures, now visibly building up.

Bayerlein and his staff were strafed, and his driver was killed. He said 'by noon it was terrible, my men were calling the main road from Vire to Bény-Bocage a fighter-bomber race-course'.[15] They were considerably shaken.

The delays inflicted upon the Panzer Lehr columns continued into the second night – 7 June. Diversions and detours through bombed-out vehicle junction points and choke points were so damaged and churned up by tracked vehicles, that wheeled traffic was unable to pass through. There were insufficient engineers and recovery vehicles to keep the traffic flow moving. The nightmare trek of Panzer Lehr was turning into a catastrophe. Losses by 19.30 that night were assessed as five tanks, 50 armoured petrol tankers – each with a 2.5 ton capacity, an important loss – 84 half-tracks and 90 wheeled vehicles.[16] The division had lost 10 percent of its vehicle strength and had yet to see action.

Aside from the psychological and material aspect, the most crucial commodity lost was time. Panzergrenadier Regiment 901 did not reach Condé-Ste-Marie, south of Caen, until 18.00 on 8 June – D+3. Its sister regiment,

902, managed to arrive during darkness the night before. The regimental command post was located a few kilometres before Brouay. Oberst Gutmann, the commander, arrived with some considerable relief to occupy a shelter trench some one and a half metres deep. Exhausted and shocked from their experience outrunning the Jabo packs on the roads, grenadiers drove into position and stumbled numbly from vehicles. After two days without sleep they had arrived. Shortly after they rolled in, the sinister drone of an Allied artillery spotter plane was heard over the CP. Almost immediately the area was bracketed with heavy naval gunfire, and artillery from both British corps. The disorientated grenadiers having arrived in the dark were buffeted and lacerated by this intense barrage for an hour. The regiment suffered heavy casualties. The division would now be short of infantry in the coming weeks, and still not a shot had been fired.

## 'Little fish! We'll throw them into the sea ...'

SS-Standartenführer Meyer, the commander of the lead regiment of the 12th SS Panzergrenadier Regiment 25, arrived at the headquarters of the 716th Infantry Division in the area of la Folie, west of Caen, shortly before midnight on 6 June. He had driven around blazing lorries burning by the roadside. Everything he saw hinted at the seriousness of his first anticipated situation report. 'Caen is a sea of flame', he observed driving through. On arrival at the bunker he had to pick his way past medics at work on the wounded from both the 716th and 21st Panzer Divisions outside, 'groaning with pain'.[1] Inside were the two commanders, Generalleutnant Richter and Generalleutnant Feuchtinger.

Richter briefed on the 716th Division situation. His command had been virtually annihilated, and he was no longer in contact with any of his regiment or battalion commanders. Some strong-points were still holding out. A telephone call interrupted the briefing. Oberst Krug, who commanded the 736th Regiment forward on the coast, had unexpectedly managed to get through. In the icy silence that descended, most managed to pick out the words, spoken hastily under fire.

*Herr General, the enemy are on top of my bunker. They are demanding my surrender. I have no means of resisting, and no contact with my men. What am I to do?*

All eyes were on the General. He responded with solemn and deliberate calmness. 'Herr Oberst, I can no longer give you any orders. You must act upon your own judgement.' He added softly 'Auf Widersehen' and replaced the receiver.[2]

The battle had entered a critical stage. There was understanding on one point. The Allies had gained a

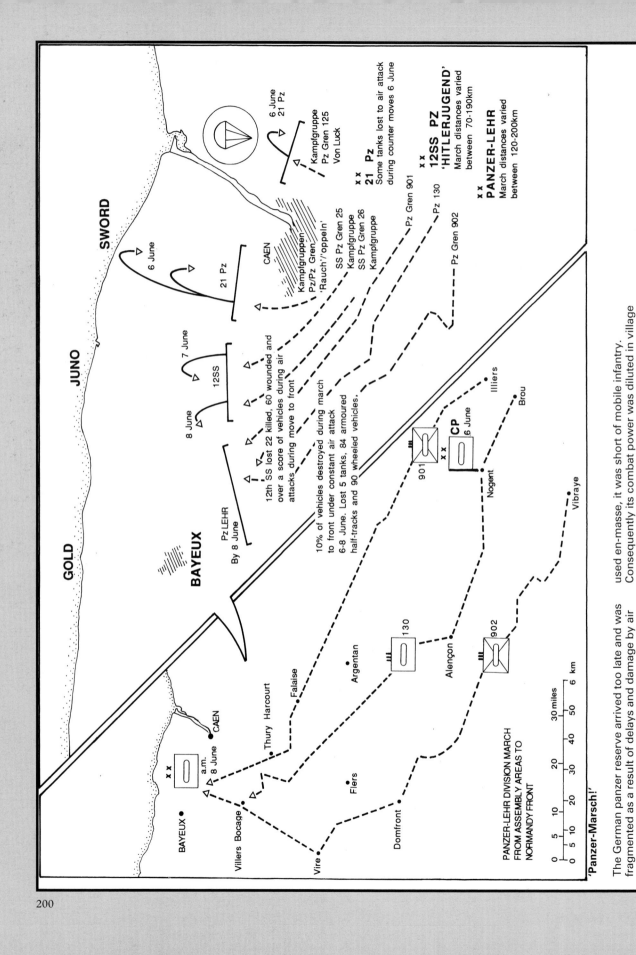

GOLD    JUNO    SWORD

6 June
21 Pz

Kampfgruppe
Pz Gren 125
Von Luck

21 Pz
Some tanks lost to air attack
during counter moves 6 June

x x
21 Pz

x x
12SS PZ
'HITLERJUGEND'
March distances varied
between 70-190km

x x
PANZER-LEHR
March distances varied
between 120-200km

6 June

21 Pz

Kampfgruppen
Pz/Pz Gren
'Rauch'/'oppeln'

CAEN

SS Pz Gren 25
Kampfgruppe
SS Pz Gren 26
Kampfgruppe

Pz Gren 901

Pz 130

Pz Gren 902

7 June

12SS

8 June

Pz LEHR
By 8 June

BAYEUX

12th SS lost 22 killed, 60 wounded and
over a score of vehicles during air
attacks during move to front

10% of vehicles destroyed during march
to front under constant air attack
6-8 June. Lost 5 tanks, 84 armoured
half-tracks and 90 wheeled vehicles.

III
901

x x
CP
6 June

III
902

130

Alençon

Nogent

Illiers

Brou

Vibraye

x x
a.m.
8 June

CAEN

BAYEUX

Villers Bocage

Vire

Thury Harcourt

Falaise

Argentan

Flers

Domfront

PANZER-LEHR DIVISION MARCH
FROM ASSEMBLY AREAS TO
NORMANDY FRONT

0   5   10   20   30 miles
0   5   10   20   30   40   50   6 km

**'Panzer-Marsch!'**

The German panzer reserve arrived too late and was
fragmented as a result of delays and damage by air
attack into inconclusive small scale assaults. Never
used en-masse, it was short of mobile infantry.
Consequently its combat power was diluted in village
fighting that resulted in stalemate.

lodgement, there was little doubt about that. Explanations were already being demanded, asking how the much vaunted coastal defences had been pierced so quickly.[3] With the failure to hold on the coast, the only sensible strategy appeared to be to hold the Allies to the landing area, yield as little ground as possible, leaving open the possibility of a counter-stroke down onto the beaches. The German command was not yet wholly committed to a race to match an Allied build-up on the fore-shore, because it had yet to conclude this really was the invasion; although those who had seen the fleet had no doubt about it. Almost 10 Allied divisions were matched against no more than 7 German divisions at the end of D-Day. Allied strength was superior because its formations had some unit integrity, although newly landed; whereas of the German divisions, two were badly battered (352nd and 716th) and elements of another three (91st, 21st and 709th) were fragmented into dispersed regimental groups, often uncoordinated and inserted into an uncertain situation. The remaining German strength consisted of battle groups inserted piece-meal throughout the day composed of approximately six battalion to regimental-size 'Kampfgruppen' despatched to points across the whole invasion frontage.[4] The initial impressions of Seventh Army and Army Group B, was that the main threat lay less in the west around the Contentin, rather more with the threatened breakthrough by the British north of Caen. It was to this area that the panzers were being sent. The role of this initial panzer thrust was therefore crucial.

German command decisions were, however, being conducted in a veritable vacuum. There was scant appreciation of the attrition that had been meted out along the fighter-bomber 'race-course track' by Jabos upon armour moving north to the coast. OB West and OKW felt that the release of three panzer divisions under command of the 1st SS Corps would probably force a decision in favour of the defence. But these deliberations appeared to pay little cognisance to realities on the ground.

On D-Day, the commander of the 1st SS Corps 'Sepp' Dietrich was in Brussels with his formation headquarters. During the afternoon he received the executive order to attack from the vicinity of Caen and drive the British into the sea. His Chief of Staff, SS-Obergruppenführer Fritz Kraemer was immediately despatched to begin coordinating measures. But he had no signals capability and was unable to speak directly to the three panzer divisions under command, a shortfall that was to continue for a further 24 hours. There was, furthermore, an incomplete battle picture. The true situation

when Meyer, the first unit commander of the newly released panzer reserve to arrive in the combat zone, was that the 21st Panzer Division was still split. Two battle groups were west of the Orne and one was in the east, all having been repelled after their first attacks. The 12th SS was in situ with a little over one third of its strength. Panzer Lehr, stung by incessant air attacks had some 70km still to travel, having reached the line of Argentan south west of Caen. The remainder of the division was scattered and dispersed in depth along numerous march routes. Therefore, the Panzer counter-thrust envisaged for 7 June would only muster a reinforced regiment from the 12th SS at first light, while the 21st Panzer contribution was not clear.

There was, in addition, friction between the commanders. In his postwar memoirs, SS-Standartenführer Meyer was to make little secret of his misgivings concerning Generalleutnant Feuchtinger's performance during D-Day. Having split his command, he lost the opportunity to bring the full weight of a panzer division to bear against Allied amphibious landings at their most vulnerable moment. A committed National Socialist, Meyer thought Feuchtinger defeatist. 'A pessimistic atmosphere reigned in the bunker', he wrote subsequently, 'it was time I disappeared'.[5] Feuchtinger thought the SS to be arrogant and over confident. Having already been mauled by Allied firepower, and impressed by their material superiority, he had suggested to Dietrich, the corps commander that two armoured divisions were not enough to take on the well entrenched British, and they should wait and strike with three formations once Panzer Lehr had arrived and assembled. He was told however to coordinate the attack with the 12th SS that night. Warning Meyer about the strength of the enemy, he received an arrogant response. Studying the map, the SS Panzergrenadier commander turned to him with a confident air and said: 'little fish! We'll throw them back into the sea in the morning.'[6]

This lack of harmony encapsulated the German response in its entirety. SS-Brigadeführer Witt, the commander of the 'Hitlerjugend' was more realistic in his assessment. He had managed to contact Meyer, and directed that only a coordinated response would be effective. 'It would be wrong to commit the division's units to the attack as they arrive', he warned, 'only a combined attack with the 21st Panzer is in question'.[7] Therefore H-Hour was to be at 12.00 the following day. But still the impact of the panzer reserve, as on D-Day, would be fragmented.

# CHAPTER 16

# VILLAGE FIGHTING

*'Each day the shelling went on and comrades whom I knew well were killed, wounded and smashed in the mind.'*
*British Soldier*

## The Centre – before Caen ... Authie.

Not only did it appear decisions were being conducted in a command and control vacuum on the German side, geography was also playing an insidious role. The invasion front, already some 80km wide, stretched from the east bank of the Orne to beyond Ste Mère-Eglise on the Cherbourg peninsula. It could broadly be divided into three sectors: west, centre and east.

The key terrain lay in the centre. Oberst Oehmichen's pre-invasion report had already identified the Caen area as potentially favourable for tanks.[1] This included the area south and south east of the city. Indeed, the 21st Panzer had been loosely located in this sector for that purpose and had already participated in one counter attack. It was the area to which the panzer reserve was being sent, and a decision sought. Furthermore it was the region of greatest crisis, because it was here the 3rd British and Canadian Divisions had made their deepest penetration. Rommel and the German High Command were, however, surprised by the breadth of the Allied landings, and the density of units they were already pushing ashore. This technological achievement, the rapid disembarkation across open beaches made possible by the prefabricated 'Mulberry' harbours supported by specialised amphibious equipments caught the defence unawares. There was no historical precedent for such an achievement, therefore, beyond rational intelligence assessment. The size of the Allied landings ought to have settled the German conundrum concerning deception. It did not. If anything, it further distracted the defence by posing the dilemma of identifying the main enemy point of effort. Should the response be to protect Cherbourg, Bayeux, or Caen?

The centre was only partially suited for armoured operations. A substantial land area already had been overrun by the Allies in the initial onrush. Left of centre, south and west of Bayeux was 'bocage' territory. This close country favoured static defence. Some 30km south

the bocage becomes broken into thickly wooded ridges and cliffs, nicknamed the 'Suisse Normande' due to its resemblance to Switzerland. This region is dominated by Mont Pinçon, a hill feature 30km south west of Caen. Eight kilometres from Caen in the same direction is Hill 112 (metres), which also dominated the surrounding area, as does also the high chimneys of Columbelle's steelworks south east of Caen. A potential tank break-out sector lay immediately south and south-east of Caen, a series of open ridges, broken only by small villages and farmhouses that stretch as far south as Falaise. But these key features, characterised by close country, woods and villages still remained to be cleared by a balanced tank-infantry force, before bursting out into the open terrain beyond.

Both sides had been convinced the invasion battle would be decided by armour. Tanks were given Allied priority on landing reflected in the large number of armoured brigades initially disembarked. The German High Command viewed the committal of its massive armoured reserve as the precursor of and instrument of victory in the west. The panzers would sweep all before them. Less thought was given to the mobility of its infantry forces. Technology – in the form of effective anti-tank guns manned by determined infantry – and the restraints of geography, were to neutralise the effectiveness of tanks. Early battles in the centre were to reflect this misappreciation of terrain that diminished the power of the offence, on both sides. After the initial impetus of the Allied assault was spent, smashing ashore, it was to be further diluted by fighting for villages, which tended to dissipate mass in a battle of attrition to secure key break-out points. Both sides were stymied by the shortfall of an appropriate tank-infantry mix to achieve their cardinal aims.

The failure to achieve a favourable force ratio of attack over defence, further contributed to the attritional character of 'village fighting'. An Allied inability to capitalise on its superiority contributed to the subsequent months-long stalemate that eventually developed around the bridgehead. To begin with, the Allies were well ahead in their aim to win the material race to dominate the invasion foreshore. An examination of available data[2]

## Geography and the Force Mix

Three of the four geographical sectors identified are not suited for armoured operations. The Germans correctly saw the area north west and south east of Caen, highlighted in the Oehmichan report as suitable for tanks, but failed to commit the armoured reserve in time. There was a shortage of mobile infantry, particularly on the German side. Both sides were armour heavy, whereas a logical study of terrain would have suggested a more balanced infantry-tank mix. The subsequent misappreciation, based upon the application of technological realities more appropriate to 1940 than 1944, was to contribute to the ensuing stalemate.

**WESTERN SECTOR**
Flooded and Bocage

Infantry country suited to defence

**CENTRAL SECTOR**
Thickly wooded Bocage

**AREA NORTH WEST
AND SOUTH EAST CAEN**
Open ridge lines and farms.
Some woods.

Tank/infantry country, favours
offence if correct tk/inf mix

**EASTERN SECTOR**
Woods and villages.
Some open areas

AREA OF THICKLY WOODED RIDGE LINES

Montebourg

Ste Mère-
Eglise

St Côme-
du-Mont

Carentan

Isigny

St Lô

Vire R.

Taute

R Douvre

Merderet R.

Cerisy Forest

Aure R.

Bayeux

Caen

Authie

Bréville

Orne

suggests that between the 6-9 June the Allies had achieved an advantage of approximately 10 divisions to six enemy, ie, almost 2:1. During this same period, two of the five defending divisions (352nd and 716th) were badly mauled, and only elements of two more panzer divisions had been despatched to support them. There was, in addition, an equivalent piece-meal reinforcement of four to five substantial regiment to brigade size battle groups sent to follow-up. This meant a substantial German shortfall of numbers at the front. The Allies, alternatively, were unable to mass their advantage at a critical point, while in the ascendency, to break-out. The Germans accepting the defence of Caen as the lynch pin, began to fill in the line from the left, moving west, as reinforcements arrived: 21st Panzer before Caen, then the 12th SS, Panzer Lehr, until eventually the 2nd Panzer Division began to arrive on 13 June. The chance to force a decision was lost in the melée of village fighting, that resulted from the piece-meal and hasty insertion of badly balanced units, unsuited to dominate the ground over which they would fight.

A further characteristic that applied, over and above a clinical analysis of force-ratio permutations, was the psychological factor. Heavy casualties were being inflicted on the Allies in the attack. Troops at the receiving end of carnage are indifferent to assessed ratios, where *perception* of success or failure is all important. Certainty of progress was not apparent to Allied troops on the ground. 'This was a very depressing period', explained one Royal Engineer driver, 'troops were being hammered constantly, every attack being costly in lives and materials to gain a few yards'. In such an atmosphere, 'rumours were rife and most of us were physically and mentally worn out'.[3] Private Richard Harris from The Suffolk Regiment in 8th Brigade dug three trenches on D-Day alone. He described the exhausting routine that began after landing.

*It was dusk and time to stand-to for one hour, after which one of us might, with a little luck, snatch two hours sleep in the bottom of the trench before it was his turn to keep watch until dawn, when again we would stand to.*

This echoed a defensive mentality. It began on D-Day and 'was to set the pattern for each of the next 70 nights, unless we were on patrol'.[4] The atmosphere in the beach-head, despite planning and efforts by senior commanders to get moving, did not mirror an imperative to advance quickly. Captain Bell, an intelligence officer in the 3rd Division, wrote in his first diary entry after D-Day:

*Three days here now. Just beginning to realise the new form of things. At first too busy dodging bombs and bullets; then too busy trying to sort out a confused battle situation. Rumours fly around. Le Havre captured say the villagers. Of course not within 30 miles of it. Tiger tanks penetrated two miles away. Also nonsense. Anything on tracks is a Tiger. Troops a bit rattled. Heavy casualties in some battalions. Several friends killed. Seems curiously natural, in these surroundings. Anyway the fighting goes on and we forget.*[5]

These are comments on a static situation. They do not give the impression of impending movement. Casualties were beginning to blunt the offensive spirit. Private Palser, an engineer driver, lamented:

*I believe the 3rd British and 3rd Canadian casualties were the highest of any infantry divisions, and even the prisoners we were taking and the damage we were inflicting did not make me feel any happier or hopeful of success while so many of our chaps were going down.*[6]

The Luftwaffe, moreover, was beginning to make its anticipated appearance, bombing beaches at night. Nineteen-year old Midshipman Pugh aboard *LCI(L) 374* recalled:

*We shot down a Jerry which came swooping down toward us with twin searchlights blazing in each wing. The flak was terrific and the plane slowly disintegrated into a burning mass and crashed into the sea about 100yds ahead of us, lighting up the force with a terrific pool of burning oil which fortunately didn't last too long.*

Raids such as these continued every night. 'Shortly after another plane was shot down into the sea', continued Pugh, 'so close that pieces of burning fabric rained down upon us like hail'.[7] Pressure was building up.

These insidious factors would become more pronounced over time. But at first, on 7 June, there was every expectation, on both sides, that an early decision might be forced. Caen seemed ripe to fall. The 3rd British Division was tasked to seize the high ground north of Caen, close the gap originally breached by the 21st Panzer Division and link in with the 3rd Canadian Division on its right. Caen, it was believed, could be taken frontally. The Canadians were instructed to push south east. It was to be one of the ironies of battle that one of the most aggressive units in the Allied lodgement area, the Canadian 3rd Division, was to be punished for pursuing the very policy required, to drive out of the bridgehead as rapidly as possible. Ignoring the 3rd British Division which appeared to be lagging on its left flank, the Canadians were driving confidently and aggressively for Carpiquet airfield south east of Caen. The leading infantry of the division's 9th Brigade were already in Authie, and Shermans of the 27th Armoured Regiment were moving into St Contest, less than three kilometres from Caen. The bulk of this Canadian armour rumbled into Buron en route for Authie to support the North Nova Scotia Highlanders. Three companies of infantry were mounted on the Shermans, another moved with the advance guard in carriers. Light Stuart tanks were reconnoitring ahead of the force, approaching Franqueville. Cambes, on the left flank, had yet to be taken by the 3rd British Division.

As often the case in battle, the situation was unclear to those about to participate in it. A British Yeomanry tank troop commander, Lieutenant David Holbrook, scouting on this flank south west of Cambes wood scanned the landscape ahead. 'Were the Canadians in contact or not?' He could not tell. 'Confusion had returned about troop dispositions.' The situation was fluid. They were inexperienced and jittery now they anticipated contact with the enemy at any moment. 'Battle was new to all the troops', he commented, 'and as the day's stress mounted there was more talk of an expected counter-attack'. The big picture in terms of the strategic objective to break out was meaningless compared to more immediate perils.

*Nothing of this large pattern was visible to the men in the confusion of D+1, as soldiers grew into veterans under the ceaseless noise and treachery of battle experience. They only moved from bewildered moments pause to catastrophe, from small triumph to inferno.* [8]

The Canadians were living a moment of 'small triumph'. Carpiquet airfield was visible to the Stuart tanks conducting reconnaissance up ahead and appeared to be clear of Germans. There was some risk of an exposed left flank, because the British had yet to catch up. Nevertheless, it was decided to push on, maintain momentum, and establish a good position north of Authie. The armour advanced.

SS-Standartenführer Kurt Meyer watched the nearest enemy tank pause about 200 metres in front of his IInd Grenadier Battalion. The Canadian tank commander raised himself from the turret, lit a cigarette, and sat back on the lid. 'My God, what an opportunity!' Meyer exhaled beneath his breath. He watched the Canadian column moving right to left across his front through binoculars. The SS-Standartenführer's regimental-size battle group, reinforced by a battalion of tanks and artillery, was poised on its start-line prior to its attack to reach the sea. They had quietly infiltrated forward during darkness. His command post was located in the Ardenne Abbey west of Caen, in sight of Authie. The attack was to go in with the 21st Panzer Division to their right, having been set by orders at 03.00. Two SS-Grenadier battalions from Regiment 25 were to spearhead the assault, grouped with a platoon of light flak and heavy weapons each. A third battalion was to attack, echeloned in depth. Panzers were grouped by companies with them. H-Hour was not due for two hours. Meanwhile a substantial enemy force was exposing its whole flank to his line of advance — now.

It had already been an eventful morning. Playing 'cat and mouse' with Allied fighter bombers, Meyer had driven the route to his CP in 100-metre spurts and dashes, thereby evading attacks. By the time they arrived, his driver had perfected a disturbing practice of waiting until the aircraft was actually howling in the dive, before violently braking and scrambling into roadside ditches. 'The grenadiers are swearing at the Jabo menace, and wish them all to the devil' remarked Meyer, echoing his own heart-felt sentiment. His command post, the Ardenne Abbey ruin, enclosed a fruit garden within its high walls. Two towers provided excellent observation. One was already occupied by his artillery forward observation officer. Meyer's commanders had been taken aback at their first sight of the massive invasion fleet, and involuntarily ducked as heavy shells 'shrieked overhead like express trains'. They could see all the way to the coast across a landscape which lay before them 'like a sand model'. Concentrations of armour were forming up west of Douvres. The activity ahead was a visible manifestation of their creeping perception of material inferiority. Meyer, observing through binoculars saw:

*The whole landscape was like an ants' nest. And what was it like behind us? – smoking rubble, empty roads and burning vehicles. The straight road from Calais to Caen is visible for kilometres, and there was no visible German combat support on it. They're waiting somewhere under cover, so that they can complete the final leg to the coast during the night.*

Thankfully, at 10.00 the first of the delayed panzers began to arrive. Fifty Mk IVs clattered into pre-recced positions along the start-line. The rest of the panzer regiment was still strung-out on the line of march. Ahead, the Canadian troops continued to file remorselessly across their line of sight. 'Not a shot rang out', Meyer observed, 'the battalion maintained excellent fire discipline'. The attacking force now faced a dilemma. H-Hour was still due in two hour's time. They either exploited this opportunity now or delayed to confer with 21st Panzer co-ordinating the attack. Tension rose. The panzer regiment commander, SS-Obersturmbannführer Max Wunche, had his command vehicle parked inside the abbey garden. It was used to relay enemy progress viewed from the observation tower directly to the panzers; two companies of which were grouped around the abbey itself.

The Canadian column, spearheaded by light tanks, proceeded unawares. They had eyes only for the airfield. On crossing the ridge line south of Franqueville they would sight one of the panzer companies waiting to advance. Meyer recalled how:

*Spellbound we stared at the spectacle! Wunche – the Panzer tank regiment commander – allowed the steady progress of the enemy tanks to continue. Nobody dared raise his voice.*

Permission to advance was sought from 21st Panzer; but it was decided as soon as the enemy vanguard drove through Franqueville the IIIrd Battalion, sheltering behind the ridge, would have no option but to assault. Should this happen, once they reached Authie the whole of the regiment would cross the start-line. The objective would be as before — the sea. Meyer watched the enemy vanguard pass through Franqueville. As the leading Canadian tanks approached the Caen-Bayeux road 'I gave Wunche the attack sign, and heard his command: "Achtung! Panzer Marsch!" go across the radio net.'

The two motionless panzer companies around the Abbey roared and lurched into exhaust-wreathed life and clattered forward on squeaking tank tracks. They drove directly into the flank of the Canadian column. Further panzers abruptly appeared over the Franqueville ridge-line, spearheading the IIIrd Battalion advance on Authie. The 'Hitlerjugend' had initiated its first major baptism of fire on the invasion front, few would survive the ensuing campaign.

*It cracked and flashed around Franqueville. The lead enemy tanks began smoking, and I saw how the crews baled out. Other tanks exploded in pieces in the air. A Panzer IV suddenly stopped, burning, tongues of flame shooting out of the turret.*

A feature of the early and confusing fighting in the Normandy bridgehead was the frequency with which attacks mounted on both sides, hastily contrived, with little intelligence, often crashed into another assault, similarly mounted, coming from the other direction. Both the Canadians and to a lesser extent the 12th SS around Authie, collided in mid flight.

Dismayed, the Canadian infantry tried to fall back on Authie and fight from there. They were given little chance because right up behind them came the IIIrd Battalion in hot pursuit. As the village was contested, the IInd and Ist Battalions of Regiment 25 crossed the start-line and drove deeply into the Canadian flank. Authie and Franqueville were taken in the initial rush. Buron a further kilometre to the north was the next objective. The 'enemy forces appeared to be completely surprised' remarked Meyer, the battle group commander. 'Artillery on both sides until now had not fired a single round.'[9] His IIIrd Battalion began to attack Buron while the IInd Battalion swept through St Contest on their right, and began to engage enemy tanks beyond.

SS-Schütze Hans Fenn, a Panzer Mk IV gunner from the 6th Company, remembers the initial euphoric success, following their sudden and startling advance from the Abbey grounds. 'We took a number of prisoners, who we sent back to the grenadiers without getting out of our tanks.' They roared around Authie and began to bear down on Buron to the north when four of the five tanks in his platoon 'immediately burst into flames'.

They had been savaged by Canadian anti-tank guns in Buron. Failing to hit any guns the surviving Mk IV locked tracks and began to slew around in the field, throwing up large clods of earth. Fenn confessed it was not a good move. They 'made the greatest mistake, turning while under anti-tank fire'. The solid shot slammed home with a resounding 'plunk' on the side, between turret and hull. Fenn relived his nightmare:

*The shell tore off the tank commander's leg – SS-Scharführer Esser – but I heard he got out of the turret later. Phosphorous shells caused the tank to instantly burst into flames all over. I was helpless. The rubber seal around my gun turret hatch melted and stuck the lid, so I couldn't immediately get out. Somehow, subconsciously I managed to reach the loader's hatch. I clearly remember falling out head-first onto the ground. I made my way back, with third-degree burns, toward our grenadiers following up. They recoiled from me on sight, as if they had seen a ghoul, which is what I must have looked like.[10]*

SS-Sturmmann Vasold, a grenadier from the 9th Company Regiment 25 advancing on Authie, recalled 'overrunning the Canadian tanks standing on the village edge' before engaging in house-to-house fighting. They attacked the Chateau St Louet west of the village, where 'several of our tanks were burning and badly wounded panzer comrades were coming back, severely burnt and missing hands'. The fight through the village continued. 'There was a to-ing and fro-ing', artillery fire came down 'and things were already getting dodgy'. They came under fire from enemy tanks in Buron. 'A bad gunner', Vasold remarked, 'sometimes in front and sometimes behind'. Attacking the source of the firing they penetrated beyond the village edge and came under heavy machine gun fire which 'forced our heads into the earth'. They realised 'we cannot go further forward here' and were forced out by the subsequent Canadian counter-attack.[11]

Meyer became concerned that the attack was stalling in Buron. There were visible signs of success: 50 Canadian prisoners of war had been gathered, arms raised, in the village of Cussy just north of his CP. Buron was subjected to intense Canadian shelling which struck both sides. Meyer, pinned down briefly in a ditch with a Canadian straggler confessed 'I had never experienced such concentrated artillery fire before'. The lead panzers bearing down on Buron were deflected by the barrage raining down, they spun around and came clattering back. Wounded from the attack, including some severely injured Canadians were laid on the decks of the returning tanks. SS-Unterscharführer Hinsberger, a IIIrd Battalion medic attempting to tend them was confronted by Meyer who 'suddenly appeared and ordered the panzers to counter attack'. The medics faced a nightmarish dilemma. They had no option but to get the wounded off, which they proceeded to do. But as Hinsberger explained:

12th SS Kampfgruppe rolling through Caen.

'And what was it like behind us? - smoking rubble, empty roads and burning vehicles' Near the Ardenne Abbey.

'Dismayed the Canadian infantry [here under fire] tried to fall back on Authie and fight from there.'

'They made the greatest mistake, turning while under anti-tank fire.' A 12th SS Panther destroyed in a counter-attack.

*Hard pressed by the heavy work, it was not possible for me and my stretcher bearers to get all the injured off the tanks, which hardly came to a stop. I was a hair's breadth away from being caught by the caterpillar treads myself.[12]*

Three of the stretcher bearers found themselves caught up in the ensuing counter attack, while the SS-Unterscharführer and his sole remaining helper did what they could for the wounded who had been roughly handled down. The rest of them were left on the tank decks, helpless and moaning with pain as the tanks clattered off into battle again. Nobody could help them.

Meanwhile the Ist and IInd Battalion advance had taken St Contest, Malon and Galmanche, advancing on Cambes. 'Up to Cambes everything went OK', said SS Schütze Emil Werner of the 3rd Company, but on entering the village 'all hell broke loose'. Two of their men were killed, but they 'still had not seen any Englishmen'. Werner's section commander was wounded, so he moved with his platoon commander SS-Untersturmführer Gescheider until the officer was struck in the cheek by an explosive bullet. 'He could no longer speak so went back.'[13] Four of five tanks in this sector were disabled, their motionless hulks marking the extent of the advance. Heavy artillery and naval gunfire descended. The IInd Battalion commander, Scapine, was blown apart by a direct hit. SS-Sturmbannführer Waldmuller decided to break off the battalion advance and go onto the defensive on the southern edge of Cambes. Meyer by now had realised 'with horror' that the 21st Panzer had been unable to support his foray and was still in Couvre, leaving his right flank wide open and menaced by Allied tanks.

By mid-afternoon the momentum of the assault had been spent. Gathered around the Abbey were 150 prisoners belonging to the 9th Canadian Brigade. Casualty assessments are variable, but agree that both sides suffered considerable losses. The North Nova Scotia Highlanders lost some 11 dead, 30 wounded and 204 missing, the Sherbrook Foresters lost 73 officers and men with between 15 and 27 tanks. Panzergrenadier Regiment 25 had 64 killed, 181 wounded and 27 missing losing as many as six to nine panzers. The 'Hitlerjugend' may not have reached the sea, but they had demolished the 9th Canadian Brigade attack. The 'Crack-Babies' as they were labelled by the German press had received their baptism of fire. Like their Canadian adversaries, who similarly found defeat difficult to accept, they were reluctant to withdraw, even with exposed flanks. A company commander described the difficulty of extricating isolated sections who, having bitterly fought their way forward, would not turn back.

*All had the will to reach the sea. It was difficult to get them back on the leash again. The order to fall back was met with disbelief, and as a result was followed only after a long delay.[14]*

Elements of two panzer divisions – the 21st and 12th SS – had tried to reach the sea on this, the second day. It was a fragmented effort that only achieved partial success. The 21st Panzer Division was halted at Epron. Another attack, this time by the Canadian 7th Brigade, broke through the 716th Division remnants to the left of Meyer's regiment. The situation was restored when the remainder of the 'Hitlerjugend' Division including Panzergrenadier Regiment 26 came up and filled the gap during darkness. The following night another SS battle group retook Bretteville-l'Orguelleuse and Putot-en-Bessin, destroying the forward companies of the Regina Rifles and Canadian Scottish. Putot changed hands again when the 7th Brigade counter-attacked the same evening and threw out the Germans. Casualties were heavy, 152 lost by the SS alone.[15] This action, which took place by night, as much due to difficulties of re-supply as the Allied air forces, typified the solidifying of a previously fluid situation. Dashes were followed by local attacks, and then limited counter-attacks. The centre was deteriorating into a battle of attrition around villages.

Generaloberst Geyr von Schweppenburg, commanding Panzergruppe West planned to start an offensive to gain the coast which would begin at 11.00 on 10 June, the first time all three panzer divisions – 'Hitlerjugend', Panzer Lehr and 21st Panzer – would be in situ. It was never launched, because an incoming Allied attack was to cause a crisis on the left flank of Panzer Lehr which distracted the effort. No longer did German orders contain the term 'drive them into the sea'. It was now a question of containing the bridgehead. The Allied superiority of 15 compared to 10 German divisions was to prove transitory. Thereafter attrition was guaranteed as German figures, coming to terms with Allied deception and despite air attacks, began to achieve almost equality by about 15 June. Stalemate was by then assured.

With the stalemate came depression and doubts. Private J. Garner, a carrier driver in the 1st South Lancs with the 3rd Division, recalled the deabilitating psychological effect of incessant shelling 'day in, day out' during this period, manning a position in a wood near le Londel before Caen. 'Thoughts of self-inflicted wounds or even complete suicide passed through the mind,' he said, 'how much more could one take?' Some men even held their arm above the slit trench parapet in the hope of securing a 'Blighty' wound.

*Each day the shelling went on and comrades whom I knew well were killed, wounded and smashed in the mind. Strong men who'd boxed or played soccer or rugger for the unit and had suffered the horror of Dunkirk were led or carried away shaking and blubbering like small children. WOs and Sergeants and even the odd officer, my heroes, disgusted themselves in my sight reduced to crying babies. I was barely 20 at the time and was deeply affected by this behaviour.[16]*

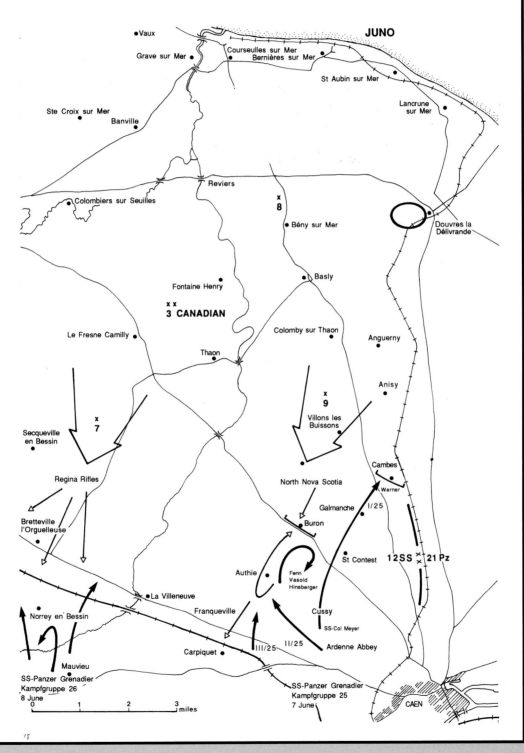

## The 'Hitlerjugend' Thrust to the Coast

Just over one-third of SS-Standartenführer Meyer's Panzergrenadier Regiment 25 Kampfgruppe - was ready to assault on D+1. They mauled the leading element of the 3rd Canadian Division, but failed to reach the sea.

**JUNO**

Vaux

Grave sur Mer

Courseulles sur Mer
Bernières sur Mer

St Aubin sur Mer

Ste Croix sur Mer

Lancrune sur Mer

Banville

Reviers

x
8

Colombiers sur Seuilles

Bény sur Mer

Douvres la
Délivrande

Basly

Fontaine Henry

x x
3 CANADIAN

Colomby sur Thaon

Anguerny

Le Fresne Camilly

Thaon

Anisy

x
9

Villons les
Buissons

Secqueville
en Bessin

x
7

Cambes

Regina Rifles

North Nova Scotia

Werner

Galmanche

1/25

Bretteville
l'Orguelleuse

Buron

St Contest

**12 SS** × 21 Pz
×

Authie

Fenn
Vasold
Hinsberger

Norrey en Bessin

La Villeneuve

Cussy

SS-Col Meyer

Franqueville

III/25   II/25

Ardenne Abbey

Carpiquet

Mauvieu

SS-Panzer Grenadier
Kampfgruppe 26
8 June

SS-Panzer Grenadier
Kampfgruppe 25
7 June

CAEN

0    1    2    3
miles

One Canadian soldier remembered his officer saying 'in this place nobody wins or loses, you just survive'. His sergeant bracketed by German artillery fire muttered 'Shit, and shit some more'.

*I asked him if he was hit and he sort of smiled and said no, he had just pissed his pants. He always pissed them, he said, just when things started and then he was okay. He wasn't making any apologies either, and then I realised something wasn't quite right with me either. There was something warm down there and it seemed to be running down my leg. I felt, and it wasn't blood it was piss.*

*I told the Sarge, I said, "Sarge, I've pissed too," or something like that and he grinned and said, "Welcome to the war".[17]*

There was some appreciation that the enemy, if he was human, was suffering as well. 'Pity, if that is what it was', remarked Garner 'came to me when we were consolidating after the bloody attack on La Londe'. He had come across a German MG42 (machine gun) team, 'young blonde and well-built', both lay dead, face downwards in a ditch.

*The No 2 had across his back the spare barrel and his arm was around the shoulders of the No 1. It saddened me even though moments before they had been trying to kill us. Funny how I have remembered the picture though I have witnessed far more horrific sights since. I can still visualise it in every detail.[18]*

This poignant embrace had resulted from the No 2 steadying the No 1, to achieve a more lethal fire platform. As the pointless – almost inconsequential – local attacks continued by both sides, it became apparent that elan alone would make little impact in this close and difficult terrain, where attack faced defence in equal numbers. Even the 'Hitlerjugend' were to experience a similar deabilitating strain. SS-Sturmmann Helmuth Pock, now working in a Field Workshop to the rear of the Ist Battalion Panzer Regiment 22, climbed a tank requiring repair. On pulling himself up 'I felt my hand touch a damp slippery substance'. The gunner was embarrassingly apologetic. 'Our Commander was killed', he said, 'his head was torn off – I know, the whole tank is soiled'. Pock, mortified, felt desperately sorry for the 'poor man', who had just been in action for the first time. 'Don't worry', he responded, 'there was nothing you could do about it'. Not surprisingly he found himself meticulously and painstakingly washing his hands, and 'for once did not have a lot to say'.[19] As with the Allies, the Germans were realising that the greatest casualties almost invariably occurred in the offence.

# The East – stalemate on the Orne … Bréville.

Both sides saw the centre – between Caen and Bayeux – as the decisive sector. The Eastern flank on the Orne was regarded as a holding action by the British, as the build up to dominate the foreshore continued. The German High Command, focussed as it was on the imperative to sweep the Allies away with a massive panzer counter-stroke, ignored the immediate logical recourse which should have been to move the nearest force mass available to interdict it, namely Fifteenth Army. Identifying the Pas-de-Calais as the main point of defence effort produced a mal-deployment in terms of holding Normandy. If flexibility had enabled a westward shift of focus, the Allies would not have achieved their initial local dominance. But the main German defence forces on the coast – static infantry divisions – by definition immobile, did not move.

Fifteenth Army on the Allied eastern flank controlled 19 infantry divisions in northern France and the Low Countries.[1] As already identified, much of the terrain surrounding the Allied lodgement was suited to a mix of tanks and infantry, often mainly infantry with tanks supporting; rarely for a panzer counter-stroke alone. Even an early thinning of these 19 divisions could have achieved a decisive impact, as only five initially slowed the impetous of the Allied assault. Although supported by the fragmented arrival of three panzer divisions, the tactical balance on the ground was often inverted. Of the available infantry that could be directly despatched to menace the eastern flank, only the 711th Division in situ was partially used, and the 346th Division in Le Havre gradually introduced over a period of four days. Reinforcements were despatched instead from the furthest geographical points, many from Brittany and the south of France.

Deception played a vital role. Army Group B headquarters was perceptibly drawn away from deriving logical deductions from the facts. It assessed 14 Allied divisions ashore on 6 June, which was broadly correct. Twenty divisions were estimated the following day. By 8 June it was calculated there were two Allied armies of eight to 10 divisions each, with an intention already identified to cut off Cherbourg, yet Army Group B assessed the enemy was only using one-quarter of his available units.[2] The War Diary records concern and tension within Fifteenth Army headquarters, worried at the prospect of an imminent threat developing against the port of Antwerp.[3] Rommel on 7 June was still suspicious that the main weight of the Allied assault will 'be elsewhere'. Despite holding 19 infantry divisions, Headquarters Fifteenth Army requested permission to close an Army Weapon Training School on the same day to supplement what it considered to be an insufficiency of force.[4] A captured US VIIth Corps operations order revealed on 8 June designs on the Contentin and Cher-

With the stalemate came depression and doubts – Canadian infantry.

*Above:* SS-Sturmmann Vasold remembered overrunning the Canadian tanks standing on the village edge. A still from a German cine-film.

Fighting east of the Orne during the early phase was infantry-dominated.

*Right:* The IInd Battalion of Infantry Regiment 857 was hanging grimly on to Bréville having captured it in a counter-attack during the afternoon. Moving up an anti-tank gun past British dead.

bourg, and a 15-division order of battle besides four to five airborne divisions. Despite this the 2nd and 116th Panzer Division deployments were blocked. Tension came to the fore during 8-12 June. On the 8th, Fifteenth Army was expecting a landing 'but not for the next few days'. It was announced the following day that landings were anticipated in Belgium during the night of 9-10 June.[5] These reports decisively shifted attention from Normandy at the very moment when every effort should have been made to meet and surpass the Allied build-up.

The background to this was a combination of 'Garbo' and 'Ultra' reports, providing the Allied deception plan with its 'finest hour'. Decrypts of the German Enigma codes confirmed by 'Garbo' convinced the German High Command of 'the imminence of an assault' in the Pas de Calais region. A summary of the report reached Adolf Hitler's command post at Berchtesgaden and von Rundstedt in France. The effect was instantaneous. Movement orders were cancelled and instructions countermanded:

*As a consequence of information which has just been received, C in C West has proclaimed a second degree alert for Fifteenth Army in Belgium and N France. The move of 1st SS Panzer will therefore be halted.*

And not only 1st SS Panzer; 116th Panzer Division was actually directed from north west Paris towards the Somme, while the 85th Infantry division, already north of the Somme but about to move south, was told to stand fast.[6] Three German divisions were immediately removed from the Normandy order of battle, and therefore from the race to dominate the foreshore, without a shot being fired. Meanwhile, 17 divisions of much needed infantry renewed a misguided focus on the Pas-de-Calais. Geography and the Allied air forces were to do the rest to promote the impending stalemate to the east of the Allied bridgehead.

The terrain east of the Orne was relatively close, with numerous hedges, woods and small villages. It was not particularly suited to armour, constrained as it was by the flooded areas bordering the Dives running broadly north-south, and the industrial areas around Columbelles, east of Caen. A number of bridges destroyed by the 6th Airborne Operation on the night of D-Day meant the main tank approaches would be from the south and southeast.

Fighting east of the Orne during this early phase was infantry-dominated. The initial D-Day armoured foray by von Luck's 21st Division Panzergrenadier battle group had been beaten off. The situation on the 6th Airborne Division perimeter after the initial dashes and conquests of 6 June, developed like the centre into local counter-attacks, which became progressively less fluid and more costly. Allied tanks, like their panzer counterparts, discovered the difficulty of operating in this rela-

tively close terrain. 'B' Squadron of the 13/18th Royal Hussars supporting a 7 PARA attack on Le Mariquet on 10 June with 13 Shermans and a reconnaissance section of Honey tanks, suffered some of the difficulties that had plagued the 21st Panzer days before. Rarely was the enemy seen. A liaison officer in a scout car attached to the 7 PARA infantry proved limited, as he was unable to accompany the paratroopers through wooded country. As they advanced 'they saw nothing ... other than a few snipers in the gliders whom they engaged'. Two tanks were ensnared and dragged to a halt when discarded parachutes from the original and re-supply drops snagged sprockets. Almost immediately the tanks burst into flames. 'They did not know what had hit them' but the troops suspected fire from Bréville. Another tank entangled in parachute silk met the same fate, hit by enemy anti-tank guns as soon as it was stationary. Six tanks were lost. Casualties within the lightly armoured Honey tanks were invariably fatal; eight from 10 crew were killed. 'It was not ideal tank country', assessed Lance Corporal Hennessey, 'because there were too many hedgerows and they were too close.'[7]

Major Taylor from 7 PARA recalled the difficulties of coordinating tank-infantry support in this terrain. 'In the afternoon we were greatly cheered to see two Shermans come up to us – the place was alive with yellow smoke, yellow triangles and red berets on sticks – but without contacting us they went straight on and were never seen by us again.' Fighting momentarily died down at their appearance, but 'I believe they got brewed up further down the road'. Taylor, a company commander was well aware of the precarious nature of their situation. 'The Germans never knew what strength we had', and seemed reluctant to close. 'They never really launched an all-out attack as we would understand it. Plenty of fire, yes, and bags of Verey lights but no men or bayonets'.[8]

Unteroffizier Werner Kortenhaus, a 21st Division panzer commander in von Luck's battle group, described how a combination of unfavourable terrain, and heavy naval gunfire, neutralised any possibility of a decisive breakthrough. 'We assembled with about 10 tanks under the trees of the avenue south of Escoville.' The difficulty, as ever, was to concentrate combat power sufficiently strong to break the dead-lock. But the ground did not allow it.

*We drove with closed ports, one tank after the other, to the right past the chateau into a large meadow, which was enclosed by hedges. There we intended switching to broad wedge formation for attack, the grenadiers behind and alongside us.*

Behind the hedge facing them was a wall. Breaking through with tanks was an option 'only at the risk of dis-adjusting our guns', not therefore practical. In front of the wall was a ditch 'very convenient for the elements defending themselves there', while artillery fire had holed the wall 'through which the defenders could easily retreat'. Kortenhaus's unremarkable conclusion was 'it was an unfavourable sector for a tank attack'. In the event this was all largely academic because 'everything happened very quickly: within a few minutes we had lost four tanks, knocked out by the naval guns'. All momentum was destroyed by the hurricane of fire that descended, 'some 30 or 40 grenadiers must have been killed by it'.[9]

Both sides were unaware of the problems of the other. Human nature often assumed the enemy was better off. Major Taylor's men, keyed-up, anticipated a major assault at any moment. 'We expected it every time things brewed up, but it never came. If they had really tried to outflank us they would have made it extremely awkward for us.' Meanwhile, Kortenhaus had concluded 'on the evening of that 9 June we realised we could no longer drive the British back into the sea'.[10]

See-saw fighting around the village of Bréville deteriorated into a battle of attrition. The 346th Division taken from the Le Havre area was inserted piece-meal against the north east side of the 6th Airborne Division perimeter. Due to the inadequate state of its transport, this 'static' division arrived in a haphazard fashion in its assembly areas having purloined civilian vehicles, bicycles, horse-drawn carts and towed motor vehicles. Heavy weapons were delayed, consequently the 75mm anti-tank guns of Regiment 857 and some ammunition arrived late. Hot food was not available to soldiers until three days after arrival. The IIIrd Battalion was in action by the evening of the 7 June. The 858th Regiment did not begin its assaults until two and a half days later, having lost two platoons' worth of vehicles to air attacks en route. One battalion pedalled 65 miles on bicycles, setting off at 23.00 on 6 June, and received no sleep, food or halts until arrival near Caen on 8 June. They were in action within an hour. The infantry strength of the 346th Division was thus haphazardly built up until by the time of the battles around Breville it fielded nine weak battalions, some dozen assault guns and two batteries of artillery. Pushing two regiments up, the 857th to the north, and 858th in the south, it tried to reach the coast between Franceville and the Bois de Bavent. Between 10-12 June a series of local advances and bitterly contested counter attacks forced a wedge into the airborne line around the Amfréville-Bréville area. Intense fighting raged around the Chateau St Côme, which represented the high tide of the German advance, easily identifiable because as the IIIrd Battalion 858th Regiment report remarked 'the open square before the Chateau was covered with dead soldiers'.[11]

Casualties on the British side had also been heavy, among the Parachute and Special Service (Commando) Brigades, and a battalion of the Black Watch from the 51st Division. Major General Gale, commanding the 6th Airborne Division, resolved to capitalise upon the exhausted state both sides had fought themselves into, by employing his last remaining reserve to capture Bréville on the evening of 12 June. All he had left was the 12th Battalion Parachute Regiment, 'B' Company from the 12th Battalion, The Devonshire Regiment and a squadron of Sherman tanks. The assault was to encapsulate the nature of the bloody fighting east of the Orne. Significantly the British were to receive all the available artillery support in the area, comprising naval gunfire and five field and one medium regiment of artillery.

Waiting in assembly areas prior to action is the most nerve-wracking aspect of any battle. Captain Sim of 'B' Company 12 PARA recalled his surprise when he was directed with his men to file into the church at Le Plein to wait, prior to the assault. Their mortality must have seemed very precarious as:

*The men sat in the pews, some spoke quietly among themselves, some smoked or sucked sweets, others gazed at the gaily painted effigies of saints … The minutes dragged by, then the platoon commanders were called out, some sergeants and corporals marched out. We continued to sit and wait.*

These subdued movements, the muted scuffle of boots in the interior of the darkening church contributed to a hospital-like atmosphere, which raised tension. Like a dentist's waiting room, or anticipating bad news, all knew the worse was yet to come. 'Soon there was a scurry and a bustle' Sim remembered. The fateful moment arrived. Quick orders were given and the battalion filed out of church in their future order of battle. 'We were going to advance into Bréville in four waves in the order "C" Company, "A" Company, a company from the 12th Devons and "B" Company; HQ Company were coming in later.' Fourth in line may improve their chances of survival, but did little to relieve nerves. Captain P.C. Berhard, commanding the second wave, was already forward reconnoitring with the CO, Lieutenant Colonel Johnson. 'Bréville looked very peaceful on that pleasant June evening' he said. The troops began to move up 'making their way in a confused stream up the narrow lane in the general direction of Breville' recalled Major Warren of The Devonshire Regiment. Many of the Devons were pushing heavy equipments along with hand carts. Most had already been involved in heavy fighting over the previous few days, few had any illusions about coming casualties.[12]

The IIIrd Battalion of Infantry Regiment 857 was hanging grimly onto Bréville, having captured it and the Chateau St Côme after fierce fighting during the afternoon. The lead platoon had been totally wiped out, and its commander Oberleutnant Streichert killed. A company of the 858th Regiment had moved up to reinforce them accompanied by some assault guns, which had already disposed of a number of Allied tanks. Breville had been considerably damaged in the fighting. Two

213

## Village Fighting around Bréville

The 12 PARA counter-attack at Bréville eclipsed the final attempt by 346th Division to force the Allied perimeter east of the Orne. No further reinforcements were commited by the Fifteenth Army which, distracted by Allied deception, focussed its 20 infantry divisions on a possible mythical assault across the Pas-de-Calais. Even a thinning out of some of this effort would have had a decisive impact on operations in Normandy. Stalemate ensued.

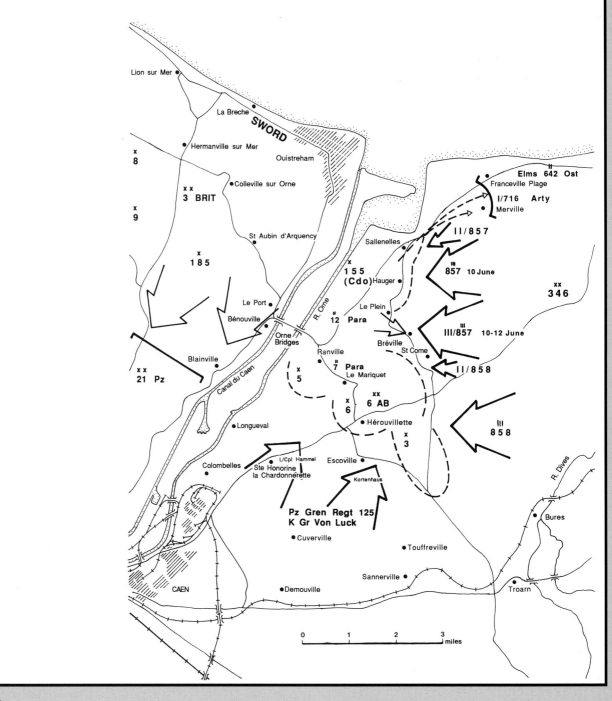

Lion sur Mer

La Breche

SWORD

Hermanville sur Mer

Ouistreham

x
8

Colleville sur Orne

xx
3 BRIT

x
9

St Aubin d'Arquency

x
185

Elms 642 Ost
Franceville Plage

I/716   Arty
Merville

Sallenelles

II/857

857  10 June

xx
346

Le Port

Bénouville

x
155
(Cdo)  Hauger

R. Orne

II
12 Para

Le Plein

Le Plein

III/857  10-12 June

Orne
Bridges

Bréville

St Come

Blainville

Ranville

II
7  Para
Le Mariquet

II/858

xx
21 Pz

Canal du Caen

x
5

xx
6 AB

x
6

III
858

Longueval

Hérouvillette

x
3

Colombelles

L/Cpl Hammel

Ste Honorine
la Chardonnérette

Escoville

Kortenhaus

R. Dives

Pz Gren Regt 125
K Gr Von Luck

Cuverville

Bures

Touffreville

Sannerville

CAEN

Demouville

Troarn

0     1     2     3
└─────┴─────┴─────┴ miles

shell-shocked remnants of companies commanded by Oberleutnants Stachel and Schweier held onto the north and west sides of the village. The soldiers, relatively inexperienced had 'already had their morale starkly reduced' by the tremendous weight of naval gunfire; 'which in certain positions had precipitated withdrawals'. Panic had broken out in one 857th Regiment battalion when subjected to an earlier tank-infantry counter-attack. Heavy casualties among officers were causing considerable difficulties. 'Crisis most often occurred', claimed the unit report, 'when several commanders in a unit were killed at the same time'.[13] They had by now developed a healthy respect for the irregular 'bush-fighting' tactics of the paratrooper snipers. Fearful casualties had also been wrought upon the initial break-in platoons on the open square in front of the Chateau St Côme, ambushed by the defenders with 'fire coming out of cellar windows and from behind hedges'. Then at 21.45 Bréville's defenders were subjected to a crippling bombardment 'from batteries of all calibres, from light field guns to heavy naval artillery'. The barrage lasted 30 minutes. The official unit report declared 'practically every square metre of ground was pounded. By 22.15 the village of Bréville was a burning smoking ruin.'[14]

'Then with a crash the show started', said Captain Sim of 12 PARA, 'and the battalion moved off slowly down the road to Bréville'. Captain Berhard in the second wave with 'A' Company believed 'it seemed impossible that anybody could live in Breville'. By 21.50 Sim said 'the noise was colossal, shells whistled over our heads to roar and rumble a little way ahead'. But things started to go wrong. Major Warren of The Devonshire Regiment hurrying down the road remarked 'the noise of our own artillery was now deafening and considerable congestion and confusion existed in the narrow lane leading to the forming up place and start-line'. Shells had begun to bracket the 12 PARA line of departure. 'Trails of white smoke from smoke shells, mortars and everything it seemed, exploded around us' recalled Sim, horrified at the realisation of what was happening. 'We hurriedly took cover in the narrow ditches beside the road, many of us hugging the walls of houses'. They had to endure their own artillery fire for some 20 minutes. The paratrooper company commander was a practical soldier, and aware of the mistakes that often occur in the conduct of hasty attacks, he commented 'it was excusable in a way as the operation was mounted at express speed'. Its consequences however were tragic, and only too apparent as 'B' Company in the third wave followed up the lead troops.

*On the way we had to pass streams of our fellows from "A" and "C" Companies. Bloody faces, limp arms, staggering and weaving our men came back. Some collapsed and remained still, some were crawling on their hands and knees.*[15]

An 'A' Company platoon was caught on the start-line and completely engulfed by a shuddering pattern of multiple orange tinged impacts. The survivors of the second wave advanced. Major Warren, who had been attempting to locate the Devonshire company, 'lay down thinking it must be Boche defensive fire'. It continued for two to three minutes then ceased. As the smoke momentarily cleared 'close to where I had been in the field on the right of the lane several men of the 12 PARA Battalion now lay killed or wounded'. Some of the wounded required assistance to get at their morphine because they 'were too badly hit to get them out themselves'. Sherman tanks were distinguishable up ahead, pouring fire onto the objective. Warren was looking for Major John Hampflyde, the Devonshire Company Commander. Stumbling onward, a few metres beyond the hedge-line that marked the start-line 'I found eight or 10 of our own men killed', among them was Hampflyde, and the man responsible for leading the attack, Lieutenant Colonel Johnson, the CO of 12 PARA.

'B' Company led by Captain Sim broke into Breville. 'There were masses of German trenches in the orchard' and 'dead Germans lay around' surrounded by discarded arms and equipment. The advancing paratroopers quickly scrambled into the comparative shelter of the enemy trenches.

*One had in it a live shivering German, on being dragged out he made a dive for one of our chaps, who immediately shot him. With surprise and horror written on the man's face he turned round to me and said "God! Look what I've done!"*[16]

Down came the anticipated counter barrage. Warren, still outside the village was convinced this was 'from our own guns'. Another nine or 10 men in 'B' Company were wounded in the shelling. The Devonshire 2IC was trying to round up stragglers, and push them forward toward the village.

*I started digging the chaps out from under odd bits of cover. Fire was now pretty intense and wounded were coming back frequently. It's incredibly difficult to get men on their feet once they have gone to cover, particularly to get them moving against a string of wounded chaps coming back.*

There was confusion and uncertainty. 'The noise was terrific and visibility at times very bad, due to smoke from shell bursts and some buildings which were blazing merrily now.' Fighting was fierce in those areas where physical contact was made. Generally one saw only fleeting glimpses of the enemy. Movement was reported to the right of the road 'so we dived into some back gardens' said Major Warren, 'and came bang up against two Germans struggling with a machine gun, they didn't see us till we fired'. A confused melée of street fighting followed. Another desperate German threw his Schmeisser at Warren's group when surprised and beset by a stoppage, 'and bolted'. Immediately 'off went the pack after him into the house', Warren following, until 'something hit me in the thigh with a wallop'. Although stunned 'I'd just pulled myself together when the Boche scrambled out of a window a few feet away and landed at my feet'. He shot him. 'An unarmed Boche served upon a plate, even my standards of pistol shooting was adequate for that.'[17] The street fighting continued into darkness as the final mopping up began. There were isolated battles between Shermans and German assault guns. Company headquarters of 'A' Company 12 PARA was wiped out by a self-propelled gun. One of its platoons was holding onto its objective to the right of the Chateau with only nine men.

A number of soldiers from the two cut-off German companies commanded by Stachel and Schweier survived the bombardment, but were stunned into a form of psychological paralysis by the intensity of the shellfire, which:

> Had never been experienced in such a form before. Heavy naval guns in particular have an extraordinary impact on morale. It is difficult for men in such a situation to resist a creeping realisation of inferiority.[18]

These demoralised remnants were struck by the combined tank and infantry attack closely supported by light and heavy machine guns, 'powerless, they were immediately destroyed'. The battalion command post, situated on the edge of the bombardment, benefiting 'from good cover from fox-holes and ditches suffered no casualties', read the after-action report. They managed to assemble a scratch-force of 20 men and conducted two counterattacks. But the CP was 'hemmed in from three sides by the enemy'. German artillery fire was called in upon the occupied Allied side of the village, but the position was untenable. 'No further reports came from Stachel and Schweier's companies', and 'a re-occupation of the village, however courageous the troops, with the remaining 20 men would be tantamount to suicide'. The battalion commander decided to withdraw eastwards between 01.00 and 02.00 on 13 June, and attempt to re-establish a new blocking line. In little over two days the IIIrd Battalion Regiment 857 had lost six of 10 officers and 62 of 75 NCOs, its manpower had been decimated from 564 to 146 all ranks.[19] The unit was burnt out.

A calm slowly descended on the village. A troop of Shermans clattered into the line of houses at the very moment the Germans began slipping away in the darkness. Major Warren described a surreal scene. 'The rest of the night passed all too slowly with its eerie light from burning houses, foul stench and the groans and cries of wounded who could not be found in the dust and rubble of smashed houses.' Captain Sim remembered a pre-

vailing gut-wrenching tension, 'while the church and two or three other houses continued to blaze and with the eerie wail of an air raid siren to cheer them up, our men waited for the Germans to counter-attack'. They never did. The waiting continued throughout the hours of darkness. An organ stop in the burning church had jammed, and continued its plaintive howling, until with a smouldering upsurge of sparks and flame, the roof finally collapsed.

Elements from the 51st Division, beginning with the 153rd Brigade, had already begun crossing the Orne into the 6th Airborne bridgehead the night before. General Gale had broken German resistance in this sector. The capture of Bréville, despite the proximity of the monolithic Fifteenth Army on its doorstep, removed the threat from the Orne river bridges. The Germans had nothing available to counter what was fast becoming an effective block on the crucial Allied left flank, enabling the build-up, to dominate the foreshore to continue unabated.

Four kilometres to the south west the Kampfgruppe 'von Luck' was ordered to assault the village of Ste Honorine on the same day the battle for Bréville was fought. After achieving initial surprise, this local attack was beaten to a standstill by naval artillery and Allied fighter-bombers. Unteroffizier Hammel lamented:

> The barrage of fire on Ste Honorine was the worst that we had experienced so far. We prayed. When we had pulled back to the village of Cuverville, a few kilometres further south, another heavy barrage of fire rained down on that village. Was there absolutely nowhere left here where one could get a breather and some sleep?[20]

As in the centre, village fighting had produced stalemate. Major von Luck, the Kampfgruppe commander, confessed 'we now finally gave up hope of making any impression on the British bridgehead, let alone of eliminating it'. The Allies failed to utilise a local superiority to break out of the lodgement; the Germans chose not to employ their massive strategic superiority in the form of Fifteenth Army located nearby, to destroy it. The race to dominate the fore-shore was fast becoming a draw.

## The West – 'Bocage' … St Côme du Mont.

On the western flank of the invasion the terrain favoured static defence. Unlike the centre, it was unsuited for armoured advances. The confluence of the Merderet and Douve rivers, flooded areas and Carentan estuary provided formidable geographical barriers to a break-out from the foreshore lodgement. This was infantry terrain. Inland from the beaches, stretching up to 80km in depth was a 'chequerboard' landscape of farmland enclosed by hedgerows forming a patchwork quilt of small fields bounded by earth banks. These overgrown hedgerows formed a veritable jungle terrain – the 'bocage' – intersected by sunken lanes and dotted with small villages. Farmhouses had often been built for defence in medieval times.

The check imposed at Omaha gave scant opportunity for any spirited short dashes that might have taken the Americans clear of this obstacle belt. Although unsuitable for tanks, close armoured fire support was still needed to methodically clear resistance to keep infantry casualties down. Tanks were delayed coming ashore, and what infantry had been landed was still insufficient in the early fluid stage of the invasion to reduce entrenched German opposition. On 7 June, Rommel alarmed by the continuing American build-up, despite the momentary success at Omaha, ordered the IInd Fallschirmjäger Corps to reinforce the base of the Cherbourg peninsula. This involved the committal of three additional infantry divisions: the 3rd Fallschirmjäger, 77th and 275th Divisions, despatched from Brittany to west Contentin. OKW committed armoured support in the form of the 17th SS Panzergrenadier Division 'Götz von Berlichingen'.

Fighting in this sector was similar in some respects, despite topographical differences, to the conflict in the centre and east. Ambitious dashes seeking early advantage were bloodily repulsed, while local commanders appeared stunned by the unexpected - a phenomena applying to both sides. The Germans were taken aback at the violence and extent of the Allied onslaught; while the latter, having overcome the vaunted Atlantic Wall, could not get a sustained push moving inland. One 26-year old American doctor treating wounded German officers remarked:

*They kept saying, it's all over for you. When our Panzers let loose, we're just gonna knock you out of France. We were really quite concerned about it.[1]*

The Americans were dismayed by the unfamiliar terrain; it was unlike anything they had trained over before. Corporal William Preston serving in the 743rd Tank Battalion of 1st Division remarked in a letter home: 'there is absolutely nothing in the books which covers this type of fighting. Every advantage of terrain lies with the enemy.' He complained:

*The small open fields surrounded by thick bushes and trees on all sides are only traps for the unwary, and as there are hundreds of these small meadows, so there are hundreds of traps to be sprung before the enemy is beaten. It makes advancing agonizingly slow, nor do I ever feel more like a goldfish in his bowl than when we advance across these fields from hedgerow to hedgerow.*

Both sides groped around in this terrain, often uncertain

where the other was, and unclear what part their action was contributing to the broad picture. 'The Battle of the Hedgerows', remarked Preston, 'continues as near to jungle fighting as anything I can think of'.[2] It was confusing and lethal to the unwary.

The 2nd Battalion of the American 115th Regiment (from the 29th Division) took the wrong turn in this maze during the middle of the night of 9-10 June, en route to Le Carretour its objective. Weary soldiers filed into fields just short of their goal to get some rest. It was the first halt the battalion had been granted following 20 hours of continuous marching and fighting. Exhausted soldiers crumpled beside hedgerows and slept, some without even removing equipment. Many chose not to dig in. As the last files of American soldiers lined the road waiting to move into nearby fields to complete a perimeter defence, they heard the sound of tracked vehicles approaching. Peering intently into the darkness, and rubbing tired eyes, they tried to identify the squat menacing shapes suddenly looming out of the darkness. They were enemy.

A column of German self-propelled guns, foot troops and trucks moving along the same Le Carretour road, retreating from the Aure river to St Lô, came across the sleeping Americans astride its withdrawal route. A burst of fire from a German Schmeisser broke the cautious silence of the bivouac area, and signalled the onset of the ensuing melée. 'All hell broke loose' declared one survivor later. 'There were tanks and Krauts everywhere – all shooting.' One tank moved into the field and 'methodically shot up all sides of it with an 88. Everybody was dead or captured but him' the soldier told investigating officers.[3] Men who had fallen asleep awoke in darkness to find their hedgerows splintering and shuddering under a hail of automatic and tank fire. German infantry began climbing over hedges and closed in, mopping up the demoralised battalion. The commanding officer was killed alongside his staff outside the command post. American survivors split into small groups and attempted to exfiltrate back to their own lines.[4] Having destroyed the battalion, the German column resumed the line of march. It was a representative example of the blind hack-and-thrust characterising operations during the first confusing days. Nobody stayed to secure the objective marked by mounds of dead from both sides; the ground had been inconsequential.

Combined attacks toward St Côme-du-Mont, protecting the causeway to Carentan, represented the first attempts by the US 101st Airborne Division staff to coordinate the actions of forces in excess of those scattered 'indian bands' that had characterised operations during the night of D-Day and the subsequent 24 hours. This was the beginning of a serious attempt to link the Utah and Omaha beachheads. In reality the task group mustered by Colonel Sink commanding the 506th Infantry Regiment, although larger than a band, was still only a motley regimental organisation in outline. It consisted of 227 men from the 1st and 301 men from the 2nd Battalions of the 506th Regiment, supplemented by a company's worth of 101st Division 'strays', 40 soldiers from the 82nd Airborne Division (way off their designated drop zones) and a platoon of anti-tank weapons.[5]

Facing them was Major von der Heydte's Fallschirmjäger Regiment 6. Having earlier lost its Ist Battalion further north around Ste Marie-du-Mont, its right flank was hanging in the air. Colonel Sink's attack force advancing south toward Vierville and St Côme-du-Mont was menacing this gap, an inter-battalion boundary between von der Heydte's IInd Fallschirmjäger battalion and the Wehrmacht IIIrd Battalion from Regiment 1058 holding in the Bse Addeville-Les Droueries area. Sink's force achieved local breakthroughs almost immediately, causing von der Heydte to comment 'the combat morale of the [Wehrmacht] battalion sank from hour to hour'. As the crisis developed he inserted two of his own Fallschirmjäger companies - the 9th and 12th - from his IIIrd Battalion in depth to restore the situation 'after panic had ensued' during a tank-infantry attack.[6] Four counter-attacks resulted in severe casualties among the 9th Company, but the line held. Oberleutnant Pöppel commanding the 12th Company forward with Oberleutnant Wagner commanding the 9th commented on the tension. 'I came across Wagner behind a hedge, in discussion with the infantrymen. To-day he doesn't seem as calm and level-headed as he usually is.' Their position was crumbling. 'Then a cry from ahead: enemy attacking with tanks!' Light infantry are particularly fearful of armour. Pöppel noticed 'the men, particularly the infantrymen, are damned jittery'.[7] He was not confident at the likely outcome.

Colonel Sink's task group advanced beyond Vierville, and was midway between Ste Marie-du-Mont and his objective, St Côme-du-Mont. It took him three hours to progress 1000yds. Momentum picked up when they were joined by six Sherman tanks from Utah Beach. 'D' Company of the 506th Regiment made the deepest penetration. 'Because of the tank's machine gun, they [the Germans] couldn't get their heads up; that was what did it' reported one observer.[8] Control was difficult to maintain. The twisting road, curtaining hedgerows and the spotty and resurgent nature of the Fallschirmjäger opposition tended to fragment the advancing columns. Four of six tanks had to momentarily return to the rear to re-fight Vierville free again. The two remaining tanks meanwhile collided with Wagner's 9th Fallschirmjäger Company, having reached the intersection which at last brought them onto the Ste Mère-Eglise-Carentan road. Any euphoria was soon cut short when the lead tank burst into flame after being struck by a *Panzerfaust*. It momentarily blocked the road, blasting out incendiary sparks and secondary explosions. The crew were incinerated. Protruding grotesquely from the turret was the shrunken fire blackened effigy of the tank commander. His ghoulish presence for the next few days was to earn

this junction the epitaph of 'Dead Man's Corner'. The advance had been halted.

Captain Joe MacMillan, the company commander, felt increasingly vulnerable as light faded. He was over-extended, and had no prospect of breaking through. Peering through the gloom, he discerned what appeared to be American supply trucks parked on the road ahead. The lead driver had his torch out and was studying a map when MacMillan came alongside. 'Don't you know you're the spear point of the American advance, out in front of the whole army?' the officer asked. The driver having jumped, responded 'Captain don't kid me'. Despite intense fighting at key points, the situation was sufficiently fluid to enable eight trucks, loaded with quartermaster supplies – razor blades, shaving cream and confectionery – to travel in convoy from Utah Beach, through the German lines and out again at St Come-du-Mont, the objective, without being fired upon. 'You better stay with me if you expect to get out alive'. Macmillan retorted, concluding the conversation.[9]

Following the onset of darkness there was another exchange of fire at the southern entrance to St Côme-du-Mont. Two American armoured vehicles penetrated as far as von der Heydte's command post. Pöppel discovered 'an enemy armoured scout car has broken through to headquarters in a dare-devil drive and is now firing across the street, although he can't see a great deal'. There was much scrambling about and 'shouting for anti-tank launchers'. Eventually Obergefreiter Fischer, a despatch rider from the headquarters hit the vehicle with a *Panzerfaust*.[10]

*But nobody dares to attack the accompanying infantry, so I get together a couple of soldiers who are standing around and move forward. Everybody is frankly shit scared in this eerie night, and I have to curse and swear at them to get them to move. When we reach the burning car, from which the ammunition is rattling and exploding heavenwards, we come across a single Yankee, completely shattered by the effect of our fire.*

The second armoured vehicle beat a hasty retreat. Oberleutnant Pöppel picked up the surviving American 'creeping around in his stockinged feet, in a terrible state'. There was no accompanying infantry, simply another confused and inconclusive clash in the dark. 'I realise', confessed Pöppel, 'that this single Ami was responsible for all the panic, and we turn back'.

Both sides resolved to attack each other at first light. Major von der Heydte intended attacking with the 10th Company from the IIIrd Battalion to restore the line. Pöppel was dubious. 'In the opinion of the men involved, this task can't be achieved with the forces we have available.' The hapless 10th Company commander concurred with this pessimistic forecast, 'less than delighted with the strength of the forces available to him. In particular he's angry that he has to attack with just two platoons.' Pöppel like everyone else, aware of their inferiority felt 'we can all sympathise with his predicament'. Fallschirmjäger Regiment 6 appeared to have lost the initiative, and Pöppel surmised, its reason:

*What has persuaded the commander to depart from the basic principles of his map exercise? Before this he always preached to us to "think big!" - but now he's simply tearing this fighting Regiment apart. It's incomprehensible.*[11]

The Americans were equally concerned to rationalise the front line. Colonel Sink decided to pull back extended elements. It was now dusk on 7 June, and the American paratroopers had been without sleep for over 48 hours. The 'friction of war' identified by Clausewitz began to hinder American preparations for the intended attack on 8 June. 'D' Company from the 506th Regiment at 'Dead Man's Corner' was roused and ordered to move back to Beaumont, retracing its steps. It took 40 minutes to wake the exhausted troops. By 02.00 they had covered the two-kilometre stretch. Fatigue was clouding the mind. A mistaken order took them a further two kilometres beyond to Angoville-au-Plain. On arrival they realised the attack plan required them to advance from a line of departure parallel to Les Droueries, which required a further slog back through the night to Beaumont. The staff, solely concerned with battle plans, lost sight of the basic welfare of the troops about to fight them. This had resulted in a pointless five-kilometre two-hour night march prior to entering battle. An observer commented: 'the wink or two of sleep afforded them in the brief pause at Beaumont was just an added torment'.[12] Sleep denial was to cause complications.

H-Hour for the new attack on St Côme-du-Mont was scheduled for 04.45 on 8 June. Led again by Colonel Sink of the 506th Parachute Infantry Regiment, it was to be conducted by elements from four battalions. In the centre, the 3/501st Infantry was to advance from north of Les Droueries to the main road south of St Côme-du-Mont. One the left the 1/401st Glider infantry would move through the 2/501st already east of les Droueries. The 1/506th and 2/506th would attack south down the road from Beaumont. Eventually the quadruple attack axis would converge on the Carentan causeway and take St Côme-du-Mont overlooking it. Four Sherman tanks were in close support. The attack was to be preceded by a massive naval bombardment.

'At about 04.30', reported von der Heydte, 'a heavy rolling barrage from every calibre including naval guns and rocket launchers descended upon the forward positions of the 9th and 10th Companies, on the 13th's fire positions and the regimental command post'. Captain Laurence Critchell of the 501st Regiment watched the concentration of fire drench the Wehrmacht battalion positions around Bse Addeville.

*A heavy artillery barrage, like saturation bombing, is one of the really terrifying forms of destruction in modern warfare. While it lasts, there is nothing a man can do to help himself. He must listen in silence generally without moving, while the heavy shells explode with a shattering thunder, so all encompassing in its violence that no doubt is left in the mind of one's chance of surviving a near miss. With each roar the earth shakes, the walls bulge, the windows rattle or burst inward as though underwater. What is worse, each explosion is anticipated by a high, thin and unearthly shriek – unearthly because it comes from something moving faster than instinct comprehends.*[13]

'The majority of the IIIrd Battalion 1058', complained von der Heydte, 'fled their positions under the impact of the barrage'. Once again two attacks were colliding in mid-stream. Pöppel confided laconically in his diary 'things get underway before dawn. Only one thing is wrong: it's not our attack, but the enemy's, hitting deep into our assembled troops.' At 05.00 phosphorous shells began raining down on the 9th and 10th company positions. Von der Heydte explained how:

*The smoke obliged our own troops to don gas masks. Some men, probably those who could not get their masks on quickly enough developed choking fits, and lapsed into an unconsciousness that for some lasted up to 6 hours. Phosphorous shells caused extremely serious injuries, while small local grass fires dried throats, mixing the fumes with the thicker smoke clouds.*

The enemy attack penetrated the forward company positions beneath the cover of this blanket 'which reduced visibility to 1-2 metres'.[14] Pöppel vainly trying to provide the forward position's fire support used binoculars and even the battery commander's telescope 'to penetrate the thick mist, but without success'. The line, shifting rearwards, could be monitored 'only roughly by listening for the exceptionally rapid fire of our MG42s'.[15]

The situation on the American side was equally chaotic. Most of the soldiers had been too tired to listen to attack orders. Hedgerows formed an obstacle course that funnelled a general convergence upon the main road axis pointing towards St Côme-du-Mont. The physical difficulty of fighting across such terrain was immense. Captain Laurence Critchell explained how centuries of cultivated growth had formed hedgerows 'into heavy tangled walls, deep rooted and almost impenetrable'. As they were often paralleled by a ditch, the only way to progress was painstakingly to belly crawl along these to reach the objective. Not surprisingly German machine guns were sited to fire along these, and the leading files were mown down. Those following had to raise themselves to traverse the corpses and in so doing were shot down. Bodies piled up and began to block the grisly thoroughfares. Critchell pointed out the dilemma:

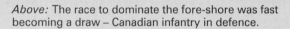

*Above:* The race to dominate the fore-shore was fast becoming a draw – Canadian infantry in defence.

*Above:* Facing them was Major von der Heydte's Fallschirmjäger Regiment 6. Exhaustion was taking its toll.

*Right:* The only way to progress was to painstakingly belly-crawl along ditches to the objective.

*Below:* The Bocage: 'There is absolutely nothing in the books which covers this type of fighting.' American infantry clearing hedgerows.

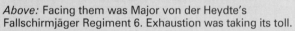

*Above and right:* The majority of the Wehrmacht battalion from the 1058th Regiment fled. These stills from a cine-film illustrate an American paratrooper unmasking the youth of his Wehrmacht captive, who is merely a teenager.

*Left:* Fallschirmjäger Regiment 6 and III/1058 began to retreat across the marshes to the rear of St Côme-du-Mont.

*Above:* To run upright, or climb over hedges was to invite death. The bitterly contested advance continued from one hedgerow to another.

*Left:* The American dead are laid out. Some 273 men were lost battling for this one village.

*For a man to crawl directly through the hedgerows was almost impossible. The twisted roots were close together and immovable. He could climb over the hedgerow, but, if he did, it was unlikely that he would be alive to reach the ground on the other side.*

There was no alternative but to follow the ditches

*Until he found a break, generally by a tree or at the junction of two hedgerows. And the enemy, anticipating an advance through these points had them zeroed in with mortars and artillery, or else mined.*[16]

The bitterly contested advance continued from one hedgerow to another. Blue haze from smokeless powder was the only identifiable enemy signature. Command and control in this jungle terrain was difficult, as was also the coordination of artillery fire. With so much artillery and mortars impacting on both sides it was a problem to identify the splash from one's own guns. Lieutenant Colonel Ballard inching toward Les Droueries with the 2/501st Regiment felt heartened when after a complicated fire adjustment, three salvoes of 8in shells from the USS *Quincy* spectacularly demolished his objective, a German fortified farmhouse. He turned to his accompanying operations officer, Captain William Pelham and said 'we've got it made!' The next concentration of 12 shells landed squarely on his own 'Fox' company, killing five soldiers and mutilating eight others.[17] It caused a momentary check.

Major von der Heydte had lost contact with his 2nd Company; and the majority of the Wehrmacht battalion from the 1058th Regiment had fled westward. Bitter hand-to-hand fighting ensued as the 9th and 10th Companies were overrun. A linear defence was briefly established left and right of the regimental CP on the eastern edge of the village, but his position was fast becoming untenable. At 07.30 he decided to retreat westwards, evacuate the village and withdraw south across the flooded marsh to Carentan and re-establish a new blocking position there. The IInd Battalion still isolated in its 'finger' configuration in the north was also ordered to retire along the railway embankment, barely visible above the level of the reed strewn marsh before Carentan. 'Contrary to the regimental commander's fears', the after-action report commented, 'the enemy allowed sufficient time for a rapid execution of these measures'. Their opponents were in no condition to hotly pursue.

Much of the problem was fatigue. Colonel Sink had given rapid oral orders to his dull-eyed battalion commanders, and under time pressure had omitted to carefully define boundaries between the advancing four battalions. These, struggling across difficult terrain, chose the line of least resistance under fire, which resulted in a shoe-horning constriction of effort as companies gradually converged on the sunken lane forming the attack axis. Units became hopelessly enmeshed just as the vanguard, Lieutenant Colonel Ewell's 3/506, was struck by desperate German counter-attacks coming up from Carentan to the south, which had the effect of covering Major von der Heydte's withdrawal to the west. The American advance careered westward in an oblique shift of effort which initially slowed, then stalled movement. Units seeking succour from enemy fire and channelled by terrain became confusingly inter-mixed. Captain Lloyd Patch, an acting battalion commander explained why:

*They were so beat that they could not understand words even if an order was clearly expressed. I was too tired to talk straight. Nothing I heard made a firm impression on me. I spoke jerkily in phrases because I could not remember the thoughts which had preceded what I said.*[18]

As the Americans tried to marshal their thoughts and reorganise their exhausted troops, the survivors of Fallschirmjäger Regiment 6 began to retreat across the marshes to the rear of St Côme-du-Mont. Confusion was to play a role here also. The regimental commander picked out a path, by chance, in the swamp enabling non-swimmers and those carrying heavy equipments to get across. But at a critical moment, and under artillery fire, remnants of the IIIrd Battalion the 1058th Regiment broke the chain of retreating Fallschirmjäger and pushed in. Those following on lost sight of the regimental commander's group and blundered into the deep water they had been seeking to avoid. Their only recourse to save themselves was to swim a 30-metre canal. Von der Heydte described the mishap:

*Only a few weapons and equipments could be taken across this swimming stretch. A succession of courageous Fallschirmjäger who refused to be separated from their weapons tried to swim across to the railway embankment with their rifles and machine guns, and were drowned.*[19]

Corporal Hehle managed to save some of these unfortunates thrashing around in panic, once they realised they had over-committed themselves in the stinking reed strewn water. At 09.00 the bridge on the Carentan causeway was blown before the majority of the stranded Fallschirmjäger could get back. This left one tenuous possibility, which was the thin thread represented by the railway embankment, just protruding above the flooded waters.

On the other side of the causeway, Oberleutnant Pöppel with the 12th Company realised as the sounds of a battle receded westward 'we were retreating slowly'. They were powerless to provide fire support:

*If we could only get a signal from the infantry, but there's nothing, absolutely nothing. It makes me want to throw up. We're desperate to help those poor fellows, but when we've no idea where the front line is we can't do a thing.*

## The Battle for St Côme-du-Mont, 7-8 June 1944

Colonel Sink's multi-axis assault converged on the one sunken road leading from Vierville to St Côme-du-Mont, deflected by the numerous hedgerows and obstacles of the 'Bocage' terrain. Confusion resulted among the exhausted attacking American airborne troops. Fallschirmjäger Regiment 6 retreated across marshes west of the village after a tenacious defence, and managed to reach Carentan which was held until the 12 June.

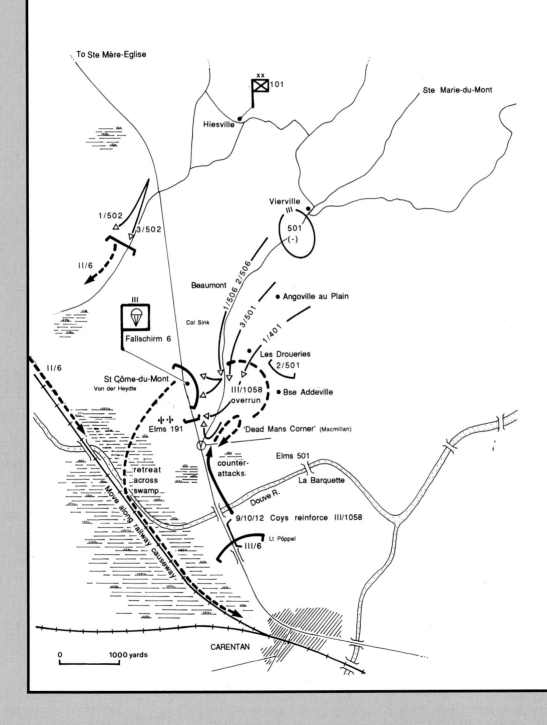

To Ste Mère-Eglise

xx 101

Ste Marie-du-Mont

Hiesville

Vierville

501 (-)

1/502

3/502

II/6

Beaumont

1/506 2/506

3/501

Angoville au Plain

III Col Sink

Fallschirm 6

1/401

Les Droueries 2/501

II/6

St Côme-du-Mont Von der Heydte

III/1058 overrun

Bse Addeville

Elms 191

'Dead Mans Corner' (Macmillan)

retreat across swamp

counter-attacks.

Elms 501

La Barquette

Move along railway causeway

Douve R.

9/10/12 Coys reinforce III/1058

Lt Pöppel

III/6

0    1000 yards

CARENTAN

The Americans had achieved success but were not fully aware of it. By late afternoon German soldiers could be seen retreating in straggling columns along the railway embankment but the Allied airborne battalions, totally mixed up with each other, had lost unit coherence and were in no condition to pursue. In fact they were relieved not to have to fight through the village. Their next task would be to storm the exposed causeway to reach Carentan. The Germans, it was assumed, would be likely to be picked off by air attack. Allied aircraft began to swoop low to investigate the files of plodding infantry, doggedly retreating across the exposed embankment. Nothing happened. The column pushed on seemingly unperturbed. Pöppel explained what happened:

> To prevent the enemy fighter bombers, who were shooting at everything under the sun, from recognizing our soldiers [they were ordered] to remove their helmets and use them to wave to the aircraft. Up to their knees or bellies in water, they weren't easy to recognize as German soldiers. Oh yes, our regimental commander von der Heydte, he can be a real fox still.

American casualties battling for just this one village were 273 men. Lieutenant Colonel Ewell's 3/506th Battalion lost 41 of 160 men in one day.[20] The German defence, of which Fallschirmjäger Regiment 6 was a part, was to fight on doggedly, despite the surprise occasioned by the invasion. Carentan fell, but not until June 12. The 'Hedgerow' war in the American western sector was also deteriorating into a village-fighting stalemate. Both sides seemed incapable of producing the local superiority required to achieve victory. Pöppel confided in his diary on 9 June:

> The fighting subsides and gives us time to reorganise. The Americans seem to need it too, otherwise they'd certainly have pressed us harder.[21]

# CHAPTER 17

# POSTSCRIPT

*'All Commanders ... are required to submit after-action reports covering the 6 June, to be shown to the Fuhrer, in which questions of surprise and the rapidity of the break-in and penetration are to be carefully addressed.'*

*Rommel*

A number of accounts, influenced by the success of Cornelius Ryan's book *The Longest Day* have suggested that the D-Day battle was won within the first 24 hours. Once ashore the Germans were unable to eradicate the bridgehead. This is too simplistic an assertion. Montgomery was well aware of the vulnerability of his situation, reflected in crisis points identified within his invasion planning parameters. In essence the aim was to win the build-up race that would occur to dominate the invasion foreshore. The Allied lodgement was still tenuous after 24 hours. Paradoxically initial Allied success sowed the seed for subsequent stalemate, when both sides became bogged down in a battle of attrition for numerous villages dominating vital ground that needed to be secured to achieve a breakout. As the panzer divisions began to arrive, haphazardly, as a result of Allied air pressure, their piece-meal insertions were fought to a standstill by Allied attacks seeking to break out. Both sides were surprised by this development. The Allies were unable to maintain momentum in the attack, the Germans could not reduce the lodgement area secured during the shock of the initial onrush. The balance of forces, infantry and tanks, committed by both sides proved inappropriate for the character of the fighting that developed. 'Bocage' proved to be a two-edged terrain feature in terms of tactical advantage. It blunted attacks going both ways. The Allies got a foothold and could not be dislodged; the same applied subsequently to the German defence, not easily overcome. Both sides' planning assumptions proved invalid as fighting developed. Although in broad terms the Allied plan worked, a number of factors conspired to produce stalemate. D-Day could not be adjudged a success until the point was reached – probably during the eight-day period of village fighting between 6-14 June when it became evident that German aims reflected in orders were concerned less with 'throwing the enemy back into the sea' than with

restoring the situation sufficiently, to gather forces for a counter-stroke. This signalled the end of the D-Day conflict – the Battle of Normandy was about to begin.

## The Germans ...

It is useful to review German reasoning accounting for their failure to win the initial build-up race. Generalfeldmarschall Rommel was required to explain to the Führer why it was that seaward defences were so quickly overrun on D-Day.

*All Commanders from divisions attacked from the sea or out of the air are to submit after-action reports covering the 6 June, to be shown to the Fuhrer, in which questions of surprise and the rapidity of the break-in and penetration are to be carefully addressed.[1]*

Awkward questions had already been raised, despite the crisis, as early as 9 June. The Chiefs of Staffs of both OB West and Army Group B were required to account for the alarm procedures that had been in place on the evening of D-Day, because 'the English have again, as in the "Nettuno" [Anzio] operation reported that German soldiers had to be hauled out of their beds in their underclothes'.[2] Generalleutnant Richter, commanding the 716th Infantry Division, was prudently giving explanations 10 days after his unit had been virtually eliminated from the German order of battle.

Richter not surprisingly chose to lay blame on factors outside his division's responsibility; claiming 'the WN [strong-points] were at full action stations, the heavy weapons manned, and staffs in their command posts'. Inland there 'was a water-tight observation net monitoring air space', while the 'particularly lively air activity' during the first half of the night, had already aroused the alertness of the troops. Readiness had not been the problem, rather the factors he listed that contributed to the rapid breakthrough.

The failure of all reconnaissance activity, both in the air and at sea was the initial shortfall highlighted. This was partly true. But as already shown, tell-tale signs of enemy activity were missed less by absence of data than by a misinterpretation of its credibility. It was not believed. Blaming bad weather was too simplistic an excuse for the failure to detect the approach of the Allied armadas. German meteorological reports did not report unfavourable weather, simply that conditions around the Pas de Calais were worse than Normandy. A credibility gap therefore contributed to reconnaissance shortfalls. The sea-state was not suitable for small craft, but German naval raids were mounted at first light. Fear of air attacks, as they were 'sitting ducks' in the face of Allied air superiority kept them in port. No German aerial photographs were taken of Allied disembarkation ports after 24 May.[3] Hauptmann Eberspacher flying a reconnaissance aircraft from KG 52 passed low over the invasion fleet at 15 metres above sea level while it was still moving. His report despatched by 05.00 appears to have been ignored.[4] Its description of the size and spread of the shipping alone would have been significant.

Richter next blamed 'the total absence of support through our own air force'. Allied air power had a decisive contribution to make in redressing the initial imbalance of forces, a point to be developed later. The Luftwaffe did indeed appear to be absent. Cornelius Ryan immortalised the audacious yet ineffective strafing run by two FW190 planes flown by Oberstleutnant 'Pips' Priller and Unterfeldwebel Wodarczyk along the British beaches on D-Day morning.[5] Grenadier Robert Vogt from Regiment 726 said:

*One single time I saw two German fighter planes, and that was at Arromanches on the morning of 6 June. Two Messerschmitts. When we saw them, we all shouted hurrah, but they were the only ones. That was it. It was so terribly depressing.[6]*

On D-Day the whole of Luftflotte (Air Fleet) 3 had only 497 serviceable aircraft, of which a mere 319 went into action. After four days 208 had been destroyed and 105 damaged.[7] Aircraft reinforcement was to some extent delayed by the perception of an imminent second landing. This initial lack of opposition enabled more Allied offensive fighter-bomber and rocket sorties to be mounted. By the evening of 7 June some 200 German fighters had been concentrated in France. The Luftwaffe was not entirely driven from the skies. Indeed one official historian of the Allied 2nd Tactical Air Force has claimed 'once reinforcements could be pushed through to this new front, the Germans were to be met in the air in increasing numbers, RAF units being engaged on a scale not met over Europe since 1940, other than at Dieppe in August 1942'. By 10 June bombers had been rushed to France, 90 from Italy and 45 torpedo bombers from southern France, bringing the total Luftwaffe operational strength in northern France to approximately 1,000 aircraft.[8] These operated mainly over the Allied beaches at night. Able Seaman John Cooper man-

ning 'B' turret aboard HMS *Warspite* gave a vivid picture of such an attack on the first night:

*"Stand to! Aircraft in sight!" was the cry from the communication number. (This dries the mouth out immediately.)*
*"Commence, commence, commence!"*
*Criss-crosses of tracers weave lazily across the sky and I hear zip-zip-zip as some fly overhead. The Fire Buzzer sounds, loud and raucous (a sound I hated as it tightened the stomach). It is quickly followed by the ear-splitter as they fire. Out fly the empties, smoking hot, to roll into the scuppers.[9]*

These air attacks produced fear, and are remarked upon by many Allied eye-witnesses on and around the beaches, but in relative terms they caused little damage.

Generalleutnant Richter next explained the failure of coastal defences to withstand the assault. Neither 'coastal obstacles nor anti-glider stakes had the anticipated effect', moreover within the 716th Division area, they were only partially completed. The huge minefields 'were prematurely detonated by the heavy naval bombardment, consequently large holes appeared in the coastal defence.' Smoke screens prevented aimed fire from being directed against ships and disembarking troops. Their own artillery was knocked out by naval guns and attacks by airborne infantry. In addition an effective anti-tank defence could not cope with the numbers of tanks landing, 'two companies of assault guns were knocked out in their field positions by the bombardment'. In short, Richter's coastal division had been overwhelmed by the violence of an echeloned frontal assault. The very effect that Montgomery had intended. What is not mentioned, primarily due to the paucity of survivors able to report it, was the degree of technological surprise achieved by the Allies. Mines were cleared less by artillery than by Hobart's 'Funnies', the Flail tanks and other specialised armoured vehicles specifically designed to overcome beach obstacles. It was an absence of these vehicles on Omaha, that was to contribute to delays there; although exiting the beach was more difficult than in the British sector. Oberst Oehmichen's Seventh Army survey revealed only about one dozen anti-tank guns along every 10 kilometres of front, but these were soon overwhelmed by the armoured support that came ashore with the assault waves. DD tanks were 'top secret', as also the other specialised equipments in the 79th Division. Their impact therefore could not be rationally anticipated in any German intelligence assessment. A further technological surprise was the scale and breadth of the landings, historically unique, therefore also beyond any credible German estimate of likely force deployments. The Allied build-up and logistic re-supply into the bridgehead, across open beaches, exceeded enemy calculable norms.

Allied deception played a crucial role, maximising

After four days, 208 German aircraft had been destroyed and 105 damaged. Many were caught on the ground as in this strafing run by an American Mustang on a Luftwaffe airfield.

surprise during the assault, and distracting German attention during the subsequent build-up. Richter, unaware like his masters at the mastery and degree of success achieved at this stage complimented the Allies on 'effective air reconnaissance and espionage (referring to captured documents) which enabled the enemy to identify weak spots in the coastal defences', enabling these to be exploited in detail. Deception, as already explained, was decisive. Fifteenth Army on the left flank of the invasion was 20 divisions strong, covering a frontage of 550km. Seventh Army was covering nearly three times that distance (1,600km) with five fewer divisions.[10] The 711th Division from Fifteenth Army failed to substantially support the 716th Division on the crucial first day. The 346th Division was inserted between 8-10 June, but was down to between 35 and 60 men per battalion, three days later.[11] Despite identifying 14 enemy divisions on the 6 June and 20 by D+1, the Germans were still convinced on 8 June that the Allies had only fielded one quarter of its available strength. (In fact only 37 were available.) An Ultra decrypt from Rommel's headquarters on 26 June read:

*In England another 67 major formations are standing to, of which, 57 at the very least can be employed for a large scale operation.*[12]

Reinforcements therefore had to be found from elsewhere, outside the Seine-Loire area. Brittany was denuded of troops, and units were moved from the south of France. As a consequence they had further to travel, and always under unremitting air attack.

The major reason for the Allied success on D-Day, alluded to by Richter, was air superiority. This had a triple impact: upon troop deployments, it contributed to the imbalance of infantry and tanks and finally crippled German command, control and logistics. The initial shock was that directed against the panzer reserve. It continued thereafter. The 17th SS Panzergrenadier Division needed five days to drive from Thouars south of the Loire to Périers in the Cherbourg peninsula, a distance of about 200 miles. Movement by rail was equally laborious. The 2nd Panzer Division left Abbeville by rail on 9 June intending to get to the front by way of Paris. So many locomotives were hit by Allied fighter-bombers that the tanks had to complete the journey on tracks by road. Eighty of 120 tanks finally limped into the line around Caumont on 18 June, having covered 300 miles in 10 days.[13] They had been preceded piece-meal by wheeled elements, lacking heavy anti-tank and self-propelled artillery. Panther tank engines were good for only 800km (480 miles), so Seventh Army therefore was warned on 14 June to anticipate large numbers of mechanical break-downs.[14]

Hermann Blocksdorff an infantryman explained the difficulty of getting his unit to the front. Having moved through Orléans from Lyons 'a French switchman crashed us into another train. The French Resistance was doing its job.' Retribution was swift.

*While we waited for a new locomotive and some new cars, the switchman was hanged from the window of his little cabin. The war was taking on new dimensions.*[15]

There was a shortage of infantry at the front. Requests were voiced for infantry reinforcement on the first day.[16] But because of the threat of further landings in Fifteenth Army's area, they were obliged to travel from far afield. If the mechanised formations were slow reaching the front, the horse and leg propulsion pace of infantry units was tortoise-like. The 276th Infantry Division left Bayonne in southern France on 12 June, it did not reach Hottot – a 400-mile journey delayed by broken bridges, air attacks and the Maquis – until 4 July. A 72-hour rail journey required no less than 22 days. The main body of the division had to march about one-third of the distance, covering approximately 20 miles each night.[17] Even infantry moving by train could only manage a haphazard pace, as Grenadier Blocksdorff recalled on 7 June:

*The journey was possible only on a stop-go basis. We would come to a stand still and take cover. We jumped out as soon as the train began to brake. When the strafing began, we were always a few hundred yards away from the standing train. We jumped back on when it started moving again. The train started slowly enough for everybody to catch up and get on.*[18]

Meanwhile at the front the panzers were bled white, fulfilling infantry tasks in unsuited terrain. The Panzer Lehr was even employing tanks on infantry-type observation post duties. Eleven days after the landings its effective strength had been reduced from 8,635 to 1,531. By 18 June Bayerlein reported 'infantry reinforcements are urgently required' because his manpower was primarily employed crewing heavy weapons; and he was losing 150 men per day. The following day Panzer Lehr declared: 'everything has been put into the frontline'.

*It can be determined by a simple calculation that when there are no more panzergrenadiers available, and that will be the case at the latest in 3 days' time, we can reckon on further advances by enemy attacks. The division losses, in terms of combat strength can be assessed as over 2,000 men.*[19]

The 21st Panzer Division similarly complained it was unsuited for its present defence role, and was being attrited by artillery. On 18 June it declared it was obliged to use most of its Panzer Mk IVs forward as anti-tank units. These being vulnerable to naval gunfire were often 'wiped out'. It also admitted that it had 'insuffi-

So many locomotives
were hit by Allied
fighter-bombers, as
shown by the lightning
attack here, that the
2nd Panzer Divisions's
tanks had to move-up
on tracks, thereby
further reducing their
mechanical durability.

The horse and leg propulsion of infantry units were tortoise-like. Reinforcements move slowly
up to the front.

Panzer units were obliged wastefully to employ main battle tanks in the infantry role. Here a panzer is employed as an anti-tank observation post.

'Shock from the massive surprise must have been the genesis of collapse.' The Germans did not recover until the weeks long following the Battle of Normandy.

*Right:* Pöppel complained 'most of our élite regiments had to go everywhere on foot like in the Middle Ages'. Both sides, but particularly the Germans, were critically short of mobile infantry.

cient panzergrenadiers available for major attack tasks'.[20]

German command and control was an early casualty to air attacks. By the second day of the invasion the 1st SS Panzer Corps, due to coordinate the activities of the 21st Panzer, the 12th SS and Panzer Lehr, at the very moment it resolved to launch a counter-stroke, admitted only four of 20 broadcasting stations were working. Panzergruppe West had lost 75 percent of its radio equipment. One spare headquarters, ZBV136, urgently required at the front was stranded in Rennes for want of shot-up locomotives.[21] Panzergruppe West was not up and working until 9 June. The following day, as a result of an 'Ultra' decrypt of its radio traffic, the headquarters was wiped out by a massive RAF bombing raid. Its commander, Geyr von Schweppenburg, was wounded and most of his senior officers killed. The headquarters was out of action for 14 days, forcing one planned counter-attack against the British to be cancelled. General Marcks commanding the 84th Corps was killed by an Allied fighter-bomber attack on 12 June, the commander of the 243rd Static Division by another four days later. These shortfalls had an inevitable detrimental impact on operations.

The German logistic chain was caught unprepared by the savagery of the Allied assault, and very nearly broken by subsequent air attacks. On 12 June, Seventh Army reported 'due to difficulties in fuel re-supply the transport situation in Contentin is seriously in question. There, the Army's convoy capacity is stretched to the absolute limit'. The shortfall of motorised transport to move infantry had been identified as early as 7 June. Constant reference is made in the Seventh Army War Diary of 3rd Fallschirmjäger Division transport difficulties, which delayed completion of its move until 22 June. On 10 June the 17th SS were pinned down due to lack of fuel, which was also affecting the deployment of IInd Fallschirmjäger Corps units. Oberst Oehmichen's identification of anti-tank shortfalls before the invasion were confirmed by the redistribution ordered on 11 June by the Commander Seventh Army that '65 percent of the close-quarter anti-tank capability (*Panzerfaust* and *Panzerschreck* - bazookas) from the 265th, 266th, the remainder of the 275th Infantry divisions, as well as the 5th Fallschirmjäger Division [in Brittany] were to be immediately withdrawn and redistributed as quickly as possible to the 84th Corps in the St Lô area'.[22] There were fundamental flaws in logistic preparedness even before the invasion, in particular, the 30-fold differential in convoy capacity between the Fifteenth and the Seventh armies. The former in northern France could carry 10,000 tons, compared to only 300 tons by the latter in Normandy.[23] This capacity tied to the Fifteenth Army was not even thinned out to the Seventh, who desperately needed it, because of the suspected fear of further landings around the Pas-de-Calais.

The re-supply requirement for a Wehrmacht division was estimated at between 600 and 700 tons daily. (Two-hundred had been considered the bare minimum at Stalingrad.) But the German logistic chain was unprepared for the total destruction of the French rail network, upon which it was based. This resulted in convoy moves of 150 to 200km and 400km for some specialised items. Even apart from air raids, 25 lorries per division began breaking down each day because of the distances travelled, which would include the further loss of the goods on board. Pressure, stretched to an elastic breaking point snapped. At the high point of the battle of Normandy the Allies were receiving the equivalent of 25 goods trains of 60 15 ton wagons daily. According to estimates, each German army received only 5 percent of its Allied equal.[24]

The consequence at the front was revealed in a Seventh Army communiqué on 12 June which announced the key town of Carentan 'has fallen to the enemy due to a shortage of ammunition'. Major von der Heydte, the regimental commander responsible for its defence, exposed a whole litany of logistic shortfalls in his subsequent report five days later. When he went into action on the first day of the invasion he was obliged to pick up his ammunition en route. Only one day's worth of first-line supply was available. His ageing transport fleet had to later seek out ammunition at dispersed depots, often covering 50km journeys under air attack only to find them closed on arrival. On one occasion his men resorted to forming a human chain passing vitally needed ammunition supplies from one truck to another across a destroyed bridge. Distribution was complicated by air-raids which attacked every vehicle in sight. His engineers resorted to using captured American mines to provide the explosives needed to blow key bridges across the enemy line of advance. Von der Heydte summed up:

*It is the overwhelming opinion of this commander that the regiment's re-supply both in Russia and Africa was never so mismanaged and conducted as in the initial days of the Normandy invasion. The soldiers felt that they were not being led and looked after, rather deserted and sold out.*[25]

His view was echoed by one of his company commanders, Oberleutnant Pöppel who complained their scant transport resources of 70 trucks were 'old and useless' and declared:

*Most of our elite regiments had to go everywhere on foot, like in the Middle Ages, carrying all the heavy guns, anti-tank guns and mortars. The General Staff seems to have thought that we paratroopers could manage with nothing more than our knives.*[26]

Generalleutnant Richter in finally assessing why the Allies broke through his 716th Division defences so quickly added 'the failure of previously thought reliable Ost battalions [of Russian auxiliaries] confronted with the enemy selected main point of effort'.[27] These poorly equipped infantry formations, the 441st Battalion around Meuvaines and the 642nd either side of the Orne fought, but as was the case with other Wehrmacht infantry battalions, stood little chance. Many chose to surrender, echoing a comment by General von Schleben commanding the 709th Division that 'we are asking rather a lot if we expect Russians to fight in France for Germany against the Americans'.[28] Interestingly, Richter chose not to include this comment in the original Seventh Army report, but it appeared in his own division statement. This may be because it summed up the primary German D-Day shortfall. Not only did the German Army choose not to commit its prime resources to crush the invasion when it was achievable, it continued to fight the following battle with its logistic arm quite literally tied behind its back.

On 6 June the German defences lacked edge. Although subsequent fighting in Normandy was to demonstrate a keener capability, it was not there during the battle of D-Day. The invasion burst upon troops whose credibility and preparedness had been stretched by numerous false alarms in the preceding months. Major Howard's force storming the Orne river bridges fell upon a garrison which considered itself conducting a virtual peacetime occupation. As the first live rounds were fired heralding the opening of a new campaign in the west, German coastal units were still conducting night exercises with blank ammunition. Not one contemporary German report dared admit it, but surprise in psychological terms was absolute.

## The Allies ...

The Allied D-Day plan worked. Deception, surprise and concentration of force resulted in the overrunning of a sizeable lodgement area within the first 24 hours. The genesis of what happened next can be seen in the pre-invasion planning. Montgomery had viewed the development of the bridgehead in terms of a race to dominate the foreshore. Critical points in the enemy ability to build up were identified at D+2 and later D+6 when a full-blooded counter-attack might come in. These fears dictated the shape and character of the formation and development of the Allied bridgehead. In planning terms it may be seen as a series of concentric lines that emanate from the beach-heads. No dramatic thrusts were considered, rather a protective edging forward from all sectors, an expanding shield, against which it was hoped the German counter stroke would dash itself. This in effect it did, the keen edge blunted by air, resulting in a fragmented and piece-meal insertion. Main Allied efforts were not viewed in terms of thrust lines out, but as the formation of defence lines able to withstand panzer attacks coming in. Criticism of the Allied plan has concentrated on the failure to achieve a rapid

breakout. As we have seen, this could not be easily achieved due to an inappropriate tank-infantry mix directed to dominate key terrain, and the inability to get momentum moving. If there was an opportunity lost, it was perhaps during the period between 6-9 June when the Allies had a pronounced local superiority, and could conceivably have secured an even larger bridgehead.

The impact of surprise has been discussed as a phenomena affecting both sides. With Allied local superiority it might perhaps have been exploited more fully. American paratroopers fighting early battles around the airborne bridgeheads remarked upon the 'lemming-like behaviour' of formed German units who retreated, deliberately ignoring the sound of guns, and the opportunity to pick off isolated and over extended American units as they fell back, 'leaving friends to a fate they need not have suffered'. The conclusion was:

*Shock from massive surprise must have been the genesis of collapse. It put the Germans within the air-head in an emotional spin from which they could not recover.*

In short 'while every hour brought greater cohesion to the Americans, the rate of disintegration in the German tactical forces accelerated far more rapidly'. If 'the enemy was temporarily victim of an acute terror which numbed response',[1] why was a break-out not achieved?

This has to some extent been answered by viewing three separate actions in some detail in the chapter on 'Village Fighting'. An early risk strategy of deep thrusts may have changed the shape of the lodgement, and enlarged it more rapidly during the crucial early days; but the urge to move quickly and decisively was circumscribed by the plan. Priority was given to joining the Allied beach-heads. A continuous British enclave was achieved by 7 June, the link between Omaha and Gold by 8 June and Utah incorporated within an 80km front on 12 June following the fall of Carentan. When the Allied fronts ceased their lateral attempts at cohesion and sought to advance outward, the British towards Caen, the American VIIth Corps to cut off the Cherbourg peninsula and the American Vth Corps towards St Lô from Omaha, the German ability to match forces in the bridgehead ensured the subsequent stalemate amid battles of attrition. Even by 8 June the Allies, having suffered 15,000 casualties with 16 divisions ashore, were experiencing a perceptible blunting of their offensive spirit.

Montgomery's plan was essentially defend on one sector – the centre – and break out in the west. The plan developed along this scheme, but not following the ambitiously predicted timings. Caen fell on D+33 not on D-Day, Cherbourg on D+22 not D+8. St Lô was not overrun until D+45 unlike the D+9 planned. The eventual break out reached Falaise on D+71, 54 days late. The plan did not fail, it took longer. Need it have taken so long is a question that has intrigued historians since.

Generalleutnant Richter, the commander of the 716th Division, outlined three fundamental failures accounting for the rapid Allied penetration inland after breaching his coastal defences. Coastal-based reserves were too weak, the panzer counter-stroke was especially delayed by the enemy's air superiority and there was no 'second position' in depth to contain the Allied onrush. Therefore, could Allied gains on D-Day alone have been greater? The extent to which the invading airborne divisions had dispersed the coastal reserve into fragmented and seemingly directionless operations when a major amphibious landing ought to have been anticipated, as a result, has already been revealed. Deception led German commanders to think otherwise, enabling the Allies to punch rapidly inland. The panzer reserve arrived too late, and there were no defences in depth. What delayed the Allies?

A contributory factor was the unexpected environmental physical and technical conditions which influenced attack and defence alike. Both sides applied the lessons of Africa, Russia and Italy to an operational theatre for which there was little experience. Moreover, the technological norms of 1940 and 1941 were applied to the more advanced realities of 1944. Although the Allies appreciated the qualitative potential of their anti-tank capability would probably match the panzers, they preferred not to take the risk, and concentrated on getting their own armour ashore first. If unsupported by infantry, they fell easy prey to the little assessed close-quarter capability of the *Panzerfaust*, in close Normandy terrain. Normandy was neither the North African desert nor the rolling Russian Steppes. Tanks could not sweep all before them, they needed to be supported by mobile infantry. It was the failure by both sides to be fully conversant tactically within the changed technological circumstances they found themselves, that contributed to the battles of attrition that were fought in and around the villages surrounding the Allied lodgement. The only room for armoured tactical manoeuvre was in the centre around Caen; and this became the main point of effort for both sides, as both matched each other.

Another reason for the failure of the Allies to push inland quickly and capitalise on their initial local superiority, was the very success of the defence for which the German commanders were later to castigate themselves. 'Static' German divisions regarded in tactical effectiveness terms as only 40 percent of a division's potential, broke up the integrity of many Allied units coming ashore. This mix-up of units required some time to resolve around Omaha, before they could continue inland. Similarly, there were vast traffic jams on the British beaches caused by German strong-points stubbornly holding out, even though they could achieve little more than eventual capitulation. In many instances it was the concentrated firepower of naval battleships that actually got assault waves off the beaches. Casualties imposed on relatively inexperienced troops coming ashore did impose a psychological check on risky advances.

The defensive nature of the plan in securing the bridgehead first, encouraged troops to dig in, rather than maintain the advance inland. It was moreover beyond the experience of Allied troops to conduct the 'Blitzkrieg'-type warfare in which many German commanders were already proficient. Training within the restricted confines of the British Isles would not have mentally or practically prepared them to conduct operations on this ambitious scale.

## The Human Factor ...

That many of the reasons for the success or failure of D-Day and the subsequent race to dominate the invasion foreshore are imponderable, is a direct reflection of the human factor. Battles are lost and won by the intervention of luck, fate and the unpredictable behaviour of human beings. A central tenet of this book has been the desire to view developments so far as possible through the eyes and comments of the participants themselves. As one Canadian soldier succinctly expressed it:

*The war, with generals looking at big maps somewhere 20 miles in the rear, that wasn't our war. Our war was only up to 400 yards in front of us, and from that farmhouse over there to that canal over there. We didn't give a shit what else was going on. Tell us what to do, no matter how stupid, and we'd do it.*[1]

Small wonder that Allied tank crews were reluctant to forge ahead when menaced by carefully concealed anti-tank guns in close terrain. Casualties might be apparent from a distance, such as the light 'click' on a tank crew man's radio net as an armour-piercing projectile struck home. 'Suddenly, across the Squadron Leader's voice came a sharp ominous click. We'd heard it before' recalled a British tank-man. 'We couldn't see the tank but we knew what the click meant.' Somebody else would take over the radio net, and the rest of the tanks would simply carry on obeying orders 'as if it were the most natural thing in the world for their comrade to depart suddenly like that – with a click as adieu'.[2] More often than not, death came suddenly and violently as recalled by Lieutenant Paul Holbrook:

*An enormous bell sounded with a clangour that threw him off his feet. The loud gong-like noise was followed by a colossal roar, and from Peters' tank soared a monstrous column of white smoke that formed a huge ring in the air. Peters leapt, a huddled figure, from the side of his tank and crawled into the side of the stack, smoke wreathed round him, his hair alight. The tank, a moment ago the home and shelter of five men, now looked a terrible sight, with flames belching out of its front hatches and engine louvres, and a pillar of fire roaring out of the turret, colossal gouts of smoke billowing across the field in curled torrents. The 88 had struck home!*

Fighting within the confines of a Sherman was a terrifying experience. Holbrook, under fire, required to double up as crew to another tank:

*Slid each round into the gun, with a hysterical sense that away across in the wood a German gunner was sliding in the shot that was to tear him limb from limb. His hair stood on end and his limbs quivered in fearful anticipation like those of a man condemned. His bowels were water with fear.*

*"God Sir, we're next! God! God!"* [3]

Allied soldiers had a healthy fear of the German '88'. 'It was a staggering thing, in size, just a beautiful piece of death for us in the tanks, or for anything,' commented one Canadian. 'In Normandy I saw one knock out eight of our tanks, one after another, and they didn't even know where the thing was hidden.' [4] It was at this level, a human perception whether one would survive or not, which often determined whether an advance was successful. Their adversaries of course were under the same pressure. Gerald Kellner, a Fallschirmjäger arriving at the front five days after the invasion in the St Lô sector said 'our losses were colossal'. His company of approximately 120 men suffered nearly 60 percent casualties. 'Every day, 10 dead, eight dead, 10 dead and so forth in our unit – but we didn't budge.' [5]

The battles of attrition around the Normandy villages had a detached surreal unreality of their own. 'From D-Day Plus Two until the final shot was fired', declared one Canadian Commando, 'I never got close enough to a real live German in action to even try to flick out his eyeball'. Rarely did they close. 'Everything was long range.' [6] Grenadier Hermann Blocksdorf fighting in an infantry regiment against British and Canadians in front of Caen echoed this sentiment:

*There could be no talk of real fighting by the enemy. If they got the slightest infantry fire, they retreated immediately and ploughed the ground with bombs for 12 to 20 hours. After that, they came with flame thrower tanks and burned everything down. Once a man was hit with the flame oil, nobody could help him. These men died a miserable death. Our hatred of the enemy grew from day to day. They only had to march in and overrun us. We were only a handful of soldiers, and it wasn't as if we could have caused them any losses.* [7]

The perception of material inferiority, a psychological pressure on the German fighting man from day one of the invasion, was inevitably to impact upon his combat stamina, and willingness to resist, against overwhelming odds. For the Allies the fear was mutual, for as the same

Canadian Commando concluded: 'a bullet or an HE shell doesn't play favourites. What it's in line with, it hits. Believe me.'

As the fighting increased in intensity, and as attrition became the only recourse once local attacks were fought to a standstill by both sides, frustrations became manifested in atrocities. There was an inevitability for this happening with immature young soldiers, such as the 'Hitlerjugend' suddenly confronted with set-backs, which their philosophy encouraged could be overcome by stern measures, or the ruthless and aggressive application of violence. Warfare is an insidiously corrupting process whereby norms transacted in an abhorrent environment of corpses, death, violence and ruin develop a perverted normalcy or acceptance of their own. Both sides had hard men, tempered by their own harsh environments; hence the clashes between the Canadians and 'Hitlerjugend'. Johnson, a Canadian soldier in the Winnipeg Rifles cut off by the 12th SS around Putot-en-Bessin described how:

*During the evening, the SS forced ten of our own men to march towards our positions while they sheltered behind them. Our men could not use their weapons against the enemy who, by this tactic, and in violation of the Rules of War, made us prisoners.* [8]

An artillery commander in the Panzer Lehr, Oberst Luxenburger, a one-armed World War 1 veteran was captured, allegedly beaten senseless by two British officers, and bound as a 'bullet-catch' to the front of a Canadian tank. He was recovered, still bound and bloody from the tank the next day, after it had been knocked out by a German anti-tank gun. He died in hospital. [9] Three Canadians were shot near the battalion command post of the II/26th from the 12th SS as reprisal. [10] There is clear evidence of atrocities committed by both sides. [11] Documentary evidence suggests certain units were not taking prisoners; this applied to the 12th SS, some Canadian and Scottish battalions and American paratroopers. More to the point, they reflected the nature of the fighting, which became increasingly unforgiving as frustrations mounted, and the human spirit further corrupted. A soldier inured to death, might accept the summary execution of a flame-thrower operator. Lieutenant Andrew Wilson described the loss of a Crocodile flame-thrower tank crew, lined up and shot against a farm wall having been overrun by an SS counter-attack.

*Wilson thought of Harvey with his big, bear-like body and a trick he'd had at parties of being able to waggle his ears. The idea of him facing an SS firing squad was utterly incongruous. He wanted to shout aloud, to do something to deny it was possible.*

His response was less disgust than fear. 'Would they

*Above:* The defensive nature of the plan in securing the bridgehead first, encouraged troops to dig in, rather than push inland. Few in any case were prepared for the initial psychological trauma of battle or casualties.

*Left:* The human factor will determine whether a plan will work or not, based upon perception of survivability. An American padre closes the eyes in death of a young German soldier, while the Fallschirmjäger medics, and prisoners, unable to save him, look on.

235

shoot all captured Crocodile crews from now on?'[12]

Some units were simply intimidated by the ferocity of their adversaries. A German infantry battalion report complained that Royal Marine Commandos 'cannot be assessed from a soldierly stand-point, they belonged to a psychologically criminal level'. This was the typical view of the ordered German mind, utterly disdainful of 'bush-fighting' methods, which they also ascribed to partisan activity, which was countered with suitably ruthless counter-measures. But the young German conscripts fighting in this particular 'static' division remarked 'they employ any stratagem or ruse, call German soldiers across in their own tongue, and finish them off with knives'.[13] A more realistic view was that of Gerald Kellner, a German Fallschirmjäger who was captured in house-to-house fighting near St Lô by soldiers from the American 2nd Division.

*Two SS men were shot right in front of my eyes – why, I don't know. At any rate, I put my hands up fast and said in English, "I surrender". We had been taught to say that. During house-to-house combat at night, you normally didn't take prisoners, so I expected to be knocked off too.*

Kellner felt himself to be lucky, he was tied up and beaten senseless by his captors.

*They sure were brutal, but you didn't feel any pain. You didn't feel anything any more. Your entire nervous system, as in my case, just shut down … my nerves and soul were totally wrung out, completely exhausted.*[14]

But he was alive.

The human factor in war is totally unpredictable. Force ratios and the impersonal application of material superiority will have a measurable impact, but in the final resort human beings produce inconsistencies that result in the dissolution of plans even as soldiers cross the start-line. The Allies were unable to achieve a rapid break-out from the Normandy bridgehead, even though opportunities to do so, given the circumstances described, were technically achievable. Similarly, the invasion of Normandy was a shock and surprise to the German defenders. All the indicators that contributed to successful deception could just as easily have led to an opposing conclusion. The human imponderable, as ever, had the decisive impact. Lieutenant Andrew Wilson described what motivated it:

*Any notion that we were fighting for our country, or to free Europe from Hitler, or to make a better world, is largely romantic. We were fighting in order to stay alive, and our loyalties were not to our country, not to our regiment even, but intensely to one another.*[15]

Soldiers fought for themselves, only secondly for a plan. Indeed the actions of single individuals might change it.

## THE RACE TO THE FORESHORE

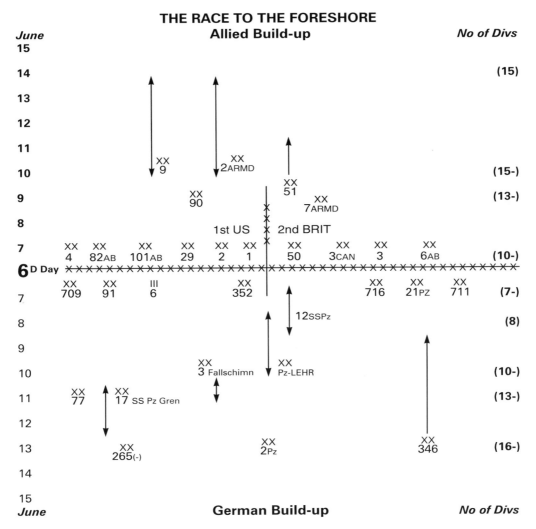

**Allied Build-up**

**German Build-up**

Sources; Ellis, Harrison, KTB H. Gr B and AOK 7

| Note: | June | Allied Divs | | German Divs | |
|---|---|---|---|---|---|
| | 6 | 9-10 | versus | 5-7 | |
| | 7 | 10(-) | versus | 8 | |
| | 8 | 11(-) | versus | 8 | Allied Superiority |
| | 9 | 13(-) | versus | 8 | |
| | 10 | 15(-) | versus | 10(-) | |
| | 11 | 15(-) | versus | 13(-) | |
| | 12 | 15(-) | versus | 13(-) | Stalemate |
| | 13 | 15 | versus | 16(-) | |

Note: Sources are crude estimate but broadly accurate

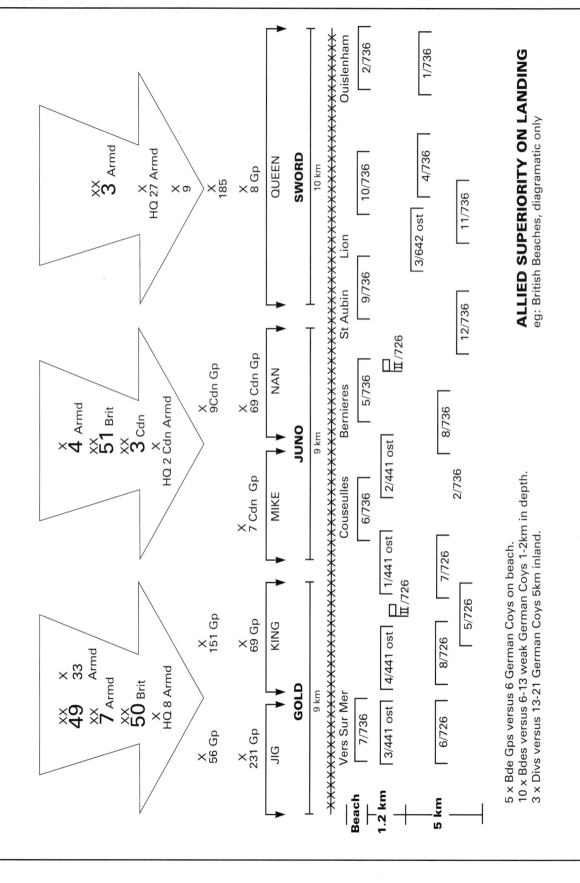

**ALLIED SUPERIORITY ON LANDING**
eg: British Beaches, diagramatic only

5 x Bde Gps versus 6 German Coys on beach.
10 x Bdes versus 6-13 weak German Coys 1-2km in depth.
3 x Divs versus 13-21 German Coys 5km inland.

## TABLES OF COMPARATIVE RANKS

| British Army | US Army | Heer | Waffen SS |
|---|---|---|---|
| Private | Private | Grenadier | SS-Schütze |
| — | Private First Class | Obergrenadier | SS-Oberschütze |
| Lance Corporal | — | Gefreiter | SS-Sturmmann |
| — | — | Obergefreiter | SS-Rottenführer |
| — | — | Stabsgefreiter | — |
| — | — | — | — |
| Corporal | Corporal | Unteroffizier | SS-Unterscharführer |
| Sergeant | Sergeant | Unterfeldwebel | SS-Scharführer |
| — | — | Fähnrich | — |
| — | Staff Sergeant | Feldwebel | SS-Oberscharführer |
| — | — | — | — |
| Company Sergeant-Major | Master Sergeant | Oberfeldwebel | SS-Hauptscharführer |
| — | — | Hauptfeldwebel | SS-Stabsscharführer |
| — | — | Oberfähnrich | — |
| Regimental Sergeant Major | Warrant Officer | Stabsfeldwebel | SS-Sturmscharführer |
| Second Lieutenant | Second Lieutenant | Leutnant | SS-Untersturmführer |
| — | — | — | — |
| Lieutenant | First Lieutenant | Oberleutnant | SS-Obersturmführer |
| — | — | — | — |
| Captain | Captain | Hauptmann | SS-Hauptsturmführer |
| Major | Major | Major | SS-Sturmbannführer |
| Lieutenant Colonel | Lieutenant Colonel | Oberstleutnant | SS-Obersturmbannführer |
| Colonel | Colonel | Oberst | SS-Standartenführer |
| — | — | — | SS-Oberführer |
| Brigadier General | Brigadier General | Generalmajor | SS-Brigadeführer |
| Major-General | Major General | Generalleutnant | SS-Gruppenführer |
| Lieutenant General | Lieutenant General | General | SS-Obergruppenführer |
| General | General | Generaloberst | SS-Oberstgruppenführer |
| Field Marshal | General of the Army | Generalfeldmarschall | Reichsführer-SS |

# ABBREVIATIONS AND GLOSSARY

| | |
|---|---|
| 2ATAF | 2nd Allied Tactical Air Force |
| 2IC | Second in command |
| AEAF | Allied Expeditionary Air Force |
| AVRE | Armoured Vehicle Royal Engineers |
| Bocage | Hedgerow countryside |
| CO | Commanding Officer |
| DD | Duplex Drive (amphibious) |
| DUKW | Amphibious vehicle |
| Fallschirmjäger | Paratrooper |
| FUSAG | First US Army Group |
| Heer | Army |
| Heeresgruppe | Army group |
| HMCS | Her Majesty's Canadian Ship |
| Kampfgruppe | Battle group |
| Kreigsmarine | German Navy |
| Landesschützen | Infantry |
| LCA | Landing Craft Assault |
| LCI(L or S) | Landing Craft Infantry (Large or Small) |
| LCM | Landing Craft Mechanised |
| LCR | Landing Craft Rocket |
| LCT | Landing Craft Tank |
| LCVP | Landing Craft Vehicle and Personnel |
| Lehr | Training |
| LST | Landing Ship Tank |
| Luftwaffe | German air force |
| Nebelwerfer | Automatic rocket launcher |
| OB West | Oberkommando West — Supreme Command West |
| OKW | Oberkommando der Wehrmacht German Armed Forces Supreme Command |
| Ost | Ost Battalions were formed from Soviet soldiers |
| Panzerfaust | Bazooka |
| Panzerjäger | Anti-tank |
| RA | Royal Artillery |
| RAC | Royal Armoured Corps |
| RAP | Regimental Aid Post |
| RASC | Royal Army Service Corps |
| RCT | Regimental Combat Team |
| RE | Royal Engineers |
| Rotte | Pair of aircraft or Sboats |
| RTR | Royal Tank Regiment |
| Schnellboot | S-boat — German motor torpedo boat |
| SP | Self propelled |
| Staffel | Squadron |
| Sturm | Storm |
| Wehrmacht | German Armed Forces —comprising the army (Heer), navy (Kriegsmarine), and airforce (Luftwaffe) |
| Widerstandsnest(er) WN | Strong point(s) |

## PREFACE

1. Broadfoot P 231-2
2. *Four Stars of Hell* Laurence Critchell P.70
3. *Flamethrower* Pxv

## 1: THE NARROW CHANNEL

### *'Wolves Circling a Wounded Dog' ... Lyme Bay 28 April 1944.'*

1. Kriegstagebuch 5. Schnellboot Flotilla 23.55hrs 28 Apr. 1944.
2. Ibid 16-27 April and 22.00hrs 28 Apr. Activity the night before was first wave of Op 'Tiger'.
3. *Rotte 1. S-100* and *S-143.*
   *Rotte 2. S-140* and *S-142.*
   *Rotte 3. S-136* and *S-138.*
   9th Flotilla *S-150, S-130,* and *S-145.*
4. KTB. 9 Flotilla 28 Apr. 00.01 hrs (German time).
   Rpt 3 Rotte.
5. Order of column: HMS *Azalea, LST 515, 496, 511, 531, 58, 499, 289, 507.* See map /chart.
6. Org for Op 'Tiger'.
7. N. Lewis *Channel Firing.* P.26-7.
8. Ibid P.69-70.
9. KTB. 9 Flotilla. 2 *Rotte.* 00.59 27/4 - 01.26.28/4.
10. Lewis P.83.
11. KTB. 9 Flotilla. 2 *Rotte.* 01.30-34.
12. Ibid. 3 Rotte 00.07-00.09.
13. Lewis P.89.
14. E. Hoyt. *The Invasion Before Normandy.* P.108.
15. KTB. 9 Flotilla. 1 *Rotte.* 00.03.
16. Ibid. 1 *Rotte.* 00.12-01.27. Beitrag 9 Flotilla 00.03-01.34.
17. Ibid 1 *Rotte* 02.14.
18. Lewis P.98.
19. Ibid P.91.
20. Ibid P.92.
21. Ibid P.93.
22. KTB. 5 Flotilla 3 *Rotte* 00.35.
23. Lewis P.98.
24. Ibid P.98.
25. KTB. 9 Flotilla 02.17.
26. Ibid. 1 *Rotte* 02.16.
27. Lewis. P.99. Eugene Rubin on *LCT 496.*
28. KTB. 5 Flotilla. 1 *Rotte.* 04.53.
29. Ibid. 'Beitrag 9 Flotilla 03.15 und Nachtragliche Auswertung.'
30. Lewis P.118.

### *'It will be All Right on the Night'.*

1. Hoyt. 122, 154-5, Lewis 237. Hoyt quotes 4 Div figure of 200 deaths on UTAH on D-Day. P.187.
2. Lewis *Channel Firing.* Hoyt *Invasion Before Normandy.* etc.
3. Lewis 117-188.
4. Ibid P.130.

5. Lt Col Jacob Bealke. 3.Bn 358 Inf Regt. 90th Inf.Div. Apr 12.1944. Quoted from A. Tapert *Lines of Battle.* P.147.
6. E. Hoyt *The GI's War,* P.290.
7. Studs Terkel *The Good War,* P.275-6.
8. B. Broadfoot. *Six War Years 1939-45,* P.286-7.
9. Hoyt.P.290.
10. N. Longmate. *The GIs,* P.293.
11. Ibid P.295.
12. G.S. Patton *War As I Knew It,* P.336.
13. R. Ingersoll. *Top Secret* (NY,1946) P.101.
14. O. Bradley *A Soldier's Story,* P.236.
15. J. Balkoski *Beyond The Beachhead,* P.1.
16. Bradley P.237-8.
17. B.C. Pohanka. Interview *Beach with No Cover, Military History* Feb 92. P.35.
18. A Moorehead *Eclipse,* P.85.
19. I.C. Hammerton *Achtung Minen!,* P.52-3.
20. A. Wilson *Flamethrower,* P.35-6.
21. P. Hennessy *Young Man in a Tank,* P.35.
22. TV Interview 'Nan-Red'. Transmitted Jun 84.
23. Hennessy. P.42.
24. N. Smith *Tank Soldier,* P.51.
25. A. Baron *From the City From the Plough,* P.11.
26. Moorehead P.83.
27. Smith P.53-4.
28. R. Neillands *The Desert Rats,* P.212.
29. J.L. Moulton. *Haste to the Battle,* P.56-7.
30. D. Eisenhower. *Crusade in Europe* P.273.
31. Moorehead P.85.
32. Ingersoll 106-32.
33. Baron P.13

## 2: THE FAR SHORE

### *... The German Army in the West.*

1. Robert Vogt. *Deutsche im Zweiten Weltkrieg,* P.361.
2. Ibid P.361.
3. Harrison P.231.
4. Ibid P.233.
5. The 326th, 346th, 348th and 19th Luftwaffe Field. Ibid P.235.
6. Ibid P.236.
7. In conversation with Lt Gen Fritz Bayerlein July 1943. 'Rommel Papers', P.453.
8. Martin van Creveld *Fighting Power,* P.87.
9. Letter Jun 1944. Hans Dollinger. *Kain, wo ist dein Bruder?* , P.256.

### *'As for as the Atlantic Wall ... It was sheer humbug.' The Defence Debate.*

1. 'Rommel Papers', P.454.
2. Ibid P.455.
3. Milton Shulman *Defeat in the West,* P.129.

### *'It is essential to prepare for hard times here ...' Normandy Defences. Spring 1944.*

1. Interview TVS 'Nan-Red' directed Graham Hurley 1984.
2. H. Speidel. *Invasion 1944,* Author's

translation.
3. P. Carell *Invasion They're Coming,* P.14.
4. Interviews 'Nan-Red' 1984.
5. G. Duboscq *My Longest Night,* P.18.
6. 'Rommel Papers', Letter dated 31 Jan 44. P.463.
7. P. Carell P.34.
8. Von Luck P.134.
9. E. Klapdor *Die Entscheidung. Invasion 1944,* P.118-9.
10. Kriegstagebuch AOK 7. Bericht *Sonderstab Oemichen* 13-5-44.
11. E. Klapdor. P.120.
12. F. Ruge. *The Invasion of Normandy,* P.328.
13. 'Rommel Papers'. Letter 19-1-44. P.462.
14. E. Klapdor P.120.
15. Marinegruppen Kommando West. Status Report 16/30-4-44. Harrison. P.262-3.
16. Reports Pemsel, Ziegelmann, and Lt Gen Richter. Ibid P.264.

### *'Your objective is not the coast. Your objective is the sea!' ... The Panzers.*

1. P. Carell. P.24.
2. Von Luck P.134.
3. Ibid P.133.
4. Ibid P.134.
5. 20kmh over 110-190km. H. Meyer *Kriegsgeschichte der 12.SS-Panzerdivision 'Hitlerjugend',* P.69.
6. Meyer. P.16-17.
7. *Signal* 1944, 'Sie Nennen Sie "Crack Babies". SS Panzerdivision "Hitlerjugend".'
8. Meyer. P.18.
9. Ibid P.19-20.
10. Ibid P.19.
11. Ibid P.43.
12. Ibid P.43.
13. Ibid P.18.
14. F. Kurowski. *Die Panzer-Lehr Division,* P.29.
15. H. Ritgen. *Die Geschichte der Panzer-Lehr Division im Westen 1944-45,* P.102.

### *Cry 'Wolf!' ... Spring 1944.*

1. R. Blinzing. *Deutsche im Zweiten Weltkrieg,* P.359 60.
2. Von Luck P.134.
3. Ibid P.134.

## 3: OBJECTIVES

### *The Race to the Fore-shore ... Objectives and Plans.*

1. D. Scott. *Typhoon Pilot,* P.99.
2. F. Ruge. *The Invasion of Normandy,* P.332.
3. These were:
   33 Static divisions.
   13 Mobile infantry divisions.
   2 Fallschirmjäger (Para) divisions.
   6 Panzer divisions (+ Reserve of 4 more Panzer/Panzergrenadier)
   Total 58 Divisions. (H. Meyer P.32).
4. 6th Airborne Division Report on operations in Normandy 6 Jun-27 Aug 44. Intelligence

Assessment Para 4 (c) and (i).
5. Taken from Montgomery's address at St Paul's School 15 May 1944. *Monty. Master of the Battlefield 1942-44*, N. Hamilton. P.573.6. Now including Panzer Lehr and 116th Panzer Division.
7. 5th Panzer (from Amiens, Toulouse, Bordeaux, Sedan and Belgium) and 8 Infantry. Hamilton, P.573.
8. Letter to wife. 19 Jan 44 'Rommel Papers'. P.462.
9. N. Hamilton, P.575.
10. R. Lewin, *Ultra Goes to War*.
11. Lewin P.305.
12. Ibid P.316.

**Realignment ... 'The situation did not look promising.'**
1. Harrison P.259.
2. James M Gavin *on to Berlin*, P.97.
3. US Doc MS-B-839. Von der Heydte.
4. M. Pöppel. *Heaven and Hell*, P.172.
5. Ibid P.173.
6. Ibid P.174.

**'The day of the dashing cut-and-thrust tank attack ... is past and gone.'**
1. Hamilton P.577.
2. Kriegstagebuch AOK 7. *Bericht Sonderstab Oemichen*. 13-5-44.
3. 'Rommel Papers'. P.468.
4. Franz Kurowski: *Die Panzer-Lehr-Division*, P.295.'Rommel Papers'. P.467.
6. Hamilton. P.577.
7. S. Badsey *Normandy 1944*, P.27.
8. Ibid Charts on P.21 and 17.
9. D. Cauldwell *JG26*, P.236-7.
10. Ibid P.241.
11. Ibid P.237.
12. *Typhoon Pilot*, P.101.
13. Ibid P.102.
14. H. Meyer *Kriegsgeschichte der 12. SS-Panzerdivision 'Hitlerjugend'*, P.44.
15. Lewin. P.314.

**4: WAITING**

**'Eternal Father Strong to Save' ... The Camps.**
1. Ed Barry Broadfoot, *Six War Years 1939-45*, P.179.
2. M. Miller 'LCT Commander', *War Monthly* No 25 P.6.
3. Baltimore News Post. Quoted Balkoski P.60.
4. Broadfoot P.179.
5. M. Miller, P.6.
6. N. Longmate. P.297.
7. Ibid P.297.
8. P. Hennessy *Young Man in a Tank*, P.50.
9. S. Sykes *Deceivers Ever*, P.121.
10. A. Moorehead *Eclipse*, P.87-8.
11. I. Grant *Cameraman at War*, P.39.
12. Hennessy P.52.
13. Grant P.39.
14. Hammerton P.67.
15. Ibid P.69.
16. A. Baron *From the City, From the Plough*, an imaginary letter from Charlie Veneables, P.104.
17. 'The World at War' Thames TV

1974. 'Morning Jun-Aug 1944'.
18. *Eclipse*, P.89.
19. Ibid P.89.
20. *Haste to the Battle*, P.54.
21. Grant P.40.
22. N. Longmate P.303.
23. Hammerton P.66.
24. N. Longmate P.303.
25. Moorehead P.91-2.
26. Hammerton P.69.
27. N. Longmate P.298.
28. Ibid P.298-9.

**Embarkation ...**
1. P. Lund and H. Ludlam *War of the Landing Craft*, P.146.
2. N. Longmate P.312.
3. Ed. Flower and Reeves. *The War 1939-45*, P.455.
4. R. Neillands. *The Desert Rats*, P.213.
5. Broadfoot P.231.
6. Miller P.7.
7. K. Lord. Paper on *Omaha Beach* 19 Jan 88. US Army Military History Institute.
8. R.H. Barry *The Allied Armada*, Purnell *History of the Second World War*, Pp 1824 and 1829.
9. J. Balkoski P.13-5.
10. Patrick P.J. Bracken *2,500 Dangerous Days*, Pp 40-1.
11. 'One Soldier's D-Day'. Based on P Hutchinsons interviews with Spandau in *War Monthly* No15, Pp 18-22.
12. Pte N. Mason 2nd Bn E. Yorks Regt Quoted Warner P.176.
13. Interview with B.C. Pohanka. *Military History* Feb 92. P.37.
14. Hennessy P.52.
15. *Images of War 1939-45*, Lt-Col Forrester P.773.

**Postponement ...**
1. Bradley P.253.
2. Ibid P.257.
3. Pohanka P.37.
4. D. Holbrook *Flesh Wounds*. P.93.
5. Grant P.40.
6. Sykes P.124-5.
7. P. Lund and H. Ludlam P.147.
8. Moulton P.57.
9. Holbrook P.98-9.
10. Sykes P.125.
11. S.J. Osborne quoted Warner P.121.
12. Grant P.41.
13. Quoted from J. Balkoski P.64.

**5: IT'S D-DAY TOMORROW**

Rhyming couplet Ginger Woodcock 9 PARA. *The Big Drop*, J. Golley, P.62.
**Manning the West Wall ... 5 June**
1. *Images of War 1939-45*, Account by Cpl Thiel. P.776. (Referred now as Thiel).
2. Pöppel P.174.
3. Thiel P.776.
4. Von Luck P.135.
5. Thiel P.776.
6. Kriegstagebuch AOK 7. 5 Jun 1944.
7. *Deutsche im Zweiten Weltkrieg*, P.361.

8. Thiel P.776.
9. Von Luck P.136.
10. Kriegstagebuch OB West. Lagerbeurteilung 29/5 - 4/6 44.
11. F. Hayn *Die Invasion*, P.16.
12. Von Luck P.136.
13. See C. Ryan *The Longest Day* influencing many other subsequent D-Day publications.
14. Wetteraussichten fur Unternehmen des Feindes in der Nacht vom 5.6. zum 6.6. 1944. Verbindungsmeteorloge OB West 4/5.6.1944 17,30h.
15. Ruge P.323.
16. Meyer P.44.
17. Ibid P.50.
18. Interview TVS 'Nan-Red' 1984.
19. Von Luck P.136-7, Carell P.32.
20. Thiel P.776, Vogt *Deutche im Zweiten Weltkrieg* P.361, Jahnke: Carell P.33.
21. Pöppel P.174.
22. Von Luck P.140.

**'We were coming over Lord' ... airfields in Southern England**
1. Figures Harrison P.279, and 6th Airborne *Report on Operations in Normandy* Appendix A.2. Letter June 1944. *Lines of Battle*, P.158.
3. Quotes and data Warner P.34-7.
4. Ginger Woodcock 9 PARA. Quoted J. Golley P.62.
5. N. Longmate P.308.
6. Weather's quotes; Warner P.45.
7. *Despatches From the Heart*, Annette Tapert P.96.8.92 Troop Carrying Squadron. Quoted *Visitors Guide to Normandy Landing Beaches*, Holt P.57.
9. Quoted Warner P.35. 13 PARA was to suffer 80 dead, 226 wounded and 54 missing by 27 Aug 44. 6th Airborne Div 'Report on Operations in Normandy' Appx 'T'.
10. J. Golley P.62.
11. *Yank* magazine. 'This was D-Day' Ralph G. Martin. Jun 30. 1944. P.183.
12. E. Hoyt *The GI's War*. P.311.
13. Warner P.35.
14. Ibid P.56.
15. Holt P.57.
16. Warner P.37.

**'What a night - dark and wet' ... the Invasion Fleet**
1. D. Holbrook P.100.
2. Hammerton P.71, Moulton P.57, Glover: *The War at Sea* ed. J. Winton P.413.
3. Quoted Warner: Triggs P.164, Sapper Mellen AVRE driver 82nd Asslt Sqn RE P.121, Webber P.188, Triggs P.164.
4. Balkoski P.63.
5. Warner P.175.
6. Balkoski P.6.
7. 'World at War'. ITV 1984.
8. Pugsley. Taken from Winton *The War at Sea*. P.408.
9. Ruge P.329.
10. Ibid P.325.
11. Ibid P.333.
12. Winton P.409-411.
13. Ibid P.414.
14. N. Smith *Tank Soldier* P.15 and 17.
15. Warner P.81.
16. Ibid P.169.
17. Hammerton P.71 and 75, Grant P.42-3.
18. Balkoski P.5.

19. Gray and Ferrara quoted from *29 Let's Go!* J.H. Ewing P.37.
20. Sykes P.133.
21. Moorehead P.94.
22. Holbrook quotes P.103 and P.107.
23. *Operation Overlord 1944-84.* ed Mark Newman. *The News* Portsmouth P.32.
24. Longmate P.307.
25. *Operation Overlord. The News* Portsmouth P.12. 1984.
26. Klapdor P.158.

## 6: SECURING THE FLANKS

### Coup de Main ... the Orne River 00.16 - 00.26 hours.
1. Interview *D-Day Plus Forty.* ITN TV production 1984.
2. Interview. Ibid.
3. Ibid.
4. Interviews Parr ibid.
5. Additional material from Stephen Ambrose *Pegasus Bridge* and the British official account *By Air to Battle.*

### The Plan ... secure the flanks.
1. OB West. Verbindungsmeteorologe H.Qu.den 5.6.1944. 17,30h.

### Go! Go! Go! ... 'a fantastic chimera of lights and flak'.
1. J. Byram, *The Unfinished Man.*
2. Taken from 'This was D-Day' Sgt R.G. Martin quoting R. Miller. *Yank* magazine. Jun 30 1944.
3. Quotes from *Soldier*, Flower and Reeves P.458.
4. Bristow quotes Warner P.28-9.
5. Clarke quoted Warner P.38.
6. Jefferson *Assault on the Guns of Merville*, P.99.
7. Warner P.38.
8. Ambrose P.125.
9. Warner P.39.
10. Ibid.
11. Jefferson P.102.
12. Ibid. P.202.
13. Warner P.40.
14. BBC *War Report*, P.60.
15. Ambrose P.126.
16. BBC *War Report*, P.60.
17. *Pegasus.* Journal of Airborne Forces. Letter P.168. Dec 92.
18. ITN interview Jun 1984.
19. Holt P.57.
20. Ibid P.61.
21. Gavin P.104.
22. *Les Paras US dans le Canton de Sainte-Mère-Eglise.* P.Jutras. P.30.
23. Quoted Flowers and Reeve P.459.
24. Compilation Gavin P.104 and ITN interview Jun 84.
25. Lt Col Vandervoort. 2nd Bn 505th Regt.
26. Holt P.61.
27. Letter Pte T Raulston 506th Regt 101st Div. 13 Jun 44. Tapert P.158.
28. L. Critchell, *Four Stars of Hell*, P.42.
29. Ibid P.42.
30. Gavin P.105.
31. Raulston letter quoted Tapert P.158.
32. *Yank* magazine. 30 Jun 44.
33. Interview ITN Jun 84.
34. Blackmon account *Images of War.* P.775.

35. BBC *War Report.* P.61-2.
36. Ibid P.62.
37. ITN interview Jun 84.
38. *Yank* Magazine 30 Jun 44.
39. Gavin P.106.
40. *Images of War.* P.775.
41. Warner P.46.
42. Ibid P.47.
43. *Instructions issued to Comd 3 PARA Bde.* Appendix C to *6th Airborne Division Report on Operations in Normandy.* 6 Jun - 27 Aug 44.

### Will it suffice? ... holding the flanks.
1. Harrison P.300. Actual D-Day losses by August were 1,259; of which 156 were known dead and 756 missing.
2. 6th Airborne Division Report on operations in Normandy. Paras 8-12.
3. Estimates ibid, Harrison and author's calculations based on quoted material.
4. The author has freely drawn upon his own 20 years active airborne experience as a serving Parachute Regiment officer, in the preparation, writing and views expressed in both this and the next chapter.

## 7: THE LONG NIGHT

### 'Condemned to inactivity' ... the Orne and the east.
1. Klapdor P.159.
2. Von Luck P.137.
3. Gefechtsbericht der H.K.A.A. 1255 fur die Zeit v. 6-9.6.44 15.00 Uh. Dated 14.6.44.
4. Jefferson P.142.
5. Richter. Gefechtsbericht über die Kampfe im Abschnitt der 716. Inf. Division am 6.6.1944. Dated 23.6.44 Page 4. Para detail taken from map Appendix 'K' from 6th Airborne Division Report.6.Gefechtsbericht des Ost-Batl.s 642 dated 14.6.44.
7. Gefechtsbericht 716 Div.P.4. Hammel quoted Von Luck P.140.
8. Jefferson P.142.
9. Gefechtsbericht 716 Div P.4.
10. Von Luck P.140.
11. Ibid. P.137.
12. Kriegstagebuch Heeresgruppe B (KTB.H.gr B) 6.6.1944. 01.40 Uhr.
13. Ibid 02.15 Uhr.
14. Von Luck P.138.
15. Gefechtsbericht 716 Div P.5.
16. Ibid. IInd Panzergrenadier Battalion from Pz Gren Regt 192, 2nd hvy arty battery of Battalion 989 and the 1st Company of Panzerjäger (Assault Gun) Battalion 716.
17. Ibid P.5.
18. Ibid P.4.
19. Von Luck P.138 and 140.
20. KTB. H.grB 03.05 Uhr 6 Jun and 03.20 Uhr.21. *Die Invasion* P.17.
22. Jefferson P.110-111.
23. Ibid P.143.
24. Carell P.48.
25. Jefferson P.143.
26. *Das Reich* magazine. Helmut Bernolt. Jul 44. Reproduced Appdx 6, Jefferson.
27. Gefechtsbericht 716 Div P.5.
28. Ibid P.6.
29. These were the 5th Company 726th Regiment reinforced by a further platoon from the 7th Company of the same

Regiment, and the 8th Company of 736th Regiment reinforced by a platoon from Ost Battalion 441. Gefechtsbericht 716th Div. P.6.
30. There are no reports of British parachute sticks dropping in this area according to official Allied accounts.

### 'The situation in the Seine Estuary is probably worse than ours' ... the West.
1. Pöppel. P.174.
2. *Images of War* P.777.
3. Auszug aus den Fernsprech - Meldebuch (Ia) der 352 I.D. Dated 5/7/44. P.2-3.
4. *Operation Overlord. The News* News Centre. Portsmouth 1984. P.22.
5. Pte John Steele who although wounded in the foot, and deafened by the church bell, was to survive. See C.Ryan: *The Longest Day.*
6. Episode based on Holt P.52-4, Carell P.39 and Jutras P.16-17.
7. Map V and VI Parachute drop patterns of the 101st and 82nd Airborne Divisions. *Utah Beach to Cherbourg* US Historical Division War Dept. 1948. These were 5 sticks of 507th Regt (20 mls off course), 6 sticks of 501st and 506th Regts (8 mls) and 8 sticks of 101st Div around St Jores.8. Pöppel P.175.
9. Gefechtsbericht des Fallschirmjäger Regts 6 Fur die Zeit von 6. bis 13. Juni 1944 (Gefechtsbericht Fsch Regt 6) dated 17 Jun 44.10. Pöppel P.175.
11. Fernsprech-Meldebuch 325 Div. 02.55, 03.10, 04.01 Uhr. Latter quote Ic 84 Corps to 352 Div 04.19 hours, dummies quote 04.35 hours.
12. Gefechtsbericht 352 Div P.2.
13. Pöppel P.175.
14. KTB H.gr B 02.15 Uhr.
15. Ibid 04.30 Uhr.
16. KTB AOK 7 Jun 6.

### 'A disturbed Beehive' ... coordinating the response.
1. Hayn P.13-15.
2. Speidel P.99.
3. Hayn, P.16.
4. Ibid P.17.
5. 502nd Regiment and 377th Field Artillery in one stick, and 2 sticks from the 508th Regiment. Assessed from Map V and VI 'Parachute Drop Patterns' from US official account 'Utah Beach to Cherbourg'.
6. Hayn P.16-17, Carell P.50-51 and author's assessment.
7. KTB H.grB 02.15 Uhr.
8. Ibid 03.50 Uhr.
9. Meyer P.52.
10. Ibid P.57.
11. Ibid P.53.
12. KTB AOK 7.6 Jun.
13. KTB H.grB 05.30, 05.50.
14. KTB H.grB 05.40 Uhr.

### Look what's coming! ...
1. Gefechtsbericht 352 Div P.2.
2. Meldung (report) 03.09 Uhr. Klapdor P.182.
3. KTB H.grB 02.15, 03.50 Uhr.
4. Gefechtsbericht der H.K.A. 1255 Fur die Zeit v.6.-9.6.44. 15.00h. A) Einsatz der Abteilung.
5. KTB H.grB 03.50 Uhr.
6. Gefechtsbericht 352 Div P.3.

7. Fernsprech-Meldebuch 352nd Div reports air attacks on two artillery bns at 03.22 and 03.30, at 03.35 on Le Guay, Pte du Hoc and Grandcamp, on naval installations 03.44 and further air-raids between 04.00-04.10 and after 05.06.
8. Interview 'Nan-Red'. ITV Jun 1984.
9. Interview. *Entscheidung Am Atlantik Wall*. Deutsche ZDF TV. Directed Lutz Becker 1984.
10. 'Nan-Red'. ITV Jun 84.
11. Fernsprech-Meldebuch 352nd Div 05.02, 05.20 and 05.32.
12. Gefechtsbericht 716 Div P.6.

## 8: THE STORM BREAKS

### 'The guns ... were too hot to be touched' ... the naval bombardment.
1. R. Capa *Images of War*. P.108.
2. Ewing P.37.
3. Ibid.
4. *History of US Naval Operations in World War II* S.E. Morison, Vol XI P.94.
5. Interview by B.C. Pohanka. *Military History* Feb 92. P.35.
6. Reeman. *A Personal Reminiscence*. 1984.
7. Capa P.108.
8. Ewing P.37.
9. Interview report 'D-Day Landing'. P.1. Feb 45.
10. Letter Jun 11. 1944. Tapert P.153.
11. Capa P.108.
12. Balkoski P.37.
13. Letter Jun 11. 1944. Tapert P.153.
14. D. Reeman *A Personal Reminiscence*.
15. *War Report*. 7 Jun BBC. P.63.
16. Morison. P.96 and 121.
17. Reeman.
18. Information via E. Grove
19. Capa P.108.
20. Ewing P.37.
21. Holbrook P.119.
22. Interview *The News* Portsmouth. *Operation Overlord 1944/1984*. P.33.
23. Andrew Cowan and Bill Herbert CBC report 12 Jun. BBC *War Report* P.74.
24. *The News*. P.32-3.
25. Interview Ibid P.33.
26. Warner P.93.
27. Ibid P.188.
28. Background material from *Hitler's Naval War* Cajus Becker P.383-4 and Carell P.76-7.
29. Morison P.106.
30. *The News*. Interview P.32.
31. Ibid. Interview P.33.

### 'The Golden City'.
1. Gefechtsbericht der 352 Inf Division P.5. Para 5.2. Ibid.
3. Fernsprech-Meldebuch der 352. I.D. 06.04, 06.14, 06.26 Uhr.
4. Background material Carell P.50-58.
5. Gefechtsbericht uber die Kampfe im Abschnitt der 716. Division am 6.6.1944. P.6.
6. Ibid.
7. Gefechtsbericht der H.K.A.A. 1255 fur die Zeit v.6.-9.6.44. 1500 Uhr. (A) Einsatz der Abteilung. P.1. The 'Nelson' and 'Maryland' class identifications were erroneous. The 'Nelson' class 'battleship' was probably the

monitor *Roberts* and the 'Maryland' class 'battleship' the British cruiser *Mauritius*.
8. Ibid. (B) Kampfauftrage. P.2.
9. Ibid P.3-4.
10. *We Defended Normandy*. (1951) P.96.
11. Jefferson P.149-50.
12. Extract from *Das Reich* magazine Jul 44, quoted Jefferson P.220.

### 'A Hollywood Show' ... Utah 06.30 hours.
1. *Yank*. (30 Jun1944.) ed Steve Kluger P.183.
2. Facts researched from Map VII US official history *Utah Beach to Cherbourg*.
3. Extract letter Jun 11 1944. Tapert P.154.
4. Morison P.98.
5. Interview. ITN 'D-Day Plus Forty'. Jun 84.
6. Tapert P.154.
7. *Utah Beach to Cherbourg* P.44-5.
8. ITN interview Jun 84.
9. S.Terkel *The Good War*, P.253-4.
10. Tapert P.154.
11. *Yank* P.185.
12. Terkel P.253.
13. Morison P.102.
14. *Yank* P.185.

### '... A peaceful summer's day on the Wannsee'.
1. Background quotes Carell P.59.
2. Fernsprech Meldebach 352 I.D. P.7.
3. Hayn. P.18.
4. Fernsprech Meldebuch 352 I.D. P.8-9.
5. Ibid. 10.00, 10.20, 11.42, and 12.05 Uhr. P.10-12.
6. Ibid 07.08 Uhr P.7, 11.47 Uhr P.12.
7. Pöppel P.175-6.
8. Gefechtsbericht des Fallschirm-Jäger-Regiments 6 fur die Zeit vom 6.bis 13. Juni 1944. P.1.9. Ibid P.2.
10. *Images of War* Interview P.805.
11. Ibid.
12. Pöppel P.177.

## 9: FIRST WAVE FOUNDERED

### 'No sign of life or resistance' ... approaching Omaha 06.15
1. Interview. Pohanka *Military History* Feb 92 P.37.
2. Ewing P.39.
3. Pohanka interview P.37.
4. Ewing P.37.
5. Captain Sabin USN. Hoyt P.328.
6. *Omaha Beachhead*. Official US history *American Forces in Action series*. P.39.
7. Lt. Saloman 2nd Ranger Bn. *Roughing it with Charlie*. E.M. Sorvisto P.33.
8. Morison *History of US Naval operations*, P.134.
9. Fernsprech-Meldebuch 352 I.D. 05.52 Uhr P.5.
10. Ibid P.6.
11. Ibid.

### 'Entire First Wave Foundered' ...
1. Interview. Thames TV 'World at War' - 'Morning Jun-Aug 1944'. 1973.
2. Sorvisto P.26.
3. Holt P.104.
4. Ewing P.41.
5. Lund and Ludlam P.169.

6. Pte Murdock. Holt P.104.
7. Interview. Thames TV 'World at War' 1973.
8. Ewing P.43.
9. Sorvisto P.32.
10. Engineer casualty figures 'Omaha Beachhead' P.42-3.
11. *Yank*. P.182.
12. Carroll quotes interview Pohanka P.38.
13. P. Hutchinson *One Soldier's D-Day.War Monthly* No13. P.20.
14. Ewing P.41.
15. Ibid.
16. HQ 1st US Inf Div G3 Journal. 6 Jun. Aboard USS *Ancon*.

### Assaulting the 'Jib' ... Pointe du Hoc. 07.10.
1. Gefechtsbericht der 352 Inf Division P.3.
2. Morison P.126.
3. Ibid P.127.
4. 1st US Div G3 Journal 6 Jun 44.
5. Interview ITN 'D-Day Plus Forty'. Jun 84.
6. R.L. Lane *Rudder's Rangers* P.80.
7. Gefechtsbericht der 352 Inf Division P.3.
8. Lane P.91.
9. Lommell interview ITN "D-Day plus Forty" Jun 84.
10. Fernsprech-Meldebuch 352 I.D. 08.19 Uhr P.8, 11.10 Uhr P.11, 12.25 Uhr P.12.
11. *Pointe du Hoc*. Small Unit Actions series. P.41.

### Coming ashore on 'Easy Red' ... Omaha 06.30 - 08.30
1. All quotations by Capa from *Images of War* P.108-110.
2. Interview report *D-Day Landing*. P.3. Feb 45.
3. Ibid P.3-5.
4. Interview Pohanka P.38.
5. He did. Only these 10 photographs survived. The remainder were accidently melted by an over enthusiastic dark-room assistant, excited at the quality of over one hundred negatives - possibly the best taken on D-Day.

### 'When, and from whom will the counter-attack ... come?'
1. Balkoski P.148.
2. Fernsprech-Meldebuch 352 I.D. P.7.
3. Balkoski P.134.
4. Fernsprech-Meldebuch 352 I.D. P.7.
5. Ibid. 07.25 Uhr.
6. Ibid. 07.45 Uhr.
7. Carell P.86-7.
8. Fernsprech-Meldebuch 352 I.D. 07.57 Uhr, 08.12 Uhr.

## 10: TANKS FROM THE SEA

### 'Out Ramps!' ... Sword 07.30.
1. Sykes P.133.
2. Hennessey P.56.
3. Holt P.169.
4. Warner P.136.
5. Hennessey quotes P.57-8.
6. *Operation Overlord 1944/84. The News* Portsmouth. P.18.
7. Major T. Wheway quotes Warner P.148.
8. Warner. P.82.
9. Interview. ITN "D-Day plus Forty". 1984.
10. A. Baron P.116.
11. Warner 82-3.

12. Interviews. 'D-Day plus Forty'.
13. Warner P.83.
14. Interview. 'D-Day plus Forty'.
15. Reeman.
16. Grant P.46.
17. Reeman. Glover. Winton P.418. Grant. P.46.
18. *Swiftly They Struck*. P.73.
19. Grant and Glover ibid. Farnborough *The Raiders*. R. Neillands P.177.
20. Glover P.419-20, McDougall P.73.
21. Grant P.47, Glover P.420.
22. Figures P. Boussel P.60, Ellis P.185-6.
23. Interviews ITN 'D-Day plus Forty'. 1984.
24. Neillands P.179.
25. *Swiftly They Struck*. P.74-5.
26. Lund and Ludlam P.155.
27. Miller P.9.
28. Glover P.421.
29. Lund and Ludlam P.155.
30. Warner P.83.
31. Lund and Ludlam P.153.
32. Warner P.184.
33. Glover P.424.

*'The appalling number of church spires' ... Juno 07.15*
1. Warner P.75.
2. Lund and Ludlam P.158.
3. Interview. ITN. Nan-Red 1984.
4. *Achtung! Minen!* P.76.
5. Interview 'Nan-Red'.
6. Interview ITN 'D-Day plus Forty' 1984.
7. Ibid.
8. Broadfoot P.237-8.
9. Hammerton P.76-7.
10. Interview 'Nan-Red'.
11. Major Morrison interview 'D-Day plus Forty'.
12. *Images of War* P. 803.
13. Interview 'Nan-Red'.
14. Broadfoot P.233.
15. Interview 'Nan-Red'.
16. Ibid.
17. *Haste to the Battle*. Moulton quotations P.60-1.
18. Ibid.
19. Interview 'Nan-Red'.
20. Interviews Travers, Square and Ward from 'Nan-Red'.
21. Moulton P.62-3.
22. Interviews Flunder and Shineton from 'Nan-Red'.
23. *Images of War*. P.802.
24. Interview 'D-Day plus Forty'.
25. Interviews the Constants and Anderson 'Nan-Red'.
26. Moulton P.65 and 67.
27. Ibid and interview 'Nan-Red'.
28. Interview 'Nan-Red'.

*Tanks from the sea ... Gold 07.25.*
1. Lund and Ludlam P.160.
2. Ibid P.161.
3. Warner P.115.
4. Lund and Ludlam P.162.
5. Warner P.199.
6. Triggs Ibid P.164-5, Foster P.264.
7. Major G Sindall Ibid. P.170-1.
8. Ibid p.265. Canadian loan officer with Dorsets.
9. Warner P.151.
10. Ibid P.146.

11. Ibid P.121-2.
12. Scaife interview 'D-Day plus Forty', Sellerie, Warner P.151-2.
13. Wright quotations Warner P.232-3. 47 Cdo losses Ellis P.175.
14. Interview Dec 1992.
15. Warner P.255.
16. Interview 'D-Day plus Forty'.

## 11: A BRUTAL DEFENCE

*Stalemate on Omaha ...*
1. Interview ITN 'D-Day plus Forty' Jun 1984.
2. Spaulding P.7, Krekorian from Ewing P.44.
3. Interview 'The World at War'. 'Morning'. Thames TV.
4. Ewing P.43-4.
5. Ibid P.49.
6. Interview 'D-Day plus Forty'.
7. Pohanka interview. Military History P.39.
8. *Omaha Beachhead*. American Forces in Action series. P.57.
9. Interview. 'The World at War'.
10. Interview. Military History P.38-9.
11. Hoyt P.348.
12. Marshall and Beer taken from Morison P.148 and 144-5 respectively.
13. Interview Military History P.38-9.
14. Letter 21 Jun 44. Tapert P.160-1.
15. Ewing P.54.
16. Morison P.149.
17. Based on Ewing account P.51-2.

*Success or Failure? ...*
1. Interview 'D-Day plus Forty'.
2. Interview *Military History*. P.40.
3. Interview 'D-Day plus Forty'.
4. Account *Omaha Beach*. 19 Jan 88.
5. HQ 1 Div G-3 Journal 6 Jun 44 aboard USS *Ancon*. Serial 28. 08.09.
6. Ibid Serial 32.
7. O. Bradley *A Soldier's Story* P.270.
8. HQ 1 Div G-3 Journal Serials 34, 50 (09.46), 63, (09.55).
9. Bradley P.271.
10. Lund and Ludlam, Loveless P.170, Allmark P.175.
11. HQ 1 Div G-3 Journal Serials 93,99, and 155 (13.41).
12. Hutchinson P.22, and Holt P.106-8.
13. Sorvisto P.32, 34 and 35.
14. Letter Jun 21.44. Tapert P.161.
15. Letter to Col Gavalas 8 Jun 44.
16. Interview Pte Al Nyland 5th Rangers 'D-Day plus Forty'.

*'They stick tight' ... the German defence Omaha.*
1. Spaulding P.8.
2. Mason: a series of quotes from letter 8 Jun to Col Gavalas, Carroll *Military History* P.40.
3. Balkoski P.136.
4. Mason letter to Col Gavalas.
5. Carell P.86.
6. Fernsprech-Meldebuch der 352 I.D.AR 352. 08.46. P.9.
7. Ibid. 09.05. P.9.
8. Ibid. 10.00 P.10, Gefechtsbericht der 352 Inf Div P.5.
9. Ibid 09.33, P.10, Gefechtsbericht 352 P.4.
10. Ibid.

11. Ibid. 11.14 p.11, 12.35 P.13.
12. Spaulding P.14.
13. Fernsprech-Meldebuch der 352 I.D. 14.03, 14.26, P.13. Gefechtsbericht P.5.
14. Ibid 17.10, P.14.

## 12: BREAK-IN

**Einbruchsraum West.** *Break-in Point West ... Gold.*
1. Richard Dimbleby 6 Jun. BBC *War Report* P.65.
2. Hansmann's report Meyer P.57-9.
3. Fernsprech-Meldebuch der 352 I.D. P.7.
4. *Deutsche im Zweiten Weltkrieg*. P.362.
5. Fernsprech-Meldebuch der 352 I.D. P.8: 08.12, 08.21, 08.25, 08.30 Uhr.
6. Ibid P.9, 08.35.
7. Meyer P.59-61.
8. Gefechtsbericht 716 Div P.7.
9. Ibid P.8.
10. Meyer P.60.
11. *Deutsche im Zweiten Weltkrieg* P.363. *Voices from the Third Reich* oral history P.363.
12. Meyer P.60.
13. Ibid P.61.
14. Fernsprech-Meldebuch 352 I.D. P.11, 11.00 Uhr, P.12, 13.17 Uhr.
15. Ibid 15.50, and Gefechts bericht der 352 Inf Div P.5.
16. Ibid P.13 Fernsprech-Meldebuch, according to IC (Intelligence Officer) report at 16.02 hours.
17. Ibid. P.14, 17.30, P.16, 21.00, 22.55 Uhr.
18. Ibid. P.14, 16.15, P.15, P.17, 23.20. Gefechtsbericht 716 Div P.8.
19. Interview 'Entscheidung Am Atlantik Wall'. ZDF TV 1984.

**Einbruchsraum Mitte.** *Break-in Point Centre ... Juno.*
1. Interview. Foster, Irish Battalion Kings Regiment. 'D-Day Plus Forty'. ITN 1984.
2. Interview ITN 'Nan-Red' 1984.
3. Interview ZDF TV 1984.
4. Meyer P.61.
5. Gefechtsbericht 716 Div P.8.
6. Ibid and Carell P.92.
7. Interview ZDF TV 1984.
8. Interview ITN 'Nan-Red'.
9. BBC *War Report* P.81.
10. Meyer P.61.

**Einbruchsraum Ost.** *Break-in Point East ... Sword.*
1. Gefechtsbericht 716 Div P.6.
2. Ibid P.6.
3. Ibid P.6-7.
4. Batteries were 3/1716, 1/1716, 1/HKAA 1260, S.Art.Abt.989. Gefechtsbericht 716 Div P.7.
5. A Jefferson P.151.
6. Gefechtsbericht 716 Div. P.7-8.
7. Ibid P.9.
8. Ibid P.10-11.

## 13: COUNTER-ATTACK

*21st Panzer attacks ...*
1. Von Luck P.141.
2. A. McKee *Caen. Anvil of Victory*. P.59.

3. Gefechtsbericht 716 Division P.7.
4. Von Luck P.141.
5. Ibid P.142.
6. Ellis P.204.
7. Hayn P.28.
8. Carell P.101.
9. Holbrook P.139-40.
10. Background material including Kortenhaus testimony of survivors taken from McKee P.61-2, Meyer P.71-2. There are different opinions over the number of tanks destroyed.
11. Von Luck P.142.
12. Ibid.
13. N. Hamilton *Monty. Master of the Battlefield 1942-1944.* P.615.
14. Warner P.149.
15. Ibid P.185.
16. Warner P.191.
17. Moulton quotes, Moulton P.70-1.
18. Warner P.139.
19. Hennessey P.63.
20. Based upon eye-witness accounts, McKee P.63 and Holbrook P.142-3.

*Assault towards Utah ...*
1. Pöppel P.178-9.
2. Gefechtsbericht Fsch Regt 6. P.2.
3. Ibid P.3.
4. Ibid and Pöppel P.179.
5. Ibid.
6. Pöppel P.181.

**14: A TENUOUS FOOTHOLD**

*... Reinforcement.*
1. Warner P.57-61 and subsequent quotes Tomblin.
2. D. Scott *Typhoon Pilot* P.109.
3. Warner P.30.
4. *The News*. Portsmouth Joly P.34 and Thoms P.33.
5. Scott P.110.
6. Ibid.
7. Warner P.52.
8. Ibid. Hollis P.107, Palser P.109.
9. These were the American 82nd, 101st, 4th, 29th, 2nd and 1st Divisions; and the British 50th, 3rd, 3rd Canadian and 6th Divisions. The 101st (US) and 82nd (US) divisions were at 38 percent and 33 percent strengths respectively.
10. Ellis P.264.
11. Harrison P.351.
12. 72,215 British and Canadian, 57,500 American across the beaches and 7,900 British and 15,500 American airborne troops. Ellis P.223.

*Beyond D-Day ... dusk 6 June.*
1. Interview 'Nan-Red'. ITN 1984.
2. Warner P.188.
3. Ibid P.192.
4. Broadfoot P.232.
5. Baron P.123.
6. Warner P.270.
7. Holbrook P.140.
8. Warner quotes Hills P.144, Garner P.182, Cadogan P.139.
9. Smith P.65.
10. Warner P.178.
11. Ewing P.60 and P.306.
12. Letter Jun 21. Tapert P.162.

13. Interview. 'D-Day Plus Forty'. ITN 1984.
14. Terkel P.256.
15. Interview *Military History* P.40.
16. Hennessey P.63.

**15: PANZER - MARSCH!**

*Where are the Panzers? ...*
1. Clostermann. *The Big Show* P.150 and P.151.
2. Scott P.110-111.
3. Quoted from personal diary in N. Hamilton. P.616.
4. Scott P.109-10.
5. Kriegstagebuch Heeresgruppe B (KTB) 09.40. 6 Jun.44.
6. H. Ritgen. *Die Geschichte der Panzer-Lehr Division im Westen. 1944-45.* P.103.
7. *Die Panzer-Lehr Division* F.Kurowski. P.32-3.
8. Letter Otto Gunsche 1981 to Meyer. Quoted P.55-6 Meyer.
9. KTB H Gr.B 10.20 (6/44).
10. Hayn P.19.
11. KTB H.Gr.B. COS to Ia OB West.
12. Ibid. 14.30, 14.32, 14.40, 14.45 hours (6/44).
13. KTB Seventh Army and Ritgen P.104.
14. K. Meyer. *Grenadiere*. P.209.
15. Ritgen P.102.

*Delays ... the 12th SS 'Hitlerjügend'.*
1. Meyer P.66.
2. Dollinger *Kain wo ist dein Bruder?* P.253.
3. Ibid. Letter 18 Jun 44. P.256.
4. M. Shulman. *Defeat in the West* P.151.
5. Pock's experiences Meyer P.66-7.
6. *Images of War* P.856.
7. Ibid.
8. Scott P.112.
9. Meyer P.69.
10. Meyer P.68-9.
11. Ibid P.67.

*A Nightmare Trek ... Panzer Lehr.*
1. Kurowski P.36.
2. Ibid P.34-5.
3. Scott P.119.
4. Ritgen. P.105.
5. Kurowski P.35 and Ritgen P.105.
6. Flying Officer Phillip Murton RAF. Interview *Images of War* P.857.
7. Kurowski P.39.
8. Ritgen P.106.
9. Shulman P.146.
10. Kurowski P.36.
11. Scott P.121-2.
12. Hartdegen quoted by Carell P.109.
13. Kurowski. P.40.
14. *Images of War* P.857.
15. Shulman P.146.
16. Kurowski P.41-2.

*'Little fish! We'll throw them into the sea ...'*
1. Meyer, K. P.210-11.
2. Ibid P.211 and Carell P.92.
3. KTB H.Gr. B 18.55 conversation COS AOK7 and H.Gr B. 4. i.e. Sturm Bn AOK7, 275 Div Kgr, Parts 711 Div, elms 265 Kgr, Fla 32, 30 Bde, Pz Ersatz 100 Bn and so on. (Details KTB AOK7 and H.Gr. B.)

5. Meyer, K. P.212-14.
6. Shulman P.144.
7. *Meyer, K.* P.214.

**16: VILLAGE FIGHTING**

*The Centre - before Caen ... Authie.*
1. Kriegstagebuch AOK 7. Bericht *Sonderstab Oemichen* 13-5-44.
2. See Appendix.
3. A.O. Palser. 246 Fd Coy RE. Warner P.108.
4. 1st Bn Suffolks 3 Div. Warner P.186.
5. Warner P.235.
6. Ibid P.110.
7. Ibid P.88.
8. *Flesh Wounds* P.178-9.
9. All Meyer quotations from *Grenadiere* P.216-18.
10. H. Meyer. *Kriegsgeschichte der 12th SS Panzerdivision 'Hitlerjugend'* P.79.
11. Ibid.
12. Ibid. P.80.
13. Ibid. P.81-2.
14. Ibid. Company Commander 1st Company I/25.
15. Ibid. P.103.
16. Warner P.182.
17. Broadfoot P.234.
18. Warner P.182.
19. Meyer, H. P.108.

*The East - stalemate on the Orne ... Bréville.*
1. Shulman P.153.
2. KTB H.Gr.B. *Verlauf* 6/6, 7/6 and 8/6/44.
3. Ibid 8/6 18.30, 20.40, 22.45 and 22.50hrs.
4. Ibid. 7/6. 11.45 and 15.00hrs.
5. Ibid 8/6 11.00 and 15.20hrs.
6. R. Lewin. *Ultra goes to war* P.317-18.
7. Hennessey P.66 and *Action by B Sqn 13/18 Hussars in sp of an attack by 7 PARA on 10 Jun 44*. Airborne Museum doc.
8. Taylor. Personal account. Airborne Museum.
9. Von Luck P.146.
10. Ibid and Taylor, Airborne Museum.
11. Erfahrungsbericht uber Einsatz. Gren Regt 857. Abt.1a. 18/6/44 and Shulman P.150.
12. Based on personal accounts: Captain Sim 12 PARA (B Coy), Captain Berhard 12 PARA (A Coy), and Maj Warren Devonshire Regt. Airborne Museum.
13. Erfahrungsbericht Gren Regt 857. 1a Meldung.
14. Ibid. P.5-7.
15. Personal account Sims 'The Capture of Bréville. 12 June.' Airborne Museum.
16. Ibid.
17. Warren account. Airborne Museum.
18. Erfahrungsbericht Gren Regt 857. P.7.
19. Ibid P.6-7.
20. Von Luck P.149.

*The West - 'Bocage' ... St-Côme-du-Mont.*
1. Terkel P.281.
2. Letter written 1 Jul 44. France. Tapert P.164.3. As related to Maj G.S. Johns a liaison officer. Ewing P.72.
3. Ewing, background material P.67-72.
4. Ewing P.72.
5. S.L.A. Marshall *Night Drop* P.267.
6. Gefechtsbericht des Fallschirm-Jäger Regiments 6 fur die Zeit von 7.bis 13.Juni 1944. P.4.7. Pöppel P.180.

8. Marshall P.273.
9. Based on Marshall account P.275.
10. Gefechtsbericht Fallschirm. Regt 6. P.5.
11. Quotes from Pöppel P.181-2.
12. Marshall P.276.
13. Critchell P.67-8.
14. Gefechtsbericht Fallschirm. Regt6. P.5.
15. Pöppel P.182-3.
16. Critchell P.69-70.
17. Marshall P.278.
18. Ibid. P.296.
19. Gefechtsbericht Fallschirm. Regt 6. P.7.
20. Marshall P.304-5.
21. Pöppel quotes: P.183, 198 and 200.

**17: POSTSCRIPT**

*The Germans ...*
1. KTB AOK7 16/6/4.
2. KTB H.Gr.B 15.30. 9/6/44.
3. See section *Manning the West Wall ... June 5.*
4. *Die Welt.* Nr.219. 19 Sep 68. P.7. Quoted Klapdor P.182.
5. Ryan P.200-201.
6. *Deutsche im Zweiten Weltkrieg* P.363.
7. Lewin P.329.

8. C. Shores *2nd ATAF* P.11-12 and 14.
9. *The News.* Portsmouth. P.33.
10. Data: Klapdor/Oehmichen Study and KTB AOK7.
11. KTB H.Gr.B. 13/6/44.
12. Lewin P.336.
13. Shulman P. 151-2.
14. KTB AOK7 14/6/44.
15. *Deutsche im Zweiten Weltkrieg* P.372.
16. KTB AOK7 6/6/44.
17. Shulman P.152.
18. *Deutsche im Zweiten Weltkrieg* P.372.
19. Bayerlein Führerbericht fur den 18.6 und 19.6.44.
20. 21 Pz Sitreps to 1st SS Pz Corps. 'Eigene taktische Lage' 17 Juni und 18.Juni.
21. KTB H.Gr.B 23.10 and 10.30 8/6/44.
22. KTB AOK7 12/6, 7/6, 10/6 and quote 11/6/44.
23. Klapdor data compiled from KTB AOK7.
24. Klapdor P.112 and *Bericht Gen v. Geyr 13.6.44 an Gen Insp. der Pz Truppen.* KTB OB West. Anlagen.
25. Gefechtsbericht Fallschirm. Regt.6. 'Versorgungsschwerigkeiten.' P.9-12.
26. Pöppel P.181.
27. All Richter's comments in this section taken from Gefechtsbericht 716 I.D.
28. Carell P.91.

*The Allies ...*
1. SLA Marshall P.294.

*The Human Factor ...*
1. Broadfoot P.210.
2. Quoted P. Fussell. *Wartime - Understanding and Behaviour in the Second World War* P.136.
3. Extracts *Flesh Wounds* P.175 and 177.
4. Broadfoot P.235.
5. *Deutsche im Zweiten Weltkrieg* P.366.
6. Broadfoot P.237.
7. *Voices from the Third Reich* An oral history. P.205-6.
8. *The Charge of the Bull* J. Brisset. P.29.
9. Kurowski P.44-5, Meyer K. P.230-1. Luxemberger was the CO of Pz Arty Bn 130.
10. Meyer P.97.
11. Mckee *Caen. Anvil of Victory* P.86-7.
12. *Flamethrower* P.60.
13. Gefechtsbericht III Bn 858 Regt. (from 346 Division) dated 15/6/44.
14. *Deutschen im Zweiten Weltkrieg* P.366-7.
15. Wilson Introduction P.XV.

# SOURCES

## ALLIED SOURCES

### Published

American Forces in Action Series:
Historical Division War Department
Washington.
- *Omaha Beachhead 6 Jun-13 Jun 1944* (1945)
- *Utah Beach to Cherbourg 6-27*

*Jun 1944* (1945)
- *Small Unit Actions* (1946)
- *Pointe du Hoc. 2nd Ra. Bn. 6 Jun 44.*

Badsey, S. *"Normandy 1944. Allied Landings and Breakout."* (Osprey, 1990).

Bagnall, N. 'Bloody Omaha' *War Monthly* (Marshall Cavendish, .
Vol.1 No.8 P.17-29).

Balkoski, J. *"Beyond the Beachhead"* (Stackpole Books, US 1989).

Baron, A. *"From the City From the Plough"* (Triad/Mayflower 1979).

Bracken, P. *"2500 Dangerous Days"* (Merlin Books, 1988).

Bradley, O. *"A Soldier's Story"* (Eyre and Spottiswoode, London 1951).

Brisset, J. *"The Charge of the Bull"* (Bates Books, 1989).

Broadfoot, B. *"Six War Years 1939-45"* (Doubleday, Canada Ltd 1974).

Byram, J. *"The Unfinished Man"* (Chatto & Windus, 1957).

Capa, R. *"Images of War"* (Hamlyn, 1964).

Clostermann, P. *"The Big Show"* (Corgi, 1979).

Crevald, M. van *"Fighting Power"*

Critchell, L. *"Four Stars of Hell"* (Jove Book, 1987).

Duboscq, G. *"My Longest Night"* (Leo Cooper, 1984).

Eisenhower, D. *"Crusade in Europe"* (Heinemann 1948)

Ellis, L. *"Victory in the West"* Vol 1: 'The Battle of Normandy', (HMSO 1962).

Ewing, J. '29 Let's Go!' (Washington Inf Journal Press, 1948).

Eyewitness *"The War Years 1939-45"* (Marshall Cavendish, 1991.
*"Images of War 1939-45"* (Marshall Cavendish, 1990-91).

Flower, D. and Reeves, J.(Eds) *"The War 1939-45."* Vol II (Panther edit, 1967).

Fussell, P. *"Wartime Understanding and Behaviour in the Second World War"* (OUP, 1989).

Gavin, J. *"On to Berlin"* (Bantam Books, US 1978/85).

Glover, D. *"The War at Sea"* ed J. Winton

Golly, J. *"The Big Drop. The Guns of Merville June 1944."* (Janes, 1982).

Grant, I. *"Cameraman at War"* (Patrick Stephens, Cambridge 1980).

Hamilton, N. *"Monty. Master of the Battlefield 1942-1944"*

Hammerton, I. *"Achtung Minen!"* (Book Guild, 1991).

Harrison, G. *"Cross Channel Attack"* US Army in World War II Series. (Office of the Chief of Military History Dept of the Army, Washington 1951).

Hawkins, D.(ed) *"War Report. D-Day to VE-Day"* (BBC Publication, Ariel 1985).

Hennessy, P. *"Young Man in a Tank"* (Tank Museum Bovington, No date).

Holbrook, D. *"Flesh Wounds"* (Buchan and Enright, London 1987).

Holt, T. and V. *"The Visitors' Guide to Normandy Landing Beaches* (Moorland Publishing Co, 1989).

Hoyt, E. *"The Invasion Before Normandy* (Robert Hale, London 1985).

Hutchinson, P. 'One Soldier's D-Day' *War Monthly*. (Marshall Cavendish, No 13. P.18-22).

Jefferson, A. *"Assault on the Guns of Merville* (John Murray, 1987).

Jutras, P. *"Les Paras US dans le Canton de Sainte-Mere-Eglise* (Heimdal, 1979).

Kluger, S. *"Yank - The Army Weekly."* (Arms and Armour, 1991).

Lane, R. *"Rudder's Rangers"*

Lefevre, E. *"Panzers in Normandy Then and Now"* (Battle of Britain Prints, 1983).

Lewin, R. *"Ultra Goes to War"* (Hutchinson, 1978).

Lewis, N. *"Channel Firing"* (Penguin, 1990).

Longmate, N. *"The GIs. The Americans in Britain 1942-5"* (Hutchinson,1975).

Lund, P.and Ludlam, H.
*"The War of the Landing Craft"* (W. Foulsham and Co, London 1976).

Marshall, S.L.A. *"Night Drop"* (Jove Book, 1984).

McKee, A. *"Caen. Anvil of Victory"*

Miller, M. 'LCT Commander' *War Monthly* (Marshall Cavendish, No25. P.1-9).

Moorehead, A. *"Eclipse"* (Sphere, 1945/78).

Morison, S. *"History of the US Naval Operations in World War II."* Vol II.

*"The Invasion of France and Germany."* (Little Brown and Co, Boston, USA. 1957/88).

Moulton, J. *"Haste to the Battle"* (Cassell, 1963).

Murdoch, C. McDougall
*"Swiftly They Struck"* (Grafton Books, 1988).

Neillands, R. *"The Raiders"* (Weidenfeld and Nicolson, 1989).
*"The Desert Rats - 7th Armoured Division

*1940-45"* (Weidenfeld and Nicolson, 1991).

Newman, M (Ed). *"Operation Overlord 1944-84"* (Portsmouth and Sunderland Newspapers, 1984).

Patton, G. S. *"War as I knew it"* (Boston 1947)

Pohanka, B. *"Beach with no Cover"* (Military History Magazine, Feb 92. P.35-40).

Reeman, D. *"D-Day - A Personal Reminiscence"* (Arrow, 1984).

Ryan, C. *"The Longest Day"*

Scott, D. *"Typhoon Pilot"* (Leo Cooper, 1982: Arrow, 1987).

Shores, C. *"2nd Tactical Air Force"* (Osprey, 1970).

Smith, N. *"Tank Soldier"* (Book Guild, 1989).

Sorvisto, E. *"2nd Ranger Bn. Roughing it with Charlie"* (Antietam National Museum, 1945).

Sykes, S. *"Deceivers Ever"* (Spellmount, 1990).

Tapert, A,(Ed) *"Lines of Battle. Letters from American Servicemen 1941-45"* (Simon and Schuster, 1987).

Terkel, S. *"The Good War"* (Ballentine, 1984).

Warner, P. *"The D-Day Landings"* (Kimber, 1990).

Wilson, A. *"Flamethrower"* (William Kimber London, 1956/84).

### Unpublished
Airborne Museum Aldershot eye-witness accounts:
- Maj J.N. Taylor, OC A Coy 7 PARA
- Capt Sim, 12 PARA. Capture of Bréville 12 Jun 44
- Capt Berhard, A Coy 12 PARA
- Maj Warren, Devonshire Regt
- 2IC, D Coy 12 Devons

Action by 'B' Sqn 15/18 Royal Hussars in support of 7 PARA attack 10 Jun 44.

Report of Operations 6th Airborne Division 6 Jun-27 Aug 44.

G3 Log 1st (US) Division 6-6-44.

Report Kenneth Lord Asst G3 1st (US) Inf Div entitled 'Omaha' in letter to US Mil Hist Institute 9 Jan 88.

Mason to Gavalas letter. HQ 1st (US) Inf Div 8 Jun 44.

Interview Lt J. Spaulding 'D-Day Landing 6 Jun 44' conducted 9 Feb 45.

Various TV Interviews from:
'The World at War'/ 'Morning Jun-Aug 1944' (Thames TV, 1974).
'D-Day Plus Forty' (ITN reports, 1984).
'Nan-Red' (ITN, 1984).

## GERMAN SOURCES

### Published

Carell, P. *"Invasion - They're Coming!"* (Harrap and Co, 1962).

Dollinger, H. *"Kain, wo ist dein Bruder?"* (Fischer Taschenbuch Verlag, Frankfurt 1987).

Hayn, F. *"Die Invasion"* (Heidelberg, 1954).

Klapdor, E. *"Die Entscheidung. Invasion 1944"* (E. Klapd or/Siek, 1984).

Kurowski, F. *"Die Panzer-Lehr Division"* (Podzun Verlag, Bad Nauheim 1964).

Liddel-Hart, B. *"The Rommel Papers"* (Hamlyn, 1953/84).

Luck, H. von *"Panzer Commander"* (Praeger NY, 1989).

Meyer, H. *"Kriegsgeschichte der 12th SS Panzer Division Hitlerjügend"* (Munin Verlag, Osnabruck 1982).

Meyer, K. *"Grenadiere"*

O'Neal, R. 'E-Boats' *War Monthly* (Marshall Cavendish, No 11. P.1-9).

Pöppel, M. *"Heaven and Hell"* (Spellmount Ltd, UK 1988).

Ritgen, H. *"Die Geschichte der Panzer-Lehr Division im Westen 1944-45"*

Ruge, F. 'The Invasion of Normandy' from *"Decisive Battles of World War II: the German View"* Ed J. Jacobs and J. Rohwer. (Andre Deutsch, London 1965).

Shulman, M. *"Defeat in the West"* (Coronet, 1973).

Speidel, H. *"Invasion 1944"* (R. Wunderlich Verlag, Tübingen 1949)

Steinhoff J., Pechel P., Showalter, D. *"Deutsche Im Zweiten Weltkrieg. Zeitzeugen Sprechen"* (Gustav Lubbe Verlag, 1989).

### Unpublished

Kriegstagebuch Heeresgruppe B. 1-15 Jun 44.

Kriegstagebuch der Führungsabteilung AOK 7 [Seventh Army] fur die zeit vom 1 Jan - 30 Juni 1944.

Gefechtsbericht über die Kampfe im Abschnitt der 352. Inf. Division am 6.6.1944.

Auszug aus dem Fernsprech-Meldebuch (Ia) der 352. I.D. Küstenverteidigungsabschnitt 'Bayeux' 6.6.44.

Gefechtsbericht über die Kampfe im Abschnitt der 716. Inf. Division am 6.6.1944.

Gefechtsbericht der Heeresküsten Artl. Abt 1255 fur die Zeit v. 6-9.6.44. 1500 Uhr.

Gefechtsbericht des Fallschirmjäger Regiments 6 fur die Zeit von 6. bis 13. Juni 1944.

Gefechtsbericht des Ost - Batl s.642.

Gefechtsbericht Batl. III/857 14.6.44.

Gefechtsbericht Batl III/858 Gren Regt, über die Zeit von 10-12.6.44 (Angriffe-und Abwehrkämpfe im Raume von Bréville) 15.6.44.

Gren Regt 857. 'Erfahrungs Bericht über Einsatz.' 19.6.44. Abt 1a and 1b.

Various reports:
12 SS: 16 Juni
21 Pz: 17, 18 Juni
Pz Lehr: 17, 18, 19 Juni
17 SS: 20 Juni

Kampfgruppe Konig "Erfahrungsbericht uber die Kampfe v. 6-20.6.44."
"Verhalten und Einsatz der Amerikaner." 22.6.44.

Kriegstagebuch der 5. Schnellbootsflotille. 16.4.44-30.4.44.

Various TV Interviews from:
'Entscheidung Am Atlantik Wall.' (ZDF, Dr Lutz Becker, Munich 1984).
'Die Deutschen im Zweiten Weltkrieg.' (BR/SWF/ORF - Joachim Hess und H Wuermeling, 1984).

# INDEX